The Future of Work in the Asia Pacific

Bringing together informed analyses on the challenges of critical skill shortages (CSS) in the Asia-Pacific region, this book provides 14 country reports to discuss the critical jobs and skills to achieve long-term policies and approaches towards realising the United Nations sustainable development goals (SDGs).

The contributors of the volume discuss the workforce projections and planning, existing programmes that address the skills and jobs needed, and workforce policy challenges that need to be addressed to achieve the SDGs. The book identifies two types of CSS present in the workforce: one being skilled labour shortages in existing industries and the second being soft skills like critical thinking and problem-solving skills. Extending the discussion beyond immediate skill shortages, the book assesses longer-term policies and approaches to tackle the 2030 United Nations Agenda for Sustainable Development.

This book will interest researchers in the fields of human resource management and development, international business, development studies, and policymakers from the Asia-Pacific region.

Subas P. Dhakal is Associate Professor at the University of New England (UNE)—Armidale, NSW.

Alan Nankervis is Adjunct Professor of Human Resource Management at Curtin University (Perth, Australia) and the Asia Pacific University of Innovation & Technology (Kuala Lumpur, Malaysia).

John Burgess is Professor at the Centre for Organisational Change and Agility, Torrens University Australia.

Routledge Frontiers of Business Management

Statistical Modelling and Sports Business Analytics
Edited by Vanessa Ratten and Ted Hayduk

China's Drive for the Technology Frontier
Indigenous Innovation in the High-Tech Industry
Yin Li

Digital Transformation in Aviation, Tourism and Hospitality in Southeast Asia
Edited by Azizul Hassan and Nor Aida Abdul Rahman

Football Entrepreneurship
Edited by Vanessa Ratten

Digitalization and Development
Ecosystem for Promoting Industrial Revolution 4.0 Technologies in Malaysia
Edited by Rajah Rasiah, Wah Yun Low, and Nurliana Kamaruddin

Air Travel Industry
Theories, Methods and Recent Issues
Edited by Azizul Hassan, Nor Aida Abdul Rahman and Nurhayati Mohd Nur

Innovation Pathways to Sustainability
Conversations Towards Complex Systems of Governance
Edited by Michael Lester and Marie dela Rama

The Future of Work in the Asia Pacific
Addressing Critical Skills Shortages for Sustainable Development
Edited by Subas P. Dhakal, Alan Nankervis and John Burgess

For more information about this series, please visit www.routledge.com/Routledge-Frontiers-of-Business-Management/book-series/RFBM

The Future of Work in the Asia Pacific

Addressing Critical Skills Shortages for Sustainable Development

Edited by Subas P. Dhakal, Alan Nankervis and John Burgess

Routledge
Taylor & Francis Group
LONDON AND NEW YORK

First published 2025
by Routledge
4 Park Square, Milton Park, Abingdon, Oxon OX14 4RN

and by Routledge
605 Third Avenue, New York, NY 10158

Routledge is an imprint of the Taylor & Francis Group, an informa business

British Library Cataloguing-in-Publication Data
A catalogue record for this book is available from the British Library

ISBN: 9781032458700 (hbk)
ISBN: 9781032458717 (pbk)
ISBN: 9781003379065 (ebk)

DOI: 10.4324/9781003379065

Typeset in Galliard Pro
by Apex CoVantage, LLC

Contents

Figures

Tables

Biography of Contributors

Jim Arrowsmith joined Massey University as Professor in the School of Management in 2008. His broad interest in the management of people at work means that he has researched and published across a portfolio of areas to do with human resource management and industrial relations. Key areas of expertise include employee engagement, variable pay, and flexible working time. Over the past few years, Jim has also acted as a consultant for the International Labour Organization, advising Pacific Island governments on issues such as the regulation of child labour, seasonal work, and employment law.

Kerry Brown is a professor at Edith Cowan University (ECU), Perth, WA. She specialises in research and publishing in organisational management; collaboration, networks and business clusters; capability, strategy, management, and policy for infrastructure asset management and major projects; public management and policy; gender and workforce issues; and employment relations. Kerry holds board memberships of Planning and Transport Research Centre (PATREC), the Asset Institute, and the Australia and New Zealand Academy of Management (2017–2023) and is ANZAM's Immediate Past President (2022–2024). She is a member of the ISO Technical Committee TC251 on Asset Management and the Asset Management Committee of IPWEA.

John Burgess is Professor at the Centre for Organisational Change and Agility. He has held previous professorial appointments at the University of Newcastle, Curtin University, and RMIT University. He has been a reviewer for the Australian, Canadian, Irish, and UAE research councils. He has held visiting academic appointments in Ireland, the UK, and Germany. He is an associate editor of the *Economic and Labour Relations Review* and is on the editorial board of *Human Resource Development Journal.* He has published extensively on insecure work, labour regulation, agency work, gig work, decent work, HRM practices of multinational enterprises, employee voice, and human resource development in Asia and Africa.

Julia Connell is a professor currently serving as an acting pro vice-chancellor and CEO at the Singapore Campus of the University of Newcastle, Australia.

She has previously held director, dean, and assistant dean roles at universities in Australia, the UAE, and Indonesia. Julia has published over 100 refereed journal articles/book chapters and co-edited 17 special issue journal volumes and nine books. Many publications focus on equity, change, people/leadership development, and new technologies. More recently, her research and publications have focused on sustainability in relation to various aspects, such as education and partnerships.

James Cooper is an independent management and education consultant with 18 years of experience in Vietnam. He has held various roles in academia and management across higher education and VET sectors with RMIT University, TAFE Queensland, and private higher education providers in Sydney. His research interests include family business, human and social capital development, and entrepreneurship with particular expertise in Southeast Asia.

Glenn P. Costin, a senior lecturer in construction technology at Deakin University's School of Architecture and Built Environment, investigates community resilience in the face of climate change. A carpenter and joiner by trade and well travelled, Glenn's academic background includes social anthropology, international relations, and education. As designer and craftsperson, his work includes new buildings, heritage renovations, extensions, boats, and artistic works. Glenn's university role is supported by 25 years of teaching in Australia's vocational education and training (VET) sector and the authoring of several books, some of which are required reading in tertiary programmes across Australian and New Zealand.

Julie I. Cunningham holds a bachelor of commerce (industrial relations) and a master of social work and completed her PhD in 2022 at the University of Wollongong researching 'International labour migration and the children left behind: Hearing the voices of young people traversing transnational parenting in Tonga'. Areas of continued research interest include the emotional work undertaken by young people experiencing transnational parenting, families, migration and the impact on care and work, Tonga and the Pacific Region, and the intersection of global inequality in labour access and family life.

Kantha Dayaram is a professor in the discipline of people, culture, and organisation at Curtin University, Australia. She is a graduate of the London School of Economics (Health Economics and Policy, UK) and the University of Durban Westville (Policy and Governance, South Africa). Her research focuses on labour and employment mobility within Sub-Saharan Africa and South Asia, the intersection between regulations, psychosocial safety, gender, and work responses to violence and harassment. Her work has been supported with national and international grants from the private, public, and not-for-profit sectors. She teaches Australian and international employment relations and global human resource management. Her work in facilitating international student engagement in Southeast Asia is supported by New Colombo Mobility grants. She received the teaching citation award for creating innovative experimental resources in postgraduate leadership and received the PhD supervision awards in 2021 and 2022. In addition to her academic work, she has been involved in consultancy work for state governments and in international accreditation reviews.

Subas P. Dhakal is Associate Professor at the University of New England (UNE)—Armidale, NSW. His research/teaching centres on applying sustainability policies and strategies to solve social, economic, and environmental challenges in Asia-Pacific/South Asia. His core area of expertise lies in the future of education and employment in the broader context of the 2030 Agenda. Subas is currently (2022–2024) serving as a regional representative (Region 1: ACT and NSW) of the Australia and New Zealand Academy of Management (ANZAM) and an editorial board member of the journal *FIIB Business Review* (2023–present).

Luis Miguel Dos Santos is Assistant Professor in the Counselling and Psychology Department at Hong Kong Shue Yan University, Hong Kong SAR. In 2021, 2022, and 2023, Dos Santos received the award as the top 2% scientific researcher in the fields of education and social sciences. His research interests include qualitative research methods, education, sociology, sex education, and career decision-making.

Lata Dyaram is Professor of Work & Organizational Psychology at the Department of Management Studies, Indian Institute of Technology Madras (IITM). Dyaram is currently the area chair (2021–till date) at the department and teaches organization theory and practice. Dyaram's research and publication interests centres on diversity, organization behaviour, and human resource management.

Apoorva Goel is a graduate student in the Department of Management Studies, Indian Institute of Technology Madras (IITM).

Shafiiq Gopee has more than 16 years of teaching experience at tertiary level and currently heads the Office of Learning and Teaching at Curtin Mauritius. His education spans across the sciences and the humanities; he holds a BSc Information Systems from the University of South Africa, an MSc Information Systems and Human Resources Management from Middlesex University, London, and a PhD Media and Information from Curtin University, Australia. He has always been passionate about the intricate relationship between people and technology, with his PhD thesis exploring the pertinent issue of digital inequality in a small island developing state. The advent of the Fourth Industrial Revolution, in particular the ramifications of the latest technological developments on the future of work, has brought another dimension to his research interest.

Sarita Hardin-Ramanan is Head of IT, Design and Communication at Curtin Mauritius. After completing a BEng in electrical and electronics engineering at the University of Mauritius, she moved to London for a master's in computer science at Imperial College before joining Curtin Mauritius for a career of more than 18 years in tertiary-level teaching and faculty management. Sarita also holds a PhD in IT governance and green IT from Curtin University, and along with IT, her commitment to work integrated learning has extended her research interests to graduate employability and the impact of AI and associated technologies on the future of work.

Nan Jiang is a senior lecturer at the School of Management and Marketing, Faculty of Business and Law, Taylor's University, Malaysia. Nan has 12 years of working experience in tertiary education and has a track record of teaching, research, and administrative engagement. Nan Jiang's publications are in the areas of the internationalisation of higher education, data mining, social media marketing, consumer behaviour, and game addiction. She is the project leader and co-researcher for several national and local grants.

Nabila Khan is a graduate student at the Department of Management Studies, Indian Institute of Technology Madras (IITM).

Pacharapong Kumjumpa is affiliated with the School of Political Science and Public Administration, Walailak University, Thailand. Pacharapong has been actively engaged in lecturing and offering guidance to students working on projects related to human resource management. His academic journey includes a prestigious master's degree in human resource management, earned with distinction from the University of Manchester in 2022, and a bachelor's degree in political science, where he graduated with second-class honours from Thammasat University in 2018. Before venturing into academia, he had professional experience as an HR practitioner in various multinational companies based in Bangkok.

Ching Ting Tany Kwee is a casual academic and PhD candidate at the University of New South Wales, Sydney, Australia. She is a registered teacher in Hong Kong and New South Wales, Australia. Her research interests include mentoring, vocational motivations and behaviours, training and professional development, online and remote learning, STEM education, and education for sustainable development. Her publications can be seen in various journals and conference proceedings. She has also received grants and funding for research projects on mentoring.

Le Li is a master student majoring in enterprise management at Shandong University's School of Innovation and Entrepreneurship, Qingdao, China. Her research interests include human resource management, business management, and strategic management.

Yi Liu has a PhD in commerce from Curtin University, Australia. She is Associate Professor in Shandong University's School of Innovation and Entrepreneurship, Qingdao, China. Her research interests include human resource management, talent management, cross-cultural students, innovation management, and knowledge management. Liu has published in journals like *Journal of Business Research*, *Journal of Knowledge Management*, and *Leadership & Organizational Development Journal*.

Ho Fai Lo is a doctoral candidate at the City University of Macau. He is currently doing a project on sexual education and sexual health for male university students and international students.

Liang Lu is Associate Professor in the School of Business Administration, Zhongnan University of Economics and Law, Wuhan, China. His research fields focus on compensation and welfare, entrepreneurship and employment, labour relationship.

Muhammad Nateque Mahmood presently holds the position of senior lecturer within the School of Architecture and Built Environment at Deakin University. With over 14 years of expertise in civil and residential construction ventures, Nateque's primary research focuses on sustainability within infrastructure projects, infrastructure asset management, and infrastructure policy.

Alan Nankervis is Adjunct Professor of Human Resource Management at Curtin University (Perth, Australia) and the Asia Pacific University of Innovation & Technology (Kuala Lumpur, Malaysia). He has previously taught and conducted research at three Australian universities and held visiting professor positions in Canada, Thailand, and the UK. His current research interests include graduate work readiness, the impact of artificial intelligence on workplaces, workforce ageing issues, and transitional HRM roles and competencies, with a particular focus on the Asia-Pacific region.

Nhat Tram Phan-Le completed graduate training at RMIT University, School of Media and Communication. Her research focuses on the use of systemic approaches to address social issues. Her areas of interest include social marketing, sustainable development, mindfulness, and health communication within the context of the South East Asian environment.

Azmeri Rahman presently serves as a part-time academic at Deakin University, Australia. Her research expertise encompasses construction procurement, multinational contracting, and supply chain management.

Vikash Rowtho is Head of Research at Curtin Mauritius. He completed his undergraduate, master's, and engineering degrees in computer science at the Riga Institute of Civil Aviation Engineers, Republic of Latvia, and has a diploma in sustainability and a PhD in education. He has worked in the education sector for over 20 years in both teaching and administration roles. With his IT, administration, and education backgrounds, his research interests include technology and the future of work, specifically how AI and related technologies will shape the future of work.

Arlene Sale is a PhD candidate at Torrens University, Centre for Organisational Change and Agility. Her research interests include employee voice, organisational change, skills development, and labour regulation in the Philippines and Australia.

Jonathan Sale is Program Director for Human Resource Management and Supply Chain Management and Lecturer in HRM at UniSA Business, University of South Australia. He teaches undergraduate and postgraduate courses on employment relations, industrial relations, and HRM and conducts research on topics such as employment skills and strategies, labour disputes settlement, labour relations policy, labour and comparative law, labour laws and labour markets, labour regulation and informal work, social security and migrant work, worker voice, decent work, and sustainable development. His study areas include Australia, Malaysia, the Philippines, and ASEAN.

Monthon Sorakraikitikul is affiliated with Thammasat Business School, Thammasat University, Bangkok, Thailand. He facilitates student learning in human resource development, organisational development, knowledge management, and business communication. He has a bachelor's degree in marketing, a MBA, and a PhD from the Asian Institute of Technology. He also serves as an external coach for executives from both public and private organisations.

Nadiah Suki joined as faculty member of Asia Pacific University (APU) of Technology & Innovation (APU) in 2003. Currently a senior lecturer in the School of Business, Nadiah draws from her collective experience in legal practice and academia to infuse industry-relevant content in her teaching. She has 20 years of teaching experience and has previously served in administrative, supervisory, and industry liaison capacity representing APU. Nadiah teaches law in the business, accounting, and IT programmes and is a certified corporate trainer in the areas of design thinking and instructional design. She is currently pursuing her doctoral studies related to employee engagement in SMEs' digital transformation.

Saskia Tjokro serves as Director of ANGIN Advisory, the most significant investment network in Indonesia, and launched the first Women Fund in the country. She leads industrial research and investment programmes focusing on capacity building in impactful SMEs. She is also on the steering committee for the Indonesia National Advisory Board for Impact Investment (Indonesia Impact Alliance), where she advocates the policy for catalytic capital in impact space. Her research interests include SMEs, sustainability, green economy, future workforce, and innovation enterprises.

Jason J. Turner is Senior Head of the School of Business at Asia Pacific University of Technology & Innovation, Malaysia. As an academic for over 20 years, he has held and holds several external positions and grants in Malaysia and abroad. His research interests are in the areas of human capital, graduate work readiness, and digital transformation, which have resulted in several books, book chapters, and peer-reviewed publications.

Peter Waring is Professor and Murdoch's Pro Vice Chancellor of Transnational Education and Singapore Dean. Peter is responsible for advancing the University's academic and strategic interests at each of its transnational education locations. He has previously held academic positions at the University of Newcastle and the University of NSW (Asia) including the positions of acting pro vice-chancellor (International) at the University of Newcastle and academic director and deputy CEO of Newcastle's Singapore operations. A qualified lawyer, Peter also holds degrees in commerce and management. He is the co-author of four books on employment relations and has published more than a hundred book chapters and articles in leading international and national journals. His research and teaching interests span the business and law fields of industrial relations, human resource management, corporate governance, and labour law. He has lived in Singapore for the past 20 years.

Samina Yasmin is a graduate student at the Department of Management Studies, Indian Institute of Technology Madras (IITM).

Acknowledgements

We thank all contributing authors, reviewers, the publisher, and copy editors for providing assistance to develop and produce this edited volume. Special thanks to Professor Peter Waring (Murdoch, Singapore) and Professor Julia Connell (Newcastle, Singapore) for organising a hybrid workshop titled 'The Future of Work in the Asia Pacific: Addressing Critical Skills Shortages for Sustainable Development'. The workshop was organised at the Murdoch Singapore Campus in February 2023, and most of the participants who attended the workshop contributed to this volume.

Abbreviations

4IR:	Fourth Industrial Revolution
5IR:	Fifth Industrial Revolution
ADB:	Asian Development Bank
ALMPs:	Active Labour Market Programs
ANGIN:	Angel Investment Network (Indonesia)
ANZSCO:	Australia and New Zealand Standard Classification of Occupations
ASEAN:	Association of South East Asian Nations
ASEAN:	Association of Southeast Asian Nations
CBS:	Central Bureau of Statistics
CLS:	critical labour shortages
COL:	critical occupations list (Indonesia)
CPV:	Communist Party of Vietnam
CSG:	critical skills gap
CSR:	corporate social responsibility
CSS:	critical skills shortages
CTEVT:	Council for Technical Education and Vocational Training
CTEVT:	Council for Technical Education and Vocational Training (Nepal)
DMW:	Department of Migrant Workers (Philippines)
FPA:	Fair Pay Agreement (NZ)
GDP:	gross domestic product
GSO:	Government Statistics Office (Vietnam)
HCT:	human capital theory
HRDC:	Human Resource Development Council (Mauritius)
ICT:	information and communications technologies
ILO:	International Labour Organisation
IMF:	International Monetary Fund
IoT:	internet of things
IPCC:	Intergovernmental Panel on Climate Change
IQA:	interactive qualitative analysis
ISCO:	International Standard Classification of Occupations
ITO:	industry training organisation

LFPR: labour force participation rate
LME: liberal market economy
LMSM: Labour mobility supply management strategy (Tonga)
LSF: living standards framework
LTB: local tourism businesses (Indonesia)
LTSSL: long-term skill shortage list (NZ)
MBIE: Ministry of Business, Innovation, and Employment (NZ)
MFA: Ministry of Foreign Affairs (Singapore)
MoCTCA: Ministry of Culture, Tourism & Civil Aviation
MoCTE: Ministry of Tourism and Creative Economy (Indonesia)
MSC: mission-critical skills (Philippines)
MyCOL: Malaysian critical occupations list
NEET: not in employment, education, or training
NPC: National Planning Commission (Nepal)
NTB: Nepal Tourism Board
OECD: Organisation for Economic Co-operation and Development
OEF: overseas Filipino workers
OTJ: on the job
PACER Plus: Pacific Agreement on Closer Economic Relations Plus
PALM: Pacific Australia labour mobility
PLMS: Pacific labour mobility scheme
PMSOL: priority migration skilled occupation list
POEA: Philippines overseas employment administration
RES: regional employer scheme
SBC: Sustainable Business Council
SDGs: sustainable development goals
SET: self-efficacy theory
SMEs: small and medium-sized enterprises
SPF: strategic partnership framework (Mauritius)
STEM: science, technology, engineering, and mathematics
THS: tourism and hospitality sector (Nepal)
TLMSMS: Tonga labour mobility supply management strategy
TSC: tourism sustainable commitment (NZ)
TTAF: Targeted Training and Apprenticeship Fund (NZ)
TTI: travel and tourism industry (Indonesia)
TVET: technical and vocational education and training
UAE: United Arab Emirates
UNDP: United Nations Development Program
UNESCO: United Nations Educational, Scientific and Cultural Organization
UNOHCR: United Nations Office of the High Commissioner for Human Rights
UNWTO: United Nations World Tourism Organisation
UNWTO: United Nations World Trade Organisation
VASS: Vietnam Academy of Social Sciences

VET:	vocational education and training
WDC:	Workforce Development Council (NZ)
WEF:	World Economic Forum
WFH:	work from home
WTTC:	World Travel & Tourism Council

Part 1

Introduction

1 The Nexus Between Critical Skill Shortages and Sustainable Development

An Introduction

Subas P. Dhakal, John Burgess, and Alan Nankervis*

Introduction

The future of work is shaped by technological advancements and the demand for and supply of critical skills supporting sustainable development. The main contention of this edited volume is that investments to overcome critical skills shortages (CSS) are necessary to advance the United Nations (UN) 2030 Agenda and accomplish various sustainable development goals (SDGs). This book focuses on various aspects of labour and skills shortages across the Asia-Pacific region in the context of the 2030 Agenda. These shortages occur when there are more vacancies than job seekers in an occupation (see Spring Professional, 2020). On the one hand, several terms are used to describe the well-reported skill shortages highlighted in the wake of the COVID-19 pandemic. These include strategic skill deficits, labour shortages, talent shortages, and skill mismatches, among others. On the other hand, the 2030 Agenda is a shared blueprint for balancing economic, environmental, and social priorities, now and into the future via the 17 SDGs and 169 targets (UNDESA, 2015). According to The Adecco Group (TAG), the common thread that binds these 17 SDGs is the world of work.

> The world of work connects all social partners and is the principal provider of livelihoods and income security. It is crucial for labour market stakeholders to come together and realise their tremendous opportunities and responsibilities to create a more sustainable future.
>
> (TAG, 2021: para 1)

In this context, this edited volume focuses on the nexus between CSS and SDGs.

Previous collections co-edited by members of this editorial team on graduate work readiness (Dhakal et al., 2018), the impact of new technology on work (Nankervis et al., 2021), an ageing population (Dhakal et al., 2019), and institutional barriers to decent work (Dayaram et al., 2020) in the region highlighted the problems of various aspects of skill shortages, skill mismatches,

DOI: 10.4324/9781003379065-2

and the challenges of developing training and education programmes that accommodate the dramatic changes in skill requirements, technology, job specifications, and structural changes in the population and labour market. Nonetheless, despite improvements in educational participation and attainment and ongoing growth in the online economy, youth unemployment and underemployment remain high, associated in part with apparent skill shortages (Cameron et al., 2019) and labour shortages. More importantly, Dhakal et al. (2019) highlighted the need for systemic reform of the education and training system in many, if not all, Asia-Pacific countries; increased engagement across key stakeholders; and a 'whole-of-life' approach to education and training that accommodates structural challenges such as new jobs and professions, changing skill requirements, and many extensive structural changes across industries and occupations.

Background to the Asia-Pacific Region

The setting for the research contained in this volume is diverse across culture, ethnicity, climate, political structure, geography, demographics, industry structure, living standards, and technology. The countries included in the study share proximity, as they are a part of the world where growth rates have been high, and they are characterised by large movements of cross-border trade, labour, students, and capital. Labour migration in and out of the Association of South-East Asian Nations (ASEAN) region is extensive. The International Labour Organisation (ILO) estimates that there are over 10 million migrant workers in ASEAN countries, two-thirds of whom are from those countries. Several countries, such as the Philippines, Indonesia, India, Nepal, Tonga, and Bangladesh, have large numbers of citizens employed externally within Asia and other locations, especially the Middle East. Several other countries, including Singapore, New Zealand, and Australia, depend on migrant labour to fill immediate and long-term labour and skill shortages.

A snapshot of the correlation between the Human Development Index (HDI) rank[1] and SDGs rank[2] in countries represented in this edited volume is depicted in Figure 1.1. Some countries are ranked highly on both metrics, and some are not. For example, Australia ranks highly in HDI (ranked #5) but significantly lower in SDGs (ranked #40). While the higher HDI rank signifies its economic prowess, the lack of commitment towards environmental issues (for example, climate action) and social issues (for example, the gap between Indigenous and non-Indigenous populations) reflects a low level of commitment and effort on the SDGs (see Schultz, 2019).

Over the past decade, the region has had to adjust to major shocks, including economic ones (the Asian Financial Crisis), the COVID-19 pandemic, and natural disasters, including floods, fires, earthquakes, and volcanic eruptions. Throughout the region, there are longer-term challenges that are shared by other regions, including population ageing and the changing climate. The Asian Development Bank [ADB] (2021) highlights the challenges associated

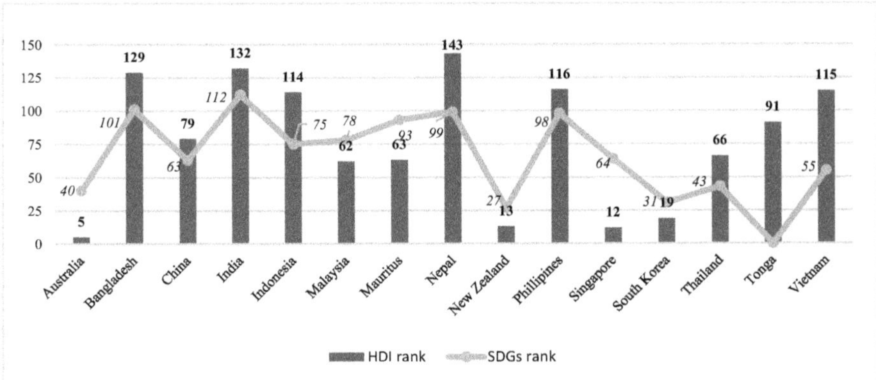

Figure 1.1 HDI and SDGs rankings of countries represented in this volume

Source: (UNDP, 2023a, 2023b)

with the transition to a green economy, improving the liveability of cities, and addressing poverty and gender equity. There are added geopolitical challenges in the region given the tensions between China and the United States, China and Taiwan, China and India, Pakistan and India, and the two Koreas. Skill shortages are present across the region in both advanced and developing economies and the structural conditions shaping skill development and the capacity to address skill shortages differ. This volume aims to evaluate how each country is addressing these longer-term skill requirements to meet the longer-term development goals embodied in the SDGs.

The Purpose of This Book

The purpose of this edited volume is to explore the nature, scope, and implications of the challenges associated with the CSS in the Asia-Pacific and beyond, and to propose a range of effective solutions to these challenges in the short, medium, and longer terms to address them and hence to contribute to the discussion that assists in achieving the desired outcomes of the UN's SDGs. Across the globe, there are acute labour and skill shortages following the opening of economies after the COVID-19 pandemic (UN, 2021a). These shortages reflect the cyclical pressures of growth and the structural adjustment processes attributed to the impact of technological change and ongoing globalisation, with its associated opportunities and challenges (TAG, 2021). While the current shortages potentially impact growth and well-being, developing skills associated with realising SDGs requires a longer-term perspective on skill planning and development. In this scenario, the country chapters in this volume reflect how various countries within the region are addressing (or not addressing) these labour and skill challenges concerning SDGs. Various country cases highlight what these nations consider innovative programmes to overcome shortages or skill development programmes, whether nationally, regionally, or by sector, in the broader context of SDGs. In order to contextualise the purpose of this edited volume, Table 1.1 exemplifies the nexus between SDGs and CSS based on scholarly and grey literature.

Table 1.1 Grey and scholarly literature on linkages between SDGs and CSS

SDGs	*Description (The Global Goals, 2023)*	*Examples*
SDG1	End poverty in all its forms everywhere.	Overcoming labour and skills shortages is a key to socio-economic development and poverty reduction (ADB, 2017).
SDG2	End hunger, achieve food security and improved nutrition, and promote sustainable agriculture.	Increasing agricultural productivity and incomes of small-scale food producers depends on the availability of unskilled, semi-skilled, and skilled labour (Shikur, 2020).
SDG3	Ensure healthy lives and promote well-being for all at all ages.	Adopting policies around the health and well-being of employees in the workplace can help attract and retain the talent pool (Rodríguez-Sánchez et al., 2020).
SDG4	Ensure inclusive and equitable quality education and promote lifelong learning opportunities for all.	Inclusive and equitable access to education, training, and lifelong learning opportunities can help reskill or upskill workers (Hamburg, 2020).
SDG5	Achieve gender equality and empower all women and girls.	Effective participation and equal opportunities at all levels across sectors, for example, engineering, can reduce critical skills shortages by luring women (Hickey & Cui, 2020).
SDG6	Ensure availability and sustainable management of water and sanitation for all.	Sustainable management of water and sanitation necessitates specialised critical skills (Capello et al., 2021).
SDG7	Ensure access to affordable, reliable, sustainable and modern energy for all.	Skilling the energy transition explores the current pathways into a clean energy career (Clean Energy Council, 2022).
SDG8	Promote sustained, inclusive, and sustainable economic growth, full and productive employment, and decent work.	Ensuring workers in the informal sector are within administrative reach and the effectiveness of social policies informed by the decent work agenda is necessary (Dhakal & Burgess, 2021).

(*Continued*)

Table 1.1 (Continued)

SDGs	*Description (The Global Goals, 2023)*	*Examples*
SDG9	Build resilient infrastructure, promote inclusive and sustainable industrialisation, and foster innovation.	Green skills provide an opportunity to build resilience and ultimately enter the path to more sustainable development (Strietska-Ilina, 2019).
SDG10	Reduce inequality within and among countries.	The cognitive biases and judgements of resource acquisition managers can keep migrants from the global south out of the organisational talent pool and inhibit career progression (UoW, 2023).
SDG11	Make cities and human settlements inclusive, safe, resilient, and sustainable.	Supporting developing countries to strengthen their scientific and technological capacity to move towards more sustainable patterns of consumption and production is key to overcoming skills shortages (Wang et al., 2019).
SDG12	Ensure sustainable consumption and production patterns.	An integrated approach to teaching science, technology, engineering, and mathematics promotes the learning of 21st-century skills and provides developing countries with the tools they need to improve people's lives (ADB, 2021).
SDG13	Take urgent action to combat climate change and its impact.	In a nutshell, very few countries have paid specific attention to the technical and vocational skill development required for the climate change transition and protection of marine and wildlife (UNESCO, 2021).
SDG14	Conserve and sustainably use the oceans, seas, and marine resources.	
SDG15	Protect, restore, and promote sustainable use of terrestrial ecosystems, sustainably manage forests, combat desertification, and halt and reverse land degradation and biodiversity loss.	
SDG16	Promote peaceful and inclusive societies for sustainable development, provide access to justice for all, and build effective, accountable, and inclusive institutions at all levels.	Initiatives such as the Global Skills Partnership (GSP) aim to mobilise technical expertise towards supporting governments, employers, workers and their organisations, educational institutions and training providers, and other stakeholders to develop and recognise the skills of migrant workers with a particular focus on women and youth ILO (2018).
SDG17	Strengthen the means of implementation and revitalise the global partnership for sustainable development.	

The 17 SDGs (Table 1.1)

> were adopted by the UN in 2015 as a universal call to action to end poverty, protect the planet, and ensure that by 2030 all people enjoy peace and prosperity. The 17 SDGs are integrated—they recognise that action in one area will affect outcomes in others, and that development must balance social, economic, and environmental sustainability.
>
> (UNDP, 2023c)

Although CSS has relevance in relation to each of the 17 SDGs, SDG#4 and SDG#8 are particularly pertinent. For instance, target 4.3 is about enhancing equal access to affordable technical, vocational, and higher education, and target 8.3 is about promoting policies to support job creation and business growth (Global Goals, 2023). The focus of SDG#8 on work conditions, processes, and policies supporting decent work has direct and indirect relevance to supporting all 17 SDGs (ILO, 2023). Within this volume, the country analysis of CSS primarily revolves around six SDGs (3, 4, 5, 8, 10, and 13).

The Extent and Scope of Critical Skill Shortages Across the Asia-Pacific

The Australian Council for Commerce and Industry (ACCI) defines skill and labour shortages as a measure 'identified from national, state or regional labour market analysis of data trends such as vacancies, industry surveys or similar (which) tend to focus on either current or forecast statistically significant shifts in demand for occupational skills' (ACCI, 2022, p. 4). The Organisation for Economic Co-operation and Development (OECD) definition focuses on the micro or organisational level, explaining that skill shortages arise 'when employers are unable to recruit staff with the required skills in the accessible labour market at the ongoing rate of pay' (Brunello & Wruunck, 2021, p. 1147). For this book, we have adopted the term 'critical skill shortages (CSS)' to emphasise the strategic contribution of these skills to global and national economies, their centrality in addressing the UN's SDGs, and the urgency with which all countries in the region need to address them.

However, there are also short- and medium-term skill (and labour) shortages explored throughout this book since short-term skill shortages contribute to losses in output, job opportunities, and income. It is essential here to delineate between critical skill shortages and, more specifically, labour shortages because the nature of many traditional jobs is changing dramatically; and new jobs are constantly being created due to structural changes in the labour market and the impacts of new technology and the pandemic, among other factors. Skill mismatches, on the other hand, have been defined as 'a gap between the (aggregate) supply and demand for skills, typically concerning a specific geographic unit (region, country or country group)' (Brunello & Wruunck, 2021, p. 1146), and are also discussed throughout this book.

Post COVID-19, many countries are experiencing critical skill shortages as their economies bounce back. The chapters in this book provide considerable detail on the scope of any specific skills deficits in their respective countries, but it is worthwhile here to record some of the overall predictions for critical skill shortages more broadly. For example, the Australian National Skills Commission (NSC, 2022) reported increased vacancies and skill shortages in Australia, New Zealand, the UK, and the United States. Many of the vacancies were linked to the pressures of supporting the health system during and post-COVID (health professionals and logistics), while others are linked to ongoing technological and socio-economic challenges and the post-recovery economy (IT specialists, cybersecurity experts, project managers, hospitality workers). Further, a recent report from the Australian Council for Commerce and Industry (ACCI, 2022) found that the Australian industry faces the 'worst skill and labour shortages in decades (which) is worsening by the day' (p. 4), citing evidence that 'a fifth of all occupations have skill shortages, at many job levels, with a quarter experiencing significant difficulty in finding suitable staff in the labour market' (p. 4).

Martin (2022), citing the National Skills Commission data, revealed that the number of occupations with skill shortages rose from 153 in 2021 to around 286 during 2022, indicating the rapid escalation of the crisis. During the same period, Workforce Australia, a government authority, predicted that the Australian industry would need to fill more than a million new jobs in the next five years, mostly with employees with vocational or higher education qualifications (Workforce Australia, 2022, p. 16). It further specified the key industry sectors requiring these employees—namely, healthcare, and social assistance; professional, scientific, and technical services; education and training; accommodation and food services; construction; public administration; and retail trade. These predictions largely accord with similar expectations from the Australian Jobs & Skills Authority (previously known as the Australian National Skills Commission) and the Australian Bureau of Statistics (ABS, 2023, p. 5) and illustrate the breadth of the skill shortages in industry and occupational applications.

From a regional perspective, a 2023 Korn Ferry report suggested that there is likely to be 'an imminent talent deficit of 12.3 million workers' (p. 1) in the Asia-Pacific region by 2030, especially in the finance and business services, information technology, media and communications, and manufacturing sectors, and notably in China and Japan. This shortage could lead to severe financial outcomes, including up to $4.238 trillion in 'unrealised annual revenue' (p. 1) due to the industry's inability to produce at capacity. The report concluded that the key problem 'is the mismatch between technological advances including artificial intelligence and machine learning, and the skills and experience workers need to leverage these advanced tools' (p. 3). In support of this prediction, an Equinix 2022 Global Trends Survey of 2,900 respondents across the region found that cloud computing specialists (29%), professionals with artificial intelligence or machine learning competencies (26%), information technology experts (26%), and data protection specialists (24%) were in the highest demand, but that soft skills such as collaboration, mentorship, reskilling, and career guidance activities were also needed (Pressley, 2022). Other observers have highlighted more specific skill shortages across the Asia-Pacific region, including a 'looming crisis in Emotional, Social & Governance (ESG) talent shortages' (Walters, 2022, p. 1), which require a combination of innovative thinking, clear articulation of corporate visions, capability to persuade and influence a range of stakeholders, highly-developed communication skills, and collaborative competencies (PWC, 2022; Walters, 2022, p. 3); and a lack of experience or skills in managing organisations' diversity, equality, and inclusion strategies (AHRI, 2023, p. 3).

Most observers of the CSS across the region agree that while there are considerable differences in their specific origins and causes in different countries, according to their levels of economic development, labour markets, and socio-cultural and political characteristics, there are some commonalities as well as a combination of short- and longer-term factors contributing to the challenge. For example, Brunello and Wruunck (2021) categorise the broad causes as 'cyclical and structural factors' (p. 1152), whether associated with global, regional, and/or national developments. Certainly, the impact of COVID-19 has caused many countries to reassess their industry structures and skills requirements in the wake of the associated suspension of migration, the loss of many jobs, and the growing attraction of 'de-globalisation' strategies, especially for developed countries and manufacturing. In the latter case, many companies decided to withdraw their international outsourcing contracts because of COVID-19-disrupted supply chains (short-term), fears of impacts on national security, and perceived declines in the provided services (longer time).

However, the key macro-causes of CSS tend to include demographic factors such as the combination of population ageing and low population growth (especially in the developed countries); long-term structural changes in the economy and in most industry sectors; declining labour force participation and workforce mobility rates; and importantly, the dramatic growth and application of new technologies such as artificial intelligence, machine learning, and robotics in almost all industry sectors, which pose enormous challenges for traditional jobs and skills, and the potential for entirely new types of jobs and skills—'a structural shift towards higher-skilled jobs (and) a reduced need for routine job functions' (Dhakal et al., 2018; NSC, 2022; PWC, 2018, 2022; ACCI, 2022; Korn Ferry, 2023). The failure of vocational and higher education institutions in many regional countries to adapt to these developments, and the absence of integrated government and industry strategies and policies (Workforce Australia, 2022, p. 8) to address them, in many but not all countries—as examples, Singapore, Malaysia, Indonesia, and, more recently, Australia have developed these—have also aggravated the impact of the CSS (Dhakal et al., 2019). The following country chapters will discuss these causative factors in more detail.

Theoretical Framework, Research Approaches, and Limitations

This edited volume brings together informed analyses of the challenges of skill shortages and skill development towards supporting SDGs in 15 selected countries. This book draws on the nexus between stakeholders and strategic workforce planning frameworks (Verma et al., 2020) to examine the CSS issue going forward. More specifically, most chapters use a broad interpretation of human capital management (HCM) theory, incorporating both social capital and emotional capital, to explore the relevant challenges and their implications for the SDGs in all the countries studied.

According to Gallo and Thompson (2000), human capital is defined as 'the sum total of all your labour force's talent (knowledge, skills, know-how and ability to innovate) serving to add value to goods and services produced' (p. 241). It includes employees' work experience, hard and soft skills, personality, education and training, health, and loyalty. As such, it can strategically embrace all the characteristics of the labour force at the macro-, meso-, and micro-levels of the national economy and can be linked to the SDGs. At the macro level, HCM theory allows for a discussion of the interconnected roles of governments, industry, and educational institutions (vocational and higher education) in single countries, and a comparison of diverse HCM and SDG applications in the countries included in this book. At meso- and micro-levels, it underpins the effective management of industry sectors and/or individual organisations.

Social capital may be defined as 'the sum of resources, actual or virtual, that accrue to an individual or a group by possessing a durable network of more or less institutional relationships of mutual acquaintance and recognition' (Bourdieu & Wacquant, 1992, p. 119), and emotional capital, or 'a tripartite concept composed of emotion-based knowledge, management skills, and capacities to feel, that links self-process and resources to group membership and social location' (Cottingham, 2016, p. 452) is naturally complementary to the broad interpretation of human capital theory. In a practical sense, Dhakal (2014) characterises social capital theory (SCT) as follows: 'the capability of actors to access necessary resources from within (intra) represents bonding social capital . . . access resources from outside (inter) represents bridging social capital' (p. 732). SCT and HCM are complementary as they both advocate for investing in harnessing networks and capabilities with expected returns in the marketplace and inform our *six central questions* for the discussion of the CSS experienced by all the countries discussed in this book. They are as follows:

1. What is meant by CSS?
2. Why have these shortages arisen, and are they a long-term or short-term issue?
3. What is the study focused on—the nation, the sector, the organisation, the occupation or profession, labour, or generic skills?

4. Where is the responsibility for addressing skill shortages, and can innovative and exciting solutions be reported?
5. How have policies addressing CSS evolved in the aftermath of the COVID-19 pandemic, and which policy developments are noteworthy?
6. How do country cases capture and demonstrate the linkages between CSS and SDGs?

Country chapters in this volume utilise a variety of research methods to address either all or selected questions mentioned earlier in diverse contexts, ranging from reviews of secondary data (including both scholarly and grey literature) and meta-analysis to broad and/or focused primary data collection, but each chapter addresses the aforementioned research questions and raises key suggestions for future research and labour market practice.

Organisation of the Book

The book comprises 18 chapters. Following this introduction, in Chapter 2, Dhakal and Mahmood present a scientometric analysis of the key research themes associated with critical labour and skill shortages. This chapter sets the tone and scope of the CSS in countries represented in this volume. These two chapters are followed by 15 country-level case studies, which provide brief country contexts and illuminate sector-specific CSS challenges, capture government and private sector responses to these challenges, and make future policy recommendations in the Asia-Pacific and Indo-Pacific regions. The order of countries is based on their performance rankings against the 17 SDGs (UN, 2024: para 1).

In Chapter 3, Arrowsmith maps New Zealand's skills gaps and examines the structural and agency factors contributing to a skills crisis in many sectors. The chapter evaluates recent governments' policy responses and strategies adopted by employers. It discusses the implications of automation and technological change for future skills needs and the country's quantity and quality of jobs. It concludes by assessing current trends and skills development strategies for meeting SDG commitments.

In Chapter 4, Dos Santos et al. explore the development of self-efficacy in cultural responsiveness among pre-service STEM educators in South Korea, addressing the global trend of teacher shortages in STEM fields. The chapter employs self-efficacy theory to examine personal and environmental factors influencing pre-service teachers' confidence in cultural responsiveness and leadership based on interviews and focus group discussions. The chapter reports that reforming teacher education to incorporate culturally responsive practices is vital for addressing the teacher shortage and aligning with SDG#4's emphasis on quality education and cultural diversity.

In Chapter 5, Burgess et al. contend that Australia's training and education system is facing increased scrutiny following a change of government in 2022. The research draws on secondary data from national agencies and national inquiries, as well as reports on skills development, by examining the extent to which the summit's recommendations have addressed the SDGs, especially those that require a long-term perspective. Findings suggest that while it is clear from the current reviews that the training and education programmes require considerable reform and funding to address SDGs, the ongoing dependence on immigration effectively poses internal and external challenges.

In Chapter 6, Sorakraikitikul and Kumjumpa explore the broad issues of skill shortages and skill mismatches in Thailand and the roles of the government, employers, and educational institutions in addressing these challenges. Based on the findings of an empirical study of employers and final-year university students, the chapter analyses the respondents' similar and different perceptions of the skills required for organisational effectiveness, and the shortcomings of educational institutions in preparing graduates with the necessary work-readiness attributes. The chapter focuses on SDG#8 and SDG#4 to explain the progress that Thailand has made and will need to pursue in the future to ensure its economic development and growth by enhancing the employability of its graduates.

In Chapter 7, Cooper and Tram examine Vietnam's market inefficiencies and subsequent ramifications for the educational supply behind demand in supplying the skills required to maintain a competitive presence. The chapter contends that since Industry 4.0 is replacing low-skilled work with an increased demand for high-skilled labour, leading to a multi-sector shortage in specialised talent, this shortage poses challenges for Vietnam's progress towards UN SDG#4 and SDG#8 and, subsequently, ongoing economic growth and development. This chapter discusses Vietnam's labour mismatch and proposes policies to encourage advanced skills development, improve access to education, and better align with industry needs.

In Chapter 8, Liu et al. explore the structural imbalance of the labour force and the mismatch between skill supply and demand in the Chinese manufacturing sector. As the largest such industry in the world, contributing around 30% to the Chinese economy, it is crucial to utilise suitably skilled workers to strategically plan current and future social and economic development. Key challenges include an ingrained preference for university qualifications over vocational skills and competencies; the need to better integrate higher education, vocational education, and industry training programmes through a more comprehensive skills certification system; and social and industrial recognition of these competencies and capabilities.

In Chapter 9, Waring and Connell examine the challenge of critical skill shortages in Singapore concerning decent work (SDG#8) and climate action (SDG#13). The chapter finds that Singapore has made steady progress concerning climate change action since embracing the SDGs. Its continuous improvement reflects the vulnerability of the low-lying city-state and the significant economic opportunity it savours by developing into a regional, if not global, hub for sustainable finance. In addition, the chapter suggests ways to foster a more productive, less injury-prone, and ethically sound working environment for migrants, which would help ensure an economically sustainable Singapore.

In Chapter 10, Dhakal and Tjokro focus on the Indonesian tourism industry. The authors contend that the Fourth Industrial Revolution (4IR) and the associated innovation and digitisation technologies have emerged as crucial industry priorities in the post-pandemic era. Nonetheless, although the inability to bridge the labour shortages and skill gaps can adversely impact local tourism businesses, the unfolding implications of the 4IR-related skills shortages in the sector remain underexplored. The chapter draws on the strategic human resource management perspective and utilises findings from an online survey and interviews to examine the nexus between 4IR and the tourism sector. The chapter demonstrates the need for tourism sector-specific policy initiatives to bridge the critical skills gap in the digital era to foster SDG#8.

In Chapter 11, Turner et al. analyse Malaysia's changing social and industrial landscape, which, like many other regional countries, is grappling with increased momentum towards digital transformation. Its impacts have led to low-skilled workers facing job losses due to their replacement by artificial intelligence technologies; on the other hand, higher-skilled employees must undertake constant upskilling to retain their well-paid positions. Using qualitative research methods as their foundation and focusing on SDG#8 with an emphasis on the information technology sector, the authors contend that these developments have been compounded by the lack of work-life balance, especially in big cities such as Kuala Lumpur, with younger employees preferring flexible occupations in the gig economy, employee disengagement, significant employee skill gaps—the so-called Great Attrition—and labour shortages in traditional industry sectors.

In Chapter 12, Rowtho et al. focus on the causes, nature, and solutions to critical skill shortages in Mauritius's information technology sector. Using a mixed methods approach, the research addresses SDGs #4, #8, and #9 in the context of the IT sector through a blend of focus groups and individual interviews with stakeholders from government, industry, vocational, and higher education to elicit the key skill shortages and effective strategies to address them in the small island state. This research aims to understand better the skill scarcity challenges facing the Mauritian IT industry. The findings suggest that the university learning experience is too academic, with insufficient opportunities to put theory into practice, learn about emerging technologies, and shape soft skills.

In Chapter 13, Sale and Sale use a qualitative approach to the Philippines—a labour-exporting country. The chapter reports on document analysis in relation to the exported labour policy, and its outcomes are analysed through the lens of decent work, as well as its indicators and patterns, as key aspects of the country's decent work performance under SDG#8. The findings suggest that the confluence of the exported labour policy, the COVID-19 pandemic, and decent work deficits contributed to the critical skill shortage of nurses and healthcare workers in 2020, which required the temporary banning of their overseas deployment.

In Chapter 14, Dhakal and Brown contend that Nepal provides a case for advancing a critical understanding of the tourism sector and the SDG#8 nexus as the country is recovering from three major crises in the past two decades: (a) the armed conflict between 1996 and 2006, (b) the 2015 earthquake, and (c) the COVID-19 pandemic. The chapter highlights that despite being a labour-exporting country, Nepal faces critical labour and skill shortages. The findings indicate that the tourism sector serves as the main engine for economic growth and opportunities, and stakeholders have observed that the absence of adequate job opportunities at the country level, and simultaneously, dismal employment conditions, inadequate education and training, and growth in emigration and immigration have all contributed to labour and skills shortages. Based on the findings, this chapter contends that steering the Nepalese socio-economic recovery back on track via tourism will be challenging without a concerted policy effort to foster innovative opportunities to overcome labour and skill shortages.

In Chapter 15, Mahmood et al. argue that despite ongoing industrialisation and structural change, a misalignment persists between workforce skills and economic development, a concern consistently voiced by the construction sector in Bangladesh. In exploring this issue, the chapter employs document analysis techniques to focus on the causes behind labour skill shortages. The chapter identifies the drivers behind Bangladesh's construction skill deficit—unveiling factors such as insufficient formal training, limited investments in education by government and industry, lack of training awareness, a significant informal labour sector, and negative migration patterns. A multifaceted approach is proposed to mitigate these issues, involving government-private sector collaboration, industry-driven initiatives, robust vocational training, and revised university programmes.

In Chapter 16, Dayram et al. argue that given India's workforce's rapidly ageing, organisations must invest in and leverage senior personnel to address skill gaps and the overall talent crunch. The authors offer a framework of critical skills for senior personnel by drawing on focus group discussions and interviews as part of an interactive qualitative analysis (IQA). The analysis underscored a shortage of digital and technological competencies among older workers.

In Chapter 17, Cunningham reviewed available studies to evaluate the social impacts of Tonga's participation in temporary labour mobility schemes. Utilising the theoretical framework of social transformation, this chapter focuses on the shortfalls of Pacific Labour Mobility schemes in achieving sustainable development outcomes. It finds that they skew population demographics, thus depleting unpaid care at home and in the community; amplify gender, age, and racial biases; provide limited opportunity for transferable skill development; and erode labour rights.

In Chapter 18, Nankervis et al. present a comparative summary and analysis of the key findings in this book. It reveals similarities and differences in how CSS are identified, the nature of the challenges of CSS in the diverse countries from the Asia-Pacific and Indian Ocean regions, and the plethora of government and private sector strategies, policies, and plans adopted in response to these challenges. The issue of CSS presents a key dilemma due to the divide in terms of the inflow and outflow of labour between developed and developing countries. The chapter contends that more resources and efforts will be needed to address the multifaceted challenges of CSS. A series of practical suggestions are included for all stakeholders involved in mitigating or minimising CSS to consider in their attempts to address SDGs.

Notes

* Corresponding author: john.burgess@torrens.edu.au.

1 The HDI is a summary measure of average achievement in key dimensions of human development: a long and healthy life, being knowledgeable and having a decent standard of living (UNDP, 2023a, para 2).

2 The SDGs ranking is a composite index based on the total progress towards achieving all 17 SDGs (UNDP, 2023b, para 1).

References

ABS. (2023, 21 February). *All regions labour market insights*. https://labourmarketinsights.gov.au/regions/all-regions-abs-sa4/?region=WA+-+Outback+%28North+and+South0

The Adecco Group. (2021). *The future of work and the 2030 sustainable development agenda*. https://www.adeccogroup.com/future-of-work/latest-insights/the-future-of-work-and-the-2030-sustainable-development-agenda

AHRI. (2023, 23 February). *The state of diversity, equity and inclusion in Australian workplaces*. www.ahri.com.au/wp-content/uploads/DEI-Report-2023.pdf

Asian Development Bank (ADB). (2017). *Japan fund for poverty reduction annual report 2017*. Author. www.adb.org/sites/default/files/institutional-document/522226/jfpr-annual-report-2017.pdf

Asian Development Bank (ADB). (2021). *ADB's support for the sustainable development goals*. Author. www.adb.org/sites/default/files/institutional-document/684471/adb-support-sdgs-2030-agenda.pdf

Australian Chamber of Commerce, and Industry (ACCI). (2022). *Overcoming Australia's labour and skills shortages through skills development, workforce participation and migration*. Author. www.australianchamber.com.au/wp-content/uploads/2022/03/ACCI-Overcoming-Australias-Labour-Shortages-24-March-2022-Final.pdf

Bourdieu, P., & Wacquant, L. T. D. (1992). *An introduction to reflexive sociology*. Chicago University Press.

Brunello, G., & Wruunck, P. (2021). Skill shortages and skill mismatches: A review of the literature, *Journal of Economic Surveys*, *35*, 1145–1167.

Cameron, R., Dhakal, S., & Burgess, J. (Eds.). (2019). *Transitions from education to work, workforce ready challenges in the Asia Pacific*. Routledge.

Capello, M. A., Shaughnessy, A., & Caslin, E. (2021). The geophysical sustainability atlas: Mapping geophysics to the UN Sustainable Development Goals. *The Leading Edge*, *40*(1), 10–24. https://doi.org/10.1190/tle40010010.1

Clean Energy Council. (2022). *Skilling the energy transition*. https://assets.cleanenergycouncil.org.au/documents/CEC_Skilling-the-Energy-Transition-2022.pdf
Cottingham, M. (2016). Theorizing emotional capital. *Theoretical Society*, *45*, 451–470.
Dayaram, K., Lambey, L., Burgess, J., & Afrianty, T. W. (Eds.). (2020). *Developing the workforce in an emerging economy: The case of Indonesia*. Routledge.
Dhakal, S. P. (2014). A methodological framework for ascertaining the social capital of environmental community organisations in urban Australia. *International Journal of Sociology and Social Policy*, *34*(11/12), 730–746.
Dhakal, S. P., & Burgess, J. (2021). Decent work for sustainable development in post-crisis Nepal: Social policy challenges and a way forward. *Social Policy & Administration*, *55*(1), 128–142.
Dhakal, S., Nankervis, A., & Burgess, J. (Eds.). (2019). *Ageing in Asia and the Pacific in changing times: Implications for sustainable development*. Springer Nature.
Dhakal, S., Prikshat, V., Nankervis, A., & Burgess, J. (Eds.). (2018). *The transition from graduation to work: Challenges and strategies in the twenty-first century Asia Pacific and beyond*. Routledge.
Gallo, J., & Thompson, P. R. (2000). Goals, measures and beyond: In search of accountability in federal HRM. *Public Personnel Management*, *29*(2), 241.
Global Goals. (2023). *The 17 goals*. www.globalgoals.org/goals/
Hamburg, I. (2020). Facilitating lifelong learning in SMEs towards SDG4. *Advances in Social Sciences Research Journal*, *7*(9), 262–272.
Hickey, P. J., & Cui, Q. (2020). Gender diversity in US construction industry leaders. *Journal of Management in Engineering*, *36*(5). https://doi.org/10.1061/(ASCE)ME.1943-5479.0000838
ILO. (2018). *Global skills partnership on migration*. Author. https://www.ilo.org/media/412556/download
ILO. (2023). *Decent work and the 2030 agenda for sustainable development*. Author.
Korn Ferry (2023, 20 February). Potential talent deficit of 47 million workers in APAC could threaten business growth. *Korn Ferry Focus*.
Martin, S. (2022, 6 October). Occupations facing skills shortages in Australia almost doubled in past year. *The Guardian*.
Nankervis, A., Connell, J., & Burgess, J. (Eds.). (2021). *The future of work in Asia and beyond: A technological revolution or evolution?* Routledge.
National Skills Commission. (2021). *National skills commission annual report 2020–2021*. Government of Australia. www.nationalskillscommission.gov.au/sites/default/files/2022-03/2021%20State%20of%20Australia%27s%20Skills_0.pdf
National Skills Commission. (2022). *2022 Skills priority list*. Commonwealth of Australia.
Pressley, A. (2022, 10 November). More than 85% of Asia Pacific businesses are reskilling IT workers in response to the growing tech skills shortage. *Insights*.
Price Waterhouse Coopers (PWC). (2018). *Workforce of the future: The competing forces shaping 2030*. Author.
Price Waterhouse Coopers (PWC). (2022). *Time for a rethink: The Asia Pacific workforce hopes and fears Survey 2022*. Author.
Rodríguez-Sánchez, J. L., González-Torres, T., Montero-Navarro, A., & Gallego-Losada, R. (2020). Investing time and resources for work—life balance: The effect on talent retention. *International Journal of Environmental Research and Public Health*, *17*(6), 1920.
Schultz, R. (2019). *Ecological determinants of health*. Paper presented at the 15th National Rural Health Conference. www.ruralhealth.org.au/15nrhc/sites/default/files/A9-1_Schultz.pdf
Shikur, Z. H. (2020). Agricultural policies, agricultural production and rural households' welfare in Ethiopia. *Journal of Economic Structures*, *9*(1), 50.

Spring Professionals. (2020). *Swiss skills shortage Index 2020.* https://ssi.springprofessional.ch/en/definition-and-effects/
Strietska-Ilina, O. (2019). Key challenges: The policy context. In O. Strietska-Ilina & T. Mahmud (Eds.), *Skills for a greener future* (pp. 59–84). International Labour Organisation. www.ilo.org/wcmsp5/groups/public/-ed_emp/documents/publication/wcms_732214.pdf
United Nations (UN). (2021a, 1 November). *Advanced economies are facing labour shortages.* Department of Economic and Social Affairs Monthly Briefing, 155. www.un.org/development/desa/dpad/wp-content/uploads/sites/45/publication/Monthly_Briefing_155.pdf
United Nations (UN). (2021b). *World economic situation and prospects: November 2021* (Briefing no. 155). www.un.org/development/desa/dpad/publication/world-economic-situation-and-prospects-november-2021-briefing-no-155/
United Nations (UN). (2024). *Sustainable development goals: 17 goals to transform our world.* www.un.org/en/exhibits/page/sdgs-17-goals-transform-world
United Nations Department of Economic and Social Affairs (UNDESA). (2015). *Transforming our world: The 2030 agenda for sustainable development.* https://sdgs.un.org/2030agenda
United Nations Development Programme (UNDP). (2016). *Human development report 2016: Human development for everyone.* Author.
United Nations Development Programme (UNDP). (2023a). *Human Development Index (HDI).* https://hdr.undp.org/data-center/human-development-index#/indicies/HDI
United Nations Development Programme (UNDP). (2023b). *Rankings 2024.* https://dashboards.sdgindex.org/rankings
United Nations Development Programme (UNDP). (2023c). *The SDGs in action.* www.undp.org/sustainable-development-goalscontent/uploads/sites/45/publication/Monthly_Briefing_155.pdf
United Nations Educational, Scientific and Cultural Organization (UNESCO). (2021). *Marine World Heritage in a changing climate.* https://whc.unesco.org/en/climate-change-marine/
University of Wollongong (UoW). (2023). *Goal 10: Reduce inequality within and among countries.* www.uow.edu.au/united-nations-sustainable-development-goals/goal-10-reduced-inequality/
Verma, P., Dhakal, S. P., & Nankervis, A. (2020). Workforce planning and development in emerging economies—A holistic approach for sustainable development. In K. Dayaram, L. Lambey, J. Burgess, & T. W. Afrianty (Eds.), *Developing the workforce in an emerging economy: The case of Indonesia* (pp. 31–42). Routledge.
Walters, J. (2022, 18 August). New research highlights the looming ESG skills shortages in APAC. *Human Resources Director.*
Wang, C., Ghadimi, P., Lim, M. K., & Tseng, M. L. (2019). A literature review of sustainable consumption and production: A comparative analysis in developed and developing economies. *Journal of Cleaner Production*, *206*, 741–754.
Workforce Australia. (2022). *National workforce strategy 2022–2027.* Commonwealth of Australia.

2 A Bibliometric Analysis of Literature on Labour and Skill Shortages

Implications for the Future of Work in the Asia-Pacific and Beyond

Subas P. Dhakal and Muhammad Nateque Mahmood*

Introduction

The future of work (FoW) research examines the drivers, processes, and outcomes of evolution associated with employees, employers, and employment. McKinsey and Company (2023) posit that FoW refers to 'an informed perspective on what businesses and other organisations need to know about how work could shift (given digitisation and other trends), plus how workforces and workplaces can prepare for those changes, big and small' (para 1). According to the European Labour Authority (ELA), the rapidly evolving diffusion of digital technologies, the transition to a climate-neutral economy, and the changing nature of workers and work have been considered the dominant phenomena of this millennium that have resulted in labour and skill shortages across developed and developing economies around the world (ELA, 2022, p. 9). The Economic and Social Commission for Asia and the Pacific's (ESCAP) report *Social Outlook for Asia and the Pacific* states that the region has a 'working-age population of over 3 billion men and women, with more than two billion making up the labour force' (ESCAP, 2022, p. v.). However, the 2018 Korn Ferry Global Talent Crunch Report projected that the Asia-Pacific region will face critical labour and skill shortages of '47 million with an economic cost of $4.24 trillion by 2030' (Korn Ferry, 2018, p. 38).

These issues have emerged as key threats that could potentially derail the UN's 2030 Agenda and aspirations to realise various sustainable development goals (SDGs), as discussed across the country cases included in this volume. In responding to these issues in Australia, Barnaba (2021) highlighted that 'education and training play a significant role in labour supply, supplemented by skilled, temporary, and other forms of supported migration' (para 2). For example, the multifaceted socio-cultural challenges, including ensuring the right mix of employment policies to generate employment opportunities within the country to curtail labour outflow as informed by the decent work agenda (see Dhakal & Burgess, 2021), have catapulted labour and skill shortages as

DOI: 10.4324/9781003379065-3

a research and policy priority worldwide, including in the Asia-Pacific region. Under the assumption that the scholarly and systematic scrutiny of the literature on labour and skills shortages can yield meaningful insights, this chapter reports on key findings of the bibliometric analysis.

This chapter has four parts. The following section provides a brief overview of the bibliometric analysis approach. The chapter then presents key findings and discusses implications for the Asia-Pacific region and beyond.

Bibliometric Analysis

The nature of and key differences between bibliometric and scientometric analyses, in which the scholarly research outputs become the focus of study, are discussed in detail elsewhere (Mahmood & Dhakal, 2022a, 2022b). Bibliometric analysis represents a quantitative evaluation of the magnitude of the impact of a specific field of study (Ellegaard & Wallin, 2015, p. 1810). Because labour and skill shortages are an integral component of the FoW agenda, unravelling variables such as prominent scholars, emerging or disappearing research themes, and the location of scholars' affiliated institutions can be helpful, particularly as bibliometric analysis of the associated literature, remains scant. As examples of the uses of bibliometrics, Saad et al. (2022) used it to develop a working framework to address the issue of skill shortages in the construction industry, and Alhloul and Kiss (2022) employed similar techniques to examine the skills and competencies of the labour force needed for Industry 4.0. It is evident that the issue has remained largely unexplored, and more importantly, an Asia-Pacific focus is non-existent. This chapter responds to this gap and examines the relevant literature of the past two decades (between 2001 and 2023) available on the Scopus database using bibliometrics.

The Scopus database was selected to collect bibliometric data because of its extensive coverage of publications (see Sankar, 2019). The literature search's first phase (global scope) used three keywords: 'labour + skills + shortages' to retrieve scholarly outputs. The search identified 921 publications, of which 878 outputs were used for the analysis after screening by the authors (such as removing non-scholarly articles). In the second phase (Asia-Pacific scope), an additional keyword ('country name') was added to extract literature specific to the countries included in this volume. Data were analysed using VOSviewer 1.6.1.13 and Microsoft Excel 2016. Both software enabled the visual representation of quantitative analysis, such as keyword maps and prominent research theme tables.

Key Findings

The key findings of the analysis appear in two separate parts. First, global labour and skill shortage trends, publication outlets, and research topics are presented. The second part presents results specific to the countries included in this volume.

Global Focus

Trend of Studies on Labour and Skills Shortages (2001–2023)

Scholarly outputs have steadily increased in the past two decades. Figure 2.1 shows a significant spike in output between 2020 and 2023. This is not surprising, as the rapid bibliometric analysis of the 'COVID-19 crisis, work, and employment' (Dhakal et al., 2021, p. 353) highlighted the impact of the pandemic on work and industrial relations worldwide and the associated unprecedented labour and skill shortages across the advanced economies during the pandemic (OECD, 2023, p. 3).

Publication Outlets/Field of Research

Of the 878 outputs in the Scopus database, 628 (71.5%) were journal articles, 137 (15.5%) were conference papers, and 113 (13%) were book chapters published between 2001 and 2023. Figure 2.2 shows the journals with over five articles on labour and skill shortages.

First, the *Construction Management and Economics Journal* had the most outputs (*n* = 11), followed by the *International Journal of Manpower* with ten outputs. The ranking of the two journals in this analysis is unsurprising given that construction is one of the top three sectors facing severe labour and skill shortages across the OECD countries (OECD, 2022a). Second, the aim and scope of the *International Journal of Manpower* (IJoM) are stated as 'an interdisciplinary journal, concerned with the utilisation, management, and planning of human resources and the economics of labour markets' (IjoM, n.d., para 2). This finding is relatively self-explanatory.

Social sciences (*n* = 386), business (*n* = 300), and engineering (*n* = 186) were the top three research fields associated with scholarly outputs on labour

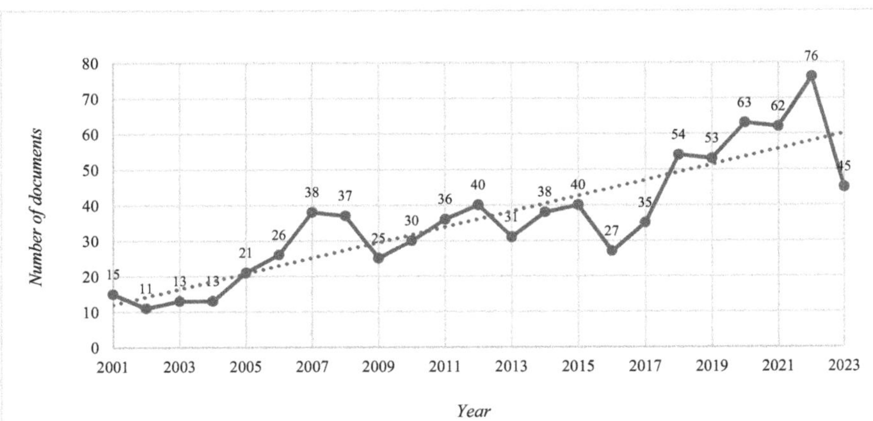

Figure 2.1 Research outputs in Scopus database (2001–2023)

Figure 2.2 Top contributing journals ($n \geq 5$)

and skill shortages. Given that proper education and training opportunities, policies, and initiatives to resolve socio-economic challenges, and investments in infrastructure development are key drivers of sustainable development (see Sachs et al., 2019), it can be contended that the emphasis on labour and skill shortages research within social sciences, business studies, and engineering disciplines is logical.

Co-occurrence Analysis of Labour and Skill Shortages-Related Research Topics

Co-occurrence analysis often involves investigating the frequency with which words appear together in a given text. Analysing co-occurring words can reveal insights into semantic relationships, word usage patterns, and thematic connections within the text (Sedighi, 2016). The co-occurrence analysis was conducted in VOSviewer, where 'unit of analysis' and 'counting method' were set as 'author keywords' and 'fractional counting' respectively. In addition, the smallest possible number of keyword occurrences was set as 3.

Of the 2140 keywords, a total of 158 met the threshold. Figure 2.3 shows the co-occurrence map of labour and skill shortages research themes. Table 2.1 complements the co-occurrence map and highlights research themes based on relative importance, ranging from skills (most important) to midwifery (least significant), as captured in the literature. The top ten list is hardly surprising, as the intertwined relationships between skills, education, employment, and migration are often part of the policy agenda in OECD countries like Australia. Themes that received the least emphasis have implications for shaping research directions on the FoW, including but not limited to labour mobility, workplace safety, and developing economies. For example, Ayentimi et al. (2018) contend that the lack of responsiveness to labour and skill shortages will likely hinder the SDGs' aspirations in developing economies of sub-Saharan Africa.

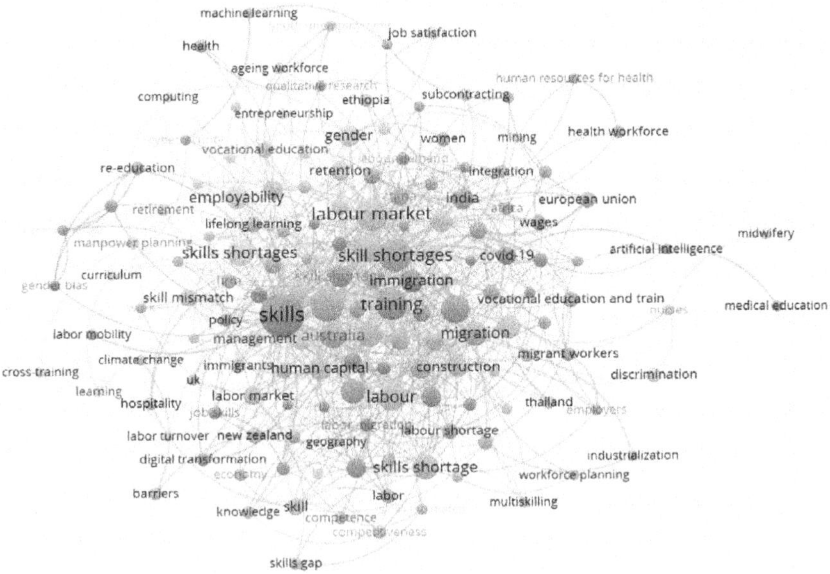

Figure 2.3 Co-occurrence map of research themes associated with labour and skill shortages

Table 2.1 Labour and skills shortages-related research themes in order of significance

Themes	*Relative importance*
Most important (top 10)	
Skills	1
Skill shortages	2
Education	3
Labour market	4
Training	5
Employment	6
Construction industry	7
Lifelong learning	8
Labour shortages	9
Migration	10
Least Important (Bottom 10)	
Human resources for health	149
Job satisfaction	150
Sub-Sharan Africa	151
Workplace safety	152
Career development	153
Developing economies	154
Cybersecurity	155
Labour mobility	156
Medical education	157
Midwifery	158

Influential Place of Scholarly Outputs and Collaborative Connections

A collaborative network analysis was conducted using a 'co-authorship' approach. The analysis focused on 'countries' as the unit of study and utilised the 'fractional counting' method for calculations. This co-authorship analysis facilitated the recognition of international collaborations regarding labour and skill shortages research. Among the 100 countries in the dataset, 52 fulfilled the prerequisites of having at least three documents and three citations, making them eligible for inclusion in the network map. Figure 2.4 illustrates that the United Kingdom (UK) was the most influential country regarding outputs associated with research institutions. The UK also displayed robust connections with the United States in the context of labour and skill shortages related to research activities. Another distinct cluster featuring strong collaborative linkages is observed between the UK and numerous European countries. In addition, the visualisation highlights a notable proportion of published studies on skill shortages originating from researchers in the Asia-Pacific region. This includes countries such as Australia, China, India, Thailand, New Zealand, Malaysia, Indonesia, Vietnam, and Singapore. Australia stands out due to its robust collaborative links in the Western sphere (Europe, Canada) and the Asia-Pacific region (China, India, New Zealand, and Indonesia).

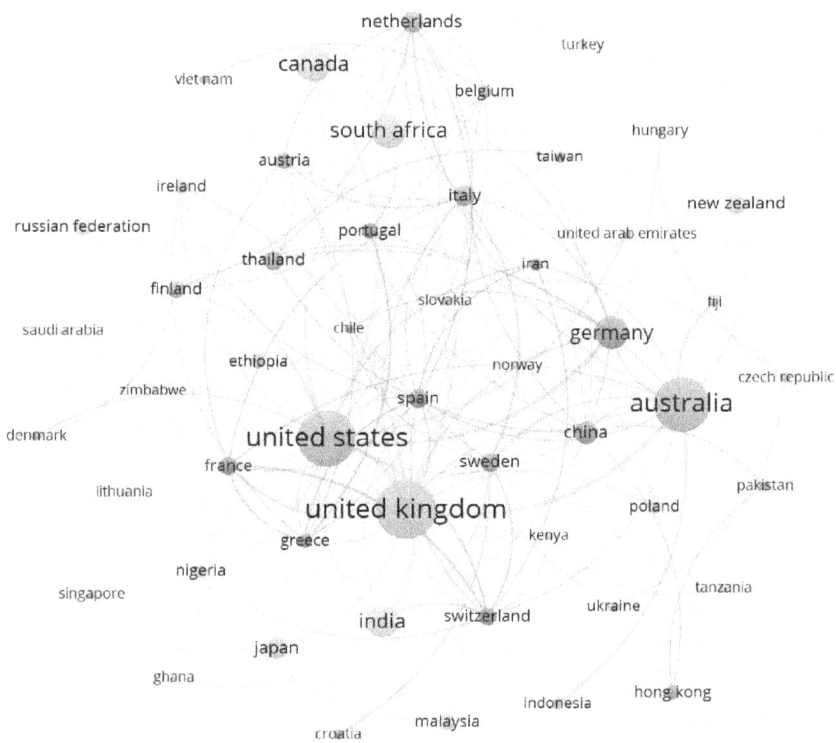

Figure 2.4 Prominent countries producing labour and skills shortages-related research outputs

Asia-Pacific Focus

Labour and Skills Shortages-Related Outputs

The number of journal articles in the 15 countries (*n* = 254) included in this volume was slightly over one quarter (29%) of the total outputs (*n* = 878). No publications on Mauritius and Tonga were in the database (Table 2.2). The fact that Australia has the highest number of outputs and has strong ties with several countries in the region (Figure 2.4) aligns with a narrative that the country aspires to strengthen its knowledge leadership profile in the Asia-Pacific region (Australian Academy of Science, 2022).

Prominent Researchers and Research Themes

Table 2.2 presents the state of labour and skill shortages literature on countries included in this volume. Of the 15 countries, Australia (*n* = 64), China (*n* = 47), and India (*n* = 42) were the top three countries in terms of the number of outputs in the database. Five outlets, the *Australian Economic Review* (*n* = 3), the *Journal of Industrial Relations* (*n* = 3), the *Worldwide Hospitality And Tourism Themes* (*n* = 3), the *Ageism In Work and Employment Journal* (*n* = 3), and the *Journal Of Asia Business Studies* (*n* = 3), published the most research on labour and skill shortages in the region. Chaturong Napathorn (Cornell University) and Peter Sheldon (University of New South Wales) were two of the prominent authors in terms of outputs (*n* = 5 each). Holland et al.'s (2007) article entitled 'Attracting and Retaining Talent: Exploring Human Resources Development Trends in Australia' was the most cited (Scopus: *n* = 70; Google Scholar: *n* = 293).

Table 2.2 Prominent researchers of the Asia-Pacific region

Country (articles count)	*Prominent authors (articles count ≥3)*	*Prominent outlet (s) (Top 3 and/or n ≥ 3)*	*Top cited article count (Scopus; Google Scholar)*
Australia (*n* = 64)	Tani, M. (*n* = 3)	*Australian Economic Review* (*n* = 3); *Journal of Industrial Relations* (*n* = 3)	Holland, P., Sheehan, C., & De Cieri, H. (2007). Attracting and retaining talent: Exploring human resources development trends in Australia. Human Resource Development International, 10(3), 247–262. (*n* = 70; 293)
Bangladesh (*n* = 1)	N/A	N/A	Mansour, S. (2017). Spatial concentration patterns of South Asian low-skilled immigrants in Oman: A spatial analysis of residential geographies. Applied Geography, 88, 118–129. (*n* = 14; 19)

(*Continued*)

Table 2.2 (Continued)

Country (articles count)	*Prominent authors (articles count ≥3)*	*Prominent outlet (s) (Top 3 and/or n ≥ 3)*	*Top cited article count (Scopus; Google Scholar)*
China (n = 47)	Sheldon, P. (n = 5); Li, Y. (n = 3)	N/A	Li, J., & Matlay, H. (2005). Graduate employment and small businesses in China. Industry and higher education, 19(1), 45–54. (n = 13; 30)
India (n = 42)	N/A	Worldwide Hospitality and Tourism Themes (n = 3)	Mehrotra, S., Kalaiyarasan, A., Kumra, N., & Ravi Raman, K. (2015). Vocational training in India and the duality principle: A case for evidence-based reform. Prospects, 45, 259–273. (n = 8;17)
Indonesia (n = 9)	N/A	N/A	Anwar, R. P. (2019). Expanding skilled-worker mobility: comparing the migration of Indonesian careworkers to Taipei, China and Indonesian nurses and careworkers to Japan In Challenges and opportunities for the ASEAN economic community, 209–240. (n = 4; 7)
Malaysia (n = 8)	N/A	N/A	Narayanan, S., & Lai, Y. W. (2005). The causes and consequences of immigrant labour in the construction sector in Malaysia. International Migration, 43(5), 31–57. (n = 26; 95)
Mauritius (n = 0)	N/A		
Nepal (n = 2)	N/A	N/A	Meinzen-Dick, R., Pradhan, P., & Zhang, W. (2022). Migration and gender dynamics of irrigation governance in Nepal. International Journal of the Commons, 16(1). (n = 6; 20)
New Zealand (n = 20)	Spoonley, P. (n = 3)	Ageism in Work and Employment (n = 3)	Chang-Richards, Y., Wilkinson, S., Seville, E., & Brunsdon, D. (2017). Effects of a major disaster on skills shortages in the construction industry: Lessons learned from New Zealand. Engineering, Construction and Architectural Management, 24(1), 2–20. (n = 26; 65)

(*Continued*)

Table 2.2 (Continued)

Country (articles count)	*Prominent authors (articles count ≥3)*	*Prominent outlet (s) (Top 3 and/or n ≥ 3)*	*Top cited article count (Scopus; Google Scholar)*
Philippines (n = 7)	N/A	N/A	Chih, Y. Y., Kiazad, K., Cheng, D., Emamirad, E., & Restubog, S. L. (2018). Interactive effects of supportive leadership and top management team's charismatic vision in predicting worker retention in the Philippines. Journal of Construction Engineering and Management, 144(10), 04018095. (n = 12; 20)
Singapore (n = 17)	N/A	N/A	Won, D., Hwang, B. G., & Chng, S. J. (2021). Assessing the effects of workforce diversity on project productivity performance for sustainable workplace in the construction industry. Sustainable Development, 29(2), 398–418. (n = 16; 22)
South Korea (n = 10)	N/A	N/A	Kwon, O. J. (2019). The diverging paths of skilled immigration in Singapore, Japan and Korea: Policy priorities and external labour market for skilled foreign workers. Asia Pacific Journal of Human Resources, 57(4), 418–444. (n = 6; 18)
Thailand (n = 14)	Napathorn, C. (n = 5)	Journal of Asia Business Studies (n = 3)	Napathorn, C. (2022). The development of green skills across firms in the institutional context of Thailand. Asia-Pacific Journal of Business Administration, 14(4), 539–572. (n = 15; 27)
Tonga (n = 0)	N/A		
Vietnam (n =13)	N/A	N/A	Montague, A. (2013). Vocational and skill shortages in Vietnamese manufacturing and service sectors, and some plausible solutions. Asia Pacific Journal of Human Resources, 51(2), 208–227. (n = 26; 58)

Discussion and Conclusion

This chapter conducted a bibliometric analysis of the scholarly literature on labour and skill shortages within the Scopus database published between 2001 and 2023. The findings indicate that the literature on labour and skill-related research has grown significantly in the past two decades, particularly during the COVID-19 pandemic. As labour and skill shortages are highly relevant to the FoW agenda and the 2030 agenda, the scholarly outputs will likely keep growing. In this context, the main contribution of this chapter is in the systematic analysis of the existing knowledge on labour and skill shortages related to scholarly outputs globally and within the Asia-Pacific region. Based on the analysis presented in the chapter, two specific matters associated with the FoW are discussed later.

Labour and Skill Shortages: An Ethical Dilemma?

It is evident from the analysis that research topics such as education, training, lifelong learning, and migration associated with labour and skill shortages have featured prominently in the literature. On the one hand, this prominence aligns with the significant attention of influential stakeholders such as governments and businesses as a way forward to address labour and skill shortages in countries like Australia (Australian Chamber of Commerce and Industry, 2022; Australian Government, 2023). Conversely, research themes such as labour mobility and ramifications for developing economies have received comparatively less attention. While temporary migration policies of developed economies help mitigate these challenges to a certain extent, they also create many ethical challenges (Ciupijus, 2010), not only for the host country but also for the country of origin. The unintended consequences of developed economies relying on labour from developing economies are a burgeoning ethical dilemma of labour mobility. Avenues of research in the future should consider these issues and examine associated ethical issues, especially in relation to the SDGs.

Increasing Research Collaboration Between Countries in the Region: Should Australia Lead?

The findings suggest that two advanced economies, the United States and the UK, are the leaders in producing labour and skill shortage-related research outputs. While Australia tops the list of countries in the region regarding research outputs, a few other countries, including China, India, and Singapore, are not far behind. However, smaller developing and emerging economies represented in this volume, such as Bangladesh, Mauritius, Nepal, and Tonga, have either negligible or no research outputs. Martinez-Fernandez and Powell (2010), for example, reported that labour outflow and the issue of manpower shortages had been under the radar in many countries in the Asia-Pacific despite overcoming the challenge of labour and skill shortages being crucial for Small Island Developing States (SIDS) and Least Developed Economies (LDCs) (OECD, 2022b; ILO, 2022). Given that the Australian government has recently funded an initiative to significantly boost the country's scientific leadership in the Asia-Pacific region (see International Science Council (ISC), 2023), perhaps the prospect of south-south collaboration within the region, in addition to envisaged north-south engagement through the ISC, warrants attention for a country that has immensely benefitted from the inflow of labour from developing countries in the region.

As with any investigation, there are limitations to the bibliometric analysis reported here (see Copyright Clearance Center, 2017). First, the limited availability of resources means that authors solely relied on the Scopus database to extract data, and research outputs that might be in another database, such as the Web of Science, were excluded. Second, although this edited volume aims to explore the nature, scope, and implications of the challenges associated with critical skill shortages, the word 'critical' was omitted in the search query due to the preliminary findings that the inclusion of the word resulted in significantly fewer outputs (878 versus 96). Studies in the future need to consider these shortcomings. Notwithstanding these limitations, the findings presented in this chapter should be useful to scholars, higher-degree research students, industry professionals, and policymakers interested in the evolution of labour and skill shortages-related scholarly outputs of the past two decades.

Note

* Corresponding author: subas.dhakal@une.edu.au.

References

Alhloul, A., & Kiss, E. (2022). Industry 4.0 as a challenge for the skills and competencies of the labour force: A bibliometric review and a survey. *Sci*, *4*(3), 34.

Anwar, R. P. (2019). Expanding skilled-worker mobility: Comparing the migration of Indonesian careworkers to Taipei, China and Indonesian nurses and careworkers to Japan. In *Challenges and opportunities for the ASEAN economic community* (pp. 209–240). Edward Elgar.

Australian Academy of Science. (2022). *Federal budget funding to strengthen Australian scientific leadership in Asia-Pacific*. www.science.org.au/news-and-events/news-and-media-releases/federal-budget-funding-to-strengthen-australian-scientific-leadership-in-asia-pacific

Australian Chamber of Commerce and Industry. (2022). *Overcoming Australia's labour and skills shortages* (Workforce Policy Position Paper). www.pc.gov.au/__data/assets/pdf_file/0007/338083/sub047-productivity-attachment.pdf

Australian Government. (2023). *Working future: The Australian Government's white paper on jobs and opportunities*. https://treasury.gov.au/sites/default/files/2023-09/p2023-447996-working-future.pdf

Ayentimi, D. T., Burgess, J., & Dayaram, K. (2018). Skilled labour shortage: A qualitative study of Ghana's training and apprenticeship system. *Human Resource Development International*, *21*(5), 406–424.

Barnaba, M. (2021). *No silver bullet for skill shortages*. www.ey.com/en_au/economics/no-silver-bullet-for-skill-shortages

Chang-Richards, Y., Wilkinson, S., Seville, E., & Brunsdon, D. (2017). Effects of a major disaster on skills shortages in the construction industry: Lessons learned from New Zealand. *Engineering, Construction and Architectural Management*, *24*(1), 2–20.

Chih, Y. Y., Kiazad, K., Cheng, D., Emamirad, E., & Restubog, S. L. (2018). Interactive effects of supportive leadership and top management team's charismatic vision in predicting worker retention in the Philippines. *Journal of Construction Engineering and Management*, *144*(10), 04018095.

Ciupijus, Z. (2010). Ethical pitfalls of temporary labour migration: A critical review of issues. *Journal of Business Ethics*, *97*, 9–18.

Copyright Clearance Center. (2017). *The limitations of keyword search*. www.copyright.com/crc/wp-content/uploads/sites/2/CCC_Keyword-Search-Tip-Sheet_FNL_WEB.pdf

Dhakal, S. P., & Burgess, J. (2021). Decent work for sustainable development in post-crisis Nepal: Social policy challenges and a way forward. *Social Policy & Administration*, *55*(1), 128–142.

Dhakal, S. P., Burgess, J., & Connell, J. (2021). COVID-19 crisis, work and employment: Policy and research trends. *Labour & Industry*, *31*(4), 353–365. https://doi.org/10.1080/10301763.2021.2005758

Economic and Social Commission for Asia and the Pacific (ECCAP). (2022). *The workforce we need social outlook for Asia and the Pacific*. www.unescap.org/sites/default/d8files/knowledge-products/Social-Outlook-2022.pdf

Ellegaard, O., & Wallin, J. A. (2015). The bibliometric analysis of scholarly production: How great is the impact? *Scientometrics*, *105*(3), 1809–1831.

European Labour Authority (ELA). (2022). *Report on labour shortages and surpluses 2022*. www.ela.europa.eu/sites/default/files/2023-03/eures-labour-shortages-report-2022.pdf

Holland, P., Sheehan, C., & De Cieri, H. (2007). Attracting and retaining talent: Exploring human resources development trends in Australia. *Human Resource Development International*, *10*(3), 247–262.

International Journal of Manpower (IjoM). (n.d.). *Aims and scope*. www.emeraldgrouppublishing.com/journal/ijm

International Labour Organisation (ILO). (2022). *Present and future of work in the least developed countries*. www.ilo.org/wcmsp5/groups/public/-dgreports/-integration/documents/publication/wcms_844025.pdf

International Science Council. (2023). *Regional focal point for Asia and the Pacific*. https://council.science/about-us/asia-pacific/#:~:text=It%20began%20its%20operations%20in,the%20results%20of%20that%20work.

Korn Ferry. (2018). *The global talent crunch*. https://focus.kornferry.com/wp-content/uploads/2015/02/The-Global-Talent-Crunch.pdf

Kwon, O. J. (2019). The diverging paths of skilled immigration in Singapore, Japan and Korea: Policy priorities and external labour market for skilled foreign workers. *Asia Pacific Journal of Human Resources*, *57*(4), 418–444.

Li, J., & Matlay, H. (2005). Graduate employment and small businesses in China. *Industry and Higher Education*, *19*(1), 45–54.

Mahmood, M. N., & Dhakal, S. P. (2022a). A bibliometric analysis of ageing literature: Global and Asia-Pacific trends. In S. Dhakal et al. (Eds.), *Ageing Asia and the Pacific in changing times: Implications for sustainable development*. Springer Nature.

Mahmood, M. N., & Dhakal, S. P. (2022b). Ageing population and society: A scientometric analysis. *Quality & Quantity: International Journal of Methodology*. https://doi.org/10.1007/s11135-022-01509-3

Mansour, S. (2017). Spatial concentration patterns of South Asian low-skilled immigrants in Oman: A spatial analysis of residential geographies. *Applied Geography*, *88*, 118–129.

Martinez-Fernandez, C., & Powell, M. (2010). *Employment and skills strategies in Southeast Asia: Setting the scene*. OECD Publishing. www.oecd.org/indonesia/45592999.pdf
McKinsey & Company (2023). *What is the future of work?* www.mckinsey.com/featured-insights/mckinsey-explainers/what-is-the-future-of-work#/
Mehrotra, S., Kalaiyarasan, A., Kumra, N., & Ravi Raman, K. (2015). Vocational training in India and the duality principle: A case for evidence-based reform. *Prospects*, *45*, 259–273.
Meinzen-Dick, R., Pradhan, P., & Zhang, W. (2022). Migration and gender dynamics of irrigation governance in Nepal. *International Journal of the Commons*, *16*(1).
Montague, A. (2013). Vocational and skill shortages in Vietnamese manufacturing and service sectors, and some plausible solutions. *Asia Pacific Journal of Human Resources*, *51*(2), 208–227.
Napathorn, C. (2022). The development of green skills across firms in the institutional context of Thailand. *Asia-Pacific Journal of Business Administration*, *14*(4), 539–572.
Narayanan, S., & Lai, Y. W. (2005). The causes and consequences of immigrant labour in the construction sector in Malaysia. *International Migration*, *43*(5), 31–57.
OECD. (2022a). *Making development co-operation work for small island developing states*. https://read.oecd-ilibrary.org/development/making-development-co-operation-work-for-small-island-developing-states_9789264287648-en
OECD. (2022b). *Too many jobs, not enough workers*. www.oecd.org/coronavirus/en/data-insights/too-many-jobs-not-enough-workers
OECD. (2023). *Ageing and employment policies retaining talent at all ages*. www.oecd-ilibrary.org/docserver/00dbdd06-en.pdf?expires=1707350246&id=id&accname=guest&checksum=2CCFB31DB41E223105521AEBD3883686
Saad, S., Alhaloul, W. S., Ammad, S., & Qureshi, A. H. (2022). A qualitative conceptual framework to tackle skill shortages in offsite construction industry: A scientometric approach. *Engineering, Construction and Architectural Management*, *29*(10), 3917–3947.
Sachs, J. D., Schmidt-Traub, G., Mazzucato, M., Messner, D., Nakicenovic, N., & Rockström, J. (2019). Six transformations to achieve the sustainable development goals. *Nature Sustainability*, *2*(9), 805–814.
Sankar, M. (2019). Mapping of research in agricultural scientist's citation analysis in google scholar, scopus and publons. *Asian Journal of Information Science & Technology (AJIST)*, *9*(2), 28–30.
Sedighi, M. (2016). Application of word co-occurrence analysis method in mapping of the scientific fields (Case study: The field of informetrics). *Library Review*, *65*(1/2), 52–64.
Won, D., Hwang, B. G., & Chng, S. J. (2021). Assessing the effects of workforce diversity on project productivity performance for sustainable workplace in the construction industry. *Sustainable Development*, *29*(2), 398–418.

Part 2

Country and Sector Studies

3 Critical Skills Shortages in New Zealand

An Evaluation of Policies

*Jim Arrowsmith**

Introduction

Developing workforce skills should be a 'win-win' for workers, employers, and society. It can support worker well-being, job satisfaction, and employability, as well as address low productivity, labour shortages, and weak economic growth. Investment in human capital, therefore, reaches across many of the UN's sustainable development goals (SDGs). This includes SDGs 1–3, addressing poverty, hunger, health, and well-being; SDG 4, on inclusive, quality education and lifelong learning; SDGs 5 and 10, around gender equality and inequalities in general; and SDG 8, on decent work and economic growth.

At the same time, providing quality vocational training is structurally constrained by employer competition and cost constraints, especially in anglophone 'liberal market' economies (LMEs) where there is weak institutional support (Hall & Soskice, 2001). Insufficient state and employer coordination around training contributes to systemic skill shortages and poor-quality work (Findlay et al., 2017). Both outcomes are reinforced in LMEs by low pay and limited employment protection around hiring and firing.

This situation is arguably acute in New Zealand (NZ), a small, geographically remote country with an economy dominated by low-value-added sectors such as commodity exports, tourism, and hospitality. Limited domestic competition and a preponderance of small and medium-sized enterprises (SMEs) inhibit innovation and investment in human capital, contributing to relatively low productivity and pay (OECD, 2022). The demise of sector-based industrial relations after the deregulatory Employment Contracts Act of 1991 also promoted a narrow and short-term response to skills shortages by employers, facilitated by declining trade union density and strength (Bryson, 2020). More recently, rapidly rising living costs have increased in-work poverty and stress and adversely impacted worker well-being, contributing to skill loss overseas through emigration (Perry, 2019). Many skilled workers leave NZ for higher-paid work in Australia, the UK, and elsewhere, which compounds the domestic skill deficit, not least as the rising cost of living has made NZ a more difficult migrant proposition. Recourse to migrant workers may also further stymie training investment in domestic talent.

DOI: 10.4324/9781003379065-5

These enduring structural problems were exposed and exacerbated by the COVID-19 crisis. In particular, the closure of the border from March 2020 until late 2022 ended the pipeline of migrant workers on both temporary visas and residency pathways. Migrant workers comprise a quarter of the workforce in many labour-intensive, technically lower-skilled sectors such as horticulture and hospitality (Conway, 2021). Employers also found it impossible to bring in high-skilled workers in occupations such as IT and construction. Tightening labour markets led to higher pay to retain and 'poach' increasingly scarce workers, especially in the post-COVID-19 inflationary environment, but there is little evidence of greater investment in training. Hence, the problem of skill shortages intensified with the pandemic.

Addressing this self-reinforcing problem of low pay, skills, and productivity has become a high priority for the government, and COVID-19 prompted responses beyond the changes to immigration settings demanded by employers. A Labour-led government was elected in 2017 after nine years of centre-right National party-led administrations. The immediate policy response included measures to significantly increase the minimum wage and in-work benefits as well as placing limits on the volume of inward migration (a priority of the coalition partner New Zealand First). The Labour Party was returned to govern alone in 2020, and strategic institutional reforms followed. This included changes to the vocational education and training system, (including unification of providers) followed by the re-introduction of sector-based industrial relations via mechanisms for 'Fair Pay Agreements' in 2022. It was argued by the then Minister for Workplace Relations that 'Fair Pay Agreements could lift industries out of a low wage, low productivity cycle by giving firms greater incentives to invest in physical and human capital (and) facilitate greater industry-wide coordination' (Lees-Galloway, 2018, p. 1). However, a National party coalition was returned to power in late 2023 and quickly reversed these policies.

Skills and the SDGs

In 2015, all United Nations members, including NZ, signed up for its initiative 'Transforming our world: The 2030 Agenda for Sustainable Development'. The 2030 Agenda seeks to improve life for current and future generations, particularly for those who are more vulnerable and furthest behind. It sets out 17 SDGs encompassing social, environmental, and economic development. Each goal has targets and indicators to drive and measure action, with 169 targets and 232 indicators overall. Companies and other organisations are also encouraged to participate, with businesses increasingly adopting the SDGs to help communicate their values and achieve better employee engagement, recruitment, and retention.

Developing workers' skills is an essential element of addressing the SDGs concerning the quality of work and life. The International Labour Organization (ILO), as the UN agency tasked with labour rights, stresses the importance of skills and lifelong learning as a key pillar of social inclusion and sustainable development in support of the SDGs. Building on the ILO Human Resources Development Recommendation 2004 (No. 194), the ILO's new Strategy on Skills and Lifelong Learning 2030 supports the development of resilient systems based on social dialogue that provide inclusive access to high-quality skills development and lifelong learning (ILO, 2023). This is vital, given rapid technological advances, demographic and climate change, and the legacy of the COVID-19 crisis, which are having profound impacts on jobs and the labour market in general.

There are three sets of considerations in this, relating to how we conceive of skills. The first concerns the supply of skills, which we address for the NZ context in the next section. As implicit in the ILO account, education and training are in themselves good things. On the other side of the equation is the demand for skills. The under-supply of skills creates problems for employers and the competitiveness of an economy, as well as for workers themselves, but a skills mismatch relating to oversupply can also lead to employee dissatisfaction and poor performance. A third issue is how we define the nature or components of skills as they relate to work. Are we sufficiently recognising—and developing and rewarding—important skills that the workforce already has?

Occupational skill broadly refers to the ability to execute the tasks required by a job. Official definitions of skill level employ hierarchies based on job complexity as indicated by tasks and duties (ILO, 2012). Proxy input measures such as education or training requirements may be used to this end. However, there are two problems with this approach in terms of how we perceive skills shortages and how the very notion of skills fits into the SDG framework. First, as Brewster and Tyson (1991, p. 15) observed, the concept of skill is 'highly ambiguous' because it refers both to 'a learned sequence of activities involved in performing a particular task' and more broadly to 'the recognised capacity to respond to the unexpected and the unpredictable'. Workers in routine jobs must still draw on higher-level skills (creative and critical thinking or communication skills) to respond to irregular and unforeseen events effectively. However, they may be classified as 'unskilled workers' because the principles of Taylorist job design (mass automated production systems) purposefully minimise discretion and involvement in their roles.

Second, and relatedly, statistical job groupings such as the International Classification of Occupations (ISCO) or local variants such as ANZSCO (the Australian and New Zealand Standard Classification of Occupations) tend to undervalue the importance of so-called soft versus technical skills. Soft skills include competencies that are difficult to specify, such as interpersonal or performative ('emotional') labour (Hochschild, 1983). Whereas automation and offshoring have eliminated swathes of repetitive and manual labour in developed countries, the growth of services has increased the number of jobs requiring these competencies. However, these are less likely to be credited as skills and therefore attract remuneration or training resources because they are conveniently viewed by employers as characteristics that are both inherent (a feature of personal maturity) and generic (generally available in the community).

Hence, many ostensibly routine jobs with limited technical training or educational development are undervalued because important interpersonal and tacit skills are unrecognised (Bolton, 2004). Female-dominated occupations such as retail and care work can require high-level communication, coordination, and problem-solving abilities (Burns, 1997), but a lack of recognition contributes to gender pay inequality (Junor et al., 2009). Furthermore, if 'soft' or 'human' skills are mislabelled as personality traits or dispositions, organisations dedicate relatively minimal training resources to developing them. It also means that skills shortages can be much higher than recognised by official statistics or by employers. These skill shortages are under-reported, even though they can be essential to effective performance, especially in client-facing service roles. One way to address this problem was pioneered in Australia and NZ using an in-depth, mixed-methods approach to job evaluation. This 'spotlight approach' is based on investigating what it is that workers do rather than the formal label or grade attached to their employment (Figure 3.1). It finds that frontline service jobs require much higher skills in dealing with people and problem-solving than are conventionally recognised in formal classifications.

Related to ambiguities around the definition of skills, it is not always clear as to what is a 'skill shortage' or what its causes may be (Richardson, 2007). A skill shortage could refer to an objective lack of suitably trained labour, reflecting factors such as past under-investment in skills development, rapid

Australian and NZ academics and stakeholders developed the spotlight skills recognition tool for the Pay and Employment Equity Unit of the NZ Department of Labour, now the Ministry of Business, Innovation and Employment (MBIE). It was designed by managers (MBIE, 2009b) to support job descriptions, recruitment and selection, and performance management and development. The method is based on job content and work process analysis. It enriches traditional job evaluation systems by adopting a 'bottom-up' and contextualised approach, interviewing people about their jobs alongside critical incident and narrative accounts. This is then used to quantify skills application, as broadly defined, highlighting otherwise intangible skill sets for interacting, relating, and coordinating activities. This analytical approach recognises the importance of on-the-job experience, not just training, in assessing required skills and redresses the undervaluing of tacit or interpersonal skills in female-dominated work.

Source: MBIE (2009a)

Figure 3.1 The 'spotlight' methodology for skills assessment

structural change, a cyclical surge in employment in a part of the economy, and/or low unemployment. It could also be that positions take a long time to be filled because the pay and working conditions on offer are unattractive, or employers are overly discerning in demanding certain personal characteristics as well as experience and technical ability. This will be perceived as a shortage by the employers concerned, even if there is an adequate supply of the skills in question within the labour force.

The New Zealand Problem

As noted earlier and evidenced in successive OECD reports, NZ is a relatively low-pay, low-skill, low-productivity wage economy. It is now also characterised by high living costs and inequality. The proportion of national income that goes to workers' wages was 59% in 2018, down from 71% in 1989 (Greer & Morris, 2019). There is also inequality in access to work as well as income. Although the pre-COVID-19 official unemployment rate was relatively low at 4.2% in 2019, it was 8.6% for Māori workers and 9.0% for Pacific people. Many people looking for work are not counted in the unemployment figures or are looking for extra hours, giving a total under-utilisation rate of 11.3% of the workforce. Youth unemployment remains a problem, with the rate of 20–24-year-olds not in employment, education, or training (NEET) at 16.0% overall but 26.7% for Māori and 23.6% for Pacific peoples. The UN (2023) notes that a problem with the stubbornly high youth NEET rate (at 12.5% of those aged 15 to 29 in 2021) is that training is focused on the already higher-skilled. Hence, as Greer and Morris (2019) note, NZ is some way off meeting the SDG goal of 'full and productive employment and decent work for all women and men'.

Part of the issue is employers' fixation with immigration to meet skill shortages and unfilled vacancies that may relate more to poor wages and employment conditions, a lack of information, or other 'labour market frictions' (Pissarides, 2011). The NZ economy has always depended on inward migration to meet its labour needs, and more than a quarter of its population is overseas-born (Productivity Commission, 2022). Stats NZ reports that between 2014 and 2019, the working-age population grew by over 60,000 each year, but in the COVID-19 years of 2021 and 2022, this fell by two-thirds. Employers responded to an increasingly competitive labour market by increasing pay, especially for blue-collar workers, and offering flexibility over working hours and location (Arrowsmith & Parker, 2023). However, once the border reopened, the clamour returned for a loosening of skilled migrant visa settings. It is not clear, however, that such a policy will be enough to address the structural skills problems in the economy.

Skills Shortages

Although COVID-19 introduced serious challenges in most sectors of the economy, one paradoxical legacy was to exacerbate recruitment difficulties.

This is partly a direct result of the border closure but also because of higher inflation and rising living costs after they were lifted. This made NZ a less attractive migrant proposition, while at the same time, the move to Australia and elsewhere became more attractive to young people and skilled workers. The Employers' Association (EMA) found in its Skills Shortage Survey 2023 that 71% of employers could not find highly skilled people, up from 40% the year before (EMA, 2023). More generally, nine out of ten employers with vacancies reported that they were struggling to fill them, and nearly a third had been advertising vacancies for over six months. Only 22% of respondents said that the situation had improved over the preceding six months, with twice as many saying it had worsened. The most impacted occupations were health professionals, construction workers, management and professional roles, as well as production operators. The survey reported that employers had responded by increasing training and upskilling (71%), 47% by looking at immigration, and 39% with enhanced youth engagement and apprenticeships. However, an obstacle to hiring apprentices or trainees was said to be insufficiently skilled staff able to train them. Recruiting migrant workers was also reported to be disadvantaged by a residency pathway policy weighed more towards university qualifications than technical skills.

Similar findings were made in a national survey of employers conducted for the Ministry of Business, Innovation and Employment (MBIE) in 2023, representing 212 businesses with 1.4 million employees (Kantar Public, 2023). More than half (55%) of respondents reported that they could not find people with the skills required, and 70% expected to retrain existing staff. Nearly half (46%) anticipated further work automation, and one in five staff redundancies lacked the skills to utilise new technologies, more so in larger firms. Three-quarters said COVID-19 had accelerated the digitalisation of work processes and that it increased opportunities to work remotely. Over half (57%) believed that the ongoing impact of COVID-19 would drive organisational transformation over the next five years.

One response by the government has been to loosen immigration requirements. The recent Labour government linked most settings to the median pay rate as a proxy for the skill level of the employment role. However, in a low-wage economy, this figure is not significantly higher than the minimum wage, at $29.66 and $22.70, respectively, in late 2023. As a result, around three in five immigrants are classified as being in lower-skilled work. There are also mounting concerns about the pace of immigration and the pressure on infrastructure and housing costs. Recent trends demonstrate record numbers both of New Zealanders leaving the country and of immigration (Dann, 2023). There was a record net migration loss of 44,800 NZ citizens in the year to September 2023. Of the 71,200 leaving NZ, nearly two in five (27,800) were aged 30 or under and over half left for Australia. However, there was also a record overall net migration increase of 118,900 in the same year. This was driven by the immigration of 163,600 non-New Zealanders, mainly from India, the Philippines, China, Fiji, and South Africa.

Skills Mismatch

A skills mismatch refers to a gap, either over or under, between a person's qualifications and abilities and their job requirements. A poor fit between skills and job demands for workers and their employers contributes to low job satisfaction, motivation, and performance (Rihova, 2016). Skills mismatch also acts as a brake on labour productivity by exacerbating allocative inefficiencies in the economy (McGowan & Andrews, 2015).

The skills mismatch in NZ is the highest in the OECD, a product of distortions concerning firms, workers, and state policy (OECD, 2022). First, the dominance of SMEs in the economy means that recruitment, selection, and work practices can be less sophisticated due to scale and management capability constraints in many firms. Second, worker mobility is inhibited by massive disparities in housing costs that present entry barriers to the major cities. Relatively high inward migration also contributes to skills mismatches, as many migrants to NZ tend to be over-educated for their roles, at least for some time following relocation (Poot & Stillman, 2023).

A third consideration is that state active labour market policy interventions (ALMPs) are underdeveloped, reinforcing systemic labour market frictions (Pissarides, 1990). Unlike other OECD countries, there is no social insurance for displaced workers, and redundancy notice periods and compensation are not mandated by law. Average notice is short by international comparison, at around one week for blue-collar workers, two weeks for white-collar workers, and one month for the fifth of workers covered by a collective agreement (OECD, 2017). This reduces costs for employers but leaves little time for dismissed workers to find a new job while still employed. Furthermore, displaced workers are also time-pressured to find any form of paid work once made redundant as they bear the costs of being laid off. Only one-third of the unemployed in NZ receive unemployment benefits because these are means-tested (OECD, 2022). Local offices of Work and Income, NZ's public employment service, are also rarely involved in supporting redundant workers. This lack of state assistance for job search, retraining, or short-term employment subsidies will likely intensify skills mismatches as technological change accelerates job displacement. Equally, advisory services for young people in schools are underdeveloped. The New Zealand Productivity Commission (2017, p. 360) observes that 'careers education and guidance in schools is highly variable, frequently delivered far too late, and at its worst appears not to reach some students'.

Training Under-Provision

It has been estimated that 250,000 people employed in industries covered by an industry training organisation (ITO) are under-qualified for the jobs they do, and when extended to the entire workforce, that figure rises to around 330,000 (Cox & Khan, 2015). Nevertheless, there was a steady decline in learner numbers in vocational education and training after 2010 (Parker et al., 2021). Between 2015 and 2020 the number of trainees fell from 105,540 to 76,749, though the number of apprentices increased from 42,005 to 61,890. The latter was partly due to a new $380 million government scheme introduced in 2020 and running to 2024. It aims to support up to 36,000 apprentices annually via a two-year wage subsidy to around 18,000 employers.

According to the Survey of Working Life (2018), an occasional supplement to the Household Labour Force Survey, most training is informal and on-the-job (OTJ). While six out of ten employees had undertaken work-related training in the 12 months prior to the survey, three-quarters of these had undertaken OTJ training. Formal training is focused on young apprentices or updating the skills and qualifications of the already highly skilled. This again reflects the predominance in the economy of SMEs, which tend to have less access to training resources and expertise and may fear labour loss if workers accumulate transferable skills. Larger firms too often look externally to respond to changing skills needs, with 77% of businesses surveyed by MBIE looking to hire solutions to meet skills gaps (Kantar Public, 2023). The same research suggests that just over half of the current workforce will require training to meet evolving skills demands, whereas only a third of the workforce has completed training. Only one in four businesses ensures all their employees receive the necessary training, with most focusing on it according to criteria relating to performance (56%), expected replacement difficulty (47%), and the likelihood of an employee staying in the longer term (37%).

Hence, the OECD (2023b) finds that the NZ vocational education and training (VET) system has not been fit for purpose. Provision tends to focus on a narrow set of fields and occupations with limited attention to transversal skills. Older learners are not well catered for, and training methods lag behind the possibilities of technology, such as simulators and virtual reality. NZ ranks low in youth enrolled in vocational programmes, at around 10% of 15–19-year-olds compared to the OECD average of nearly 40%. All of this compound the problems of skill shortages and skills mismatch and have prompted major institutional reforms.

The Policy Response

The return of a Labour-led government in 2017 heralded a series of VET policy reforms aimed at preparing organisations and their employees for the rapidly changing future of work. The Aotearoa New Zealand Skills Pledge was launched in May 2019 by the then prime minister and her business advisory council, committing signatory employers to double their investment in reskilling and training hours by 2025 and to report annually on progress. Though this commitment was severely disrupted by COVID-19, a focus on training needs was maintained by initiatives such as the Future of Work Tripartite Forum, which in 2022 agreed on a shared definition of a Just Transition.

Major institutional reform of the VET sector proceeded with the Education (Vocational Education and Training Reform) Amendment Act 2020. This merged the 16 polytechnics and nine sector-based industry training organisations (ITOs) into a new national institute, Te Pūkenga. Stronger industry input and oversight are exercised through Regional Skills Leadership Groups and six Workforce Development Councils (WDCs). The WDCs retain the qualification and standards development function of the former ITOs but also have an expanded remit to cover all VET, not just workplace learning. They also provide a stronger strategic role in the skills system by providing advice on public investment in VET, including in response to issues such as sustainability, workforce supply, equity, and the needs of Māori. The new system is designed to enhance social partner involvement to help focus on delivering the skills that employers need and ensure more consistency in provision across the country while providing greater support for trainees. Work-integrated learning will also become an increasingly important part of the vocational education system.

COVID-19 also provided a platform to enhance state support on the grounds of boosting economic recovery. A policy of Fees Free Tertiary Education and Training had already been introduced on 1 January 2018 for first-time tertiary learners in their first year of provider-based study or their first two years of work-based learning. During the COVID-19 period, the government announced a further series of enhanced funding measures, including $320 million for trade training for critical industries and $412 million to help employers retain their apprentices (Gerritsen, 2023). In addition, the Targeted Training and Apprenticeship Fund (TTAF) was introduced to financially support learners with up to NZD 6,500 per year (Beehive, 2020). The TTAF was directed towards industries where skill needs were expected to be acute during the post-COVID-19 recovery. These include primary industries, conservation, construction, community work, manufacturing, engineering, road transport, and information technology. The 2020 budget also provided the Ministry of Social Development with a $400 million boost to support those in disadvantaged groups and communities. A year later, the government announced a 13.4% increase in VET spending by 2024 (Parker et al., 2021).

A key goal of these reforms was to build a better sector-based training focus between providers, employers, and policymakers. One example is the development of the Sector Workforce Engagement Programme (SWEP), a cross-government initiative that aims to improve employers' access to skilled labour and support job seekers into work. The initiative works across industries such as horticulture and viticulture, dairy farming, road freight transport, construction, tourism, hospitality, and aged residential care. In the first few years since it was established as a pilot in 2016, more than 3,000 people were supported into recognised training while in employment (Business Advisory Council, 2019). Such initiatives have been enhanced by innovations such as 'micro-credentials' of around 5 to 20 credits that may be credited towards a nationally recognised qualification. There are more than 200 approved micro-credentials, including qualifications for farming, veterinary science, administration, transportation, construction, health, hospitality, and IT, which aim to encourage wider recourse to formal training (NZQA, 2022).

A second example is industrial relations reform, which aims to bring trade unions back into sector-based conversations and negotiations around pay and working conditions, including training. As sector-level agreements that also cover small and medium-sized businesses, Fair Pay Agreements (FPAs) could help disseminate best practices around workforce management, training, technology use, and health and safety. According to the OECD (2019, p. 29), FPAs 'could play a significant role in enhancing labour market security and strengthening workers' labour market adaptability'. The FPA Act received Royal Assent on 1 November 2022. By late 2023, no FPAs were in place, though the establishment process was underway in six sectors—hospitality, grocery, bus transport, early childhood education, commercial cleaning, and security. Trade unions also have a voice through membership in each of the six sector WDCs, providing an active role in setting skill standards, developing qualifications, and providing the government with advice on workforce development policies specific to their industry. However, it is early days in terms of awareness and impact. In the EMA Survey (2023), most respondents (83%) were unaware of a WDC established for their industry, and of those that were, only 17% had engaged in skill needs and workforce planning discussions with their relevant WDC.

The general election held in October 2023 led to the exit of the Labour government and the return of a National-led coalition with the New Zealand First and Act parties. New Zealand First has traditionally been opposed to high levels of immigration, but National and Act see this as a way to ease labour costs for employers. National has a number of policies geared towards encouraging overseas labour, which include raising the limit and reducing employer obligations towards seasonal workers; raising the upper age limit for working holiday visas to 35; allowing migrant workers to pay domestic rates for training; abandoning the median wage requirements for work visas; and allowing international students to work more hours while studying. National and Act parties are also committed to significant cuts in the public sector workforce.

Most immediately, the new government repealed the Fair Pay Agreements (FPA) Act just two months after the general election. It also announced a process of disestablishing Te Pūkenga to be completed by 2024 on the basis that centralisation increased bureaucracy and thereby slowed innovation and increased costs. It is intended that it be replaced with eight to ten individual training providers. However, it is not clear how the longer-term problems associated with underfunding, including shortages of course tutors for apprentices, will be addressed (Gerritsen, 2023).

Business, Skills, and the SDGs

Interestingly, most of the preceding Labour government's initiatives have been met with a generally positive response by businesses, especially by larger firms that see benefits from a more actively coordinated training policy. Even FPAs had not sparked undue antagonism as they might place a more effective floor under 'unfair competition'. The impetus in sectors like construction to cautiously welcome policy changes also derived from chronic labour shortages due to unique factors such as the 2011 Christchurch earthquake rebuild and reconstruction following adverse weather events, including Cyclone Gabriel in 2023. A Construction Skills Action Plan was launched in October 2018, co-developed by government agencies and an industry group of leading employers across the sector.

In the hospitality and tourism sectors, too, employers have been concerned about addressing their 'image problem' of low skills and precarious work by developing and marketing clearer career pathways around decent work. The Tourism Sustainability Commitment (TSC) was launched by the Tourism Industry Association in November 2017, explicitly setting out how individual businesses could achieve to help the industry reach the SDGs. It was refreshed in August 2020, by which time over 1,400 businesses and organisations had signed up. One of the 12 commitments refers to being an 'employer of choice' or 'attracting, supporting, and developing the workforce we need to flourish and succeed'. This includes paying a living wage and investing in staff training and development, supported by regular reviews and staff involvement.

New Zealand companies are also engaging with the SDGs through membership of the Sustainable Business Council (SBC), a Global Network Partner of the World Business Council for Sustainable Development. Members of the SBC make a commitment to reduce their greenhouse gas emissions and build sustainability into their purchasing decisions, as well as review employment conditions such as fair and equal pay and opportunities for disadvantaged groups. They are also required to introduce annual reporting practices, outlining their progress on environmental, social, and governance (ESG) and related economic issues, which are reviewed every two years. In 2020 there were 100 SBC member organisations, representing 28% of NZ's private sector GDP and 10% of the NZ workforce. The New Zealand Stock Exchange also updated its Code in 2017, requiring a listed issuer to report on ESG factors and practices as part of its non-financial reporting or, if a board decides not to report on these, explain why this is appropriate.

Within companies, the HRM function can be important in advocating for SDGs alongside corporate social responsibility (CSR) professionals (Sarvaiya & Arrowsmith, 2023). The professional association HRNZ introduced its first portfolio of activities linked to SDG week in 2022. It has focused on six SDGs (3, 4, 8, 10, 12, and 13), introducing relevant targets. In the 2023 SDG week, HRNZ declared that

> we are resolute in engaging HR professionals and businesses in transformative conversations surrounding sustainability. Our core intention is to establish a profound connection between HR Professionals and people leaders and the pursuit of sustainability. Moving beyond the conventional perception of 'green and clean' sustainability, we aim to highlight the importance of nurturing and caring for people as an integral part of our sustainability journey.

This commitment recognises a concern of CSR with investment in people and decent work, alongside 'external' environmental concerns, which the HR function can help implement and embed through its recruitment, promotion, training, and employee involvement practices (Sarvaiya & Arrowsmith, 2023). A major constraint is that firms focused on profit and shareholder value often tend to have a more short-term and instrumental view of their human resources. A further barrier to investment in 'human capital' is that the time and financial costs of training are real and immediate, but potential returns can be remote and uncertain and are rarely evaluated (Aguinis & Kraiger, 2009).

More fundamentally, as is also recognised in the HRNZ position, though much of the training policy debate focuses on reinforcing the skills base in the labour force, there is little point in developing skills if workers and their employers cannot apply them (Arrowsmith & Parker, 2012). As Russo et al. (2023) note, what is necessary are effective human resource strategies that, in the terminology of the 'AMO' model, enhance workers' motivation and opportunity as well as their ability to perform. In practice this means a clearer focus on worker well-being, job design, 'voice', and management selection and development that promote better people management capabilities. Training alone is insufficient to optimise skills utilisation and performance.

The Emerging Technological Challenge

Any SWOT analysis concerning the future of skill shortages must begin with consideration of technological change. This is accelerating due to incredible technological advances and societal changes, including the ageing workforce and the COVID-19 pandemic, both of which intensified automation (Acemoglu & Restrepo, 2017; Chauhan, 2021). The exponential growth in computer power, the internet, and advanced robotics promises huge possibilities for humankind but also raises fears that digitalisation is already driving labour substitution and inequality (Långstedt & Arrowsmith, 2023). On the one hand, as these technologies replace repetitive tasks, they effectively help upskill the employment structure through a process of 'skill-biased technological change' (Berman et al., 1998). There are also major social benefits if productivity gains are shared in the form of higher incomes or reduced working time as well as more meaningful work. Technology is also driving innovation and improvements in the price and quality of products and services provided to consumers. Automation could also help respond to global challenges such as demographic change, which is contributing to labour shortages and increasing the 'dependency ratio' in many countries, as well as addressing climate change by developing the 'green economy'.

Alternatively, new technologies could make work more structured, intense, and impersonal, such as through algorithmic management, and prompt large-scale economic dislocation. This negative view is of a future of work characterised by increased unemployment and job insecurity. It was long ago predicted by Braverman (1974), who forecast the large-scale displacement and proletarianisation (de-skilling and casualisation) of white-collar and professional work as soon as technologically feasible. Zuboff (1988) similarly observed how early computerisation was used to control more than liberate workers from routine tasks.

New technology has facilitated the growth of casual work in NZ, as elsewhere. Smartphone technology has led to the rapid rise of the digital gig economy characterised by temporary and freelance work. While gig work presents novel opportunities for autonomy and control for workers with scarce and marketable skills, by driving casualisation, it also reduces employment standards, including training and career development, for large numbers of lower-skilled workers (Vallas & Schor, 2020). Platform work is also strongly linked to reduced worker well-being due to an enhanced sense of powerlessness and loneliness, as well as financial stress and long working hours (Glavin et al., 2021). Regulation is therefore important to maintain labour standards, such as those that occurred in NZ with its restrictions on the use of zero-hour contracts imposed by the Employment Relations Amendment Act 2016.

A current challenge for skills and jobs is also presented by the deployment of generative artificial intelligence (AI) tools. This is likely to impact clerical jobs most immediately and, therefore, female workers, displacing some while augmenting the work of others (Gmyrek et al., 2023). However, a lack of appropriate skills remains a major barrier to wider AI adoption in NZ, and this is a product of business underinvestment in training (OECD, 2023b). The education sector's domestic pipeline of advanced ICT skills is also weak. Poor mathematics achievement limits the proportion of school students who can obtain the university qualifications needed for ICT careers. This encourages employers to compete for experienced workers or import labour from abroad rather than invest in their own career pathways (OECD, 2022).

Increasingly rapid technological change means that a focus on workforce upskilling and reskilling is imperative, but even businesses making significant training investments find their efforts are hampered by two important problems: limited measurement and evaluation of what works and a lack of information about how to generalise and scale up successful programmes (Jorge Tamayo et al., 2023). Policymakers, too, are failing to systematically get to grips with building a positive ecosystem for skills development in response to rapidly unfolding and often unpredictable challenges posed by paradigmatic change such as the green transition (OECD, 2023a). The threat that AI poses in terms of deskilling work and reducing jobs and pay is more likely to be realised in countries that do not sufficiently invest in their innovative capabilities, that is, human capital and related institutional and technical infrastructure, which go beyond organisations and require government action (Hayton, 2023).

Conclusions

Investment in human capital is generally good for workers, employers, and society. However, in LMEs such as NZ, firms driven by 'shareholder value' tend to be short-term, cost-focused and uncollaborative with other firms in the sector, the state, and employee representatives. NZ also has additional structural barriers in its product and labour market that inhibit VET and contribute to skill mismatches and shortages. This includes its small, remote, oligopolistic economy; the offshoring of manufacturing; and the deregulation of collective bargaining; the dominance of SMEs in low-skill, low-productivity sectors; high living costs and fewer career opportunities that fuel a 'brain drain' and a reliance on migrant workers. COVID-19 has only added to these problems.

After 2017, Labour governments introduced a series of policies to address the problem of low workforce skills, which were linked to low pay, productivity, and 'skill shortages' in the economy. On the demand side, this included efforts to make labour a valued rather than disposable asset, including infrastructure spending to reduce unemployment and other reforms to raise wages and employment costs, such as a rapidly rising minimum wage and better employee benefits. On the supply side, major VET reform was undertaken with the merger of 16 Polytechnics and Institutes of Technology and a massive increase in Trades and Apprenticeships investment. This was accompanied by measures to increase employer coordination and tripartism, such as 'Fair Pay Agreements' to set minimum sector standards by industry-wide bargaining, the replacement of ITO with tripartite Workforce Development Councils and Skills Leadership Groups, and tripartite Industry Transformation Plans to improve innovation, productivity, and the quality of work in eight major sectors.

It remains to be seen what the legacy of this will be on the stock and distribution of skills in the NZ economy, not least because a three-year electoral cycle and coalition politics, favoured by the proportional representation system, make profound institutional change difficult to sustain. The incoming National-led government took immediate steps to terminate two of its predecessor's flagship reforms in Te Pūkenga and FPAs. COVID-19 also placed a brake on some relevant initiatives. In its first and only government review of progress towards the SDGs (MFAT, 2019), lofty claims were made:

> New thinking is required to achieve the vision encapsulated in the SDGs. Rather than measuring progress in purely economic terms. New Zealand is developing a broader set of measures—the Living Standards Framework (LSF)—that puts sustainable intergenerational wellbeing at the centre of policy-making and the management of our resources.

The more immediate pressures introduced by COVID-19 largely put paid to that.

Skill needs are rapidly changing under challenges such as the climate crisis, COVID-19, demographic change, new technologies, and global political instability. Technical and vocational education and training (TVET) have arguably never been so important in ensuring that young people and adults are equipped to play a full part in an increasingly dynamic society. This includes a renewed focus on recognising and rewarding the development of intangible, tacit, and 'soft' skills such as communication, problem-solving, and interpersonal skills related to emotional intelligence, which are likely to be in increasing demand in our rapidly changing economy. If this is not addressed, we will have the prospect of another layer of structural and critical skills shortages to contend with.

Note

* Corresponding author: J.Arrowsmith@massey.ac.nz.

References

Acemoglu, D., & Restrepo, P. (2017). *Secular stagnation? The effect of aging on economic growth in the age of automation*. NBER Working Paper Series 23077. doi: 10.3386/w23077.

Adalet McGowan, M., & Andrews, D. (2017). *Skill mismatch, productivity and policies in New Zealand: Evidence from PIAAC* (OECD Economic Department Working Papers). OECD Publishing.

Aguinis, H., & Kraiger, K. (2009). Benefits of training and development for individuals and teams, organizations, and society. *Annual Review of Psychology*, *60*, 451–474.

Arrowsmith, J., & Parker, J. (2012). Good work and good workplaces. In J. Bryson & R. Ryan (Eds.), *Human resource management in the workplace* (pp. 172–203). Pearson.

Arrowsmith, J., & Parker, J. (2023). Employer perspectives on the living wage and minimum wage during Covid: Evidence from New Zealand. *Labour & Industry*, *33*(1), 102–122.

Beehive (2020, 2 June). Release of initial list of supported training to aid COVID-19 recovery. Press Release. Retrieved August 19, 2021. https://tec.govt.nz/news-and-consultations/archived-news/release-of-initial-list-of-supported-training-to-aid-covid-19-recovery/

Berman, E., Bound, J., & Machin, S. (1998). Implications of skill-biased technological change: International evidence. *Quarterly Journal of Economics*, *113*(4), 1245–1280.

Bolton, S. (2004). Conceptual confusions: Emotion work as skilled work. In C. Warhurst, I. Grugulis, & E. Keep (Eds.), *The skills that matter* (pp. 19–37). Palgrave Macmillan.

Braverman, H. (1974). *Labor and monopoly capital: The degradation of work in the twentieth century*. New York: NYU Press.

Brewster, C., & Tyson, S. (Eds.). (1991). *International comparisons in human resource management*. Pitman.

Bryson, J. (2020). The role of trade union collective voice in the access to training for workers in New Zealand. *International Journal of Training and Development*, *24*(1), 231–244.

Burns, P. M. (1997). Hard-skills, soft-skills: Undervaluing hospitality's 'service with a smile'. *Progress in Tourism and Hospitality Research*, *3*, 239–248.

Business Advisory Council. (2019). *A future that works*. Prime Minister's Business Advisory Council. www.mbie.govt.nz/dmsdocument/26404-a-future-that-works-report-harnessing-automation-for-a-more-productive-and-thriving-new-zealand-pdf

Chauhan, A. (2021). Robotics and automation: The rescuers of COVID era. In D. Oliva, S. A. Hassan, & A. Mohamed (Eds.), *Artificial intelligence for COVID-19* (pp. 119–151). Cham: Springer.

Conway, P. (2021, 2 July). What role will migrant workers play in the future of New Zealand? *Stuff*. www.stuff.co.nz/business/the-monitor/300332934/what-role-will-migrant-workers-play-in-the-future-of-new-zealand

Cox, M., & Khan, M. (2015). *The workforce within scope of the ITOs—Profile and projections overview report* (Berl Economics Report Number 5553). NCVER. www.voced.edu.au/content/ngv%3A71194
Dann, L. (2023, 15 November). Leaving home: Record net migration loss of NZ citizens in year to September. *New Zealand Herald.*
Employers and Manufacturers Association (EMA). (2023). *Skills shortage survey.* https://emalive.co.nz/documents/advocacy/Skills-Shortage-Survey-Results-2023.pdf
Findlay, P., Warhurst, C., Keep, E., & Lloyd, C. (2017). Opportunity knocks? The possibilities and levers for improving job quality. *Work and Occupations, 44*(1), 3–22.
Gerritsen, J. (2023, 18 October). Te Pūkenga apprentice training 'a disaster'—trades businesses. *RNZ.* www.rnz.co.nz/news/national/500442/te-pukenga-apprentice-training-a-disaster-trades-businesses
Glavin, P., Bierman, A., & Schieman, S. (2021). Über-alienated: Powerless and alone in the gig economy. *Work and Occupations, 48*(4), 399–431.
Gmyrek, P., Berg, J., & Bescond, D. (2023). *Generative AI and jobs: A global analysis of potential effects on job quantity and quality* (ILO Working Paper 96). ILO.
Greer, G., & Morris, M. (2019). *The people's report on the 2030 agenda and sustainable development goals: An alternate report for Aotearoa New Zealand.* www.sdg.org.nz/peoples-report
Hall, P. A., & Soskice, D. (2001). *Varieties of capitalism: The institutional foundations of comparative advantage.* Oxford University Press.
Hayton (2023). The future is algorithmic (Core 11). *Warwick Business School,* 33–35. https://online.flippingbook.com/view/441896271/34-35/
Hochschild, A. R. (1983). *The managed heart: Commercialization of human feeling.* University of California Press.
ILO. (2012). *International standard classification of occupations: ISCO-08.* Author.
ILO. (2023). *The ILO strategy on skills and lifelong learning 2030.* Author.
Jorge Tamayo, J., Doumi, L., Goel, S., Kovács-Ondrejkovic, O., & Sadun, R. (2023, September–October). Reskilling in the age of AI: Five new paradigms for leaders—and employees. *Harvard Business Review.*
Junor, A., Hampson, I., & Smith, M. (2009). Valuing skills: Helping mainstream gender equity in the New Zealand state sector. *Public Policy and Administration, 24*(2), 195–211.
Kantar Public. (2023). *2023 NZ future of work survey.* MBIE.
Långstedt, J., & Arrowsmith, J. (2023). Values, work and well-being in artificial intelligence society: Exacerbating dilemmas in human resource management. In M. Filimowicz (Ed.), *Algorithmic ethics: Algorithms and society* (pp. 22–38). Routledge.
Lees-Galloway, I. (2018). Improving the employment relations and standards system: Fair pay agreements. *MBIE.* www.mbie.govt.nz/dmsdocument/3251-improving-the-employment-relations-and-standards-system-fair-pay-agreements-pdf
McGowan, M. A., & Andrews, D. (2015). *Skill mismatch and public policy in OECD countries.* OECD.
Ministry of Business, Innovation and Employment (MBIE). (2009a). *Spotlight: A skills recognition tool—background research report.* Author. www.employment.govt.nz/assets/Uploads/tools-and-resources/publications/8f5dce509a/spotlight-research-report.pdf
Ministry of Business, Innovation and Employment (MBIE). (2009b). *Spotlight: A skills recognition tool user guide 1. Introduction for managers.* www.employment.govt.nz/assets/Uploads/tools-and-resources/publications/a5724739a2/spotlight-Introduction-for-Managers.pdf
Ministry of Foreign Affairs and Trade (MFAT). (2019). *He waka eke noa: Towards a better future, together. New Zealand's progress towards the SDGs.* Author.

New Zealand Productivity Commission (NZPC). (2017). *New models of tertiary education, inquiry report.* NZPC.
New Zealand Qualifications Authority (NZQA). (2022). *Register of NZQA-approved micro-credentials.* Author. www.nzqa.govt.nz/nzqf/search/microcredentials.do.
Organisation for Economic Cooperation and Development (OECD). (2017). *Back to work New Zealand—Improving the re-employment prospects of displaced workers.* Author.
Organisation for Economic Cooperation and Development (OECD). (2019). *OECD economic surveys: New Zealand.* www.oecd.org/economy/surveys/new-zealand-2019-OECD-economic-survey-overview.pdf
Organisation for Economic Cooperation and Development (OECD). (2022). *OECD economic surveys: New Zealand 2022.* Author. www.oecd.org/economy/surveys/New%20Zealand-2022-OECD-economic-survey-overview.pdf
Organisation for Economic Cooperation and Development (OECD). (2023a). *Assessing and anticipating skills for the green transition.* Author.
Organisation for Economic Cooperation and Development (OECD). (2023b). Building Future-Ready Vocational Education and Training Systems.
Parker, J., Arrowsmith, J., Barney, A., & Junaid, F. (2021). *Working life in New Zealand.* Eurofound. www.eurofound.europa.eu/en/resources/article/2023/new-zealand
Perry, B. (2019). *Household incomes in New Zealand: Trends in indicators of inequality and hardship 1982 to 2018.* Ministry of Social Development.
Pissarides, C. A. (1990). *Equilibrium unemployment theory.* Blackwell.
Pissarides, C. A. (2011). Equilibrium in the labour market with search frictions. *American Economic Review, 101*, 1092–1105.
Poot, J., & Stillman, S. (2023). *The importance of heterogeneity when examining immigrant education-occupation mismatch: Evidence from New Zealand* (CReAM Discussion Paper No 23/10). Motu Publications.
Productivity Commission. (2022). *Immigration by the numbers.* www.productivity.govt.nz/research/immigrationbythenumbers/
Richardson, S. (2007). *What is a skill shortage?* NCVER.
Rihova, H. (2016). *Using labour market information: Guide to anticipating and matching skills and jobs.* Publications Office of the European Union.
Russo, G., van Houten, G., & Consolini, M. (2023). *Fostering skills use for sustained business performance: Evidence from the European Company Survey.* Publications Office of the European Union.
Sarvaiya, H., & Arrowsmith, J. (2023). Exploring the context and interface of corporate social responsibility and HRM. *Asia Pacific Journal of Human Resources, 61*(2), 300–323.
UN (2023). *Sustainable development report 2023.* https://dashboards.sdgindex.org/static/profiles/pdfs/SDR-2023-new-zealand.pdf
Vallas, S., & Schor, J. B. (2020). What do platforms do? Understanding the gig economy. *Annual Review of Sociology, 46*, 273–294.
Zuboff, S. (1988). *In the age of the smart machine.* New York: Basic Books.

4 Cultivating Culturally Responsive Self-Efficacy in South Korean Pre-service STEM Teachers

Addressing Skill Shortages in Education

Luis Miguel Dos Santos, Ching Ting Tany Kwee, and Ho Fai Lo*

Introduction

With a global trend of STEM teacher shortages (UNESCO, 2022), it is foreseeable that such shortages will become more critical for South Korea over the following decades. Over the past few decades, the South Korean government, non-profit organisations, and universities have established and expanded the number of scholarships and support and potential teacher training programmes for pre-service teachers to join the teaching and education profession (G.-L. Lee et al., 2009; Park, 2010). As such, South Korea generally has a good track record in teacher selection and recruitment. Over the past decade, about 80% of teachers have had teaching as their first career choice (OECD, 2019). Furthermore, teachers in South Korea have relatively competitive salaries, making it a relatively attractive profession for graduates. Primary school teachers have ranked the third highest teacher salary, which is 1.24 times the salary of other professionals with similar qualifications (UNESCO, 2022).

However, such commendable statistics do not shield South Korea from the pressing challenge of a teacher shortage. Indeed, a confluence of factors is intensifying this scarcity of educators within the nation. First, similar to other OECD countries, about one-third of the teachers in South Korea are aged 50 or above (OECD, 2019). Second, South Korea has a low proportion of teachers who feel satisfied with their employment except for salary (OECD, 2019). Scholars (Klassen & Chiu, 2010; Lent et al., 2011) suggested that job dissatisfaction and stress directly correlate with the early attrition problem.

Moreover, there are peculiar challenges in recruiting and retaining STEM educators. A primary concern is the allure of job opportunities in alternative sectors, which effectively divert STEM professionals away from academic institutions and towards industry roles. Since the 1980s, the South Korean government has strongly encouraged the development of information technology, computer sciences, and engineering (Arnold,

DOI: 10.4324/9781003379065-6

1988). Consequently, many traditional-aged (18–24) students and adults (25 years or older) have decided to study and receive their educational qualifications and training in STEM, especially information technology. As a result, many technologically oriented companies and organisations, such as Samsung, LG, and Lotte, employ well-trained university graduates, master's degree holders, and doctoral degree holders. However, this does not benefit small and mid-sized companies and organisations, including educational institutions, and exacerbates the disparity in talent distribution (Won & Park, 2020).

Such plight directly impacts the goal of providing quality education, as per SDG 4, underscoring the importance of increasing the number of teachers and ensuring they are well-trained, motivated, and capable of meeting a diverse student body (UN, 2021). While South Korea predominantly consists of a Korean-majority population (Bae et al., 2019; Shen, 2019), the increasing mobility of international exchange programmes at various educational levels has led to a notable rise in the number of international students in both secondary and tertiary education institutions (Jon, 2012; Kang & Hwang, 2022). However, 70.1% of South Korean teachers believe they are not confident enough to cope with the challenges in a culturally diverse classroom, ranking 49 out of 50 (UNESCO, 2022). This demographic shift necessitates the development of culturally responsive pedagogies, a strategy crucial for leveraging the diverse cultural capitals of students to augment their educational outcomes (Sleeter, 2012; Lambert & Lambert, 2019). Furthermore, acknowledging and embracing cultural diversity not only celebrates inclusivity but also aids students for whom the language of instruction is not their first language, thereby reducing their cognitive load and consequently enhancing their learning effectiveness in STEM subjects (Barron et al., 2021; Song et al., 2023). However, recent statistics indicate a significant challenge: due to the predominantly homogeneous population, South Korean educators often lack confidence in their cultural competency, which is essential for implementing such culturally responsive pedagogies (OECD, 2019). This shortcoming contrasts with one of the critical criteria for quality education as outlined in SDG 4, which emphasises cultural responsiveness in celebrating and respecting cultural diversity (UN, 2021). The educators' lack of confidence in this area thus emerges as a potential threat to achieving the goal of truly inclusive and effective quality education.

The gaps in achieving SDG 4 delineate a context for an in-depth examination of the factors contributing to self-efficacy among pre-service teachers and educators in South Korea. Scholars (Bandura, 1986, 1997) posit that heightened self-efficacy contributes to individual educators' professional development and the sustainable teaching workforce. The confidence and competencies of educators in executing culturally responsive pedagogies (Chen, 2022; Kart et al., 2023) are integral to mitigating attrition issues and bolstering teacher retention. This study explores the strategies that enable female pre-service educators to develop the cultural responsiveness and leadership competencies required to inch closer to realising SDG 4, quality education, and SDG 5, gender equality. It is guided by the research question—what personal and environmental factors contribute to self-efficacy in cultural responsiveness among female STEM pre-service educators in South Korea? And how?

Theoretical Framework: Self-Efficacy Theory

Self-efficacy theory (Bandura, 1986, 1997) was adopted as the theoretical framework to guide this study, whereby the development of self-efficacy alongside its relationship with one's motivation, behaviours, and social environment was explored. According to Bandura's self-efficacy theory (1986, 1997), there are four sources of self-efficacy, namely mastery experiences (successful past experiences), vicarious experiences (observing similar success of others), social persuasion (encouragement or praises from others), and emotional and physiological states (positive emotions). Figure 4.1 captures the factors related to the four sources of cultural responsiveness self-efficacy in Korean STEM educators.

Self-efficacy is a valuable predictor of motivation, confidence, and persistence in career decisions and actions (Lent et al., 1994; Brown & Lent, 2019). Bandura's (1986, 1997) conceptualisation of self-efficacy suggests that higher levels of self-efficacy in individuals correlate with a greater likelihood of achieving success. This success, in turn, acts as a reinforcing mechanism, bolstering an individual's resilience and perseverance in the face of career challenges. Prior research (Siwatu, 2007; Isaac et al., 2012; Siwatu

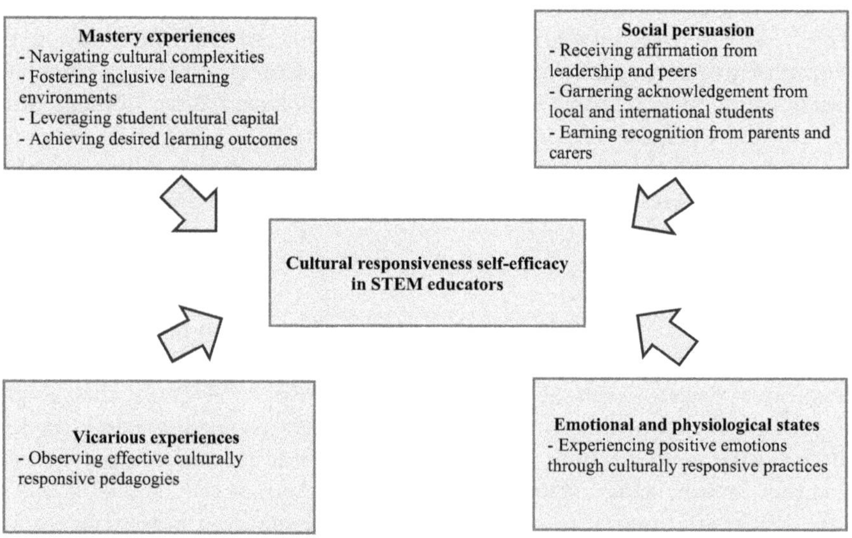

Figure 4.1 Factors contributing to the development of cultural responsiveness self-efficacy in Korean STEM educators

et al., 2016; Miralles-Cardona et al., 2022) has effectively utilised self-efficacy Theory to evaluate existing practices and develop interventions aimed at sustainable equity or instructional strategies. For instance, Mirrales-Carondona et al. (2022) employed this theory to examine teachers' beliefs in their capabilities, focusing on how their confidence in gender knowledge, skills, and awareness evolves to shape their teaching practices and sustain gender equity over time.

Similarly, Siwatu (2007) explored pre-service teachers' culturally responsive teaching outcome expectations about various personal and contextual factors, thereby establishing their self-efficacy. These studies underscore the utility of self-efficacy theory in identifying individual and contextual factors that contribute to the development of self-efficacy, particularly in achieving desired teaching outcomes such as adopting culturally responsive pedagogies and navigating inclusive learning environments. Furthermore, it facilitates an understanding of how educators can continuously develop their culturally responsive teaching methods throughout their careers, aligning with the evolving demands of the educational landscape.

Data Collection and Analysis

The embedded nature of self-efficacy within participants' lived experiences, where personal and environmental factors are intricately intertwined and not consistently explicitly recognised by the individuals themselves, warrants a qualitative approach with a small sample size (Larkin et al., 2006; Smith et al., 2021). A cohort of fewer than 15 participants is deemed appropriate for delving deeply into the sense-making processes of the individuals, uncovering the subtle yet influential elements within their professional development experiences that shape the evolution of self-efficacy in STEM pre-service teachers and educators (Alase, 2017; Smith et al., 2021). For instance, a study examining the self-efficacy of ten teachers and their experiences can be instrumental in identifying conditions for successful teacher collaboration that bolster their teaching efficacy (Chong & Kong, 2012). While a small sample size may face limitations in terms of generalisability (Yip et al., 2022; Yip, 2023), its strength lies in the potential to discern factors that contribute to sustainable practices in both teaching and career development, intricately linked to broader social and cultural contexts, paving the way for future research. The selection criteria for participants in this study are defined as follows:

- Participants must be South Korean citizens verified by their official identification documents.
- They should be at least 18 years of age.
- Additionally, they must be actively enrolled in an initial teacher education programme, specifically focusing on STEM subjects, at a South Korean university.

The primary data for this study were collected through two semi-structured interviews and a focus group activity with each participant. Drawing upon Bandura's self-efficacy theory (1986, 1997), the research team devised a set of interview questions tailored for the individual semi-structured interviews (Seidman, 2006). Due to COVID-19 restrictions during data collection, nine participants engaged in face-to-face interviews, while five participated in online sessions. Participants were invited to a focus group activity after these interviews to facilitate deeper discussion and sharing. During these sessions, participants were encouraged to share personal items, such as photographs and reports relevant to their experiences and perceptions of self-efficacy (Creswell, 2012; Merriam & Tisdell, 2016). To ensure accuracy and participant agreement, transcripts of the interviews and focus group discussions were sent back to the participants for member-checking before data analysis (Creswell, 2012; Merriam & Tisdell, 2016).

The researchers employed open, axial, and thematic coding during data analysis (Creswell, 2012; Merriam & Tisdell, 2016). Initially, the general inductive approach (Thomas, 2006) was used to categorise the data—the research team utilised NVivo software to manage and analyse the transcripts. The initial data coding was conducted through open coding, identifying various themes and subthemes. Further analysis involved axial coding to refine the themes and establish relationships. A codebook was developed to facilitate the dialogic reliability check, discussion, and mutual critique among research team members regarding the hypothesis and framework underpinning the coding process, ensuring consistency in the understanding and interpretation of the codes (Åkerlind, 2005).

Furthermore, this study received ethical approval from Woosong University. The research team adhered to protocols for handling sensitive data, ensuring the anonymity and confidentiality of the participants. Following the identification of 12 themes and 23 subthemes through open and axial coding, thematic coding was applied, aligning closely with the sources of self-efficacy stated in self-efficacy theory (1986, 1997). This rigorous approach further distilled the data into a concise set of themes and subthemes that directly respond to the research questions, offering targeted insights into the specific personal and contextual factors influencing self-efficacy among STEM pre-service teachers and educators in South Korea.

Findings

This section presents and discusses the findings in response to the research question: What personal and environmental factors contribute to self-efficacy in cultural responsiveness among female STEM pre-service educators in South Korea? How? Table 4.1 encapsulates the identified themes and subthemes that illuminate the personal and environmental factors fostering the development of self-efficacy in cultural responsiveness within this demographic.

Table 4.1 Themes and subthemes pertaining to personal and environmental factors influencing self-efficacy in cultural responsiveness among STEM pre-service educators

Themes and Subthemes
Personal Factors Contributing to Cultural Responsiveness Self-Efficacy in STEM Pre-Service Educators
• Engaging Reflective Practices in Adopting Culturally Responsive Pedagogies
Environmental Factors Contributing to Cultural Responsiveness Self-Efficacy in STEM Pre-Service Educators
• Navigating Institutional Barriers to Culturally Responsive Pedagogy in STEM Education
• Navigating the Challenges of an Exam-Centric Curriculum in Cultivating Culturally Responsive STEM Education
• Work-Integrated Learning in Bridging Industry Experience and Classroom Teaching

Personal Factors Contributing to Cultural Responsiveness Self-Efficacy in STEM Pre-Service Educators

This study identifies specific personal factors contributing to the development of self-efficacy in cultural responsiveness among STEM pre-service educators, highlighting the crucial role of individual reflective practices in embracing diverse cultural contexts within STEM teaching.

Engaging Reflective Practices in Adopting Culturally Responsive Pedagogies

This study's findings show that reflective practices are integral for pre-service STEM educators in understanding and adopting culturally responsive pedagogies. When engaging in reflective practices, the participants start by observing the differences in the learning styles between international and Korean students. They begin from their concrete experiences in the classroom, thinking reflectively about how they can adapt their instructions and teaching materials to facilitate their students' learning (Kolb & Kolb, 2018; Lehane, 2020).

> *It is always assumed that science or math is universal. They are just symbols . . . and most manuals or materials are in English. . . . Our math can be a bit more challenging for some learners. But it does not mean that they [international students] do not have relevant concepts. . . . I provided my students a vocabulary list of the translated words in also their native language. . . . I saw the impact there and they were more active in discussion and volunteer information.*
>
> (Participant #8)

Translanguaging can effectively scaffold the materials and deploy their entire repertoire of linguistic and semiotic resources (Otheguy et al., 2015; Pierson & Grapin, 2021). This is especially important in classrooms with English language learners (ELLs); this involves respecting and incorporating the native languages of students into the learning process (Beres, 2015; Yuvayapan, 2019). By engaging in reflective practice, the observation of such learning needs of the students allows the participants to draw upon their funds of knowledge to think over the appropriate pedagogies (Radhakrishnan et al., 2021; Kharlay et al., 2022). On the other hand, adapting the materials to make them familiar to international students can be helpful. Another participant shared insights into making content more universally relatable:

> *Some word problems are really very Korean context, like building names, cities, and even K-pop. Of course, it is good to showcase to them some part of our amazing cultures and heritage . . . but we can also have some more 'international bits'. . . . Like I got a class with some students from the US. . . . Of course, they come here for exchange because they like Korean culture, or mostly I should say K-pop . . . but it is good to include something they know, like we do Newtonian mechanics, we used some examples about the US buildings or even their brands of cars.*
>
> (Participant #1)

This strategy of contextualising STEM content demonstrates an engagement in abstract conceptualisation from their learning experiences (Kolb & Kolb, 2018; Radhakrishnan et al., 2021). Another participant also provided some benefits of such adaptations, stating that culturally responsive pedagogies aim to engage students by connecting learning to their experiences and cultural backgrounds.

> *I can see the improvement there. . . . It's not just changing the names of brands from Siemens to Samsung. It is about how this may look familiar to them, and they find even if they learn STEM here, it is still relatable to them. . . . It makes me feel successful. . . . I can teach even international students. . . . If I'm gonna teach again, I'll put this on my plate.*
>
> (Participant #11)

The success achieved by pre-service STEM educators in engaging students through culturally relevant STEM content fosters a proactive cycle of experimentation (Kolb & Kolb, 2018; Radhakrishnan et al., 2021). These educators are keen to explore this approach further in their future teaching, confident in its effectiveness and practicality. This enthusiasm is rooted in their positive experiences connecting STEM learning with students' cultural backgrounds and community contexts, which they believe enhance the overall educational experience. The successful past experiences from the mastery of experiences as a source of self-efficacy can make the pre-service STEM teacher confident in translating that into another context in their future teaching to attain the outcomes of teaching (Lent et al., 1994; Bandura, 1997).

While adopting reflective practices can enhance pre-service STEM educators' self-efficacy through successful experiences and positive reinforcement, this often occurs individually without formal support or encouragement from their teacher training programmes. The prevailing environment in higher education, which tends to be suppressive rather than supportive of developing cultural responsiveness, poses a significant barrier. Consequently, this lack of institutional support limits the potential growth of educators in this area. The upcoming section will delve into the environmental factors within teacher training settings and curriculum design, examining how they negatively impact pre-service STEM teachers' ability to teach in a culturally responsive manner.

Environmental Factors Contributing to Cultural Responsiveness Self-Efficacy in STEM Pre-service Educators

Although South Korea is one of the educational destinations and hubs for international students who want to study and complete their education in the East Asian environment (Jon et al., 2014; Alemu & Cordier, 2017; Ayhan et al., 2022), this study's findings reveal that a significant gap exists in the incorporation of culturally responsive pedagogies within the curriculum. The prevailing teaching approaches, largely traditional and examination-focused, do not adequately address the diverse needs of a globalised student body. This disconnection between the educational system's practices and the requirements of a multicultural learning environment hampers the development of essential skills among pre-service STEM educators.

Navigating Institutional Barriers to Culturally Responsive Pedagogy in STEM Education

A primary issue in pre-service teacher training programmes within higher education institutions is the notable absence of structured training in culturally responsive pedagogies. This deficiency is compounded by the fact that many teacher trainers lack the requisite expertise and strategies to effectively address the increasing cultural diversity brought about by the influx of international students. Consequently, this gap in teacher education curricula and faculty preparedness hinders the development of essential skills among future educators, which are vital for navigating the complexities of an increasingly globalised student population. One participant pointed out a distinct lack of focus on cultural responsiveness in teacher education:

> *When I first heard of culturally responsive pedagogies, I thought it was just something about learning English or something in developing countries, and it is not a Korean thing . . . because my university and my previous*

education . . . did not have strong . . . teaching and learning materials about these areas [cultural competencies].

(Participant #1)

Another participant highlighted the broader issue within the education system, pointing out that despite educational efforts, the specific needs of international students were often overlooked:

Korea and its government invest many resources in . . . education . . . the training in Korea is useful . . . but . . . many professors . . . and even students are not ready for international students . . . because many professors continue to use the Korean teaching style . . . many international students cannot follow the teaching.

(Participant #14)

When further asked what is meant by the 'Korean teaching style', the participants generally defined it as 'rote-learning', 'lecture', 'teacher-centred', and 'chalk-talk'. However, if educators ignore such differences in learning styles, it can potentially cause them to fail to achieve their teaching outcomes.

My experience is a bad one. . . . It showed and told me that the traditional way as the only way didn't work . . . there are no ways to ask questions in our lecture. . . . Korean professors tend to speak all over the lecture . . . they do the math on the board and we just copy, copy, and copy . . . and students usually do not have any chances to ask . . . but many of my international classmates want to ask . . . but the professors . . . dislike the questions . . . and believe the international students . . . disgrace their [professors'] teaching . . . that makes the lectures so . . . dead.

(Participant #6)

The teacher trainers' responses reflect how the broader social and cultural contexts of understanding students' learning styles and needs can be potentially hampered. In Asian educational contexts, there is a strong emphasis on student respect and discipline towards teachers and classroom norms (Kwee, 2023; Yip, 2023). Regarding international students, Korean educators often anticipate similar behaviour from them. Consequently, actions such as posing questions during a lecture, which may be commonplace in other educational cultures, are sometimes perceived as disruptive or atypical behaviours by Korean educators. This cultural difference in classroom etiquette highlights a potential area of misunderstanding and cultural adjustment for Korean educators. This can be more intensified when it comes to STEM. For instance, when some students come from international backgrounds, their learning styles can be diverse, as they expect learning to be more interactive, practical, and scaffolded, especially in STEM subjects.

[In] my science curriculum lectures . . . my professors told us that we should not employ and conduct lab experiments with secondary school students . . .

because it can be dangerous . . . professors believe that videos and PowerPoint presentations can completely replace the hands-on experiences and lab experiments . . . it might work in South Korea . . . but my classmates from the United Kingdom . . . do not understand and do not accept . . . many classmates argued with the professors.

(Participant #7)

STEM education relies on hands-on experiences and laboratory experiments from teachers and professors (San-Valero et al., 2019). However, it is expected that South Korean schools and universities tend to employ top-down teaching and learning strategies and approaches (Skedsmo & Huber, 2019), which significantly limit the motivations, experiences, and achievements of students (Pečiuliauskienė & Belakoz, 2019). Another participant also mentioned a scenario in which the idea of being culturally responsive by including culturally relevant examples for international students was rejected by the tutors when they were doing some scenario-based learning and discussions during tutorials:

My tutor . . . I didn't want to name him. . . . He disagreed that we should use some examples related to the international student's backgrounds to make those word problems in math more relatable. That's . . . sickening . . . He said math is math everywhere. . . . I'm not sure whether I want my classroom to be that. . . . I don't think it works, but there is no way out. . . . That's our culture . . . We have to follow our supervisors. . . . We can't challenge them . . . . if the older generations do not make any changes, we cannot reform the curriculum.

(Participant #11)

Another participant expressed similar concerns, reflecting on the disconnection between university education and the practical needs of a more internationalised classroom:

I felt like . . . we disappointed them [international students] . . . many international students and foreign professors are in my university . . . it is a perfect start . . . because many people believe in Korean education . . . and they believe Korea can offer them the right education. . . . I haven't seen anyone do that before. . . . I'm not sure I could do that. . . . Perhaps I would also fail them in future. . . . I don't want to be one of them.

(Participant #14)

This sentiment points to a disparity between the theoretical aspects taught at the university and the realities observed in diverse classroom settings. The frustration experienced by this pre-service STEM teacher stemmed from an inability to meet the students' varied learning needs. According to Bandura's self-efficacy theory (1986, 1997), the lack of vicarious experiences, such as being unable to observe successful role models implementing culturally responsive pedagogies, can negatively impact the development of self-efficacy.

This situation can significantly diminish pre-service teachers' confidence in effectively managing a culturally diverse classroom. Consequently, it also affects their motivation to pursue a career as a STEM teacher.

Navigating the Challenges of an Exam-Centric Curriculum in Cultivating Culturally Responsive STEM Education

Apart from the constant rejection the pre-service STEM teachers faced in their initial teacher training to adopt culturally responsive pedagogies, another challenge they faced was the STEM curriculum. Like many Asian countries, South Korea is also predominated by an examination-oriented curriculum (Lee & Butt, 2014). With the pressure of meeting standards quantified by test and examination marks, teacher trainers at higher education continue to ensure their graduates are equipped with such skills to meet their future employers' standards, which hampers their development of cultural competencies. One participant explained:

> *[I]n my secondary chemistry lectures . . . my professors continued to focus on the test skills and how to prepare for the national exams . . . the Korean professors do not want our students to understand the meaning of the materials . . . they [Korean professors] only want our students to have good grades . . . these professors do not understand teaching . . . they only care about the scores.*
>
> (Participant #2)

The pressure on teachers and students to achieve high test scores can lead to a narrowing of the curriculum. Teachers might feel compelled to concentrate solely on test-related content, leaving little room for higher-order thinking skills needed for incorporating cultural elements or addressing students' unique cultural needs and backgrounds, which future STEM educators feel are essential. For instance,

> *[C]ritical thinking and inquiries are important elements in science learning . . . but the current [Korean] teaching style usually limits students' critical thinking and inquiry . . . I grew up in a top-down classroom . . . [Korean] students can only listen to our teachers . . . we [students] knew our teachers made a mistake . . . but we could not argue . . . because she [teacher] is our teacher.*
>
> (Participant #4)

Another evidence of being culturally responsive is critically evaluating or challenging assumptions related to cultures, languages, or ideologies in the curriculum or daily sciences. In such an exam-oriented curriculum, especially when university teacher trainers share this mindset, collaborative learning, such as problem-based learning, is not encouraged. According to self-efficacy theory (Bandura, 1986, 1997), such rejection can be a negative verbal persuasion that hampers the development of cultural responsiveness among future educators, as they feel that such development is not very encouraged. This can be seen in another example from a participant:

> *For example, when we consider building constructions, it is only about functionality like energy saving or making the office space more efficient, there is no room to think over inclusion or how to consider the needs or even embrace the diverse cultural groups. . . . Even though I tried to voice out that the professor is just saying that it is not needed, and students only need to consider space and energy or those parameters to gain marks. . . . But you know the real world is not like this.*
>
> (Participant #2)

Such frustration is intensified when the participants often find that such a way is not a sustainable learning method in response to the following educational context.

> *I believe that is a trend that we have to align our curriculum and learning styles with other parts of the world. Of course, results are important and an indicator, but we also have to consider other strategies to use to make our classroom more effective. Especially science or technology is like cross-nation collabouration. . . . Just like in Microsoft, there are employees from all around the world. . . . It is something that we should have in STEM education, that if our future students stay in STEM, they know that skill how to think scientifically, collabourate scientifically.*
>
> (Participant #5)

In line with self-efficacy theory (Bandura, 1986, 1997), the lack of training of pre-service STEM teachers, together with the lack of awareness of teacher trainers at the university level, leaves these pre-service teachers lacking in mastery experiences, making them feel unprepared to navigate the cultural complexities they have already foreseen in their future classrooms, be it in secondary or university contexts. As such, the lack of this source of self-efficacy makes them believe they may be unable to achieve their future teaching goals. Such a lack of past experiences and training in cultural responsiveness triggered the educators' initial shock when teaching international students.

Work-Integrated Learning in Bridging Industry Experience and Classroom Teaching

Apart from majoring in education, some participants also pursue their major in one of the STEM subjects. They mentioned that opportunities for work-integrated learning experiences, such as internships or practicums in industry, made them realise the importance of cultural responsiveness in quality education.

My internship experiences . . . taught me that working with people from different cultural backgrounds requires some sensitivities. . . . It's not just like coding is a common language, but there are protocols . . . we need to consider ways to explain stuff . . . like using the right examples. For myself, that means using fewer idioms . . . or slang. Trying to research some relatable examples in their cultures to explain. . . . I wish my teachers taught me that when I was in high school. More practice, the better.

(Participant #5)

The positive affection that the participants gained boosted their self-efficacy and belief that if they and their future students are empowered with such cultural responsiveness, they will achieve similar success in the future. According to self-efficacy theory (Bandura, 1986, 1997), such positive affection, alongside mastery experiences, boosts self-efficacy, making pre-service teachers believe that if they empower students with a similar skill set, they will also be culturally responsive and attain similar success as they did. Such contentment in fulfilling the goal of education makes them feel that it is worthwhile to continue with education.

I think there is something more important than examinations. . . . Being communicative, thinking out of the box, being empathetic . . . that's what we need for a global citizen. I know it's hard . . . for my students to imagine working with foreigners. They may think of Americans . . . or . . . even Japanese. . . . They may not think about other people from different nations, like Indonesia, Chile . . . but that's true that we always have some projects around . . .. I know that even in high schools, they have some practical experiences that they can have a taste of and learn how to do those conversations right. Not being hubristic, you know . . . that is what a teacher should do.

(Participant #4)

On the other hand, real-world situations make the participants realise the importance of such cultural competencies in coping with the STEM workplace, which they, on the other hand, as an educator, believe is crucial for them to empower younger generations (Leonard et al., 2019; Purzer & Leftwich, 2023). This reminds them of the mission and vision of teaching; when they can empower their students with such skills, they feel more likely to continue their careers as STEM teachers.

Discussion

As mentioned in the introduction, there is a global shortage of teachers, particularly in the STEM fields (UNESCO, 2024). Our findings illuminate a critical aspect of this issue: the absence of culturally responsive elements in initial teacher education. This gap is crucial in classroom teaching and in preparing educators for an increasingly globalised world. For example, Participant #2's remarks highlight the curriculum's narrow focus: '[M]y professors continued to focus on test skills . . . only caring about scores.' This approach limits the scope for developing critical thinking and inquiry skills essential for culturally responsive teaching.

Furthermore, as described by participants, the traditional 'Korean teaching style' (rote-learning, lecture, teacher-centred) fails to accommodate diverse learning styles. It hampers the development of culturally responsive competencies. As such, from the participants' experiences, we identified potential challenges in enhancing pre-service STEM teachers' cultural responsiveness. These challenges stem from a lack of awareness among higher education teacher trainers and the prevalent examination-oriented curriculum. This deficiency hinders the development of mastery experiences in culturally responsive pedagogies, adversely impacting pre-service teachers' self-efficacy.

However, this study also uncovers positive influences on self-efficacy among pre-service STEM teachers. Reflective practices and work-integrated learning experiences offer valuable insights. For example, Participant #5's internship experience underscored the importance of cultural sensitivity in a professional setting, enhancing their belief in the necessity of cultural responsiveness in education. Participant #4's comments about the need for communication skills and empathy in fostering global citizenship further emphasise the importance of these competencies in a globalised educational context.

To enhance the cultural competencies of pre-service STEM educators, the following recommendations for the initial teacher education providers are proposed:

1 **Embedding reflective practices in teacher education**: Integrating structured reflective practices centred around cultural responsiveness into teacher education programmes is essential. This approach can significantly enrich the teaching methodology by encouraging educators to introspect and adapt their teaching to diverse cultural contexts. This practice not only enhances the pedagogical skills of future teachers but also prepares them to navigate and appreciate the varied cultural backgrounds of their students.
2 **Embracing diversity in learning approaches**: Moving beyond an exam-centric paradigm, teacher education should embrace a diversity of learning styles and interactive methods. This shift is crucial for developing a more inclusive and effective teaching strategy that resonates with students from various cultural backgrounds. It fosters an environment where students feel seen, heard, and understood, enhancing their engagement and learning outcomes.
3 **Diversification of curriculum and assessment**: Reforming the curriculum to include a broader range of assessment methods beyond standard examinations is necessary. Such a diversified approach accommodates different learning styles. It nurtures a more holistic understanding and appreciation of cultural differences among students. This methodology promotes a more inclusive educational environment that values and integrates cultural diversity.

4 **Integrating work-integrated learning into STEM curricula**: Incorporating practical, work-integrated learning experiences within STEM education can significantly enhance cultural competencies. This hands-on approach allows students to apply theoretical knowledge in real-world settings, fostering a deeper understanding of cultural nuances in professional contexts. Equipping educators with the skills to supervise these experiences effectively is equally important, ensuring that students derive the maximum benefit from these opportunities.

Implementing these suggestions can align pre-service STEM educators' training with students' diverse needs, fostering a more inclusive and effective educational environment. Additionally, these changes imply the necessity for reform and evaluation in higher education, ensuring trained teachers are well-equipped to deliver quality education in line with SDG4's objectives of celebrating cultural diversity among learners.

Conclusion

This study offers valuable insights into pre-service STEM educators' challenges and opportunities in South Korea, particularly in culturally responsive teaching. The findings reveal significant gaps in initial teacher training programmes, especially in equipping educators with the skills necessary to address the diverse needs of an increasingly globalised classroom. These gaps manifest in teacher trainers' lack of awareness and an examination-oriented curriculum that limits the development of essential teaching competencies. Despite these challenges, the study also highlights the potential of reflective practices and work-integrated learning experiences in fostering cultural responsiveness and self-efficacy among pre-service teachers. These findings have important implications for educational policy and curriculum reform, underscoring the need for a more inclusive and culturally aware approach to teacher education. The study contributes to the broader discourse on quality education, as outlined in SDG 4, by emphasising the importance of cultural diversity and responsiveness in teaching. However, the study's limitations, including a small sample size and a focus on South Korean educators, suggest further research in diverse educational contexts to fully understand the nuances of culturally responsive teaching in STEM education.

Note

* Corresponding author: lmdossantos@hksyu.edu

References

Åkerlind, G. S. (2005). Variation and commonality in phenomenography research methods. *Higher Education Research & Development*, *24*(4), 321–334.

Alase, A. (2017). The interpretative phenomenological analysis (IPA): A guide to a good qualitative research approach. *International Journal of Education and Literacy Studies*, *5*(2), 9. https://doi.org/10.7575/aiac.ijels.v.5n.2p.9

Alemu, A. M., & Cordier, J. (2017). Factors influencing international student satisfaction in Korean universities. *International Journal of Educational Development*, *57*(1), 54–64. https://doi.org/10.1016/j.ijedudev.2017.08.006
Arnold, W. (1988). Science and technology development in Taiwan and South Korea. *Asian Survey*, *28*(4), 437–450. https://doi.org/10.2307/2644737
Ayhan, K. J., Gouda, M., & Lee, H. (2022). Exploring Global Korea Scholarship as a public diplomacy tool. *Journal of Asian and African Studies*, *57*(4), 872–893. https://doi.org/10.1177/00219096211035800
Bae, H., Choo, H., & Lim, C. (2019). Bullying experience of racial and ethnic minority youth in South Korea. *The Journal of Early Adolescence*, *39*(4), 561–575. https://doi.org/10.1177/0272431618776121
Bandura, A. (1986). *Social foundations of thought and action : A social cognitive theory*. Prentice-Hall.
Bandura, A. (1997). *Self-efficacy: The exercise of control*. Worth Publishers.
Barron, H. A., Brown, J. C., & Cotner, S. (2021). The culturally responsive science teaching practices of undergraduate biology teaching assistants. *Journal of Research in Science Teaching*, *58*(9), 1320–1358. https://doi.org/10.1002/tea.21711
Beres, A. M. (2015). An overview of translanguaging. *Translation and Translanguaging in Multilingual Contexts*, *1*(1), 103–118. https://doi.org/10.1075/ttmc.1.1.05ber
Brown, S. D., & Lent, R. W. (2019). Social cognitive career theory at 25: Progress in studying the domain satisfaction and career self-management models. *Journal of Career Assessment*, *27*(4), 563–578. https://doi.org/10.1177/1069072719852736
Chen, S.-Y. (2022). To explore the impact of augmented reality digital picture books in environmental education courses on environmental attitudes and environmental behaviors of children from different cultures. *Frontiers in Psychology*, *13*. https://doi.org/10.3389/fpsyg.2022.1063659
Chong, W. H., & Kong, C. A. (2012). Teacher collabourative learning and teacher self-efficacy: The case of lesson study. *The Journal of Experimental Education*, *80*(3), 263–283. https://doi.org/10.1080/00220973.2011.596854
Creswell, J. W. (2012). *Educational research: Planning, conducting, and evaluating quantitative and qualitative research* (4th ed.). Pearson.
Isaac, C., Kaatz, A., Lee, B., & Carnes, M. (2012). An educational intervention designed to increase women's leadership self-efficacy. *CBE—Life Sciences Education*, *11*(3), 307–322. https://doi.org/10.1187/cbe.12-02-0022
Jon, J.-E. (2012). Power dynamics with international students: From the perspective of domestic students in Korean higher education. *Higher Education*, *64*(4), 441–454. https://doi.org/10.1007/s10734-011-9503-2
Kang, J., & Hwang, K. (2022). Belonging otherwise: Chinese undergraduate students at South Korean universities. *Globalisation, Societies and Education*, 1–14. https://doi.org/10.1080/14767724.2022.2095504
Kart, A., Groß Ophoff, J., & Pham Xuan, R. (2023). Pre-service teachers' attitudes about teaching and learning in multilingual classrooms. Insights from the Austrian-wide summer school programme in 2021. *Language, Culture and Curriculum*, *36*(3), 276–292. https://doi.org/10.1080/07908318.2022.2138426
Kharlay, O., Wei, W., & Philips, J. (2022). How do I teach? Exploring knowledge of reflective practice among in-service EFL teachers in Ukraine. *Teachers and Teaching*, *28*(2), 188–205. https://doi.org/10.1080/13540602.2022.2062709
Klassen, R. M., & Chiu, M. M. (2010). Effects on teachers' self-efficacy and job satisfaction: Teacher gender, years of experience, and job stress. *Journal of Educational Psychology*, *102*(3), 741–756. https://doi.org/10.1037/a0019237
Kolb, A., & Kolb, D. (2018). Eight important things to know about the experiential learning cycle. *Australian Educational Leader*, *40*(3), 8–14. https://search.informit.org/doi/10.3316/informit.192540196827567
Kwee, C. T. T. (2023). Chinese immigrant teachers' motivation for teaching heritage language in Australia: A qualitative study. *International Journal of Instruction*, *16*(1), 333–356. https://doi.org/10.29333/iji.2023.16119a

Lambert, C. F., & Lambert, C. (2019). How do they teach? The Jamaican Immigrant teacher pedagogy. *Caribbean Journal of Education*, *41*(2), 84–109. https://doi.org/10.46425/c541025877

Larkin, M., Watts, S., & Clifton, E. (2006). Interpretative phenomenological analysis giving voice and making sense in interpretative phenomenological analysis. *Qualitative Research in Accounting and Management*, *3*(2), 102–120.

Lee, G.-L., Myers, D. A., & Kim, K. J. (2009). Kindergarten teachers' professional training and their social status in Korea. *Journal of Early Childhood Teacher Education*, *30*(3), 263–271. https://doi.org/10.1080/10901020903084363

Lee, J., & Butt, G. (2014). The reform of national geography standards in South Korea—trends, challenges and responses. *International Research in Geographical and Environmental Education*, *23*(1), 13–24. https://doi.org/10.1080/10382046.2013.858404

Lehane, L. (2020). Experiential learning—David A. Kolb BT. In B. Akpan & T. J. Kennedy (Eds.), *Science education in theory and practice: An introductory guide to learning theory* (pp. 241–257). Springer International Publishing. https://doi.org/10.1007/978-3-030-43620-9_17

Lent, R. W., Brown, S. D., & Hackett, G. (1994). Toward a unifying social cognitive theory of career and academic interest, choice and performance. *Journal of Vocational Behavior*, *45*(1), 79–122. https://doi.org/10.1006/jvbe.1994.1027

Lent, R. W., Nota, L., Soresi, S., Ginevra, M. C., Duffy, R. D., & Brown, S. D. (2011). Predicting the job and life satisfaction of Italian teachers: Test of a social cognitive model. *Journal of Vocational Behavior*, *79*, 91–97. https://doi.org/10.1016/j.jvb.2010.12.006

Leonard, J., Barnes-Johnson, J., & Evans, B. R. (2019). Using computer simulations and culturally responsive instruction to broaden urban students' participation in STEM. *Digital Experiences in Mathematics Education*, *5*(2), 101–123. https://doi.org/10.1007/s40751-018-0048-1

Merriam, S. B., & Tisdell, E. J. (2016). *Qualitative research: A guide to design and implementation.* John Wiley & Sons. https://doi.org/10.1097/NCI.0b013e3181edd9b1

Miralles-Cardona, C., Chiner, E., & Cardona-Moltó, M.-C. (2022). Educating prospective teachers for a sustainable gender equality practice: Survey design and validation of a self-efficacy scale. *International Journal of Sustainability in Higher Education*, *23*(2), 379–403. https://doi.org/10.1108/IJSHE-06-2020-0204

OECD. (2019). *TALIS 2018 results (Volume I): Teachers and school leaders as lifelong learners.* OECD Publishing. https://doi.org/10.1787/1d0bc92a-en

Otheguy, R., García, O., & Reid, W. (2015). Clarifying translanguaging and deconstructing named languages: A perspective from linguistics. *Applied Linguistics Review*, *6*(3), 281–307. https://doi.org/10.1515/applirev-2015-0014

Park, K. (2010). Mathematics teacher education in Korea. In *Reforms and issues in school mathematics in East Asia* (pp. 181–196). Brill. https://doi.org/10.1163/9789460912283_012

Pečiuliauskienė, P., & Belakoz, A. (2019). School students' motivation for learning sciences: How is it influenced by self-confidence in science and inquiry-based teaching approach? *Pedagogika*, *134*(2), 121–134. https://doi.org/10.15823/p.2019.134.8

Pierson, A. E., & Grapin, S. E. (2021). A disciplinary perspective on translanguaging. *Bilingual Research Journal*, *44*(3), 318–334. https://doi.org/10.1080/15235882.2021.1970657

Purzer, S., & Leftwich, B. M. (2023). Journal of pre-college engineering education research (J-PEER) annual report from 1 January 2022, to 31 December 2022. *Journal of Pre-College Engineering Education Research (J-PEER)*, *13*(1). https://doi.org/10.7771/2157-9288.1395

Radhakrishnan, D., Capobianco, B. M., & DeBoer, J. (2021). Kenyan engineering teachers building reflective practice. *Reflective Practice*, *22*(5), 697–711. https://doi.org/10.1080/14623943.2021.1961126

San-Valero, P., Robles, A., Ruano, M. V., Martí, N., Cháfer, A., & Badia, J. D. (2019). Workshops of innovation in chemical engineering to train communication skills in science and technology. *Education for Chemical Engineers*, *26*, 114–121. https://doi.org/10.1016/j.ece.2018.07.001

Seidman, I. (2006). *Interviewing as qualitative research: A guide for researchers in education and the social sciences* (3rd ed.). Teacher College Press.

Shen, S. (2019). Teaching 'multiculturally': Geography as a basis for multicultural education in Korea. *Multicultural Education Review*, *11*(1), 37–58. https://doi.org/10.1080/2005615X.2019.1567092

Siwatu, K. O. (2007). Pre-service teachers' culturally responsive teaching self-efficacy and outcome expectancy beliefs. *Teaching and Teacher Education*, *23*(7), 1086–1101. https://doi.org/10.1016/j.tate.2006.07.011

Siwatu, K. O., Chesnut, S. R., Alejandro, A. Y., & Young, H. A. (2016). Examining pre-service teachers' culturally responsive teaching self-efficacy doubts. *The Teacher Educator*, *51*(4), 277–296. https://doi.org/10.1080/08878730.2016.1192709

Skedsmo, G., & Huber, S. G. (2019). Top-down and bottom-up approaches to improve educational quality: Their intended and unintended consequences. *Educational Assessment, Evaluation and Accountability*, *31*(1), 1–4. https://doi.org/10.1007/s11092-019-09294-8

Sleeter, C. E. (2012). Confronting the marginalization of culturally responsive pedagogy. *Urban Education*, *47*(3), 562–584. https://doi.org/10.1177/0042085911431472

Smith, J. A., Flowers, P., & Larkin, M. (2021). *Interpretative phenomenological analysis: Theory, method and research* (2nd ed.). Sage Publications. https://doi.org/10.1002/9780470776278.ch10

Song, C., Shin, S.-Y., & Shin, K.-S. (2023). Optimising foreign language learning in virtual reality: A comprehensive theoretical framework based on constructivism and cognitive load theory (VR-CCL). *Applied Sciences*, *13*(23), 12557. https://doi.org/10.3390/app132312557

South Korea: Record Growth in International Student Enrolment. (2018). https://monitor.icef.com/2018/02/south-korea-record-growth-international-student-enrolment/

Thomas, D. R. (2006). A general inductive approach for analysing qualitative evaluation data. *American Journal of Evaluation*. https://doi.org/10.1177/1098214005283748

UN. (2021). *The sustainable development goals report 2020*. https://doi.org/10.4324/9781003099680-3

UNESCO. (2024). *Global report on teachers: Addressing teacher shortages and transforming the profession*. https://www.unesco.org/en/articles/global-report-teachers-addressing-teacher-shortages-and-transforming-profession

Won, J. Y., & Park, M. J. (2020). Smart factory adoption in small and medium-sized enterprises: Empirical evidence of manufacturing industry in Korea. *Technological Forecasting and Social Change*, *157*, 120117. https://doi.org/10.1016/j.techfore.2020.120117

Yip, S. Y. (2023). Positionality and reflexivity: Negotiating insider-outsider positions within and across cultures. *International Journal of Research & Method in Education*, 1–11. https://doi.org/10.1080/1743727X.2023.2266375

Yip, S. Y., Saito, E., & Diamond, Z. M. (2022). Professional identity and agency in immigrant teachers' professional transition to work in Australia. *Australian Educational Researcher*. https://doi.org/10.1007/s13384-022-00600-w

Yuvayapan, F. (2019). Translanguaging in EFL classrooms: Teachers' perceptions and practices. *Dil ve Dilbilimi Çalışmaları Dergisi*, *15*(2), 678–694. https://doi.org/10.17263/jlls.586811

5 Australia's Labour Market and Skill Needs

John Burgess, Alan Nankervis, and Kantha Dayaram*

Country Background

Australia is geographically one of the largest countries within the Asia-Pacific region, but it has a low population density. Despite its size, it is heavily urbanised, with the population concentrated in a few cities, which, apart from Perth, Darwin, and Adelaide, are located on the east coast. Australia was colonised by the British in the early 19th century, and the legal and administrative system was modelled on Britain's Westminster system (Parliament of Western Australia, 2023). There is a central government, six state governments, and two territory governments. In terms of the indicators of economic progress, Australia ranks higher than the OECD average in per capita income and outperforms the average global quality of life indicators (Cameron & Burgess, 2023; OECD, 2021).

The population is culturally diverse, with immigrants being drawn predominantly from Europe, but in more recent decades, from South Africa, Asia, and South America. Educational attainment is relatively high with the human capital index (HCI) also high relative to countries in the region and against other advanced economies (World Bank, 2022). The HCI 'measures the amount of human capital that a child born today can expect to attain by age 18. It conveys the productivity of the next generation of workers compared to a benchmark of complete education and full health' (World Bank, 2022, p. 1). Despite the high average living standards, Indigenous Australians lag in all development indicators, including income, living standards, health, and education (LeRoy-Dyer, 2020). To address some of these issues, a national referendum in late 2023 will determine whether Indigenous Australians will have more influence on related government policies and processes.

The key features that are relevant to the discussion of skills development are as follows:

1 There is a fragmented education sector with responsibilities shared between the central and state governments. However, the long-term trend is towards greater centralisation through the fiscal controls exercised by the Federal

DOI: 10.4324/9781003379065-7

government. Centralised co-ordination and control extend throughout the system from school education to universities (Department of Education and Training (DEET), 2018; Hutchens, 2020).

2 The post-secondary education sector has undergone major changes over the past decades characterised by reduced funding for the sector, the restructuring of the technical education sector, and the inclusion of private providers, and the increasing fiscal pressure on universities through reduced funding that forces universities to impose fees and raise revenue from international students (Shah et al., 2019; Qi & Ma, 2021).
3 The long-term use of migrants to fill skill shortages for both skilled and unskilled labour across all sectors of the economy (Coates & Reysenbach, 2022). While skilled migration was severely restricted during the pandemic, the new Federal government proposes to significantly increase it through a more focused immigration strategy (Australian Chamber of Commerce and Industry (ACCI), 2022; Workforce Australia, 2022).
4 There are programmes in place through the National Skills Commission (NSC) and subsequently by its recent replacement, Jobs and Skills Australia (JSA), to identify skill needs and skill shortages for the purpose of informing training, education, and immigration policy and for developing longer-term training and education programmes (Workforce Australia, 2022; Australian Industry Group (AIG), 2023).
5 The population and workforce are ageing (Baird & Williams, 2022), and the retirement of the baby boomer generation has placed pressure on the labour market and contributed to a skills shortage. However, in part to offset the shortage, the participation rates of females and older (60 years and above) workers are increasing (Baird & Williams, 2022; Australian Bureau of Statistics (ABS), 2023).
6 The pre-school education system has grown as has the provision of training and opportunities for those with disabilities. In both cases the changes are linked to improving access to the workforce for women and the disabled (Australian Human Resource Institute (AHRI), 2023a, 2023b).
7 Following a change of Federal government in 2022, the new government held a Jobs and Skills Summit that invited key stakeholders to contribute to the development of a skills and training programme that, in part, incorporated the UN SDGs (Australian Government, 2022). There is direct engagement with the SDG agenda and its links to education and training.

The purpose of the chapter is to outline the policy programme towards skills development, link this to the UN SDGs, and discuss future challenges for skills development. The chapter initially discusses the nature and measurement of skill shortages, largely in terms of filling job vacancies and upgrading workforce skills. This reflects an emphasis on the economic goals of the SDGs—growth, productivity, and employment. However, there is a broader skills shortage agenda that is linked to social and environmental aspects of the SDGs that are discussed later in the chapter. To support the analysis, the chapter draws on secondary information that includes reports, policy documents, and public discussion.

The Economy

Australia had two decades of continuous growth, low unemployment, limited inflation, strong trade growth, and rising living standards until the COVID-19 pandemic (ABS, 2015). The services sector is the largest in terms of output and employment, accounting for approximately 70% of gross domestic product (GDP) and 75% of paid employment (Cameron & Burgess, 2023). However, mining and agriculture, despite their small employment shares, are the largest sources of export income (ABS, 2021). On a comparative basis, Australia's economy was largely unaffected by the global financial crisis and the Asian financial crisis (ABS, 2015). During the COVID-19 pandemic, constraints restricted growth and employment; however, many organisations supported operations through work-from-home arrangements (Dayaram & Burgess, 2021). Nevertheless, there was extensive disruption to national and international supply chains, and an increase in unemployment which is currently declining.

Post-pandemic there has been steady growth, falling unemployment, and increased export income driven by commodity price increases, but this has been tempered by increasing inflation and interest rates (Export and Finance Australia, 2022). Energy prices have increased because of supply disruptions linked to the conflict in Ukraine, with the consequence of higher inflation. During 2022 the inflation rate exceeded 7%, which was the highest rate in more than 30 years. For 2023 the forecasts for the economy are tempered by global developments that will impact Australia. These include high inflation, increasing interest rates, and financial instability, with several global banks requiring financial support or being taken over to support the stability of the banking system; lower rates of economic growth in China (Australia's largest trading partner); the decline in international tourism visitors and international students from China; the ongoing disruption to global supply chains linked to political instability; periodic crises linked to climate change; and within the region, the ongoing confrontation between China and the United States (Lowe, 2023).

The Labour Market

Following the COVID-19 pandemic, there has been an improvement in and tightening of the labour market. The June quarterly report on the labour market (NSC, 2022) highlighted that

- total employment rose to a record high,
- the participation rate and the employment-to-population ratio also rose to record highs,

- the unemployment rate fell to its lowest rate since 1974 (at 3.5%), and
- internet job advertisements reached their highest level since 2008.

A recent complementary industry study found that from a sample of 600 employers, 46% intended to increase staff numbers compared with only 16% planning on redundancies, with the public sector projecting both higher employment levels and higher pay than the private sector (AHRI, 2023b, p. 5). Nearly half of the sample (46%) reported ongoing sourcing and recruitment difficulties, and employee turnover remained relatively low (12%). Unlike earlier periods of employment growth, the net increase in jobs was taken up by full-time jobs, while part-time jobs declined (NSC, 2022). Another significant finding was that the strongest growth in jobs occurred in high-skill occupations, with the trend being a compositional shift towards high-skill jobs (skill level 1). The NSC commented:

> The shift towards higher skill levels through the COVID-19 period has been an acceleration of a long-term trend as the workforce continues to become more highly educated and employment has transitioned towards services-based industries. Since February 2020, the share of total employment accounted for by Skill Level 1 occupations has increased by 2.4 percentage points to 34.7% in May 2022, while the share of total employment accounted for by Skill Level 5 occupations has fallen by 1.6 percentage points to 14.2%.

The tightening labour market was also the result of the decline in migrant workers, tourists, and students throughout the COVID-19 pandemic. Students and tourists were previously a source of low-paid and temporary jobs in hospitality, health, agriculture, and retail. As a result, with the recovery in the economy, unfilled job vacancies were present across all sectors, from the high skilled to the low skilled.

The NSC (2021b) reported that in terms of sector employment growth post 2020 there was strong employment growth in five industries: health care and social assistance (up by 231,200 or 12.9%); professional, scientific, and technical services (up by 152,300 or 13.2%); retail trade (up by 116,500 or 9.3%); construction (up by 77,300 or 6.5%); and financial and insurance services (up by 71,200 or 15.3%).

In terms of occupational growth post 2020, the NSC (2021b) reported that the trend towards high-skilled jobs continued as the largest job gains were recorded for professionals (up by 314,900 or 9.9%), managers (up by 244,900 or 15.2%), and community and personal services workers (up by 71,400 or 5.0%), while the largest falls were for labourers (down by 97,500 or 7.7%) and clerical and administrative workers (down by 20,100 or 1.1%). A subsequent report from the Australian Bureau of Statistics confirmed these projections, adding more specific sub-categories such as medical, education, and training professionals; public sector administrators; accommodation and food service workers; and construction staff (ABS, 2023). However, the latter group has been impacted more recently by difficulties in the building and construction sector, leading to the demise of several high-profile building companies, compounded by continuing high inflation levels and a shortage of building products.

Skill and Education

Australia has a high rate of participation across all levels of education. Along with Singapore and New Zealand the participation rates in tertiary education for both males and females are among the highest in the Asia-Pacific region. Additionally, over the last decade there have been large inflows of international students, with Australia, New Zealand, and Singapore being major destinations for international students prior to the COVID-19 pandemic (Cameron & Burgess, 2023).

The Australian Qualifications Framework (AQF, 2016) accredits qualifications from across the tertiary education sector, including school qualifications (AQF, 2016). It has 10 levels and links school, vocational, and university education qualifications into one national system (AQF, 2016). This allows progress from one level of study to the next, and from one institution to another, if individuals satisfy entry requirements (Department of Employment, Education and Training (DEET), 2017). The AQF enables choice and flexibility in career planning. All qualifications in the framework are designed to help prepare students for further study and connection to an adult vocational life (DEET, 2017). The AQF defines and describes all nationally recognised qualifications (AQF, 2016), forming a single qualification framework from certificate I level through to senior secondary certification to doctoral level (DEET, 2017).

DEET is accountable for national policies and programmes that assist Australian citizens in accessing the quality of early childcare and childhood education, school education, higher education, vocational education and training, as well as international education and research (DEET, 2017). School education is similar across the Australian nation with only minor variations between states and territories and is required between the ages of 6 and 16 (year 1 to year 9 or 10) (DEET, 2017). Compulsory school education comprises 11 years in total and is divided into primary school for seven to eight years, commencing at the kindergarten/preparatory level, moving into secondary (or high) school for another three to four years, with years 11 and 12 not being compulsory (DEET, 2017).

Table 5.1 shows the number of Australians enrolled in various education sectors. In terms of qualifications, over 11 million people in Australia reported having a non-school (vocational or tertiary) qualification, a 19.8% increase since 2016; 5.5 million people reported having a bachelor's degree or higher, a 30.7% increase since 2016; and 4 million people reported having certificate I to IV, a 10.6% increase since 2016. The most common field of study for

Table 5.1 Formal education enrolments, 2022

Number of individuals	*Preschool*	*Primary school*	*Secondary school*	*Vocational education*	*Tertiary education*
Attendance rates	484,185	2,075,224	1,629,624	601,901	1,185,450
Qualifications				3,962,732	5,464,631

Source: Australian Bureau of Statistics (2022)

non-school qualifications was business and management (1,144,084 people), followed by teacher education (836,410) and nursing (608,276).

Tertiary education embodies the academic and vocational/technical pathways in higher education (including universities) and includes vocational education and training (VET). The VET system has undergone major changes, and a critique of the VET system and its policies can be found in Montague et al. (2018). Under the AQF, students who successfully prove that they are proficient within a group of competencies can be awarded a VET qualification such as certificate I, certificate II, certificate III, certificate IV, diploma, and advanced diploma. The certificate levels align with levels of attainment, with a certificate I graduate requiring supervision, and certificate IV graduates being regarded as supervisors/managers of others. Certificate III is common among apprentices, with nearly 40% of students taking courses at that level and 30% at a higher level. The remaining 30% are enrolled in courses at lower levels or in non-AQF programmes (CEDA, 2016). The awarding of higher education (HE) qualifications (bachelor's degree to PhD) is the domain of universities predominantly, but some vocational education (VE) institutions can also award degree-level certificates (DEET, 2017). The AQF comprises 13 national qualifications in three sectors, with several cross-sectoral linkages (AQF, 2016).

Major Changes and Challenges to the Skill Development Framework

The demographic and structural changes outlined have contributed to skills shortages. Major structural developments include the changing skills and employment profiles associated with the fourth industrial revolution technologies (Mumme & Cameron, 2019), the aging of the population and workforce and the need to attract and retain older workers (Baird & Williams, 2022), and the ongoing growth in high-skill jobs in the service sector (NSC, 2021b). In turn, the COVID-19 pandemic placed pressure on several sectors such as health and logistics, while the restrictions on overseas students and migrants contributed to the skills shortage (Dayaram & Burgess, 2021; Qi & Ma, 2021). Previous studies highlighted graduate work-readiness challenges (Montague et al., 2018) together with the increasing growth of short-term and insecure employment (Campbell & Burgess, 2018). Graduate work-readiness challenges indicate a mismatch between the supply and demand for graduates, while short-term and insecure employment is unlikely to attract training or support career development.

Montague et al. (2018) outline key changes to the tertiary education system which include privatisation/contracting out of the training or TAFE sector and the reduction in public funding for the sector. In the university system there have been increases in student fees and reduced government funding, leading to the growth and dependence on onshore and offshore international students to make up the funding shortfall (Qi & Ma, 2021). As with other countries in the region, there is a persistent problem of graduate unemployment and underemployment, with long delays in transitioning from tertiary education into regular employment (Mumme & Cameron, 2019). A review by Phillips KPA Ltd. (2018) of the AQF framework noted systemic problems, including the failure to accommodate micro-credentials, flexible delivery options, and mechanisms to assist learners to construct their own programmes, sometimes across sectors, to meet individual learning needs. The report commented that 'the AQF is also impacted by and impacts upon related policy areas such as workforce planning, skills development and migration policy and cannot be viewed as a stand-alone educational instrument' (Phillips KPA Ltd., 2018, p. 9).

The COVID-19 pandemic forced major changes to the education and training system, notably the move towards flexible delivery and at-home learning, and major downsizing and job losses in the higher education system which was deemed as being ineligible for protection from the Federal government *Jobseeker Scheme* that was designed to support jobs during the pandemic, despite the decline in overseas students studying in Australia (Dayaram & Burgess, 2021).

The TAFE system has been under pressure with declining funding, apprenticeships, and completion rates, even in areas deemed to have skill shortages. Since 2022 the Federal government has initiated several inquiries into the education and training system. The data indicate a decline in apprenticeships and a falling rate of apprenticeship completion, even in areas identified as having skill shortages. Around 40% of those occupations deemed to be suffering from skill shortages require apprenticeship training, and the number of completed apprenticeships had declined from around 57,000 in 2012 to 20,000 in 2021 (O'Conner, 2023). Both the number of apprenticeship priority occupations and the financial support for apprentices and employers participating in programmes were increased. To address this, a few reforms emerged that included a new service model for the delivery of TAFE training. The key elements of the new model are as follows:

> Provide every apprentice with a structured assessment at commencement of their training to identify individual needs and the additional supports needed to give the apprentice the right foundation for success. Make mentoring more accessible earlier and provide specialised support to improve outcomes for First Nations apprentices, apprentices with a disability, those

> who live remotely, women in male-dominated trades and others who experience additional barriers to completing their apprenticeship. Ensure more proactive support from services over the course of the apprenticeship, with an increased focus on supporting completions. This includes the first two years, when wages are typically at their lowest and apprentices are at the highest risk of dropping out. Support employers to create a positive learning environment and workplace culture that encourages apprentices to succeed, especially for employers who are under-resourced or inexperienced, and taking on an apprentice for the first time.
>
> (O'Conner, 2023)

Skill Shortages Assessment

The National Skills Commission (NSC) formerly produced an annual skill priority list, which was constructed from official labour market data, employer surveys, and consultation with key stakeholders. The list was used to inform policy in training, education, and immigration. Occupations were classified as either being in shortage or without shortages. There was a further classification based on future demand estimates: strong, moderate, or soft. The data are broken down by state and territory, and by metropolitan and non-metropolitan regions. In 2022 the occupations with a strong skill shortage were registered nurses, software and application programmers, aged and disabled carers, and construction managers (NSC 2022).

Following a change of government in 2022, the NSC was replaced by Jobs and Skills Australia (JSA) (Australian Government, 2022). JSA releases a quarterly report that assesses skills shortages across occupations and states. The elements of the skills assessment are as follows.

> The percentage of advertised occupation vacancies filled (fill rate) is a key metric from the Survey of Employers who Recently Advertised (SERA) and provides a valuable proxy for identifying occupations and parts of the labour market in potential shortage. Generally, lower fill rates imply greater employer difficulty with filling vacant positions and a higher likelihood of occupations in shortage. In contrast, higher fill rates imply fewer challenges (in general) with filling vacancies and a lower likelihood of shortages. The metric is consistent with the definition of shortage used for developing the annual Skills Priority List (SPL). Moreover, analysis of SERA data is pivotal to informing the SPL. Additional metrics are also reported on. These include average number of total applicants, qualified applicants, and suitable applicants per vacancy; and average years of labour market experience sought by employers. The extra information provides further context to fill rate changes overtime, including the links between these measures and the fill rate. A new metric, the 'suitability gap', is introduced in the report to shed further light on skill gaps from the employer's perspective.
>
> (JSA, 2023, p. 2)

From the March 2023 report the following national data were presented: fill rate (63%), applicants per vacancy (14.1), qualified applicants per vacancy (4.7), suitable applicants per vacancy (2.4), and suitability gap (2.3). In general, a skills shortage would be manifested by falling fill rates and reductions in the qualified and suitable applicants per vacancy. The suitability gap indicates that while applicants may be qualified, they lack other job requirements such as work experience and soft skills. A skills gap may reflect few job applicants, few qualified job applicants, and/or few suitable job applicants. This reflects the number of applicants, their qualifications, and the other conditions that are required to fill each vacancy.

The Australian Jobs and Skill Framework

As an example of the ways in which countries in the Asia-Pacific region have approached critical skills shortage challenges, the Australian government has developed a relatively comprehensive and integrated framework for the identification and resolution of these issues. The NSC was established to address the looming deficits in crucial employee skills and the increasing difficulties associated with labour shortages against the backdrop of the COVID-19 pandemic and the temporary cessation of skilled worker migration. The NSC's role was 'to provide expert advice and national leadership on the Australian labour market and current, emerging, and future workforce skills needs' (NSC, 2022, p. 17). Additionally, the Minister for Skills and Training noted the strategic role of the NSC: 'by investing in skills, we can capitalise on the demonstrable connection between a trained and skilled workforce and a more productive economy' (Martin, 2022, np).

In order to achieve these lofty ideals, its focus was on three long-term outcomes, namely 'to make an enduring and relevant contribution to labour market information; to improve the quality, accessibility and relevance of vocational education and training (VET); and to contribute to a labour market that effectively aligns skills needs with education and training' (NSC, 2022, p. 17). The NSC strategy necessarily embraced stakeholder engagement and communication with industry, unions, higher education, and VET institutions across Australia.

During 2020–2022, the NSC produced annual reports listing the skills priorities across industries based on the existing Australian Skills Classification, which divides work skills into core, technological, and specialist competencies, and nominated the industries and occupations with the most serious labour and skills shortages. As an example of their findings, the 2022 NSC list of industries most affected currently and into the future included (inter alia) community and personal services, healthcare, accommodation and food services, professional and scientific, and education and training sectors. Within these sectors and beyond, the occupations with the greatest shortages embraced such diverse jobs as technicians and tradespeople, doctors and nurses, care workers, clerical and sales employees, professionals, labourers, and truck drivers; and the broad areas of skill shortages were categorised as 'care, computing, cognitive, and communication' (NSC, 2021a, p. 17).

Other observers confirm these findings but with some additional or diverse occupations and their requisite skills. Hays (2022), for example, largely agreed with the NSC's findings about occupations in demand but added more specific examples, including information technology project managers, civil engineers, human resource positions such as talent acquisition and payroll officers, software developers, executive assistants, welders, digital producers, legal counsel, forklift operators, urban and town planners, and customer service representatives, to name but a few. Martin (2022) also added dentists, surgeons, emergency medicine specialists, and teachers in primary, secondary, and special needs settings, not to mention university lecturers and researchers, many of whom were displaced or replaced by online teaching during the pandemic.

Of the critical skills listed by the NSC and other reporters, digital skills, encompassing baseline, specific, and 'cutting edge' or emerging skills (Hope et al., 2021), are regarded as being crucial to Australia's future economic and industry growth. As Hope et al. (2021, p. 1) suggest, these skills 'can ensure success for people in the labour market, enable transitions between jobs, and create new opportunities for Australia to lead in the development of digital technologies into the future'. However, they further suggest that all these levels of digital skills remain under-developed and that they will need to be prioritised for Australia 'to be on par with other like countries' (ibid). In support of this assertion, their report compares Australia's demand for these skills with those from Canada, New Zealand, the United States, and Singapore. Over the period 2013–2020, Hope et al. (2021) estimated that the percentage of jobs that required digital skills in Australia and New Zealand was around 30%, and well below the 45–50% of vacancies in the United States, Canada, and Singapore requiring digital skills, concluding that Australia still 'lags somewhat behind'.

Cognisant of the increasing urgency to upskill employees amidst a looming labour shortage, the Federal government's Jobs and Skills Summit in September 2022 proactively sought to address these challenges. Emphasising the need for collaboration between federal and state governments, industry, and unions, the new government focused on practical strategies to move past data collection and analysis to resolve the underlying issues. It also transitioned from an enterprise bargaining model of industrial relations to multi-employer bargaining, funded more vocational education and training courses, supported wage rises, especially for lower-paid workers, and replaced the NSC with JSA, which seeks to strengthen the nexus between skills and the present and future jobs which demand them (Butler, 2022; Tamaray, 2022). In addition, the government launched a new five-year workforce strategy detailing its new approach to the skill shortages which embodied a projected migration increase, especially in relation to skilled workers (Workforce Australia, 2022).

SDG Priorities and the Skills Summit

The UN (2022) Sustainable Development Goals have a close link with effective education and training programmes. Through education and training, both individual and community living standards can be improved. The economic argument and evidence are conclusive that investment in education, on average, pays off for individuals and communities (Cameron & Burgess, 2023). While growth can support improved living standards, reduce poverty and hunger, and improve well-being, it is not sufficient to address inequality, discrimination, water quality, the environment, and the quality of the health system. There are also objectives that require infrastructure (health and education) and investment in workforce development to address goals such as innovation, water and air quality, and environmental sustainability. Immediate policy priorities are driven by the state of the labour market as indicated by unemployment or unfilled vacancies. These drive training, education, and migration policies. However, many of the SDGs require longer-term policy development and, as such, are surrounded by uncertainty. It raises the question of what steps are proposed in the training and education policy programme to address these long-term SDGs (Australian Government, 2022).

The broad objectives of the skills summit embodied an SDG agenda:

> [T]he consensus reached at the Summit, immediate actions will be taken to build a bigger, better trained, and more productive workforce—to help deliver secure jobs with growing wages, boost incomes and living standards and create more opportunities for more Australians. The Summit has also laid out priorities for further work and future action.
>
> (Australian Government, 2022, p. 2)

The summit communique set out an agenda that included immediate actions, areas for further work, and complementary existing commitments. The SDGs identified included improving diversity and equality, increasing productivity, job creation, skills development, and enhancing job access for disadvantaged groups. Recognising that addressing the skill shortages entails harnessing the talents and skills of all workers, the design and implementation of strong diversity, equality, and inclusion (DEI) strategies was highly recommended to all public and private sector employers. To date, the outcomes of this imperative have largely been disappointing. As a recent industry survey revealed, 'there is a clear gap between employer awareness, intent and action' with respect to DEI programmes, and current policies 'focus largely on gender, and to a lesser extent, Indigenous Australians, and ignores other disadvantaged workers' (AHRI, 2023b, pp. 4–5). As evidence, the survey found that only 45% organisations have defined policies in this area, very few have established effective targets or measures, and only half regard DEI as a priority area to resolve skill shortages (AHRI, 2023b).

On training and skills development, proposals that the summit agreed to include the following:

- A $1 billion one-year National Skills Agreement that will provide additional funding for fee-free TAFE in 2023, while a longer-term agreement that drives sector reform and supports women's workforce participation is being negotiated.
- Acceleration of the delivery of 465,000 additional fee-free TAFE places, with 180,000 to be delivered, with costs shared between the states and territories on a 50:50 basis.
- Establish the JSA work plan in consultation with all jurisdictions and stakeholders to address workforce shortages and build long-term capacity in priority sectors.
- Explore options to improve the apprenticeship support system and drive up completions.
- Include specific sub-targets for women in the Australian Skills Guarantee.
- Up to 20,000 additional Commonwealth-supported university places for under-represented groups in areas of skills shortages.
- Train 10,000 new energy apprentices and fund a new energy skills programme.

The Skilled Migration Review

Skilled immigration has been both a long- and short-term policy solution to Australia's skills shortages. Employers can resort to skilled migrant visas if the occupations they seek to fill are on the skills shortage list. The report of the panel to review the skilled migration programme was released in 2023 (Australian Government, 2022). The migration programme is complex and encompasses many different visa classifications in addition to skilled migration. These include family reunion, refugees, tourists, and students. With respect to the effectiveness of the migration programme in meeting current and future skills needs, the report identified weaknesses in the current programme that included (Australian Government, 2022):

- A lack of data inhibits effective assessment of the system as does the absence of any evaluation plan or data strategy to underpin the migration system's ability to improve, and the ability for it to be reviewed.
- There is growing international competition for highly skilled migrants, and Australia will need to sharpen its approach to attract migrants who can meet future needs.
- The occupation lists underpinning the employer-sponsored visas are unresponsive and outdated.
- Current settings for temporary skilled migration are inefficient and create the risk of migrant worker exploitation.

- Australia has a large population of 'permanently temporary' migrants without a pathway to permanent residence.
- Australia is not focused enough on capturing high-potential international students.
- Migrant skills recognition is complicated and burdensome.
- Challenges in regional Australia, including skills shortages, cannot be addressed purely by migration.

Linking Australia's Skill Needs to the SDGs

Following the 2016 National SDG Summit, the Australian Government, in partnership with non-governmental organisations, the university sector, and the private sector, uses an Australian-based SDG website to track and guide its targets through 2030. For instance, SDG 4 (quality education) has nine targets, with target 4.3 ensuring that by 2023 all women and men will have access to affordable, quality technical, vocational, and tertiary education. The Federal Department of Education and Training targeted language, literacy, and numeracy by linking the programme with SDG 4 (quality education), SDG 8 (promote decent work and economic growth), and SDG 5 (gender and equality). The programme specifically targets job seekers and provides 800 hours of free, accredited training (DEET, 2017). It reports that in 2016–2017, the programme provided 36,563 job seekers with six hundred hours of training. While some gains have been made in investing towards skills development in the vocational sector, Australia has a fair way to go in meeting its SDG targets. A recent 2023 survey found 46% of female students finished their studies with a debt of $20,000-$50,000 that was a rise of 14% in three years. It also found that 70% of men compared to 59% of women earned more than $60,000, and 35% of men compared to 21% of women earned more than $100,000 (Cassidy, 2023).

In addition, in the 2022 budget, the Australian government committed $42.8 million towards the design and transition to the new Indigenous Skills and Employment (ISE) programme (National Indigenous Australians Agency, 2022) that also targets SDG 8 (decent work and economic growth), SDG 10 (reduced inequalities), and SDG 17 (partnerships for the goals). While the outcomes of the ISE programme are yet to be audited, this programme's primary focus is on co-designing with local communities and stakeholders' involvement.

Other reports on inclusive skills development and employment outcomes show a lag in SDG targets, such as the Diversity Council Australia's research findings that despite a shortage of talent, more than 3 million people continue to look for employment (Diversity Council Australia, 2022). The report highlights a need for concentrated effort towards DEI talent attraction and skill development. Similarly, a June 2023 report on labour shortage and migrant skills recognition has called for reforms that simplify migrant recruitment and labour supply concerns across 286 occupational categories (Mostafa, 2023).

The report proposes recommendations (inter alia) to fix a fractured skills and qualifications recognition system, increase public-private partnerships, and modify English language requirements.

Discussion and Conclusions

Australia faces considerable skill shortages, currently and into the future. Despite high rates of participation in post-secondary education and an extensive skilled migrant programme, skill shortages persist. A recent change of national government precipitated several reviews of the skill development and augmentation programme. Consequently, several policies have been introduced to support the TAFE/VET and university sectors and modify the skilled migrant programme. Through migration, skilled and unskilled job shortages have been addressed in both the short and long term. Consequently, Australia is a major destination for students and skilled and unskilled labour from the region. While it is clear from the current reviews that the training and education programmes require considerable reform and funding if they are to effectively address SDGs, the ongoing dependence on immigration poses internal and external challenges. Internally, wage suppression, jobs that do not meet minimum employment standards, and reduced training, and the use of temporary and at-call labour that does not attract investment in training since attachments are short term (White, 2022; AIG, 2023). Externally, this is contributing to the brain drain and skill shortages in regional economies.

Note

* Corresponding author: john.burgess@torrens.edu.au.

References

ACCI. (2022). *Overcoming Australia's labour and skills shortages: Through skills development, workforce participation and migration*. Better Australia.

AHRI. (2023a, February 23). *The state of diversity, equity, and inclusion in Australian workplaces*. Melbourne: Australian Human Resources Institute. https://www.ahri.com.au/wp-content/uploads/DEI-Report-2023.pdf

AHRI. (2023b). *AHRI's Quarterly Australian Work Outlook a forward-looking view of the Australian labour market* (2nd Quarter). Melbourne: Australian Human Resources Institute. https://www.ahri.com.au/wp-content/uploads/AHRI-report_15.5.23.pdf

Australian Bureau of Statistics. (2015, May) *Education and work, Australia*. Australian Bureau of Statistics Canberra. www.abs.gov.au/ausstats/abs@.nsf/mf/6227.0

Australian Bureau of Statistics. (2021). *Australian industry earnings*. www.abs.gov.au/statistics/industry/industry-overview/australian-industry/latest-release

Australian Bureau of Statistics. (2022). *People and education*. www.abs.gov.au/statistics/people/education#:

Australian Bureau of Statistics. (2023, February 21). Labour market insights. https://www.abs.gov.au/statistics/labour/employment-and-unemployment/labour-force-australia/feb-2023

Australian Government. (2022). *Jobs and skills summit outcomes.* file:///E:/strategic%20skills%20asia/Jobs-and-Skills-Summit-Outcomes-Document.pdf
Australian Industry Group (AIG). (2023, 27 January). Deep dive: Solving the skills shortage crisis. www.aigroup,com.au-economics-intelligence
Australian Qualifications Framework. (2016). *Australian qualifications framework.* Australian Government. www.aqf.edu.au/
Baird, M., & Williams, A. (2022). Ageing, work, care in Australia: Progress and prospects in meeting Sustainable Development Goals of inclusive growth and gender equality. In S. Dhakal, A. Nankervis, & J. Burgess (Eds.), *Ageing in the Asia Pacific in changing times* (pp. 51–70). Springer.
Butler, J. (2022, 3 October). Common ground and concrete steps: Five takeaways from Labour's jobs and skills summit. *The Guardian.*
Cameron, R., & Burgess, J. (2023). Employment and labour markets. In D. Kapur, L. Kong, F. Lo, & D. Malone (Eds.), *The oxford handbook of higher education in the Asia-Pacific region* (pp. 66–92). Oxford University Press.
Campbell, I., & Burgess, J. (2018). Patchy progress? Two decades of research on precariousness and precarious work in Australia. *Labour and Industry, 28*(1), 48–67.
Cassidy, C. (2023, March). Female university graduates have bigger HECS debts but earning less than men, research reveals. *The Guardian.* www.theguardian.com/australia-news/2
Coates, B., & Reysenbach, T. (2022). Why boosting permanent skilled migration won't fix the worker shortage. *Grattan Institute.* https://grattan.edu.au/news/why-boosting-permanent-skilled-migration-wont-fix-the-worker-shortage/
Committee for the Economic Development of Australia (CEDA) (2016). *VET: Securing skills for growth, committee for economic development of Australia, Melbourne.* www.ceda.com.au/research-and-policy/research/2016/08/vet- skills-for-growth
Dayaram, K., & Burgess, J. (2021). Regulatory challenges facing remote working in Australia. In D. Wheatley, I. Hardill, & S. Buglass (Eds.), *Handbook of research on remote work and worker well-being in the post-COVID-19 era* (pp. 202–220). IGI Global.
Department of Education and Training. (2018). *Through growth to achievement: The report of the review to achieve educational excellence in Australian schools.* Commonwealth of Australia.
Department of Employment, Education and Training (DEET). (2017). *SDG skills.* https://sdgs.org.au/project/skills-for-education-and-employment-see-program/
Diversity Council Australia (2022). *DCA's inclusive recruitment report. Australia's got talent—Inclusive recruitment the key to unlock the potential of those overlooked and underleveraged.* Author. dca.org.au
Export and Finance Australia (2022). *Higher global inflation and interest rates add risks to exports.* www.exportfinance.gov.au/resources/world-risk-developments/2022/february/australia-higher-global-inflation-and-interest-rates-add-risks-to-exports/
Hays (2022). The *most in-demand skills in 2022.* www.haystalentsolutions.com/-/the-most-in-demand-skills-in-2022
Hope, A., Yemm, N., Nguyen, G, Ali Raza, M., Sparke, E., Buhagier, & Neumann, R. (2021). *Digital skills in the Australian and international economies.* National Skills Commission. https://www.jobsandskills.gov.au/sites/default/files/2022-03/ABS%20Paper%20-%20Digital%20Skills.pdf
Hutchens, G. (2020). University fee changes announced by Dan Tehan combine market-based economics with social engineering. *ABC News.* www.abc.net.au/news/2020-06-22/university-fee-changes-dan-tehan-capitalist-economics-analysis/12377498
Jobs and Skills Australia. (2023, March). *Skills shortages quarterly.* www.jobsandskills.gov.au/reports/skills-shortage-quarterly-march-2023

Leroy-Dyer, S. (2020). Across the world: Black Lives Matter. *Advocate: Journal of the National Tertiary Education Union*, *27*(2), 10–20.
Lowe, P. (2023, 8 March). *Keynote address to the financial review business summit 2023.* Reserve Bank of Australia.
Martin, S. (2022, 6 October). Occupations facing skills shortages in Australia almost doubled in past year. *The Guardian.* www.theguardian.com/australia-news/2022/oct/06/staggering-occupations-facing-skills-shortages-in-australia-almost-doubled-in-past-year
Montague, A., Connell, J., & Mumme, B. (2018). Graduate employability in Australia: Time for a VET and HE overhaul? In R. Cameron, J. Burgess, & S. Dhakal (Eds.), *Transitions from education to work: Workforce ready challenges in the Asia Pacific* (pp. 166–187). Taylor and Francis.
Mostafa, R (2023, 19 June). Migrant groups urge reform of Australia's 'broken' skills recognition process. *Guardian Online.* www.theguardian.com/australia-news/2023/jun/19/migrant-groups-urge-reform-of-australias-broken-skills-recognition-process
Mumme & Cameron (2019). The future of work in Australia: Preparing graduates for changing work patterns that require new skill sets. In J. Burgess, P. Verma, S. Dhakal, & A. Nankervis (Eds.), *The transition from graduation to work* (pp. 65–84). Springer.
National Indigenous Australians Agency (NIAA). (2022). *New indigenous skills and Employment program tailored to community needs.* www.indigenous.gov.au/news-and-media/announcements/new-indigenous-skills-and-employment-program-tailored-community-needs
National Skills Commission (NSC). (2021a). *The state of Australia's skills 2021: Now and into the future.* Australian Government.
National Skills Commission (NSC). (2021b). *The transformation of Australia's labour market.* Australian Government.
National Skills Commission (NSC). (2022). *Skills priority list: Key findings report.* Australian Government.
OECD. (2021). *Better Life Index.* www.oecdbetterlifeindex.org/countries/australia/X
Parliament of Western Australia. (2023). *History of parliamentary democracy in Western Australia.* www.parliament.wa.gov.au/
Phillips KPA Ltd. (2018). *Contextual research for the Australian qualifications framework review.* Final report. Phillips KPA Limited, Melbourne.
Qi, J., & Ma, C. (2021). Australia's crisis responses during COVID-19: The case of international students. *Journal of International Students, 11*, 94–111. www.proquest.com/scholarly-journals/australias-crisis-responses-during-covid-19-case/docview/2635271546/se-2
Shah, M., Yen Vu, H., & Stanford, S.-A. (2019). Trends in private higher education in Australia, perspectives. *Policy and Practice in Higher Educatio*n, *23*(1), 5–11. https://doi.org/10.1080/13603108.2018.1521348
Tamaray, P. (2022). *After much anticipation, parliament passes.* 'Jobs and Skills Australia' Bill, HRD.
UN. (2022). *Sustainable development goals.* https://sdgs.un.org/goals
White, L. (2022, 14 December). How to combat labour shortages in 2023. *Human Resource Development.*
Workforce Australia. (2022). *National workforce strategy 2022–2027.* Commonwealth of Australia.
World Bank. (2022). *Human capital country brief: Australia.* https://thedocs.worldbank.org/en/doc/7.

6 Employability Skills in Thailand

The Need for Sustainability

Monthon Sorakraikitikul and Pacharapong Kumjumpa*

Introduction

Throughout Asia there is a labour market challenge of graduate work readiness as new graduates find it difficult to access employment since they do not possess the hard and soft skills to fill workforce vacancies (Dhakal et al., 2019). As a result, graduates take time to access a job in their field of specialisation or are forced into employment that does not utilise their skills. Thailand is no exception; it reformed its education policy in 2019 to address its rapidly challenging environment due to adopting new technologies for living, working, and learning. The policy focuses not only on reforming university curricula towards 21st-century skills for the workforce but also on enhancing workers' employability (Dhamnimitr, 2014). This policy tries to ensure that graduates from the Thai education system can be employed and have a better quality of life, with graduates better prepared for work with professional skills. It is expected that graduates will be employed very soon after graduation.

One recent study of employability and graduates' skills in the information technology (IT) sector found that graduates were generally employed within five months of graduation. The three key skills that equipped them best for work included programming skills, system development, and soft skills (Rahmat et al., 2012). However, the mismatches in skills issue were discussed in various fields, such as business and accounting, banking, engineering, and nursing (Abbasi et al., 2018). In developing employability skills, the process needed to involve various stakeholders such as students, teachers, curriculum designers, employers, and the government.

Thailand has adopted the UN's sustainable development goals (SDGs) and included them in the Thailand National Strategic Plan (National Strategy Secretariat Office, 2018). Relevant to this chapter's discussion is SDG 8—promote sustained, inclusive, and sustainable economic growth, full and productive employment, and decent work for all. Consistent with SDG 8.6, the country wanted to reduce the proportion of youths not in education, employment, or training, because if young people were in the education system, they would develop their skills and be work-ready. Then, this would stimulate economic growth and productivity. In addition, the programme supports SDG 4.4 that

DOI: 10.4324/9781003379065-8

calls for an increase in the number of young people and adults with relevant skills, including technical and vocational skills, for employment, decent jobs, and entrepreneurship (Office of the National Economic and Social Development Board, 2021). The Thai government is interested in and supportive of the development of appropriate workforce (or employability) skills.

From the supply side of the labour market, if colleges and universities can equip their students with enhanced employability capabilities, they can enhance their employment opportunities as graduates. Researchers suggest that it is the responsibility of tertiary education to enhance the employability of their students (Abbasi et al., 2018; Rahmat et al., 2012) Employers could then obtain competent and work-ready employees, which would improve business operations, result in higher productivity, and stimulate economic growth. However, an important issue remains of matching skills from both supply and demand sides of the labour market, since a skill gap will constrain economic growth (Abbasi et al., 2018; Dhamnimitr, 2014). Some authors have suggested that these skill gaps derive from 'structural reasons such as skill mismatches' (Sivasomboon, 2017), talent shortages (Staffing Industry Analysts, 2016), and substandard education system curriculum (Fernquest, 2017). These issues call for thorough educational reform and graduate work-readiness policies to better prepare Thai graduates for entry into the job market (Promsit, 2019, pp. 206–207). These and other related topics are discussed later in the chapter.

The OECD concluded that the skills imbalance in Thailand was the results of skill shortages. At the occupational level, cognitive skills, social skills, and technical skills, particularly, were reported as being in short supply (Vandeweyer et al., 2020). As a result, the Thai labour market has experienced a significant labour mismatch. Many workers were employed in an occupation that did not match their educational qualification, while other industries faced an over-qualification situation where employees possessed skills that were not being applied, especially in sales and service workers, plant and machine operators, wholesale and retail industry, and the accommodation and food service sector. Under-qualification was also found among managers and clerical support workers in the entertainment and recreation sectors (Vandeweyer et al., 2020). These findings highlighted the critical issue in achieving SDG 4.4. As workers are an essential engine for economic growth and sustainability, obtaining the right skills and competencies for a particular job is a key challenge for Thailand.

This chapter investigates the skills that employers are looking for in new staff while exploring the perspectives of employability from the perspective of both Thai managers and current students, especially those from the sciences and social sciences. Managers who have experience in supervising newly hired staff and current students who wanted to find a job were represented in the research sample. This chapter begins with an overview of Thailand's economy, labour market, and industry structure and is followed by a discussion of the concept of employability. The data collection and analysis are presented, followed by the results, and the chapter ends with the discussion and conclusions.

Research Objectives

1 To identify the skill gap between the expectations and current skills of newly hired employees from managers' (employers') perspectives.
2 To identify the differences between managers' expectations for the position (new hires) and current students' expectations of skill requirements.

Country Overview

Thailand is an upper-middle-income country (United Nations, 2023), and in 2022, Thailand's gross domestic product (GDP) was around 495 billion US dollars. The inflation rate was 6.1%, and GDP per capita was around 7,089.7 US dollars per person. Thai household debt accounted for 88% of GDP, which also came from domestic private investment (Office of the National Economic and Social Development Board, 2023). In the private sector, most economic activities were created by a small group of large firms which have greater productivity, compared to small and medium enterprises. Thailand was on the way to recovery from the economic slowdown from the COVID-19 pandemic during 2020–2021.

More than 800,000 jobs were created in 2022 (United Nations, 2023). In the second quarter of 2023, the number of employed people totalled 39.7 million. Most jobs are located in the non-agricultural sectors, namely hotel and restaurant, construction industry, wholesale and retail trade, transportation, and storage. The average wage is between 400 and 440 USD per person per month. The number of migrants was 2.1 million over 2000–2022, most of whom work in the service sector (Office of the National Economic and Social Development Board, 2023).

Globally, Thailand is 12th in terms of agricultural output, 18th in manufacturing output, 19th in purchasing power, and 21st in industrial output (Thailand Board of Investment, 2023). In 2023, Bangkok, the capital of Thailand, was ranked as the second best place to be a digital nomad (ETHRWorld Southeast Asia, 2023). For remote workers, this reflected cost-efficient living, agreeable weather, and good digital connectivity.

Employability

Employability is an individual's responsibility to develop and make oneself ready for work (Chorkaew, 2016) and is a precondition for the career success of prospective employees. Employability comprises a variety of skills and abilities (Rahmat et al., 2012). This perspective views employability as an individual's capability and willingness to work (Cheng et al., 2022), and possessing appropriate academic skills, connectivity skills, personal characteristics, and exploration skills (Rahmat et al., 2012).

Employability is also associated with lifelong learning to ensure that the workers can develop themselves and remain employed despite changing conditions of work. Thus, employability is not specific to a particular job or position; it is the concept of the ongoing development of workers' competencies (Chorkaew, 2014). In this case, employability relates to the labour market and employees' chance to maintain and find new employment (Cheng et al., 2022).

Programming skills, system development skills, and soft skills are the significant skills that have helped graduates from IT-related fields to find a job in the IT industry (Rahmat et al., 2012). Other studies have identified a broader range of skills applicable to other industry sectors which graduates often lack, including creativity, innovation, general communication skills (including language proficiency in English and Chinese), problem-solving, critical thinking, and related cognitive capabilities (Promsit, 2019, pp. 210–211).

In response to the increasing opportunities with the growing number of Chinese-owned businesses, many universities in Thailand now offer Chinese language programmes to increase the chances for graduates to get employment. In this regard, internships, work experience, and outside activities can enhance Thai students who studied Chinese to have more opportunities to practise language skills and absorb business practices from the world outside the classroom (Jiracheewewong et al., 2019). One study showed that employers also look for skills outside the classroom, and, in particular, languages. The skills that were highly associated with employability included nonverbal communication, a positive personality, and attitude traits related to self-learning, such as being open-minded, service-oriented, and willing to learn new things (Jiracheewewong et al., 2019).

There are various gaps which occur during the hiring of new staff and developing their work competence. Previous research in Thailand has investigated employee employability from either the supply or demand side of the labour market. This chapter addresses the gap in relation to both sides to find the suitable future skills that need to be developed. Then the chapter evaluates the skill gap from the perspectives of managers or supervisors of new employees and current students.

Data Collection and Analysis

This chapter aims to identify the skill gap by comparing the mean scores in the research towards the related to perceived skills from the managers/supervisors and current students. The first group (the demand side) includes managers or supervisors in an organisation, with at least one year's experience, and who are working with at least one subordinate. The second group (the supply side) includes current students in the third year of an undergraduate degree at the university who have plans to apply for a job after graduation. The information collected from both groups is then compared to assess the differences between their perceptions of the skill sets that are essential in obtaining and performing a job.

The research was conducted via a web-based survey undertaken during March–July 2023. The researchers sent the invitation with a survey link to the target groups to ask for participation, using convenience sampling (Cohen et al., 2017). The researchers also asked the target samples to send the survey link to other qualified persons that they know to participate in the survey as 'snowball sampling' (Cohen et al., 2017).

There were 215 completed responses in the first group (N_1). After checking, no missing data were found, and all 215 responses were usable. In the second group, current students (N_2), there were 258 responses from the survey. After checking the responses, 221 completed responses were considered usable.

G*Power was used for sample size estimation. With a significance criterion $\alpha = .05$ and power = .95, the minimum sample size needed with this effect size is N = 45 in comparing the mean score from the same group (Faul et al., 2007). In comparing the mean scores from different groups, the sample size estimation with a significance criterion $\alpha = .05$ and power = .95 was N = 176 (Faul et al., 2007). Thus, the obtained sample sizes $N_1 = 215$ and $N_2 = 221$ were more than adequate to analyse the data.

Employability was the focus to identify the critical skills gaps. In this research employability was composed of three conditions and 24 skills that were identified in prior research (Chorkaew, 2014, 2016). The first skill set included the competencies in performing tasks (17 items), namely Thai literacy, English literacy, numeracy, technology skills, communication skills, interpersonal skills, teamwork skills, service skills, collecting and organising information skills, problem-solving skills, planning skills, innovative thinking, systems thinking, responsibility, being resourceful, flexibility, and having self-esteem.

The second skill set included the following competencies: ability to adapt to a changing environment, ability to adapt to a rotation if required, self-promotion in obtaining and relaying information to maintain awareness of working conditions, and learning skills that contribute to the ongoing improvement and expansion of operations and outcomes.

The third skill set were competencies relevant for obtaining new employment (three items), including job search ability, self-presentation skills, and the ability to transfer and adapt to new workplaces (Chorkaew, 2014, 2016).

Data were obtained through self-reporting, as with previous research projects on this topic (Cheng et al., 2022; Chorkaew, 2014). A four-point Likert scale was applied to assess all questions of employability. In assessing the 'expectation', the four-point scale included highly expect, expect, partially expect, and none. A four-point Likert scale to measure perception towards 'current skill' included abundant, some, fair, and none. In the first group (demand side), managers were asked to provide their responses to the following questions.

1 To what extent do you expect newly hired employees in your organisation to possess these skills?
2 To what extent do you think the newly hired employees possess these skills?

The current students were asked to assess the employability skill requirements of the expected positions for which they would apply. The question asked of the new graduates was 'What do you expect the level of employability to be for the position you want to apply for in your prospective organisation?' A four-point Likert scale was applied with the following choices: highly expected, expected, partially expected, and none.

Data were analysed with descriptive statistics, and mean score differences with t-tests. In the research objective 1, data were from the managers' side. This was considered by testing the mean difference from the same sample group. A paired sample t-test was applied in these cases. In research objective 2, where the data came from different groups, managers and current students, two-group independent-sample t-tests were performed. The average age of the manager/supervisor group was 36.93 years ($SD = 8.00$) and the average age of third-year students was 21.14 years ($SD = 0.71$). The respondents' characteristics are shown in Table 6.1.

Table 6.1 Respondent characteristics

Characteristics	*Manager/ Supervisor*		*Students*		*Full sample*	
	n	%	N	%	*n*	%
Gender						
Male	76	35.4	58	26.2	134	30.7
Female	124	57.7	155	70.1	279	64.0
Prefer not to say	15	6.9	8	3.6	24	5.3
Size of the organisation[a]						
< 10 employees	11	5.1	19	8.6	30	6.9
11–50 employees	43	20.0	45	20.4	88	20.1
51–250 employees	54	25.1	84	38.0	138	31.6
251–1,000 employees	49	22.8	54	24.4	103	23.6
> 1,000 employees	58	27.0	19	8.6	77	17.6
Location[a]						
Bangkok area	153	71.2	130	58.8	283	64.9
Central part of Thailand	35	16.2	42	19.0	77	17.6
North	5	2.3	9	4.1	14	3.2
Northeastern	8	3.7	3	1.4	11	2.5
Eastern	5	2.3	7	3.2	12	2.7
Western	1	0.5	0	0	1	0.2
South	8	3.7	6	2.7	14	3.2
Aboard	0	0	24	10.9	24	5.5
Type of Organisation[a]						
Business	151	70.2	185	83.7	336	77.0
Public	42	19.5	7	3.2	49	11.2
State enterprise	14	6.5	22	10.0	36	22.0
Not-for-profit	8	3.7	7	3.2	15	3.4

Note: [a] (For student) as the expectation towards desired job from the third-year students.

In the group of managers or supervisors, there were 215 respondents, of whom 57.7% were female, and 27% worked in large organisations with more than a thousand workers. This was followed by 25.1% who worked in an organisation with 51–250 employees. Around 70% were from an organisation in the Bangkok area. More than half worked in the position as the line functional manager (junior level), followed by 22.3% senior-level managers. A quarter were from the banking and finance/insurance sector, and the rest were from various industries such as computing and telecommunications, health services, retail/wholesale, and production and sale of industrial goods.

In the group of the current students who were in their third year at university, there were 221 respondents, of whom 70.1% were female and 82% studied social science, while 18% studied sciences. Thirty-eight percent expected to work in an organisation with 51–250 employees, followed by 24.4% who wanted to work in an organisation with 251–1,000 employees. Nearly 59% (58.8%) wanted to work in the Bangkok area, while only 19.9% wanted to work in the central part of Thailand. Most of the sample (83.7%) expected to work for a business organisation.

Results

This section reports the results from testing the mean score differences according to the three research objectives to identify the critical skills gaps.

Managers' Perspectives

The first part tested the mean score from a manager's perspective, comparing their expectations with the current skills of the newly hired employees. The significant difference provides information on the skill gap within the newly hired staff in the work environment (Table 6.2). Table 6.2 shows the results of testing the mean score differences between the expectations and current skills of newly hired employees. The results were derived from a paired simple t-test with 0.5 significant level. There were 16 skills out of 24 in which the mean scores were different. There are 11 skills from competencies in performing tasks that were different, including numeracy, communication skills, teamwork skills, collecting and organising information skills, problem-solving skills, planning skills, innovative thinking, systems thinking, responsibility, being resourceful, and flexibility. Three skills from the remaining competency included the ability to adapt to a changing environment, self-promotion, and learning skills that contribute to ongoing improvement and expansion of operations and outcomes. Another two skills for obtaining new employment were job search ability and self-presentation skills.

There were 3 of the 16 skills in which the current skills of newly hired employees were higher than managers' expectations—namely, self-presentation skills ($M = 2.86$), numeracy ($M = 2.83$), and job search ability ($M = 2.55$). This indicated that from the managers' viewpoint, newly hired staff demonstrated

Table 6.2 Skills gap of newly hired employees

Skills	*Managers' expectation n = 215*		*Newly hired staff skills n = 221*		*t(214)*	*P*	*Cohen's d*
	M	*SD*	*M*	*SD*			
Thai skills	3.46	0.563	3.45	0.547	0.319	0.750	0.58
English skill	2.64	0.715	2.74	0.720	-2.13	0.034	0.68
Numeracy	2.65	0.694	2.83	0.693	-3.36	0.001*	0.79
Working with technology skills	3.13	0.667	3.16	0.679	-0.44	0.658	0.77
Communication skills	3.33	0.571	3.11	0.679	4.25	0.000*	0.78
Interpersonal skills	3.24	0.680	3.21	0.654	0.47	0.634	0.85
Teamwork skills	3.50	0.554	3.24	0.693	4.95	0.000*	0.77
Service skills	3.20	0.714	3.20	0.692	1.76	0.079	0.81
Collecting and organising information skills	3.09	0.691	2.88	0.749	3.53	0.001*	0.86
Problem-solving skills	3.10	0.700	2.87	0.766	3.48	0.001*	0.94
Planning skills	2.95	0.689	2.78	0.740	2.96	0.003*	0.87
Thinking innovatively	2.96	0.722	2.72	0.796	4.29	0.000*	0.84
Systems thinking	3.05	0.654	2.84	0.734	3.51	0.001*	0.87
Responsibility	3.73	0.475	3.35	0.673	7.15	0.000*	0.78
Being resourceful	3.06	0.688	2.80	0.742	4.51	0.000*	0.81
Flexibility	3.32	0.636	3.12	0.700	3.31	0.001*	0.86
Having self-esteem	3.16	0.688	3.07	0.752	1.63	0.104	0.87
Ability to adapt to a changing environment	3.25	0.613	3.01	0.680	4.08	0.000*	0.85
Ability to adapt to a rotation if required	2.60	0.767	2.65	0.777	-0.89	0.372	0.83
Self-promotion in obtaining and relaying information to maintain awareness of working conditions.	3.11	0.582	2.92	0.735	3.36	0.001*	0.81
Learning skills that contribute to ongoing improvement and expansion of operations and outcomes	3.21	0.612	3.03	0.679	3.41	0.001*	0.77
Job search ability	2.37	0.791	2.55	0.740	-3.07	0.002*	0.86
Self-presentation skills	2.73	0.685	2.86	0.703	-2.19	0.029*	0.87
Ability to transfer and adapt to new workplace	3.23	0.613	3.17	0.636	1.12	0.264	0.79

these three skills more effective than their expectations. With the remainder of the 13 significant skills, the top 3 skills mean score of managers' expectations included responsibility (M = 3.73), teamwork skills (M = 3.50), and communication skills (M = 3.33). The lowest three skills mean scores were job search ability (M = 2.37), numeracy (M = 2.65), and self-presentation skills (M = 2.73).

The table also shows that of the 13 skills, the level of managers' expectations was higher than the newly hired staff demonstrated. This finding indicated that there was a gap that new staff needed to bridge to meet their manager's expectations. There were eight skills in which the mean scores were similar to expectations, including Thai skills, English skills, working with technology skills, interpersonal skills, service skills, self-esteem, ability to adapt to a rotation if required, and ability to transfer and adapt to a new workplace. Managers' perspectives of these eight skills were at the same level as the current skills of newly hired employees.

When we look at the effective size of the difference, as reported by Cohen's d score (Cohen, 2013), the 16 skill gaps were categorised as being large in size. The highest value of Cohen's d score was problem-solving skills (d = 0.94), followed by planning skills and system thinking, showing the same Cohen's score (d = 0.84). The third highest Cohen's score was collecting and organising information skills (d = 0.86). The lowest Cohen's score was teamwork and learning skills that contribute to ongoing improvement and expansion of operations and outcomes (d = 0.77).

To answer the first research objective, the skill gaps between the expectation and current skills of newly hired employees from the managers' perspective included 16 skill gaps. Three skills of newly hired employees were higher than managers' expectations—namely, self-presentation skills, numeracy, and job search ability. For the rest of the 13 skills, managers' expectations were higher than employees' current skills. All these 16 skills were in the 'large different' category.

Comparing Managers' and Students' Perspectives

The second part of the analysis compared mean scores from managers' expectations of the position (newly hired staff) and current students' perspectives towards the desired position. The results provided a clearer picture of the skill gap between demand and supply sides (Table 6.3).

When comparing mean scores from different groups, the independent sample t-test was applied. Table 6.3 compared mean scores between managers' expectations of the newly hired staff and current students' expectations about the required skills for work. The results showed that 22 out of 24 skills mean scores were different between the two groups. With respect to one skill, Thai language skills, the findings indicated that the mean score from the managers' expectations (M = 3.46) was higher than current students' expectations (M = 2.86). The rest of the mean scores from the 21 skills from the current students' expectations were higher than their prospective managers. The highest mean scores were communication skills and teamwork skills (M = 3.64), followed by problem-solving skills (M = 3.60), and flexibility (M = 3.58). The lowest three mean scores were ability to adapt to a rotation if required (M = 2.78), job search ability (M = 2.80), and numeracy (M = 2.86).

Table 6.3 Skills gap of current students

Skills	*Managers* *n* = 215		*Students* *n* = 221		*df*	*t*	*p*	*Cohen's d*
	M	*SD*	*M*	*SD*				
Thai skills	3.46	0.563	2.86	0.820	390.820	8.93	0.000*	0.70
English skill	2.64	0.715	3.34	0.617	434	−10,95	0.000*	0.66
Numeracy	2.65	0.694	2.86	0.820	434	−2.98	0.003*	0.76
Working with technology skills	3.13	0.667	3.34	0.617	434	−3.39	0.001*	0.64
Communication skills	3.33	0.571	3.64	0.534	434	−5.80	0.000*	0.55
Interpersonal skills	3.24	0.680	3.49	0.637	434	−4.05	0.000*	0.65
Teamwork skills	3.50	0.554	3.64	0.552	433.565	−2.64	0.008*	0.55
Service Skills	3.30	0.714	3.22	0.751	434	1.08	0.280	0.73
Collecting and organising information skills	3.09	0.691	3.41	0.631	434	−5.03	0.000*	0.66
Problem-solving skills	3.10	0.700	3.60	0.544	434	−8.33	0.000*	0.62
Planning skills	2.95	0.689	3.46	0.628	427.921	−7.96	0.000*	0.65
Thinking innovatively	2.96	0.722	3.38	0.682	430.870	−6.26	0.000*	0.70
Systems thinking	3.05	0.654	3.38	0.619	431.071	−5.54	0.000*	0.63
Responsibility	3.73	0.475	3.76	0.469	434	−0.66	0.508	0.47
Being resourceful	3.06	0.688	3.52	0.592	434	−7.56	0.000*	0.64
Flexibility	3.32	0.638	3.58	0.547	420.930	−4.62	0.000*	0.59
Having self-esteem	3.16	0.688	3.35	0.668	434	−2.85	0.004*	0.67
Ability to adapt to a changing environment	3.25	0.613	3.53	0.568	434	−4.91	0.000*	0.59
Ability to adapt to a rotation if required	2.60	0.767	2.78	0.769	434	−2.48	0.013*	0.76
Self-promotion in obtaining and relaying information to maintain awareness of working conditions	3.11	0.582	3.45	0.590	433.917	−6.07	0.000*	0.58
Learning skills that contribute to ongoing improvement and expansion of operations and outcomes	3.21	0.612	3.53	0.568	434	−5.57	0.000*	0.59
Job search ability	2.37	0.791	2.80	0.831	434	−5.51	0.000*	0.81
Self-presentation skills	2.73	0.685	3.29	0.687	434	−8.58	0.000*	0.68
Ability to transfer and adapt to new workplace	3.23	0.613	3.51	0.615	434	−4.66	0.000*	0.61

Two skills in which the mean scores were not different were service skills and responsibility. The service skill mean score was lower than responsibility in both groups: the managers' expectation (M = 3.33) and current students' expectation (M = 3.22). The mean score of responsibility was the highest score in each group, with the managers' expectations (M = 3.73) and current students' expectations (M = 3.76). Even these mean scores were not significantly different, as both managers and students gave the highest important skill to responsibility.

From the 22 skills, the highest Cohen's score was job search ability (d = 0.81), indicating large effect size. The rest of the 21 skills were in the medium category. The top skills in the medium category were numeracy and ability to adapt to a rotation if required (d = 0.76). The lowest skills were communication skills and teamwork skills (d = 0.55). These helped in answering the second research question that aimed to identify the skill gap between managers' expectations of the position (newly hired staff) and current students' expectations. There were 22 out of 24 skills in this survey in which mean scores were different. Only with the score for Thai language skills was the managers' expectation higher than the students' expectation. The rest of the 21 scores showed that students' expectations were higher than that of the manager group. Job search ability was also indicated as the large effect size. Most of the skills were in the medium effect size category.

The research faced some limitations. The first limitation is the stability of observation as the method was based solely on the respondents' opinions. The results may change over time. The respondents may receive new information after they completed the survey and thus their opinions may not be the same. Second, each respondent may also interpret their own skills differently from others as the data from this research were based on self-assessment (Cohen et al., 2017). Third, this is cross-sectional data, which were based on the results at this point in time, so no changes through time are assessed (Cohen et al., 2017). For jobs or industries that require advanced technical skills and knowledge, further research may consider investigating the ability to apply technical knowledge in addition to the other employability skill sets.

Conclusion and Discussion

The research revealed the following three findings. The first finding is from the managers/supervisors' viewpoint, compared with the expectations and current skills of newly hired employees. There are 16 significant employability skill gaps with medium to high levels of difference. There are 11 skills in the performing task skill set, including problem-solving, systems thinking, planning, collecting and organising information, flexibility, innovative thinking, being resourceful, numeracy, communication skills, responsibility, and teamwork skills. There are three skills from the remaining employed set, including ability to adapt to a changing environment, self-promotion, and learning skills for improvement. Two skills from the competencies for obtaining new employment included self-presentation and job search ability. In this group, three skills that managers considered that the new hired staff performed better than expectation are numeracy, job search ability, and self-promotion from the new employment skills set. The rest of the 13 skills represented significant differences, and managers' expectations were higher than the newly hired staff performed. This indicates that as newly hired staff, there are significant skill gaps that they need to improve to meet a manager's expectations.

The second finding draws on the differences between the two groups—managers' and current students' expectations. There are 22 significant employability skills gaps. Most of the differences are at the middle level, except 'the ability to adapt to rotation' which demonstrates a high level of difference. Two skills that do not indicate differences in expectations are service skill and responsibility. Only with 'Thai language skills demonstrated' was the managers' expectation higher than that of the current students. A manager wants the staff member to perform at a higher level than the students anticipated. With respect to the remainder of the 21 skills, the results show that current students' expectations are higher than those of the managers. These suggest that students expect to perform these employability skills at a higher level than is expected by their managers.

Thai higher education institutions need to prepare their graduates with the essential skills for job entry. However, both government agencies and higher education institutions need to monitor the skill requirements for job access and the skill gap. This requires greater co-operation between the key labour market stakeholders (Abas-Mastura et al., 2013; Dhakal et al., 2029). Improving graduate work readiness through the development of key job skills would satisfy Thailand's SDG Goal 4.4 to increase the number of young people and adults who have relevant skills, including technical and vocational skills, for employment, decent jobs, and entrepreneurship; and Thailand's SDG 8—promote sustained, inclusive, and sustainable economic growth, full and productive employment, and decent work for all.

The results from this research highlight the importance of higher education institutions to monitor and sustain the employability skills of their graduates (Abas-Mastura et al., 2013; Abbasi et al., 2018). Higher educational institutions also need to ensure that the basic skills requirements such as language, responsibility, numeracy, and communication are met. Government policy could focus more on supporting educational institutions to equip students with skills for both work and life. The outcome of a graduate skill set needs to be broadened and evaluated to assess its success. Moreover, the government may consider supporting both new graduates and employing organisations through subsidies or funding to develop a skill set during the first year of employment to develop work readiness. This policy would motivate and give a chance for unemployed people to develop and utilise their skills to provide the desired performance for an organisation. It could also help to motivate an organisation to hire more workers. In summary, there would be the development of the required skills from the supply side and transfer of graduates with the right skills to the demand side.

This chapter has focused on employability skills that will equip the workers to acquire and appropriately perform in their chosen job. The findings suggest that there is an imbalance of various skills as perceived by both sides of the labour market, with both over and under expectations being reported. Further significant steps need to be considered to support the achievement of Thai SDG 4.4, notably by ensuring that graduates possess the technical skills required to work with new technologies.

Note

* Corresponding author: monthon@tbs.tu.ac.th.

References

Abas-Mastura, M., Imam, O. A., & Osman, S. (2013). Employability skills and task performance of employees in government sector. *International Journal of Humanities and Social Science*, *3*(4), 150–162.

Abbasi, F. K., Ali, A., & Bibi, N. (2018). Analysis of skill gap for business graduates: Managerial perspective from banking industry. *Education + Training*, *60*(4), 354–367.

Cheng, M., Adekola, O., Albia, J., & Cai, S. (2022). Employability in higher education: A review of key stakeholders' perspectives. *Higher Education Evaluation and Development*, *16*(1), 16–31.

Chorkaew, S. (2014). Human resource development interventions and employability enhancement: A Perspective of the Thai public sector on government employees. *NIDA Development Journal*, *54*(2), 31–66.

Chorkaew, S. (2016). Employability: The new deal of short-term employment. *NIDA Development Journal*, *56*(2), 1–17.

Cohen, J. (2013). *Statistical power analysis for the behavioral sciences.* Academic Press.

Cohen, L., Manion, L., & Morrison, K. (2017). *Research methods in education.* Routledge.

Dhakal, S., Prikshat, V., Nankervis, A., & Burgess, J. (2019). *The transition from graduation to work.* Springer.

Dhamnimitr, P. (2014). Educational policy agenda in the 21st century: Alternative policy or survival policy of Thailand. *Mahidol Integrated Social Science Journal*, *1*(1), 148–169.

ETHRWorld Southeast Asia. (2023, 5 April). *The best places to be a 'Digital Nomad' in 2023: Research.* https://hrsea.economictimes.indiatimes.com/news/employee-experience/the-best-places-to-be-a-digital-nomad-in-2023-research/99246964\

Faul, F., Erdfelder, E., Lang, A. G., & Buchner, A. (2007). G* Power 3: A flexible statistical power analysis program for the social, behavioral, and biomedical sciences. *Behavior Research Methods*, *39*(2), 175–191.

Fernquest, J. (2017). University over-enrolls, graduating students punished. *Bangkok Post.* www.bangkokpost.com/learning/advanced/1284471/university-over-enrolls-graduating-students-punished.

Jiracheewewong, E., Yongxia, M., & Han, X. (2019). The determinants for best employability skills and job opportunities for undergraduate students majoring in Chinese in Thailand. *Education and Urban Society*, *51*(7), 989–1004.

National Strategy Secretariat Office. (2018). *National strategy 2018–2037.* Office of the National Economic and Social Development Board.

Office of the National Economic and Social Development Board. (2021). *Thailand's SDG progress report 2016–2020*. Author.
Office of the National Economic and Social Development Board. (2023). *Thailand's social outlook of Q2/2023*. Author.
Promsit, S. (2019). Graduate work-readiness in Thailand. In S. Dhakal, V. Prikshat, A. Nankervis, & J. Burgess (Eds.). *The transition from graduation to work: Challenges and strategies in the twenty first century Asia Pacific and beyond*. Springer Nature.
Rahmat, M., Ahmad, K., Idris, S., & Zainal, N. F. A. (2012). Relationship between employability and graduates' skill. *Procedia-Social and Behavioral Sciences, 59*, 591–597.
Sivasomboon, B. (2017). *Thailand's skill problem is slowing down its high-tech push*. https://www.bloomberg.com/news/articles/2017-07-18/skills-gap-tests-thai-junta-s-goal-of-forging-innovative-economy (Accessed: 30 November 2023).
Staffing Industry Analysts. (2016). *Thailand—lack of skills, unrealistic expectations are key factors in unemployment*. http://www2.staffingindustry.com/row/Editorial/Daily-News/Thailand-lack-of-skills-unrealistic-expectations-are-key-factors-in-unemployment-37307
Thailand Board of Investment. (2023, 23 June). *Thailand's ranking*. www.boi.go.th/index.php?page=thailand_rankings&language=en\
United Nations. (2023). *2022 UN Thailand results report*. Thailand. https://thailand.un.org/en/259712-2023-un-thailand-annual-results-report
Vandeweyer, M., Espinoza, R., Reznikova, L., Lee, M., & Herabat, T. (2020). *Thailand's education system and skills imbalances: Assessment and policy recommendations*. https://dx.doi.org/10.1787/b79addb6-en

7 Skills Shortages in Vietnam

James Cooper and Nhat Tram Phan-Le*

Introduction

Despite having made significant progress towards implementing the United Nations (UN) sustainable development goals (SDGs), Vietnam still faces challenges in addressing shortages in vital skills, which could hinder progress towards achieving them. The UN 2030 Agenda for Sustainable Development identified productive employment, basic social services, and universal social protection as key pathways to sustaining Vietnam's development (UNDP, 2023). Within these three areas the World Bank has provided strategic advice for Vietnam on workforce preparation for future jobs. These include major investments in universities and advisory services on skills development (World Bank, 2022), which aligns to SDG 4—ensuring inclusive and equitable quality education and promoting lifelong learning opportunities for all (UNDP, 2023).

This chapter applies human capital theory (Mincer, 1958; Schultz, 1959, 1961; Becker & Collins, 1964) to identify the underlying and related factors impacting skill development as the country advances towards a developed nation status. Human capital theory is limited by primarily focusing on the supply side of the labour market and by assuming an economic model of individuals with rational decision-making abilities and full information (Marginson, 2019). This chapter addresses those limitations by also considering the demand side of the labour market and its role in incentivising progress towards a high-skill economy. In addition, it analyses the relationship between investments in education and economic growth. By doing so, the chapter aims to propose government initiatives that support effective labour market outcomes. In this context, critical skills are regarded as insufficient skills across the workforce to enable the realisation of growth and employment targets, and thus hamper the achievement of SDGs #4 and #8 linked to jobs, growth, and incomes.

The methodological approach of the study analyses labour market indicators using available data provided by Vietnam's Government Statistics Office (GSO) and other government sources such as the World Bank (WB), the United Nations (UN), and International Labour Organisation (ILO) reports.

DOI: 10.4324/9781003379065-9

This is complemented by current and relevant academic work identifying skill deficiencies impacting Vietnam's sustainable economic performance. It analyses specific sector labour shortages in Vietnam through lenses provided by UN SDGs 4 and 8, which promote quality education/lifelong learning opportunities and advance decent work/productive employment respectively. It aims to discuss sector-specific skills required for achieving the SDGs in Vietnam, the current state of realisation of the SDGs, workforce projections and planning, and workforce-related policy challenges that should be addressed to achieve SDGs that are of national significance.

Human Capital Theory

The concept of human capital has its roots in classical economic theory and remains a significant focus in modern economies (Forrester et al., 2016; Kalimullin et al., 2016). It is a foundational element in the assessment and approaches to sustainability for global organisations. While Adam Smith initially implied the recognition of human capital by highlighting the significance of skills and talents in personal success and societal advancement (Turekulova et al., 2016), the development of human capital theory, which occurred two centuries later, extends beyond individual attributes. This theory encompasses the broader aspects of social systems, educational quality, health care, and crime prevention within the context of the development process (Schultz, 1961).

Since then, human capital theory has undergone continuous development and has been the subject of ongoing debates among scholars. Kendrick (1976) elaborated on the concept, separating tangible from intangible capital, such that the key components of human capital include individual, collective, and public. Others, such as Kritskiy (1991), aligned human capital classification with economic function. Korchagin (2012) then provided social and technological perspectives of human capital and explained the gradual development as an economic concept, including investment ensuring public safety; training of effective elites; development of a civil society; higher effectiveness of institutional care; investment in living standards; and external capital flows. Meanwhile, Simkovic (2013) presented social, biological, cultural, and psychological perspectives through economic interactions.

The World Economic Forum (WEF) describes human capital as a 'key factor for growth, development and competitiveness' (World Economic Forum, 2017, p. 13), working through multiple pathways. As such, the WEF assesses human capital across elements of capacity (formal education of current generations), development (future-focused and next-generation formal education), deployment (skill application), and know-how (breadth and depth of specialised skills). In this chapter, these issues are important to the study of skill shortages and skill development in Vietnam. Human capital theory emphasises the importance of investing in people, focuses on the role of education and training in economic development (ILO, 2019b), and as such, can provide insight into methods to address skill shortages, enabling opportunities to examine challenges and opportunities in implementing improvement programmes, and offer recommendations to policymakers and other stakeholders.

The United Nations Development Programme and Human Capital Development

Central to the UN SGDs, the United Nations Development Programme (UNDP) encompasses 165 countries which are coordinating efforts towards achieving the 2030 Agenda for Sustainable Development. This agenda provides 17 SDGs built upon the Millennium Development Goals to mobilise a globally united effort to end all forms of poverty, fight inequalities, and tackle climate change, while ensuring that no one is left behind (Weiland et al., 2021). Within the 17 SDGs, SDG 4 seeks to ensure inclusive and equitable education and promote lifelong learning, but several of the other goals include elements of education, indicating the importance of this goal to the achievement of the overall agenda. This journey towards decent work for all is primarily included under SDG 8. Therefore, most labour-related indicators pertain to SDG 8 and cover a range of aspects including both the quantity and quality of employment (ILO, 2019a).

Leveraging human capital theory, the WEF contends that the world of work is the common denominator to the achievement of the SDGs as the principal provider of livelihoods and security and is central to connecting all social partners (Adecco Group, 2021). The WEF stresses the policy urgency of investment in human capital (WEF, 2022) based on research indicating that adult lifelong learning attracts only 0.5% of global GDP, while the Organisation for Economic Cooperation and Development (OECD) forecasts that around 1.1 billion jobs are likely to be radically transformed over the coming decade (WEF, 2022). Meanwhile, the WEF 2017 *Global Human Capital Report* highlights gaps within and across nations in preparing people for the future of work. Education, in its various forms, represents an investment in human capital. It provides people with knowledge and skills crucial to upward social mobility, improving employment prospects, reducing poverty, and improving overall health and well-being.

Country Background

With a population of 98.5 million, situated by the South China Sea and bordered by China, Laos, and Cambodia, Vietnam is one of the world's most successful transition stories. Following decades of economic mismanagement and through the *Doi Moi* (renovation) initiatives of 1986, Vietnam's economic rise has been remarkable, with growth among the fastest in the world since 1990 (World Bank, 2018). GDP per capita reached around US$3700 in 2021, a 360% increase since 2002 (World Bank, 2022). During this period poverty rates decreased from 14 to 3.8% (World Bank, 2022). This growth was underpinned by factors including an expansion in manufacturing, increased foreign direct investment, export growth, and a rapidly growing services sector.

However, this rapid growth likely exacerbates significant challenges related to the critical skill shortages (CSS) necessary for achieving the UN SDGs. Along with improvements in infant mortality and health comes an increase in life expectancy. This, combined with a declining fertility rate, means that an aging population is an impending threat. Vietnam's workforce is aging with changes to industry structure such that the percentage of workers aged 15 to 24 has declined from 18.3% to 10.1% since 2010, while the percentage of workers over 50 has risen from 20.3% to 26.8% (World Bank, 2022).

The process of urbanisation has improved literacy and the labour rate, while population growth has delayed poverty reduction (Pham & Riedel, 2019). Unemployment since 2015 had remained relatively stable at around 2.2%, but as a likely outcome of the COVID-19 pandemic, the number of unemployed people increased to 2.48% in 2020 and 3.2% in 2021. Unemployment is higher in urban areas at around 4.3% and has increased more dramatically since 2019 when compared to rural employment; it is currently recorded at 2.5% (Nguyen et al., 2019). Unemployment has increased, especially in the Southeast of Vietnam and the Mekong Delta, across both urban and rural sectors. Unemployment among the 15–24-year-old age group is presently at 8.55%, with the highest rates being located in the southeast and Mekong Delta areas (Nguyen et al., 2019). The overall literacy of the Vietnamese working population has improved from 93.7% in 2010 to 95.7% in 2021. While female literacy (94.5%) remains lower than males' (96.9%), the gap between gender literacy rates has closed from 4.3% to 2.4% since 2010 (GSO, 2021). The gap in literacy between urban and rural areas, however, is somewhat more stubborn, and despite improvements in rural locations, there remains a gap of 3.9% when compared to urban literacy rates.

The WEF *Global Human Capital Report* (WEF, 2017) outlines national dimensions of human capital and its future development. Vietnam was ranked 64th out of 130 countries in 2017 (Table 7.1). While ranking highly in terms of present levels of workforce deployment, this may conceal issues associated

Table 7.1 Human capital index comparison

Country	*Overall index*		*Capacity sub-index*		*Deployment sub-index*		*Development sub-index*		*Know-how sub-index*	
	Score	*Rank*	*Score*	*Rank*	*Score*	*Rank*	*Score*	*Rank*	*Score*	*Rank*
Norway	77.12	1	80.46	13	72.18	24	82.63	6	72.22	6
Vietnam	62.19	64	62.26	85	81.12	6	63.62	53	50.21	80
Australia	71.56	20	78.44	20	66.2	63	80.24	9	61.36	29
Thailand	66.15	40	65.5	77	80.99	7	63.68	66	54.33	51
Yemen	35.48	130	34.95	122	34.26	130	34.39	130	38.43	127

with underemployment (World Bank, 2019). The 2019 report ranked Vietnam 48th out of 157 countries; however, disaggregation of the global human capital index (HCI) highlights how child health and education deficiencies today will impact next-generation labour productivity, suggesting larger gaps in future worker productivity. (World Bank, 2019). Examination of the HCI sub-indices highlights Vietnam's relative weakness in capacity and know-how in particular, while the development stub-index could be considered in the mid-range in a global context. For Vietnam, the deployment index is particularly strong, suggesting a highly skilled workforce; however, the remaining indices indicate that skills are not matching industry demand. Here, a capacity sub-index ranked at 85 measures expected educational quantity such as expected years of schooling and quality in terms of graduate skill relevance; while the know-how sub-index, ranking 80, measures the availability of specialised skills such as those in areas associated with science, technology, engineering, and mathematics (STEM). When combined with a development sub-index measuring skill accumulation through experience, ranked 53, it suggests that Vietnam needs to focus on educational quality and graduate skill relevance in addition to further investment in on-the-job training.

Between 2010 and 2019, Vietnam has seen a shift in employment from agriculture towards manufacturing and market services as the economy industrialises. From 2010, the employment share in agriculture has fallen from 48.5% of adult workforce to 29.2% in 2019. Meanwhile, employment in manufacturing increased from 14.3% to 22.3%, and employment in market services rose from 20.1% to 27.2%. Employment in construction and non-market services also rose through this period, albeit to a lesser extent (O'Higgins & Viegelahn, 2021). The sector shifts towards the higher-productivity manufacturing sector suggested positive impacts on poverty reduction, but the employment shift towards the services sector has likely had negative impacts, as benefits from services may fail to flow through to the rural poor in particular. This suggests a net effect negatively impacting progress towards SDG 1 and poverty reduction in Vietnam.

As of November 2022, Vietnam had experienced 43,166 deaths attributed to the COVID-19 pandemic (WHO, 2022). While still able to maintain a degree of economic growth, COVID-19 containment efforts have exacerbated existing inequalities across a range of dimensions, especially in income, employment, and gender (Huynh, 2021). Relative to the bottom 10% of wage earners, the top 10% of wages increased from 5.2 times during the last quarter of 2019 to 7.4 times by the end of 2020. Of the total contraction in wage employment, 71.7% was attributable to five sectors: agriculture, manufacturing, wholesale and retail trade, accommodation and food services, and education (Huynh, 2021).

Critical Skill Shortages

The abundance of low-wage workers and factors such as political stability make Vietnam an attractive destination for foreign direct investment (FDI). Despite

Doi Moi's initiation of a movement away from a centralised economy, Vietnam remains a one-party socialist state under the Communist Party of Vietnam (CPV) (Truong & Rowley, 2014). As such, significant political decisions remain reserved by the CPV and are implemented by government. As a consequence, and unlike more advanced ASEAN countries, stakeholders such as the business community are likely excluded from consensus-building processes (Ohno, 2013). Despite some transfer of fiscal and administrative authority to provincial levels, including the licensing and management of FDI projects (Malesky, 2004), these are often unaccompanied by institutional autonomy and financial resources (Anh, 2016). High unionisation of wage earners notwithstanding, all unions reside within the Vietnam General Confederation of Labour (VGCL) under the leadership of the CPV with little ability to contest employers on behalf of their members (Schmillen & Packard, 2016). As a result, employers report satisfaction in access to low-wage workers (Goodwin et al., 2014), supporting notions that Vietnam's education system has been effective in delivering fundamental skills.

However, the heavy reliance on FDI to provide scale and drive development also puts significant pressure on labour supply and quality. According to Lanvin et al. (2019), Vietnam ranks 87 out of 119 countries in terms of talent attractiveness, retention, and development, with 40% of FDI firms reporting frustration in finding skilled workers. In particular, the information technology sector was undersupplied by 78,000 persons, with expectations of a 500,000-person shortfall of the required 1.2 million by 2020 (Kiet, 2018). These deficiencies detract from Vietnam's attractiveness as an FDI destination, particularly in sectors dependent on high technology. Pennings (2020) notes the under-utilisation of Vietnam's human capital and a decline in the HCI from 0.69 to 0.37 despite improvements in education, indicating a mismatch in skills and knowledge supply. Meanwhile, Richiardi et al. (2023) report only 9% of occupations in Vietnam are classified as highly skilled. That is, employment in Vietnam remains predominantly lower and medium skilled (World Bank, 2018), while the population is becoming more educated; but at the same time, high-skill positions cannot be filled from the available labour pool

Rapid technological change means that firms must innovate to remain competitive, which requires advanced skills. The Vietnamese commercial landscape, however, is dominated by small and medium enterprises (SMEs), frequently family-owned (Cleine, 2013), which often operate informally (Cling et al., 2012) and lack the scale and access to finance necessary to adapt. Market inefficiencies mean educational supply remains behind demand in providing the skills required to maintain competitive presence. Vu (2020) cites Industry 5.0 as replacing low-skilled work with increased demand for highly skilled labour. There is a multi-sector shortage of engineers and managers and a 20% annual growth in tourism, requiring 40,000 workers against a current supply of 15,000, of which only 12% are higher education graduates.

Labour migration and a growing outbound student market pose a twofold challenge in retaining the skilled workforce within Vietnam and encouraging their return to the country. While most highly skilled workers trained abroad have no intention to return home, as many Vietnamese are seeking opportunities to develop their career overseas, there is an increasing 'brain drain'. There is a growing outbound student market, with 63,703 students studying abroad in 2017 (Trines, 2017). Outbound skilled migration in Vietnam has increased rapidly, with the current net migration rate for Vietnam in 2023 being –0.935 per 1,000 population, a 2.07% increase from 2022 (Macrotrends.net, 2023). The challenge of the brain drain, particularly among highly skilled workers, is becoming increasingly significant for Vietnam in the era of rapid globalisation. To address this issue effectively, Vietnam needs to revamp its policies to compete with other nations, not only to attract its skilled expatriates back but also to entice talent from around the world.

However, the Vietnamese government's efforts to cultivate a pool of highly skilled workers have not been successful. Vietnam has been implementing Resolution 27 on building a pool of highly skilled workers, but it is evident that the policies have failed. One of the most significant issues is the misallocation of individuals with valuable professional expertise into managerial positions, resulting in a significant loss of talent (Nguyen, 2016). These talented individuals are not appropriately deployed, hindering their ability to advance and to showcase their capabilities. There are challenges in the provision of sufficient finance to support science, technology, culture, and artistic endeavour, all of which require skilled workers (Trang, 2022).

Addressing Skill Shortages

The Vietnam Academy of Social Sciences (VASS) defines skilled labour as 'any labour with special skills, training, knowledge, and abilities in their field', while referring to highly skilled labour as

> generally characterised by advanced education (college and higher), the possession of knowledge and skills to perform complicated tasks, as well as the ability to adapt quickly to technological changes, and a creative application of knowledge and skills acquired through training in their field.
>
> (Vu, 2019, p. 1)

While the 2016–2020 Socio-Economic Development Plan makes fleeting references to the UN Agenda for Sustainable Development (Nishitani et al., 2021), Vietnam has since indicated an increasing commitment to the sustainable development framework. In 2017, the country adopted a National Action Plan on the 2030 Agenda, and early in 2019, it launched the Vietnam Sustainable Development Statistical Indicators list as a tool to make the SDG framework specific to the national context and to secure commitment from relevant institutions. Further, Vietnam has been upgrading its data collection capacity to support the monitoring of the SDGs, especially with respect to labour market issues. Vietnam's Labour Force Survey, one of the most advanced in emerging Asian nations, has since January 2019 embraced modern standards adopted by the 19th International Conference of Labour Statisticians (Dang et al., 2023). While the desire to improve data collection and measurement towards SDG achievement is admirable, Vietnam does have many businesses operating informally with likely consequences for statistical reliability.

Labour market and business informality remain a problem in Vietnam. Typically less-skilled informal workers have limited social protection, are lower paid, and are highly vulnerable to economic disruption. Huynh (2021) reported a 9.4% spike in the number of low-paid workers in the informal sectors of the Vietnamese economy during the last quarter of 2020. The first quarter in 2021 saw a further 1.1% increase, up 1.8% against the same period last year, leading to a total of 57.1% of workers informally employed (Government of Vietnam, 2022). This renders any improvement and monitoring of human capital difficult.

Skill Supply and Demand Perspectives

The human capital theory perspective assumes that market mechanisms are efficiently functioning to match the supply of skills with demand. Therefore, the responsibility for determining skill development lies with individuals and the market. Consequently, the role of government is in removing market failures that create obstacles and barriers to individual investment in education and training (Stevens, 1996). As a result, a preferable government focus would be to improve labour market information systems; forecast likely future labour demand, support training and education infrastructure; and improve information flows and accuracy across the labour market (Packard & Van Nguyen, 2014; Rihova, 2016). That is, from a human capital theory perspective, the role of government is to create and implement policies that support market adjustment and functioning. Vietnam's efforts towards data collection, the labour force survey, and cooperation with the ILO on forecasting 2010–2020 sector and occupation employment demands align with this approach (ILO, 2011).

On the other hand, a demand-side discussion cautions that market supply approaches are susceptible to demand fluctuations and future disruptive developments such as technological change, climate change, changes in industry composition, and subject to social and political influence (Brown et al., 2001). Research suggests that government has a significant role in influencing skill demand through macroeconomic policy to support labour demand, and through the infrastructure and funding of education (Ashton & Sung, 2014; Brown et al., 2015). Such action assumes that government has the capability to foresee future skill requirements and learn through a process of dynamic capacity development (Ohno, 2009) to craft effective policy and to generate the skills required to meet current and future labour market needs (Ashton et al., 2005). For emerging industrialised nations such as Vietnam, Ashton et al. (2005) contend that government intervention is preferable to allowing market mechanisms to determine skill provision. This is due to the suggestion that centralised controls support fast responses to changing conditions and through leverage of government economies of scale in skill production. Here, education and training can be aligned to ensure that skill production supports current and future labour market requirements linked to stages of economic development. Hauge (2019) and Ashton et al. (2005) use the examples of central government intervention and planning of skills development in Singapore, Taiwan, and South Korea to illustrate this point. However, unlike those Asian economies, in Vietnam, the ability to plan and accurately forecast has been held back by data deficiencies, the strength of the informal sector, and persistent skill shortages that have escaped effective policy adjustment (Gillespie, 2002; Fforde, 2009).

Addressing Current Skill Shortages

While Vietnam has made significant progress towards SDGs 4 and 8, a challenge that remains is to address the mismatch between the supply and demand of skills. Based on the political, social, educational, and economic context discussed earlier, this study proposes a systemic transformation that encompasses both the supply and demand sides of Vietnam's skilled labour. Vietnam's education system, a lack of technological infrastructure, low levels of research and development expenditure, and supply and demand mismatches are the key reasons for skill deficiencies. A supply-side agenda is suggested, stressing the need for educational reform, including progress towards the accreditation of technical and vocational education and training (TVET) providers and greater investment in the TVET sector. However, reforms to the training system require delegation and a collaborative effort across the key stakeholders, including the government, the education system, and industry partners.

From a supply perspective, it is crucial to focus on enhancing access to education, particularly tertiary education, to address professional skill shortages and, at the same time, reduce reliance on informal jobs. Globally, 94% of those with less than primary education are engaged in informal work, while only 24% of tertiary-educated workers hold informal jobs. In Vietnam, the corresponding shares (in 2019) were 95% and 14% respectively (O'Higgins & Viegelahn, 2021). This strong association between low education levels and informal employment underscores the existing labour market inequalities. That is, individuals with lower education levels are likely to be engaged in informal work, which often lacks job security, fair wages, and social protections. Enabling more individuals to pursue higher qualifications can lead to a more skilled and competitive workforce, and with ongoing industry transformation away from agricultural employment, this potentially reduces the overall reliance on informal jobs (O'Higgins & Viegelahn, 2021). Additionally, promoting relevant and up-to-date vocational training programmes is vital in equipping individuals with practical skills that are in demand in the industry. These programmes can address specific skill shortages in the labour market, ensuring a better match between the skills of job seekers and the needs of employers.

In addition to addressing accessibility to tertiary education, the quality and relevance of education play a crucial role in reducing skill shortages in Vietnam. Despite improvements in access to education, concerns around the quality and relevance of the educational experience in Vietnam persist, and there is evidence of significant graduate work readiness challenges. Therefore, increased participation in tertiary education will not solve the skill gaps if the programmes are not aligned to the skill needs of the labour market (Huynh, 2021). At issue is the quality of the tertiary education sector and the lack of engagement of the key stakeholders, especially employers, in developing the programmes within the sector (Huynh, 2021). The education sector faces challenges in keeping pace with global advancements and competitiveness. This limitation can restrict the full potential of the educated workforce to contribute effectively to the country's economic and social development (World Bank, 2020). One of the contributing factors to the weakness of the sector is the reliance on bureaucratic state leadership within the education system. The centralised decision-making process may impede flexibility and innovation, hindering the sector's ability to adapt to rapidly changing economic demands and technological advancements.

This issue can be addressed by increasing institutional autonomy for universities. This autonomy can permit more effective responses to market demands, foster research and innovation, and offer programmes tailored to the evolving needs of industries and the labour market. A more flexible and autonomous university system can also help bridge the gap between education outcomes and the requirements of the job market, ensuring that graduates are well-prepared and equipped with relevant skills and knowledge. While autonomy offers numerous advantages, the existing government structure in Vietnam restricts universities from achieving autonomy unless they forego financial support from the state (Tran et al., 2023). As a result, it is recommended that Vietnamese higher education institutions (HEIs) adopt a policy that grants them greater autonomy while making essential modifications (Tran et al., 2023). One potential solution is to introduce partial financial autonomy, contingent on the implementation of a performance-based funding system.

Perhaps more contentious is the debate around the role of government in the TVET sector. The World Bank does not support exclusive government control in the provision of TVET (Almeida & Cho, 2012), insisting that businesses are better informed on training needs (Psacharopoulos, 1994) and should be integrated into the training system. This might be achieved through training subsidies, accreditation for employer-led training, apprenticeships supported by off-the-job training, and/or other financial incentives aimed at individuals and businesses potentially linked to unemployment benefits and welfare. At the same time the quality of training requires certification and accreditation, and this again requires effective stakeholder engagement.

In Vietnam, addressing skill deficiencies through partnership between education institutions and industries is of utmost importance as the demand for skilled labour fails to keep up with industry needs. Skilled labour has struggled to meet industry needs, satisfying only 20% of skilled job growth between 2009 and 2014, while relatively concentrated in sectors including education and training (30%), state administration and national security (19%), and social work (8%) in the face of rapid modernisation, World Trade Organisation (WTO) acceptance, and international integration (Vu, 2020). To bridge the skills gap and foster a more skilled and competitive workforce, it is imperative to establish strong partnerships between educational institutions and industries. Collaboration between universities and businesses can lead to the development of tailored training programmes, apprenticeships, and internships that equip students with practical and relevant skills demanded by the job market. By aligning educational curricula with industry needs, graduates can be better prepared to contribute effectively to the workforce, reducing the gap between skill supply and demand (Nguyen et al., 2019).

Moreover, it is crucial for industries to prioritise and invest in training and development initiatives and for government to encourage that investment. By taking an active role in developing their workforce, companies can bridge the gap between the skills required by the job market and the skills possessed by potential employees. This investment in training programmes, upskilling, and continuous learning opportunities will not only equip employees with the necessary competencies but also empower them to adapt to evolving industry demands and technological advancements (Huynh, 2021). Moreover, fostering a culture of learning and professional growth within the workforce will enhance employee engagement and retention, reducing the turnover of skilled workers. A successful example of this approach can be seen in Samsung's operations in Vietnam. The company invests heavily in training its vast assembly workforce, significantly reducing employee turnover, and improving employee retention. Moreover, Samsung collaborates with universities to provide free courses at night within its factories, enabling workers to enhance their skills and knowledge in areas like language proficiency, electronic engineering, and accounting (Sheldon & Kwon, 2023). Such efforts by industries to invest in the development of their workforce play a pivotal role in fostering a skilled labour force, contributing to the overall economic growth and prosperity of Vietnam.

The government can enhance such efforts through measures such as tax policy encouraging investment in skills and through supplementary TVET support. While TVET provision may be less than commercially attractive due to high investment costs, it remains significant as a skill development pathway (Almeida & Cho, 2012) and as a transition into work (Tan & Nam, 2012). Here, the literature refers to 'demand-driven' or 'demand-led' TVET (Martinez-Fernandez & Choi, 2012; Tan & Nam, 2012, pp. 85, 14; Tan et al., 2013, p. 14) designed for and aligned with industry needs, again implying excellence in communication and coordination between the various stakeholders.

While Vietnam has achieved progress towards SGDs 4 and 8, the actions suggested can help by improving the quality and relevance of education, reducing the reliance on informal jobs, and fostering a skilled and competitive workforce. By aligning educational curricula with industry needs and investing in the development of the workforce, Vietnam can bridge the gap between skill supply and demand, contributing to the country's economic growth and prosperity. Specifically focusing on SDG 4, the proposed solutions stress the need for educational reform, including progress towards the accreditation of TVET providers and greater investment in the sector. By enhancing access to education, particularly tertiary education, and promoting relevant and up-to-date vocational training programmes, individuals can acquire practical skills that are in demand in industry. This can address specific skill shortages in the labour market, ensuring a better match between the skills of the labour market and the needs of employers such that graduates can be better prepared to contribute effectively to the workforce, reducing the gap between skills supply and demand.

When focusing on SDG 8, the actions proposed can alleviate the reliance on informal jobs, which often lack job security, fair wages, and social protections. Improving access to higher qualifications can lead to a more skilled and competitive workforce, potentially reducing reliance on informal labour. Moreover, fostering a culture of learning and professional growth within the workforce will enhance employee engagement and retention, reducing the turnover of skilled workers. This can help companies bridge the gap between the skills in demand and the skills possessed by potential employees, contributing to the overall economic growth and prosperity of Vietnam.

Conclusion

Vietnam's appeal to FDI is driven by its abundant low-wage labour force and political stability. However, its one-party socialist state structure and limited stakeholder involvement in decision-making processes pose challenges for developing critical skills to address the SDGs. Although some authority has been delegated to provincial levels, institutional autonomy and resources remain insufficient, resulting in unmet skill demands. Despite a well-performing education system in providing basic skills, a shortage of high-skilled labour persists, particularly in technology-related sectors. The issue is exacerbated by labour migration and a growing outbound student market, contributing to a 'brain drain'. This study proposes a systemic transformation addressing both the supply and demand sides of Vietnam's skilled labour market. Recommendations include educational reforms, increased access to tertiary education, and quality improvements to align educational curricula with industry needs. Encouraging collaboration between educational institutions and industries, fostering a culture of continuous learning, and government support for upskilling initiatives are essential steps to bridge the skill gaps.

Note

* Corresponding author: jamcooper65@gmail.com.

References

Adecco Group. (2021). Why is the world of work so closely linked to the UN's sustainable development goals? *World Economic Forum*. www.weforum.org/agenda/2021/09/why-is-the-world-of-work-so-closely-linked-to-the-un-sustainable-development-goals.

Almeida, R., & Cho, Y. (2012). Employer-provided training: Patterns and incentives for building skills for higher productivity. *The Right Skills for the Job?*, 105.

Anh, V. T. T. (2016). Vietnam: Decentralization amidst fragmentation. *Journal of Southeast Asian Economies*, 188–208.

Ashton, D. N., & Sung, J. (2014). Skills in business: The role of business strategy, sectoral skills development and skills policy. *Skills in Business*, 1–232.

Ashton, D., Green, F., James, D., & Sung, J. (2005). *Education and training for development in East Asia: The political economy of skill formation in newly industrialised economies*. Routledge.

Becker, G., & Collins, R. A. (1964). *Human capital: A theoretical and empirical analysis, with special reference to education*. University of Chicago press.

Brown, P., Green, A., & Lauder, H. (2001). *High skills: Globalization, competitiveness, and skill formation: Globalization, competitiveness, and skill formation*. Oxford University Press.

Brown, P., Lauder, H., & Sung, J. (2015). *Global value chains and the future of high skills: Evidence from Singapore and implications for the UK*. UK Commission for Employment and Skills.

Cleine, W. (2013). *KPMG launches family business practice in Vietnam and Cambodia, Vietnam Investment Review*. Retrieved 29 August 2018, from www.vir.com.vn/kpmg-launches-family-business-practice-in-vietnam-and-cambodia-23947.html

Cling, J.-P., Razafindrakoto, M., & Roubaud, F. (2012). To be or not to be registered? Explanatory factors behind formalizing non-farm household businesses in Vietnam. *Journal of the Asia Pacific Economy*, *17*(4), 632–652.

Dang, H.-A. H., Nguyen, C. V., & Carletto, C. (2023). Did a successful fight against COVID-19 come at a cost? Impacts of the pandemic on employment outcomes in Vietnam. *World Development*, *161*, 106129.

Fforde, A. (2009). Economics, history, and the origins of Vietnam's post-war economic success. *Asian Survey*, *49*(3), 484–504. http://dx.doi.org/10.1525/as.2009.49.3.484.

Forrester, S. V., Ustinova, G. H., Kosyakova, I. V., Ronzhina, N. V., & Suraeva, M. O. (2016). Human capital in the innovative conditions. *International Electronic Journal of Mathematics Education*, *11*(8), 3048–3065.

Gillespie, J. (2002). Transplanted company law: An ideological and cultural analysis of market-entry in Vietnam. *International & Comparative Law Quarterly*, *51*(3), 641–672.

Goodwin, J., O'Connor, H., & Quinn, M. (2014). Training and labour needs of young workers in Vietnamese organisations. *Education + Training*, *56*(1), 35–46.

Government of Vietnam. (2022). *General statistics office*. www.gso.gov.vn/en/data-and-statistics/2022/07/infographic-labour-and-employment-in-second-quarter-and-6-months-of-2022/

GSO. (2021). *Statistical yearbook of Vietnam*. Statistical Publishing House. www.gso.gov.vn/en/data-and-statistics/2022/08/statistical-yearbook-of-2021/

Hauge, J. (2019). Should the African lion learn from the Asian tigers? A comparative-historical study of FDI-oriented industrial policy in Ethiopia, South Korea and Taiwan. *Third World Quarterly*, *40*(11), 2071–2091.

Huynh, P. (2021). *COVID-19 and rising wage inequality: Trends and challenges in Thailand and Viet Nam.*Geneva: ILO.

ILO. (2011). *Vietnam employment trends 2010.* National Centre for Labour Market Forecast and Information, Bureau of Employment Vietnam Employment Trends 2010 ILO Office in Vietnam, 2011. ISBN: 978-92-2-124619-0(print) 978-92-2-124620-6(web pdf)

ILO. (2019a). *Decent work and sustainable development goals in Viet Nam—Country profile.* www.ilo.org/hanoi/Whatwedo/Publications/WCMS_730825/lang--en/index.htm

ILO. (2019b). *Decent work and the sustainable development goals in Vietnam, country report.* www.ilo.org/wcmsp5/groups/public/-asia/-ro-bangkok/-ilo-hanoi/documents/publication/wcms_730825.pdf.

Kalimullin, A. M., Yungblud, V. T., & Khodyreva, E. A. (2016) Characteristic features of innovation project management aimed at university human resource development. *International Journal of Environmental and Science Education, 11*(9), 2237–2253.

Kendrick, J. W. (1976). The formation and stocks of total capital. *NBER Books.*

Kiet, A. (2018). No title. *Hanoi Times.*

Korchagin, Y. A. (2012). Human capital and innovative economy in Russia. *Centre of Regional Economic Research.*

Kritskiy, M. M. (1991). Chelovecheskiy kapital [Human capital]. *Leningrad, Lengosta Publ.*

Lanvin, B., Monteiro, F., & Armanio, M. (2019). Entrepreneurial talent for competitiveness. In *The global talent competitiveness index* (pp. 3–37). INSEAD.

Macrotrends.net (2023) Vietnam Net Migration Rate 1950–2023. *Macrotrends.net.* www.macrotrends.net/countries/VNM/vietnam/net-migration.

Malesky, E. (2004). Leveled mountains and broken fences: Measuring and analysing de facto decentralisation in Vietnam. *European Journal of East Asian Studies, 3*(2), 307–336.

Marginson, S. (2019). Limitations of human capital theory. *Studies in Higher Education, 44*(2), 287–301.

Martinez-Fernandez, C., & Choi, K. (2012). An overview of skills development pathways in Asia. OECD Local Economic and Employment Development (LEED) Working Papers, (12), 13.

Mincer, J. (1958). Investment in human capital and personal income distribution. *Journal of Political Economy, 66*(4), 281–302.

Nguyen, C. H. (2016) Development and brain drain: A review of Vietnamese labour export and skilled migration. *Migration and Development, 3*(2), 181–202.

Nguyen, N. D., Ngoc, N. B., & Montague, A. (2019). Enhancing graduate work-readiness in Vietnam. In *The transition from graduation to work: Challenges and strategies in the twenty-first century Asia Pacific and beyond* (pp. 221–237). Springer.

Nishitani, K., Nguyen, T. B. H., Trinh, T. Q., Wu, Q., & Kokubu, K. (2021). Are corporate environmental activities to meet sustainable development goals (SDGs) simply greenwashing? An empirical study of environmental management control systems in Vietnamese companies from the stakeholder management perspective. *Journal of Environmental Management, 296*, 113364. https://doi.org/10.1016/j.jenvman.2021.113364.

O'Higgins, N., & Viegelahn, C. (2021) *Informal employment in Viet Nam: Trends and determinants* (1st ed.). ILO.

Ohno, K. (2009). Avoiding the middle-income trap: Renovating industrial policy formulation in Vietnam. *ASEAN Economic Bulletin, 26*, 25–43.

Ohno, K. (2013). *Learning to industrialize: From given growth to policy-aided value creation.* Routledge.

Packard, T. G. and Van Nguyen, T. (2014) *East Asia Pacific at work: Employment, enterprise, and well-being.* World Bank Publications.

Pennings, S. (2020). *The utilization-adjusted human Capital Index.* Policy Research Working Paper No. 9375. World Bank.
Pham, T. H., & Riedel, J. (2019). Impacts of the sectoral composition of growth on poverty reduction in Vietnam. *Journal of Economics and Development*, *21*(2), pp. 213–222.
Psacharopoulos, G. (1994). Returns to investment in education: A global update. *World Development*, *22*(9), 1325–1343.
Richiardi, P. S., Ghani, S., & Toan, P. N. (2023). Trade and decent work in Viet Nam. In *Integrating trade and decent work* (pp. 183–208). International Labour Organization.
Rihova, H. (2016) *Using labour market information: Guide to anticipating and matching skills and jobs: Volume 1.* Publications Office of the European Union.
Schmillen, A. D., & Packard, T. G. (2016). Vietnam's labour market institutions, regulations, and interventions: Helping people grasp work opportunities in a risky world. World Bank Policy Research Working Paper 7587.
Schultz, T. W. (1959). Investment in man: An economist's view. *Social Service Review*, *33*(2), 109–117.
Schultz, T. W. (1961). Investment in human capital. *The American Economic Review*, *51*(1), 1–17.
Sheldon, P., & Kwon, S. H. (2023). Samsung in Vietnam: FDI, business—government relations, industrial parks, and skills shortages. *The Economic and Labour Relations Review*, *34*(1), 66–85.
Simkovic, M. (2013). Risk-based student loans. *Washington and Lee Law Review*, *70*, 527.
Stevens, M. (1996). Transferable training and poaching externalities. In A. L. Booth & D. J. Snower (Eds.), *Acquiring skills: Market failures, their symptoms and policy responses* (pp. 19–40). Cambridge University Press.
Tan, J.-P. et al. (2013). *What matters in workforce development: A framework and tool for analysis.* SABER Working Paper Series 6, World Bank Group.
Tan, J.-P., & Nam, Y.-J. J. (2012). Pre-employment technical and vocational education and training: Fostering relevance, effectiveness, and efficiency. In *The right skills for the job?: Rethinking training policies for workers* (p. 67).
Tran, T.-V., Pham, T. P., Nguyen, M. H., Do, L. T., & Pham, H.-H. (2023). Economic efficiency of higher education institutions in Vietnam between 2012 and 2016: A DEA analysis. *Journal of Applied Research in Higher Education*, *15*(1), 199–212.
Trang, N. M. H. (2022). Educational migration in Vietnam: Challenges and new opportunities. *ДЕМИС. Демографические исследования/DEMIS. Demographic Research*, *2*(1), 127–141.
Trines, S. (2017). *Education in Vietnam, world education news and reviews.* https://wenr.wes.org/2017/11/education-in-vietnam.
Truong, Q., & Rowley, C. (2014). Vietnam: Post-state capitalism. In M. A. Witt & G. Redding (Eds.), *The Oxford handbook of Asian business systems* (pp. 283–305). Oxford University Press.
Turekulova, D., Ydyrys, S., Dalayeva, T., & Altybay, Z. (2016). The classification of human capital types and their comparative characteristics. *International Journal of Economic Perspectives*, *10*(4).
UNDP. (2023). *United Nations Sustainable Development.* https://sdgs.un.org/
Vu, D. (2020). Current skilled labour shortage in Vietnam. *Vietnam Academy of Social Sciences*, *4*, 192. http://en.vass.gov.vn/noidung/tintuc/Lists/TinTucHoiNghiHoiThao/View_Detail.aspx?ItemID=875.
Vu, T. P. D. (2019). Current skilled labour shortage in Vietnam. *Journal of Vietnam Academy of Social Sciences*, *4*.
WEF. (2022). Reskilling revolution: Preparing 1 billion people for tomorrow's economy. *World Economic Forum*, 1–8. www.weforum.org/impact/reskilling-revolution-preparing-1-billion-people-for-tomorrow-s-economy/.

Weiland, S., et al. (2021). The 2030 agenda for sustainable development: Transformative change through the sustainable development goals? *Politics and Governance*, *9*(1), pp. 90–95.

WHO. (2022). *World Health Organization*. Retrieved 16 November 2022, from https://covid19.who.int/region/wpro/country/vn

World Bank. (2018). *Vietnam's future jobs. Leveraging mega-trends for greater prosperity*. World Bank.

World Bank. (2019). *Vietnam. Insights from disaggregating the Human Capital Index*. World Bank

World Bank. (2020). *Improving the performance of higher education in Vietnam, policy notes*. Author. https://doi.org/10.1596/33681.

World Bank. (2022) *Vietnam overview*. Retrieved 14 November 2022, from www.worldbank.org/en/country/vietnam/overview

World Economic Forum. (2017). *The global human capital report*. www.weforum.org/reports/the-global-human-capital-report-2017/.

8 Skills Shortages in the Chinese Manufacturing Sector

Yi Liu, Le Li, and Liang Lu*

Introduction

As the largest developing country in the world with a population of 1.4 billion, China has always been a responsible country, striving to contribute to the development of the global economy. The President of China, Xi Jinping, has pointed out that 'manufacturing is the lifeblood of the national economy' (The Paper, 2020, p. 1). As the main contributor to the national economy, in 2022, the added value of China's manufacturing industry reached 33.5 trillion yuan (about 4.6 trillion US dollars), accounting for nearly 30% of the global proportion and maintaining its position as the world's largest manufacturing country for 13 consecutive years (Ministry of Industry and Information Technology of the People's Republic of China, 2023). The added value of China's manufacturing industry accounts for 27.7% of its gross domestic product (GDP), which is crucial for the smooth operation of the national economy (China's National Bureau of Statistics, 2023). The United Nations Industrial Organisation believes that manufacturing is a key driving force for sustainable development, as it pointed out:

> [I]n the face of the impact of emergencies such as the COVID-19 epidemic, the manufacturing industry not only provides support for economic resilience but also plays a fundamental role in promoting common prosperity. The manufacturing industry has also achieved innovation and multiplier effects, promoting the development of other economic sectors. Industrialisation and achieving Sustainable Development Goal (SDG)9, which is to build resilient infrastructure, promote inclusive and sustainable industrialisation, and promote innovation, are also crucial to the realisation of many other SDGs.
>
> (United Nations Industrial Development Organization, 2021)

Thus, it can be seen that the development of the manufacturing industry is particularly crucial for achieving SDG 9.

However, in recent years, on the one hand, several developments have posed significant challenges to global public health, disrupting China's

DOI: 10.4324/9781003379065-10

economic prosperity level (World Bank, 2022), and weakening the manufacturing industry's growth potential (World Bank, 2017). On the other hand, China's ageing population has gradually eliminated the demographic dividend, which affects economic growth and leads to labour shortages. Moreover, for China, there is still a gap between the skills of low-educated individuals and market demand, while the skills structure of high-educated individuals is disconnected from the market, and the issues of an imbalanced labour structure and mismatches between skill supply and demand are becoming increasingly concerning (JP Morgan Chase, Tsinghua University, and Fudan University, 2016).

As one of the industries with a significant mismatch in the supply and demand structure between labour and employment positions, manufacturing is also facing labour shortages and severe skill shortages (Li & Wang, 2021). It is also facing challenges such as international competition in the field of intelligent manufacturing. As a broad concept, intelligent manufacturing aims to optimise production and product transactions by making full use of advanced information and manufacturing technologies (Kusiak, 1990) to significantly 'upgrade . . . the design, production, management, and integration of the whole life cycle of a typical product' (Zhong et al., 2017, p. 618). China's manufacturing industry has important advantages such as its large scale, complete system, and strong resilience, to achieve the goal of moving towards the high end of the global value chain and transforming from a manufacturing power to a world manufacturing powerhouse, China must appeal to all sectors of society, from the government to enterprises, to pay more attention to the issue of skill shortages.

The existing research has proposed corresponding policy recommendations with different focuses to achieve SDG 9 in the manufacturing sector. Among others, Li and Rong (2021) indicated the importance of green manufacturing, and Qiu (2022) suggested digitalisation, while Han et al. (2021) pointed out the need for intelligent transformation. This refers to the application of artificial intelligence technology in the manufacturing industry to achieve automation and intelligent production, using intelligent robots, intelligent warehousing, and intelligent logistics. There are also relevant discussions on the implementation of the SDGs in China. Lan et al. (2018) established a four-step 'adaptive governance' framework to promote the realisation of SDGs. Xie et al. (2021) analysed the realisation and implementation of China's SDGs by comparing the policy tools used by Japan and South Korea. Based on the Global Indicator Framework, which is used to monitor progress in the implementation of the SDGs at the global level, Shao et al. (2021) have coordinated and screened China's relevant key indicators to build its localisation evaluation index system to promote China's achievement of the SDGs. Furthermore, the existing literature also examined the capability of China's Belt and Road Initiative to implement SDG 9 from the perspective of international capacity cooperation (Liu, 2019; Abdelhak et al., 2022). For all that, there seems to be a lack of relevant research on the relationship between China's manufacturing sector and the SDGs of the United Nations, particularly from the perspective of a labour skills shortage.

According to the Organization for Economic Cooperation and Development (OECD, 2017), 'skills' are defined as cognitive and non-cognitive abilities. These abilities (for example, technical skills) are required for a specific job, profession, or department. 'Shortage' refers to the existence of job vacancies in certain positions that require the same type and quality of labour under current wage rates (Arrow & Capron, 1959). The concept of 'skill shortage', due to its close correlation with technological progress and as an interdisciplinary concept, is not easy to measure, and therefore, there is no universally applicable definition (OECD, 2003). As Chinese scholars Sheng and Cheng (2020) believe, skill shortages refer to the inability of employers to recruit suitable employees with the necessary skills for the jobs at the current wage level in the relevant labour market. From a supply-side perspective, skill shortages emphasise a structural mismatch between the quantity and quality of skilled labour and employer demand (Richardson, 2009). Based on previous research, this chapter selects the most common definition and argues that a skill shortage refers to the inability of organisations with specific skill requirements to attract employees who meet the job requirements of the National Training Agency (NTA). However, the challenges remain unsolved because it is difficult for enterprises to recruit skilled talents who meet the job requirements, and the existing employees do not have sufficient skills to be competent for the job.

To address the research gap, this study uses a qualitative method to assess the effects of policies or strategies initiated by the government and implemented by organisations, to analyse policy facilitators and barriers at the macro-, meso-, and micro-levels, and thus to explore the current situation and challenges of skill shortages in the manufacturing sector. It also makes relevant policy recommendations to overcome the skill shortage in specific sectors in China.

Research Approach

Understanding China's current position in addressing the SDGs in the manufacturing industry requires the review of relevant national policies and related documents. A systematic review and analysis of the relevant policies and their implementation outcomes exposed the challenges in addressing the SDGs in general and in the manufacturing industry in particular. This approach enables the convergence of information from different pieces of evidence and credible data sources, including state and provincial level policies.

China has been at the forefront among nations in addressing the UN's SDGs. Indeed, on 25 September 2019, the Special Representative of President Xi Jinping, State Councillor and Minister of Foreign Affairs Wang Yi, attended the United Nations Sustainable Development Goals Summit and made a statement suggesting that 'China will work tirelessly with the rest of the international community to realise the Sustainable Development Goals for

2030 and bring a better future to all' (People's Daily Online, 2019). To fulfil the promise made by President Xi at the United Nations Sustainable Development Summit in 2015, in March 2016, China incorporated the SDGs into the '13th Five-Year Plan' and the country's medium- and long-term overall development planning (Xinhua News, 2016a). Under the active promotion of China, the Group of Twenty (G20) summit in September 2016, for the first time, put sustainable development issues, which was the formulation and implementation of the 2030 Sustainable Development Agenda Action Plan, at the core (Xinhua News, 2016b). Subsequently, the Chinese government once again highlighted its position on participating in the realisation of the UN's SDGs and determination with the implementation of the 2030 Sustainable Development 'Code Country Plan'. More recently, with the release of the 14th Five-Year Plan, China has put more emphasis on addressing the SDGs (Liu, 2021b).

In terms of SDG-related research in China, a large number of studies were found in the disciplines of climate change (Liu, 2021a), with some in education (Guo et al., 2022), technology (for example, artificial intelligence) (Wang et al., 2023), corporate sustainability, and social responsibilities (Hou et al., 2022). There is still much unknown about how skill shortages affect the manufacturing industry in achieving SDG9 in China. On a wider spectrum,

> for SDG9, China has made notable progress in pursuing an innovation-based approach, drawing on Fourth Industrial Revolution technologies, to drive industrialisation and infrastructure expansion. However, there is room for improvement in harnessing innovations for resource efficiency and greater adoption of clean and environmentally sound technologies by industry.
>
> (UNSDG, 2020, p. 5)

On a narrower spectrum, using clean and environmentally sound technologies requires an educated, skilled, and innovative workforce. China, however, is facing an acute skills shortage (Li & Yuan, 2016). According to the *Manufacturing Talent Development Planning Guide* released by the Ministry of Human Resources and Social Services, China will face a talent demand gap of nearly 30 million workers by 2025 in 10 key areas of China's manufacturing industry, or a 48% shortage of skilled workers to meet demand (Fang, 2017; Boland et al., 2022, p. 1).

This study employed systematic review procedures developed by Peters et al. (2015) to further address the research questions. There are four steps, including (a) identification, (b) screening, (c) eligibility, and (d) synthesis. In the first step, several relevant studies were identified through available databases, such as Emerald, ProQuest, Wiley, and EBSCO, as well as Google Scholar databases. Some keywords used in searching included China, skill shortage, education, workforce, SDGs, government, and workplace. Several relevant reports from government websites were also identified simultaneously.

In the second step, the studies collected in the first step were screened to decide if they contained relevant information. The third step required assessing whether the studies collected in the second step provided answers, viewpoints, statistics, or analysis vital for answering the research questions. Finally, the selected studies were synthesised to draft possible answers to the research questions.

Current Situation of China's Manufacturing Industry

Currently, China's labour force ranks highest globally (Sina Finance, 2021). However, skill shortages are particularly prominent in China due to insufficient quantity and structure. Also, there is a lack of emphasis on cultivating and developing highly skilled talent teams. Such phenomena are most severe in the manufacturing industry.

Imbalance in Skill Supply and Demand

The low quality of labour and a lack of skilled talent are the biggest obstacles to China's goal of becoming a strong manufacturing powerhouse. According to the Ministry of Education, Ministry of Human Resources and Social Security. and Ministry of Industry and Information Technology of the People's Republic of China (2016), the talent gap in the top ten key areas of China's manufacturing industry exceeded 19 million in 2020, and this number will be close to 30 million in 2025, with a gap rate up to 48%, but there is still a shortage of 'blue-collar technology'. Additionally, the China Labour Market Information Network Monitoring Center reported that since 2005, the demand/supply ratio (reflecting the ratio of job vacancies to job seekers) for various skilled human capital in China has been greater than 1. By 2021, the demand/supply rates for senior technicians, technicians, and senior skilled personnel had risen to 3.05, 2.7, and 2.51 respectively. From these numbers, it can be seen that there is an increasingly widening trend in the supply and demand gap of skilled human capital in China. The labour force in the manufacturing industry is mainly composed of off-farm workers (Yang et al., 2021), with relatively low skill quality. Due to the impact of education and knowledge levels, it may be difficult for them to adapt to technological progress and meet the requirements of high-end links in the industrial chain. Arguably, skill shortages or employee skill gaps can negatively affect a country's economic growth, particularly in the manufacturing industry (Dou, 2016).

Structural Mismatch of Skills

Although a full range of talent resources in China is at the forefront, due to the obvious structural problems in the skilled talent team, including age structure and training structure, the 'quality' of talent in China is not strong enough.

Significant Age Structure Disparity

The Innovation Strategy Research Institute of the China Association for Science and Technology surveyed the 'High Skilled Talent Team' by targeting manufacturing technical workers, industrial enterprise managers, and vocational college students (Huang et al., 2023). The results in Figure 8.1 show that more than half of the skilled talents in the manufacturing industry are between 31 and 40 years old, with 73.4% being over 31 years old. Overall, the age of highly skilled talents in China is relatively old, and the shortage of highly skilled young talents is relatively severe.

Unreasonable Talent Cultivation Structure

The structural issue of talent cultivation, which can be affected by institutions and enterprises, is the key to constraining the cultivation of highly skilled talents (Wen et al., 2022). In China, some people's mindsets are influenced by the concept of valuing academic qualifications over skills in the belief that education can improve or even change people's living conditions by having a good job with better pay (for example, improved material conditions). Hence, the value of education remains focused on the evaluation system based on academic qualifications, causing limited educational resources for academic education, thereby adversely affecting the investment in vocational education, which leads to an imbalance between the education and training systems. Accompanied by the overall low educational structure of skilled talents in China's manufacturing industry, the proportion of skilled talents with a college degree or below is as high as 69.0% (Huang et al., 2023). Moreover, the current vocational education policy is still based on theoretical learning

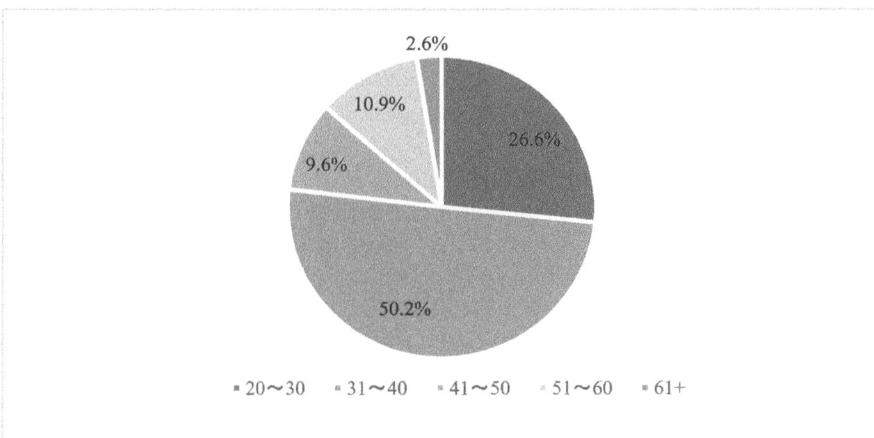

Figure 8.1 Investigation and research on the highly skilled talent team

Source: Huang et al. (2023).

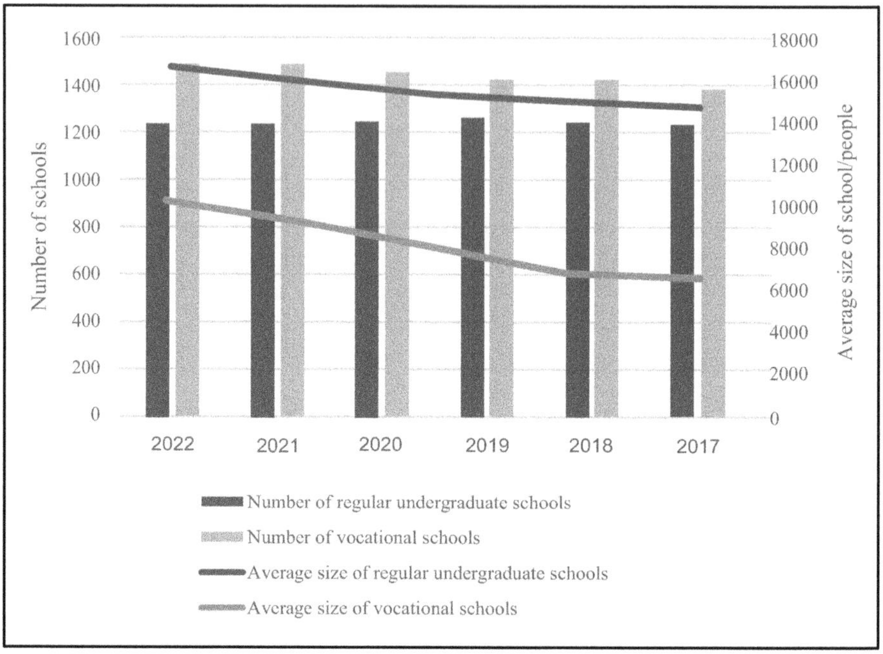

Figure 8.2 Regular undergraduate schools and vocational colleges in China from 2017 to 2022

Source: Ministry of Education (2017–2022)

on campus, supplemented by an internship and practical training, resulting in poor alignment between vocational education talents and the actual needs of enterprises (Ye, 2023). Figure 8.2 shows the difference between the number and average size of regular undergraduate and vocational schools in China.

Low Emphasis on Skilled Talents

As early as 2005, the China Skilled Talents Professional Reputation Survey results showed that 52.7% of people believed that skilled talents had a low social status and were not respected. As many as 67.7% of people expressed unwillingness to send their children to technical schools for study, resulting in difficulty in ensuring the quality of students in technical schools and a lack of successors for highly skilled talents (Lu, 2006). For skilled talents, on the one hand, the average annual salary in the manufacturing industry is much lower than that in the information transmission, software, and information technology services, as well as the financial sector (China's National Bureau of Statistics, 2022), and there is a certain lag in talent services such as life, employment, and continuing education security (Huang et al., 2023). On the other hand, skilled talents lack opportunities to participate in business management and decision-making consultation at both the workplace and the overall social level as well as opportunities to be included in local talent rewards and commendations. They are often overlooked in regional high-level talent plans and social organisation positions (Ma et al., 2022). Collectively, these factors have led to a low emphasis on skilled talents in China.

Analysis of the Causes of Problems in China's Manufacturing Industry

Through the analysis of China's manufacturing industry, the causes of such problems, including an imbalance in skill supply and demand, skill structure mismatches, and a low emphasis on skilled talents, were summarised into four main reasons: (a) insufficient institutional integration, (b) imperfect training mechanisms and modes, (c) the worsening problem of population ageing, and (d) the unformed skill evaluation and certification system.

1 Insufficient Institutional Integration

The national institutional environment influences the skill supply of industries by shaping a country's skill formation system. The government has committed to promoting the development of vocational education, from the integration of engineering and education to the cooperation between industry, academia, and research and then to the deep integration of industry and education. The government hopes to promote deep integration by continuously improving the system and mechanisms for integrating industry and education to achieve an organic connection between the education, talent, industry, and innovation chains. However, it has not met expectations, and one of the reasons is the partial absence of government roles and functions. Arguably, the shortage of skills has institutional roots.

Pursuing a degree or diploma has led to deviations in the educational philosophy and positioning, leading to 'non-professionalisation' and 'non-technicalisation'. Moreover, the low enthusiasm of enterprises for skill training can hinder the growth of skilled talents. For example, some enterprises are not willing to pay for their workers to attend training courses because of the perceived high costs, coupled with uncertain returns (for example, poaching by competitors). These circumstances potentially contribute to the under-skilling, skill shortages, and skill gaps at the enterprise level.

2 Imperfect Training Mechanism and Model

Cultivation Mechanism

Some vocational education majors are large and comprehensively 'universal', disconnected from enterprises' needs and industrial upgrading. The training method is still centred around books and classrooms, emphasising the instillation of theoretical knowledge and lacking practical skills. This method is not conducive to cultivating innovation and entrepreneurship awareness, making it difficult for talent cultivation to reach the production line. Also, due to unclear responsibilities, gaps between the competent departments of vocational education are overlapping, resulting in weak educational conditions, slow equipment updates, and 'empty shelves' in constructing training bases (Huang et al., 2023).

Training Mode

This mainly reflects the joint training model of the school and enterprise. The direction of reform for state-owned enterprises to divest themselves in the function of 'running society' has led to the separation of enterprises and universities. Such separation caused losses in talent cultivation. Currently, most school-enterprise cooperation is limited to basic training models such as entrusted training (a system in which the employing department entrusts the schools/institutions to cultivate students) and practical internship training. Such training modes result in a mismatch between the education system and the labour market. In this regard, enterprises need to cultivate highly skilled talents equipped with the necessary skills; hence, this training mode needs to be further improved. Specifically, training programmes at all levels must be designed to closely align with the labour market needs. However, most training institutions are established to obtain utilitarian certificates, making it difficult for rural areas and impoverished populations to obtain effective training resources (Liu, 2021a). Thus, lifelong learning programmes at higher education levels and continuous government investment in training across different regions in China can potentially reduce the skilled talent gaps.

3 The Worsening Problem of Population Ageing

Over the past 40 years of reform and opening up, China has promoted the development of the manufacturing industry by relying on the labour cost advantage brought by the demographic dividend. However, the National Health Commission shows that since becoming an ageing society in 2000, the proportion of elderly people aged 60 and above in China reached 18.9% in 2021, and the proportion of elderly people aged 65 and above reached 14.2%, which has achieved the threshold of a moderately ageing society (Chinese Government Website, 2022). The labour force, as one of the important factors in social production, is bound to have a serious impact on China's economic and social life due to the reduction of the working-age population and the increase in labour costs (Ma & Yang, 2021). Such phenomena can potentially affect economic growth and slow down the pace of technological innovation (Catalano & Pezzolla, 2016). In addition, the trend of an ageing population structure also poses challenges to the continuous cultivation and supply of skilled talents.

4 Skill Evaluation and Certification System Not Fully Formed

At present, the major problem is that even if the skills of workers in their job positions have reached the level of senior workers or above, they cannot be recognised as corresponding professional qualifications due to the failure to keep up with the evaluation work promptly, resulting in their abilities and abilities not being fully reflected (Ye, 2023). Limited certification systems can also lead to migrant workers being 'skilled without status', reducing the incentive for skill accumulation (Yang et al., 2021). In addition, highly skilled talents have not received sufficient attention from society. This is particularly true for young people, as for them, the importance of social status even exceeds material conditions, and their career orientation is gradually shifting towards realising their values, social respect, and status improvement (Huang et al., 2023), which is not conducive to attracting young employees. High-skilled youth can provide sustained development momentum for the manufacturing power strategy, which will further increase structural issues in the manufacturing industry.

Suggestions for Improvement Measures in China's Manufacturing Industry

While the existing problems in China's manufacturing industry and the possible reasons have been analysed, it is imperative to discuss the necessary improvement measures. The goal of SDG 9 is to build a flexible infrastructure, promote inclusive and sustainable industrialisation, and promote innovation, which is closely related to the development of China's manufacturing industry. Hence, this chapter has discussed some suggestions and measures in combination with SDG 9 to help the Chinese government, enterprises, and education departments overcome the talent shortage in the manufacturing industry.

Implementation of Relevant Policies by Governments at All Levels

Skilled talents play a crucial role in the development of the manufacturing industry, and governments at all levels need to play a leading role and integrate them into the overall planning of social development. In light of the national conditions, China has successively issued a series of supporting documents (for example, *Made in China 2025*, *A Guide to the Development Planning of Manufacturing Talents*, and *Several Policies and Measures on Promoting the Expansion of Foreign Investment with Emphasis on Manufacturing Industry, Stabilizing the Stock and Improving the Quality*) and pointing out the directions for solving skill shortages. However, in the process of implementation, the governments (state and provincial levels) need to develop policies and regulations that are more in line with industry and local realities with a particular focus. For example, in response to the trend of an ageing workforce structure in China's manufacturing industry, it is necessary for the government to introduce corresponding guiding policies to promote the rational employment of elderly skilled talents in the manufacturing industry. In addition, the government also needs to consider adjusting the education structure and providing more training funds and inclusive policies towards skilled talent training and vocational education (Huang et al., 2023).

Improving the Education and Training System for Skilled Talents

The report of the 20th National Congress of the Communist Party of China pointed out the importance of 'accelerating the construction of a strong manufacturing country' and 'promoting the high-end, intelligent, and green development of the manufacturing industry' (Ministry of Foreign Affairs of the People's Republic of China, 2022). The skilled talent team is the core driving force for achieving the strategic goal of becoming a manufacturing powerhouse. It is an important force supporting 'Made in China' and 'Created in China'. Special attention should be paid to cultivating skilled talents, which will especially help promote innovation in SDG 9 with the possibility of addressing SDG 4. Indeed, China intends to 'cultivate a greater number of master scholars, science strategists, first-class scientists, and innovation teams, your scientists, outstanding engineers, master craftsmen, and highly skilled workers' (Reports to the 20th National Congress of the Communist Party of China, 2022, p. 31). This section proposes the direction of talent cultivation from two aspects.

School-Enterprise Cooperation

Cultivating skilled talents was one of the key topics discussed during the 2023 Chinese People's Congress, and the government work report also proposed the need to develop vocational education vigorously. As the main talent output channel for the development of the manufacturing industry, vocational education aims to cultivate high-quality, skilled talents and is the main battlefield for managing skill shortages. The most mainstream concepts are 'school-enterprise cooperation' and industrial integration. This notion was discussed in detail in the Reports to the 20th National Congress of the Communist Party of China (2022, p. 29), China will

> promote collabourative innovation in vocational education, higher education, and continuing education and promote integration between vocational education and general education, between industry and education, and between science and education . . . better establish vocational education as a category in the educational system . . . do more to develop basic disciplines, emerging disciplines, and interdisciplinary subjects and speed up the development of world-class universities and strong disciplines with Chinese features . . . better guide and regulate the development of private schools.

A detailed and specific explanation is given next.

Flexible Educational Model

Actively promoting the reform of the mixed ownership education model, supporting and encouraging private and even foreign capital to enter the field of vocational education will, to some extent, make up for the shortage of educational funds. Meanwhile, it will be helpful to carry out closer school-enterprise collaborative education and gradually improve the skill talent training system. Achieving such an outcome requires government coordination, industry guidance, vocational colleges' autonomy and flexibility, and active participation of social forces. This relatively flexible educational model can also dynamically set majors, adjust and optimise curriculum systems, and reform talent cultivation models promptly according to industry needs.

Closer Cooperative Relationships

Vocational schools need to strengthen cooperation and communication with enterprises. The school is close to the requirements of the enterprise, and the enterprise can increase its enthusiasm and fully cooperate. Conditional enterprises can also join vocational education teachers to establish enterprise universities. Both parties can effectively utilise the school-enterprise cooperation model to promote the increase of corresponding practical teaching sections and truly achieve the integration of theory and practice. Such an initiative can make the trained, skilled talents more targeted, more in line with job requirements, and more suitable for the long-term development needs of the enterprise.

Comprehensive Professional Settings

On the other hand, vocational schools should keep up with the technological era and be forward-looking in their professional settings (Wen et al., 2022). The Double High Plan, jointly issued by the Ministry of Education and the Ministry of Finance, proposes to create a group of internationally advanced vocational colleges by 2035. This requires vocational colleges to fully integrate with the actual development of society while realising their advantages to strengthen the professional setting and disciplinary layout of key manufacturing fields; reinforce the application of new technologies, new knowledge, and new processes; and implement the three-level training requirements of skilled talents. Also, there is a need to promote the comprehensive improvement of the quantity and quality of skilled talents and thus use the power of aggregation to create a favourable situation where high-quality skilled talents continue to grow. This initiative is also of great significance for achieving SDG 9.

Audiences for Skill Training

China can also rely on vocational colleges or vocational training institutions and enterprises to carry out multi-level and multi-type retraining for migrant workers, retirees, and other groups with low or easily neglected skills to improve the knowledge structure and skills-matching ability. Moreover, practical and feasible measures can be formulated to ensure their effective employment, which helps to develop potential human resources comprehensively, expand the supply capacity of skilled talents, and improve the quality and efficiency of skill matching.

Establish a Scientific Skill Evaluation Mechanism

All sectors of society need to actively guide a positive social evaluation trend and establish an image of manufacturing skilled talents as professional, practical, and skilled craftspersons. It is necessary to improve the technical ability-oriented, performance-focused, and professional ethics-oriented skill talent evaluation system and establish a skill talent evaluation system based on professional standards, guided by work processes and on professional abilities. For example, by establishing certification systems such as skill levels, job qualifications, and professional and technical titles (Huang et al., 2023), problems such as the 'ceiling' and 'with skills but no status' in worker development can be solved. There is a need to strengthen policy supply, supplement corresponding incentive measures, and continuously improve all skilled talents' income and welfare benefits (Luo, 2020).

Conclusion

This chapter argues that to achieve the SDGs of the United Nations, China, especially its manufacturing sector, needs to address the challenges of skill shortages, including the imbalance of skill supply and demand, the mismatch of skill structure, and the lack of attention to skilled personnel. This chapter analyses the possible reasons from different perspectives and provides targeted suggestions for the government, enterprises, and other entities to address talent shortages in the manufacturing industry. For China, the manufacturing sector is seen as the tool for revitalising the country and the foundation for building a strong economy. At present, the structural imbalance and skill supply and demand mismatch hinder the realisation of SDG 9. Consequently, the government can strive to minimise the negative impact of skill shortages by building resilient infrastructure, promoting inclusive and sustainable industrialisation and promoting innovation to achieve SDGs.

The skill shortages in China's manufacturing industry are profound and urgent and cannot be ignored. This chapter argues that insufficient institutional factors, imperfect training mechanisms and models, severe population ageing issues, and insufficient formation of skills evaluation and certification systems are the roots of the problem. To effectively minimise the challenges posed by the shortage of manufacturing skills while promoting sustainable economic growth, it is necessary for the government to take some countermeasures. For example, functional departments and governments at all levels need to promote the implementation of relevant policies further, improve the education and training system for skilled talents (for example, develop new training models and mechanisms, expand training scope), and establish a scientific skill evaluation mechanism to promote the formation of inclusive and sustainable industrialisation and innovation. Indeed, the governments have issued and taken a series of major measures to control the impact of skill shortages. These efforts can increase the opportunities for China to achieve SDG 9 (e.g. build resilient infrastructure, promote inclusive and sustainable industrialisation and promote innovation).

Note

* Corresponding author: liuyi969@sdu.edu.cn.

References

Abdelhak, S., Awal, I. M., Nee, A. Y. H., & Ogbeibu, S. (2022). The Belt and Road Initiative (BRI): A mechanism to achieve the ninth sustainable development goal (SDG). *Journal of Cleaner Production, 372.*

Arrow, K. J., & Capron, W. M. (1959). Dynamic shortages and price rises: The engineer-scientist case. Quarterly Journal of Economics, *73*(2), 292–308.

Boland, B., Dong, K., Blanchette, J., & Hass, R. (2022). How China's human capital impacts its national competitiveness. *Center for Strategic and International Studies*, 1–15. Retrieved 29August 2023, from www.csis.org/analysis/how-chinas-human-capital-impacts-its-national-competitiveness

Catalano, M., & Pezzolla, E. (2016). The effects of education and ageing in an OLG model: Long-run growth in France, Germany and Italy. *Empirica*, *43*(4), 757–800.

China's National Bureau of Statistics. (2022, May 20). In 2021, the average annual salary of urban nonprivate sector employees was 106837 yuan [EB/OL], 20 January 2023. http://content-static.cctvnews.cctv.com/snow-book/index.html?item_id=16532587752187739599

China's National Bureau of Statistics. (2023). *National Bureau of Statistics article, interpreting the 2022 China economic "Annual Report"*. https://baijiahao.baidu.com/s?id=1758036389757877262&wfr=spider&for=pc

Chinese Government Website. (2022). *2021 National aging career development bulletin*. Retrieved 25 July 2023, from www.gov.cn/xinwen/2022-10/26/content_5721786.htm

Dou, Z. Y. (2016). *Research on human capital accumulation in the context of transformation and upgrading of China's manufacturing industry*. Shanghai Academy of Social Sciences.

Fang Y. Z. (2017, February 14). *Notice of the three departments on printing and distributing the guidelines for the development of manufacturing talents*. Government of China. www.gov.cn/xinwen/2017-02/24/content_5170697.htm

Guo, Z., Xu, L. H., & Wang, S. Y. (2022). Research on the demand characteristics and training trends of engineering science and technology talents for sustainable development education. *Engineering Science*, *2*, 179–188.

Han, M. H., Tang, Y. Q., & Zheng, D. L. (2021). A study on the realistic dilemma and policy support of the intelligent upgrading of China's manufacturing industry. *Journal of the Party School of the Communist Party of China Ningbo Municipal Committee*, *43*(4), 110–116.

Hou, M., Wang, Q. N., & Gong, J. Y. (2022). Entrepreneurship, organizational resilience and sustainable development of small and medium-sized enterprises—the moderating role of environmental uncertainty. *East China Economic Management*, *36*(12), 120–128.

Huang, C., Shi, L., & Yang, L. H. (2023). Reflections on accelerating the growth of China's skilled talent team under the strategy of building a strong manufacturing country. *Today's Science Park*, (2), 1–8.

JP Morgan Chase, Tsinghua University, and Fudan University. (2016). *Research on the skills gap in the Chinese Labour Market*. School of Economics, Fudan University. http://www.econ.fudan.edu.cn/dofiles/all/20161121160023663.pdf

Kusiak A. (1990). *Intelligent manufacturing systems*. Prentice Hall Press.

Lan, X., Weng, L. F., & Yu, H. Z. (2018). Addressing policy challenges in implementing sustainable development goals through an adaptive governance approach: A view from transitional China. *Sustainable Development*, *26*(2), 150–158.

Li, Q., & Yuan, Z. G. (2016, October). Skills shortages in the Chinese Labour Market. *JP Morgan*. https://china.usc.edu/sites/default/files/skillsgap-in-chineselabour-market-exec-summary.pdf

Li, S. H., & Rong, F. Y. (2021). Green transformation and upgrading of China's manufacturing industry: Policies, practices, and trends. *Globalization*, (5), 103–114 + 136.

Li, S. Q., & Wang, H. C. (2021). The impact of artificial intelligence on manufacturing labour in the context of an ageing population: Evidence from China. *Science and Technology Management*, *42*(7), 3–17.

Liu, L. (2021a). Problems and countermeasures in the cultivation of skilled talents in state-owned enterprises. *Talent Resource Development*, (11), 80–82.

Liu, X. D. (2021b). *China's sustainable development goals and policy priorities during the "14th Five-Year Plan" period*. www.ydylcn.com/skwx_ydyl/initDatabaseDetail?siteId=1&contentId=11263480&contentType=literature

Liu, Y. (2019). China's implementation of goal 9 of the 2030 agenda for sustainable development: International capacity cooperation under the Belt and Road Initiative. *Chinese Journal of Urban and Environmental Studies*, *7*(1), 65–85.

Lu, Y. (2006, May 11). The shortage of highly skilled talents challenges "Made in China". *Economic Information Daily* (005).

Luo, Z. (2020). Why there is an urgent need for highly skilled youth in the construction of a strong manufacturing country. *People's Forum*, *656*(2), 84–87.

Ma, H. M., & Yang, Y. (2021). The impact of population ageing on the quality of manufacturing development in China. *Macro Quality Research*, *9*(6), 44–58.

Ma, H. Y., Jiang, L. J., & Zhu, Z. Z. (2022). Basic experience, main dilemmas, and breakthrough paths in the cultivation of highly skilled talents in the new era. *Education and Career*, *2022*(8), 44–49.

Ministry of Education. (2017–2022). *Statistical bulletin on the development of global education*. http://www.moe.gov.cn/jyb_sjzl/sjzl_fztjgb/

Ministry of Education, Ministry of Human Resources and Social Security, Ministry of Industry and Information Technology of the People's Republic of China. (2016). *Guidelines for talent development planning in the manufacturing industry*. https://www.gov.cn/xinwen/2017-02/14/content_5167903.htm

Ministry of Foreign Affairs of the People's Republic of China. (2022). *Full text of the report to the 20th National Congress of the Communist Party of China*. Retrieved 25 July 2023, from www.fmprc.gov.cn/eng/wjdt_665385/zyjh_665391/202210/t20221025_10791908.html

Ministry of Industry and Information Technology of the People's Republic of China. (2023). *Vice Director of the Planning Department of the Ministry of Industry and Information Technology, Chang Guowu: In 2022, China's manufacturing industry accounted for nearly 30% of the global proportion, ranking first in the world for 13 consecutive years*. https://baijiahao.baidu.com/s?id=1762040681636056959&wfr=spider&for=pc

OECD. (2003). *OECD employment outlook*. Author.

OECD. (2017). *Getting skills right: Skills for jobs indicators*. Author.

People's Daily Online. (2019). *Wang Yi's speech at the United Nations Sustainable Development goals summit*. https://baijiahao.baidu.com/s?id=1645606295061323228&wfr=spider&for=pc

Peters, M. D. J., Godfrey, C. M., Khalil, H., McInerney, P., Parker, D., & Soares, C. B. (2015). Guidance for conducting systematic scoping reviews. JBI Evidence Implementation, *13*(3), 141–146.

Qiu, Y. (2022). Factors influencing the digital transformation of the manufacturing industry. Economic Research Guide, (24), 53–55.

Reports to the 20th National Congress of the Communist Party of China. (2022). *Hold high the great banner of socialism with Chinese characteristics and strive in unity to build a modern socialist country in all respects*. Retrieved 25 July 2023, from https://view.

officeapps.live.com/op/view.aspx?src=https%3A%2F%2Fwww.fmprc.gov.cn%2Feng%2Fwjdt_665385%2Fzyjh_665391%2F202210%2FP020221025833535574835.doc&wdOrigin=BROWSELINK

Richardson, S. (2009). What is a skill shortage? Australian Bulletin of Labour, *35*(1), 326–355.

Shao, C. F., Chen, S. H., Gao, J. L., He, Y., & Zhou, H. L. (2021). Design of China's sustainable development evaluation index system based on SDGs. *China Population, Resources and Environment*, *31*(4): 1–12.

Sheng, S. M., & Cheng, Q. (2020). Exploring the causes of skill shortage and skill mismatch in the context of the new economy. *Journal of Shangrao Normal University*, *40*(4), 91–95 + 105.

Sina Finance. (2021). *Latest population data: China's 894 million labour force ranks first in the world! Is the situation in India not optimistic?* https://baijiahao.baidu.com/s?id=1699529030742862527&wfr=spider&for=pc

The Paper (2020). *Keeping in mind the instructions, thanksgiving, and striving forward | Shaanxi Automobile Group: "Four New" Leading to a High Quality Development Fast Track.* https://m.thepaper.cn/baijiahao_12097133

United Nations Industrial Development Organization (UNIDO). (2021). *Industrial development report 2022: Overview of the future of industrialization in the post-epidemic era.* Author.

UNSDG. (2020). *United Nations sustainable development cooperation framework for the People's Republic of China, 2021–2025.* Retrieved 29August 2023, from https://unsdg.un.org/sites/default/files/2020-11/China-UNSDCF-2021-2025.pdf

Wang, Z. Y., Deng, Y., Zhou, S. A., & Wu, Z. B. (2023). Achieving sustainable development goal 9: A study of enterprise resource optimization based on artificial intelligence algorithms. *Resource Policy*, *80*.

Wen, S. K., Yang, X. M., & Jiang, Q. (2022). The problems and countermeasures of cultivating high-quality technical and skilled talents in the context of 'intelligent manufacturing'. *Journal of Handan Vocational and Technical College*, *35*(4), 54–57.

World Bank. (2017). *Encountering trouble? The future of manufacturing-oriented development.* www.shihang.org/zh/topic/competitiveness/publication/trouble-in-the-making-the-future-of-manufacturing-led-development

World Bank. (2022). *World Bank report: The COVID-19 and multiple obstacles disrupt the normalization of China's economic growth.* www.shihang.org/zh/news/press-release/2022/06/08/covid-19-outbreaks-and-headwinds-have-disrupted-china-s-growth-normalization-world-bank-report

Xie, H. L., Wen, J. M., & Choi, Y. (2021). How the SDGs are implemented in China—A comparative study based on the perspective of policy instruments. *Journal of Cleaner Production*, *291*, 125937.

Xinhua News. (2016a). *Outline of the 13th five-year plan for national economic and social development of the People's Republic of China.* Retrieved 12 November 2016, from http://www.china.com.cn/lianghui/news/2016-03/17/content_38053101.htm

Xinhua News. (2016b). *G20 Hangzhou summit.* Retrieved 12 November 2016, from http://www.g20.org/hywj/dncgwj/201609/t20160906_3392.html

Yang, P., Wang, X., & Liu, Y. (2021). *Yunbo manufacturing 2025 and skills shortage governance.* China Institute of Education Finance Science, Peking University (Supplementary Report on China's Education Finance Policy Consultation (2015–2019): 6).

Ye, W. (2023, March 6). *Cultivating highly skilled talents to assist in "Made in China". Introduction to China's High-Tech Industry* (002), p. 1.

Zhong, R. Y., Xu, X., Klotz, E., & Newman, S. T. (2017). Intelligent manufacturing in the context of industry 4.0: A review. *Engineering*, *3*, 616–630.

9 Towards a Sustainable City-State? Critical Skill Shortages in Singapore

Peter Waring and Julia Connell*

Introduction

As an innovative, modern small island state, Singapore has embraced the United Nations Sustainable Development Goals (SDGs) and the concept of sustainability more generally. The city-state strongly contributes to the SDG ASEAN working group, including as its Chair, and in 2018, the Singapore government undertook a Voluntary National Review of the country's progress against the 17 SDGs, with a second voluntary review published in July 2023. While the country's active commitment to the 2030 agenda is commendable, shortages of the critical skills required to progress on key indicators threaten its ability to realise its aspirations. Singapore faces very significant demographic and labour market problems, which, if left unaddressed, will make it very difficult for the country to lead the region in progress towards the SDGs. In this chapter, we examine the challenge of critical skill shortages with respect to two SDGs of primary importance to the city-state—namely decent work (SDG 8) and climate action (SDG 13). In recent years, Singapore has endeavoured to position itself as a leading example of sustainability efforts in Southeast Asia. As a small tropical low-lying island nation at the end of the Malayan peninsula, its embrace of environmental best practices (especially climate change mitigation) could perhaps be anticipated. Yet environmentalism is also arguably etched into the city-state's DNA as a historic and familiar guiding principle. In 1965, when it was ejected from the Malaysian Federation, its very survival as a sovereign nation depended on developing sustainable water, housing, and economic policies.

Appreciation for the environment and pursuing economic development while preserving nature is a complex and difficult balance for an island that is just 720 square kilometres in size and has one of the highest population densities in the world. Despite these challenges and many competing priorities, in 1967, the country's founding father, Lee Kuan Yew, envisaged 'a garden city beautiful with flowers and trees and as tidy and litter less as can be' (Lee, 1967, p. 4) as he would later caution that 'a blighted urban jungle of concrete destroys the human spirit' (Lee, 1995). His vision was reflected in law-making in the newly independent state. For example, the second reading speech of

DOI: 10.4324/9781003379065-11

the Environmental Public Health Bill in 1968 declared, 'the improvement in the quality of our urban environment and the transformation of Singapore into a garden city—a clean and green city—is the declared objective of the government'.

More than 50 years on, this commitment to the environment has been given added urgency considering overwhelming scientific evidence of anthropocentric climate change (IPCC, 2023). Singapore's geography makes it especially vulnerable, but as with water, the country is positioning itself to turn this exposure into opportunity through its climate policy leadership, which will be detailed later in this chapter. However, critical challenges in meeting these ambitions are specific skill deficits that will need to be overcome. Historically, Singapore's education and training systems have been geared towards supporting rapid industrialisation—initially focusing on manufacturing, chemicals, marine, and aviation industries. Then, in the 1990s and 2000s, there was a greater focus on transforming Singapore into a services-based economy with a strong emphasis on developing tertiary industries such as finance. The shift to a low-carbon economy will once again challenge education and training systems to respond rapidly. Making progress against SDG 8, decent work, is also made more difficult in the context of Singapore's rapidly ageing population and its historical dependency on large numbers of temporary foreign workers.

Country Background

Singapore's survival as an independent city-state in a world of nation-states seems as improbable as its subsequent rise into what is possibly the world's most successful entrepot. Fuelled by a pragmatic policy mix, the Singapore government has successfully courted international capital to the 720 square km red dot that boasts no natural resources other than its approximately 5.7 million population and a strategic location for shipping and air travel at the end of the Malayan peninsula. This makes Singapore one of the world's most densely populated independent countries. Over 75% of Singapore's multiracial population has Chinese heritage, with Malays and Indians comprising the remainder. Consequently, the city-state has a population with a rich mix of religions and languages—English, Malay, Mandarin, and Tamil (BBC, 2018).

Singapore has come a long way over the past 50 years. In the early days of its independence, the country faced high unemployment, poor infrastructure, and housing shortages. A range of strategies have led to contemporary Singapore possessing a skilled workforce, a pro-foreign investment and export orientation, and a thriving free-market economy that attracts international investment funds on a large scale despite its high-cost operating environment (World Bank, 2022a). This business-friendly regulatory environment contributes to the city-state's ranking as one of the world's most competitive economies (World Bank, 2022a). Moreover, Singapore has been highly rated in the *Ease of Doing Business* survey for some years—currently being ranked number two in 2022, just behind New Zealand (Trading Economics, 2022). The World

Bank ranks Singapore as the best country in the latest World Bank's *Human Capital Index*. This is mainly due to its policies (discussed later in the chapter), which are targeted at developing human capital (World Bank, 2022b).

Labour Market Overview

Since Singapore gained independence from Britain in 1965, the absence of natural resources has focused the ruling party's attention on education and skill development to drive waves of industrialisation and modernisation, supplemented by a high dependence on low-wage/low-skilled labour from the region. For example, Singapore's trade-driven economy relies strongly on employing foreign workers. In 2013, the government forecast that by 2030 immigrants will make up more than 50% of the residential population (BBC, 2018). Singapore has a particularly high dependence on foreign labour across most economic sectors, especially in the construction, marine engineering, and manufacturing industries.

In 2022, the total labour market reportedly comprised 3.54 million employees, down from 3.75 million in 2019 (pre-COVID-19). O'Neill (2022) reports that the number of employed in Singapore is forecast to continuously decrease between 2022 and 2023 by a total of 0.1 million people, estimated to amount to 3.49 million people in 2023. These demographic challenges include one of the lowest total fertility rates in the world (TFR: 1.2 versus Japan's 1.3) and an Old-Age Support Ratio, which has fallen from 8:1 in 2000 to 5:1 in 2015 and is set to decline further to 2:1 by 2030.

Singapore's Ministry of Manpower reports that labour market recovery improved in the second quarter of 2022, with 'total employment reaching 99.5% of the pre-pandemic level in December 2019' (MoM, 2023). These figures include resident and non-resident employment, with resident employment 4.2% above the pre-pandemic level in June 2022. Non-resident employment improved when border restrictions were relaxed in April 2022 but remained 10% below the pre-pandemic level, and unemployment rates remained low (overall: 2.1%, resident: 2.9%, citizen: 3.0%) (O'Neill, 2022).

The Singapore Workforce

The *Skills Demand for a Future Economy Report* was released by the Singapore government in 2022 and identifies a range of skill requirements for the projected future economy. Primarily, a focus on green, digital, and caring economies led to the identification of multiple technical skills, and three critical core skills clusters considered essential for business transformation. These include 'Thinking Critically', 'Interacting with Others', and 'Staying Relevant' (SkillsFuture, 2022b).

Sustainable Development Goals

The Sustainable Development Report (formerly the SDG Index and Dashboards) is a global assessment of countries' progress toward achieving the

United Nations SDGs (2022). It complements the official SDG indicators and voluntary national reviews.

According to the Singapore SDG dashboard, its overall score is 71.72/100, and its ranking is 60 out of 163 countries. Also on the dashboard is a 'spill-over' score, which relates to each country's actions that can positively or negatively affect other countries' abilities to achieve their own SDGs. The Spillover Index assesses such spillovers along three dimensions: environmental and social impacts embodied in trade, economy, and finance, and security. A higher score means a country causes more positive and fewer negative spillover effects. Singapore scores 33/100 on the spillover score. Of the 17 UN SDGs, Singapore has achieved five, is moderately achieving eight, is stagnating on two, and is decreasing on one—(SDG 15) life on the land. For SDG 15 (reduced inequalities), the dashboard indicates that information is unavailable. Overall, the indications are that much more remains to be done, particularly in relation to SDG15, which relates to the protection, restoration, and promotion of the sustainable use of terrestrial ecosystems, sustainably managed forests, combating desertification, and halt and reversal of land degradation and halt biodiversity loss.

These challenges and the unquestionable impacts of climate change on natural and man-made systems, along with the experience of the COVID-19 pandemic fresh in the minds of citizens and policymakers, mean that the challenge of sustainability confronts Singapore. This challenge is particularly acute as a small, low-lying state that relies on other states for water and energy. Hence, the SDGs primarily focused on in this chapter will be SDG 8 (decent work) and SDG 13 (climate action). These goals are especially relevant to Singapore's particular challenges and the policy activity in which it has been most active.

There is a strong willingness among Singapore's policymakers to address these challenges with ingenuity and strategic foresight. The predilection of the ruling party to embrace 'green policies' most likely stems from the leanings of its founders, especially the former Prime Minister Lee Kuan Yew, whose indomitable influence over Singapore's development extended to its parks and even the choice of trees planted. The city-state's impressive achievement in closing its water loop is yet to be matched by similar success in renewable energy, although substantial progress has been made, which is detailed further. Singapore's 2030 Green Plan (if successfully implemented) will at least meet commitments under the Paris Accord.

The 2030 Green Plan (Singapore Green Plan, 2022) is a comprehensive policy response and a 'whole-of-nation' strategy to transition to a low-carbon economy. The plan details various initiatives and ambitious policy targets to meet and exceed the Paris Accord climate commitments. The key initiatives and goals include the following:

- Quadrupling solar energy deployment by 2025 and importing 35% of energy from renewable sources
- Eliminating new diesel car registrations from 2025 and no new internal combustion engine car registrations from 2030
- Planting one million more trees between 2021 and 2030

- 'Greening' 80% of Singapore's buildings (by Gross Floor Area) by 2030
- Reducing landfill waste (per capita, per day) by 30% by 2030 and working towards achieving a 20% reduction by 2026

Complementing the Green Plan was introducing a Carbon Tax in Singapore in 2019. Singapore was the first country to introduce such a tax and plans to steadily increase to SGD50–80 a tonne by 2030.

> Singapore also sees regional opportunities to develop itself as a hub for sustainable finance. It has taken the first steps in this regard by investing $1.8 billion in 2021 to 'invest in public market investment strategies that have a strong green focus'.
>
> (MFA, 2023, p. 48)

The Singapore government has also attempted to lay the ground rules for Green Bonds by publishing the Singapore Green Bond Framework. An additional initiative to promote transparency in ESG reporting is 'Project Greenprint', which will invest in a digital registry to record corporate ESG disclosures (MFA, 2023, p. 48).

The 2030 Green Plan's success depends on addressing critical skill shortages in Singapore and acknowledging that a new generation of jobs is required to meet the United Nations SDGs. However, the country's ageing population, low birth rate, and restricted migration represent significant impediments to achieving the SDGs. A further challenge is the country's continued reliance on low-skill, low-wage migrant labour, which disincentivises employers from investing in capital and high-skilled labour.

The Way Forward

'Skill shortages' are generally assessed through industry or national-level surveys of employers to identify current skill deficits or skills that employers predict will be in demand in future (National Skills Commission, 2023). In the context of this chapter, we define 'Critical Skill Shortages' as a current or future skills deficit that is critical to achieving desired progress against the SGDs. The methodology comprised a systematic review of relevant literature, including published and 'grey' literature. There are various suggestions as to the approach this might take. In this case, we will follow Khan et al.'s (2003) suggestions regarding taking a series of five steps: framing the question(s), identifying relevant publications, assessing the quality of studies, summarising the evidence, and reporting on the findings.

Analysis was conducted using a range of literature, including academic research, government reports, and statistics reports. The research questions focus mainly on two areas:

1 How effective are the policies and strategies being adopted to address the critical skill shortages in Singapore likely to be? This question required an

analysis of the policies and strategies in Singapore and comparing and contrasting the policies and strategies being adopted elsewhere.
2 Given current demographic change and long-run labour market trends, how do skill-related policies and strategies align with the Singapore government's Green Plan and the UN SDG targets?
3 Given the evidence, what recommendations can be made, and conclusions drawn?

In this chapter, our contribution focuses on identifying the sustainability challenges facing Singapore and the steps that policymakers have made towards addressing these, with particular reference to jobs and critical skill shortages. Our analysis also seeks to explain how these challenges are impacted by structural features of the Singapore economy, including its high dependence on foreign labour, the impact of demographic change, and its exposure to global supply chains. Our chapter will also comment on the skills Singapore needs to meet the UN SDGs and recommendations to address the challenges identified. The next section will focus on Singapore's performance with respect to two fundamental and interconnected SDGs—SDG13 (climate action) and SDG 8 (decent work).

SDG 13 (Climate Action)

Singapore's Ministry of the Environment and Water Resources published *Singapore's Climate Action Plan: A Climate-Resilient Singapore for a Sustainable Future* in 2016. Using modelling from the Centre for Climate Change Singapore and the UK's Met Office Hadley Centre, the report predicted that daily mean temperatures would rise between 1.4 degrees to 4.6 degrees Celsius, creating a sharper contrast between the traditional dry and wet months experienced in Singapore. In turn, this would increase risks to Singapore's coastline from flooding and damage to biodiversity, increase the likelihood of diseases such as dengue, increase the frequency of damaging extreme weather events, negatively impact Singapore's infrastructure, and increase the process of imported foods (p. 8). The report details the infrastructure that Singapore will require to adapt to high temperatures and rising sea levels. It also outlines efforts to improve food security and habitat management. The report did not consider the workforce or the skills that would underpin the actions in mitigation.

The Committee of the Future Economy noted in 2017 that 'given the threat of climate change, Singapore should play its part in contributing to global efforts to improve environmental sustainability' (p. 14). This included greater deployment of solar photovoltaics, investment in research and development of renewable energy storage solutions, and improved food security and water resilience (p. 99). However, while the report acknowledged and detailed the need to develop skills (especially digital skills) across various sectors, it did not identify the skills required to combat climate change.

Singapore undertook a 'Voluntary National Review' of progress across the SDGs in 2018, which outlined, among other things, its approach to environmental sustainability and climate action (MFA, 2018). Among the key achievements listed are the following:

- Singapore is among the 20 most carbon-efficient countries in the world.
- 72 hectares of rooftop gardens and green walls.
- Solar photovoltaic deployment grew from 0.4 megawatts in 2008 to 143 megawatts in 2017, with plans to reach 350 MW by 2020 (p. 26).
- 2017—two consortiums appointed to implement utility-scale energy storage systems.
- Whole-of-nation approach to mitigating climate change.

A key initiative announced in the submission and described earlier was adopting a carbon tax which was implemented in 2019 across all sectors of the economy. Singapore plans to reduce emissions intensity by 36% from 2005 to 2030 (p. 48). In July 2023, Singapore's Ministry of Foreign Affairs published the findings of its second voluntary national review. The review presents a picture of significant progress with respect to climate change mitigation efforts, including

- 700 megawatts of installed solar power capacity as of the second quarter of 2022—this represents double the 2020 goal.
- Setting a goal of 2 gigawatts of solar energy by 2030.
- Establishment of a 285-megawatt energy storage system—the largest in Southeast Asia.
- Working with countries in the region to deliver low-carbon electricity—for example, the Lao PDR-Thailand-Malaysia-Singapore Power Integration Project provides 100 megawatts of renewable hydropower from Lao PDR to Singapore (p. 16).
- Publication of a National Hydrogen Strategy.
- A Green Economy Agreement was signed with Australia, the first of its kind designed to reduce trade barriers for renewable energy, among other initiatives.

With respect to progress against SDG 13 goals, the Voluntary Review suggests that approximately 60% of the goals have seen good or fair progress. This includes the sub-goals of

- resilience and adaptive capacity
- climate change policies
- climate change planning and management.

Interestingly, the Voluntary Review notes that there is insufficient data on the subgoal of 'climate change awareness' to be able to describe progress

(MFA, 2023, p. 63). The Voluntary Review acknowledges that 'exciting new economic opportunities will emerge as Singapore transitions to a low carbon economy'. These are stated to include not only engineering and renewable energy production but also the services sector, such as carbon accounting, trading, and 'green finance'. There is, however, tacit acknowledgment that the achievement of progress towards the 'Green Economy' is reliant on the development of new skills. The Voluntary Review notes that the government already offers reskilling and upskilling programmes such as the 'Career Conversion Programme for Clean and Renewable Energy Professionals' (p. 33). This is presented as an 'opportunity' rather than a challenge in the Voluntary Review.

Of the three emerging economies (digital, caring, and green) that the Singapore government identified in the 'Skills Demand for a Future Economy Report', the green economy appears to be the smallest in terms of employment size currently, but it is growing quickly. An analysis of job post data indicated that 3,000 jobs advertised in 2018 could be classified as 'green economy' jobs. By 2021, this had ballooned to 19,000 job postings—a compound average growth rate of 93%. This rapid growth signals a need for the authorities to scale education and retraining initiatives to address this demand rapidly.

The 'Skills Demand for a Future Economy' (2022) report notes that the green jobs with the highest demand are in green infrastructure and mobility (demand growth of 194%) and resource circularity and decarbonisation (demand growth of 129%). Within the green infrastructure domain, the occupation with the highest demand growth was green facilities management at 2300%. Interestingly, the report notes that demand for green skills was evident and growing throughout various industry value chains—from construction and manufacturing to banking and finance. The transition from internal combustion vehicles to electric cars was also noted to be driving demand for automotive technicians with 'EV' technical and safety skills.

As a major transportation hub, especially for shipping and aviation, there is also likely to be strong demand from those sectors in Singapore as employers seek to use low-carbon or renewable energy fuels. This will lead to a significant retraining and upskilling need in these industries. Aside from 'green economy' specific jobs, the *Skills Demand for a Future Economy* report notes that many existing jobs will require some level of 'green skills' as private and public sector organisations introduce more sustainable practices and, in some cases, seek 'green finance' to undertake business activities. This means that demand for generic or foundational knowledge and skills, as well as more complex/sophisticated and specific green skills, may form part of an emerging skill deficit.

The picture that emerges from the *Skills Demand Report for a Future Economy* and the Voluntary National Reviews on SDG progress that Singapore has undertaken is of a very significant, and, some might say, radical make-over of the Singapore economy. This transformation has been gathering momentum as both government and business adopt sustainable practices and strategic postures designed to address local environmental and climate change challenges, and to take advantage of new green economic opportunities. In doing so, though, significant pressures and skills deficits are building in the local labour market that may only be partially addressed through government initiatives.

SGD 8—Decent Work

SDG 8 (decent work and economic growth) concerns promoting inclusive and sustainable growth, full and productive employment, and decent work for all. In addition, several 'sub-goals' include young people and persons with disabilities and equal pay for work of equal value. Decent work is a broad term that covers different dimensions, such as employment (paid or unpaid), social protection, and workers' rights. The Sustainable Development Report (Sachs et al., 2023) states that although some progress was being made globally prior to the pandemic in 2020, all the SDGs are now behind the 2030 agenda. This includes SDG 8, where it is indicated that no one global region is on track to achieve this SDG. East and Southeast Asia, in general, are reportedly facing significant challenges regarding SDG8, where progress is largely stagnating, whereas the SDG dashboard for Singapore indicates that SDG8 is moderately improving. That said, there is a lack of information around areas such as 'victims of modern slavery', which is challenging when the intention is to measure progress.

In 2022, two billion workers were reportedly in precarious jobs without social protection. While global unemployment is predicted to fall to below pre-pandemic levels in general, this is not the case for low- and middle-income countries (United Nations webpage). Hence, workers from low- and middle-income countries are likely to continue to seek work in higher-income economies, such as Singapore, for the foreseeable future. Singapore is one of the few high-income economies that relies extensively on migrant labour. Hence, while migrant workers may undertake work that is considered 'low skilled', it is critical to Singapore's economy by supporting a range of sectors. Sectors range from construction to domestic work whereby migrant workers build homes, offices, and roads; help care for children and elderly; and produce commodities used both domestically and abroad (Bal, 2017).

As pointed out earlier in this chapter, Singapore undertook a voluntary national review (NVR) of its progress concerning the SDGs, with findings published in the *Building a Sustainable, Resilient and Inclusive Singapore* report (2023). The foreword by Prime Minister Lee Hsien Loong stresses the need for digital transformation to empower people and promote inclusive sustainable development, stating, 'we have therefore stepped-up efforts to bridge the digital divide and enhance digital skills and training for all segments of society' (NSC, 2023, p. 5). However, although the section on SDG 8 reports that Singapore has 'has made progress on reducing inequalities, with the Gini coefficient falling to its lowest level (since 2000) in 2021, and households in the 11th to 20th percentile seeing the largest real growth of 5.5% in income', there is no mention of migrant workers. The ambition of positioning

Singapore as a global business, innovation, and talent hub for advanced manufacturing is also outlined under SDG 8, suggesting a three-pronged strategy to enable local enterprises to adopt Industry 5.0 technologies with the intention of strengthening the pipeline of skilled local talent for the sector. Hence, while promoting inclusivity and equality is laudable, it applies only to the Singaporean workforce, while largely excluding the approximately 1.3–5 million migrant workers the city-state relies on.

Conversely, the report *'Lost in the Garden City' Singapore's Migrant Worker System in the Age of the Sustainable Development Goals by Transient Workers Count Two* (TWCT, 2023) reports on the experiences of low-wage migrant workers (primarily Bangladeshi and Tamil work pass holders) in Singapore and the barriers imposed on the migration system that impede true progress with regard to SDGs 1, 8, 10, and 16. The continued reliance on low-skilled, low-wage labour does not incentivise training and skill development investment and further impedes the country's SDG performance. Forrester and Kim are cited in the report stating that Singapore's approach to the SDGs and sustainability is 'significantly undermined by the practice of cherry-picking goals based on existing state priorities' (TWCT, 2023, p. 2).

Such arguments are problematic, given that associations between migration management and the SDGs have been the focus of academic discourse since their initiation, with connections established between all 17 SDGs and migration management (TWCT, 2023). As of June 2022, Singapore had 1.3 million work pass holders of all visa types working in the city-state—more than 20% of the population of 5.637 million—of those workers, 1.11 million are reportedly low-wage migrant workers (Ministry of Manpower, 2022a).

Workers from various countries, such as Bangladesh, China, and Vietnam, take on difficult and often dangerous jobs in construction and the maritime industry, working outdoors for long hours in difficult weather conditions without a minimum wage. These labourers are transported from their dormitories to their work sites in the back of open trucks without seatbelts—a dangerous practice resulting in injuries and even fatalities at times (Chen, 2023). In 2021, a worker fell from the back of a truck and fractured his leg, leaving him unable to work—he subsequently sued his company and won. Employers are now required to buy medical insurance, and the workplace fatal injury rate decreased in Singapore as it was ranked seventh best for this category in the OECD in 2018 it increased in 2022 compared to 2021, as the rate per 100,000 workers was 1.3, when compared to 1.1 in 2021 (MoM, 2022b). Of the 16 fatalities reported to the Ministry of Manpower's List of Workplace Fatalities (Jan to Jun 2023), almost all worked in construction, transportation, and storage or manufacturing.

Foreign Domestic Workers (mostly women) in Singapore are also excluded by Singapore's approach to the SDGs (TWCT, 2023). Migrant domestic workers in Singapore do not benefit from regulated working hours; they do not have a minimum wage, and women migrant workers are deported if they are found to be pregnant (International Labour Organisation, 2020). Moreover, while Singaporean employers often restrict the movement of domestic workers, resulting in their isolation and limited ability to seek help, if they have valid grievances, they are allowed to find another employer (International Labour Organisation, 2020).

Often migrant workers are excluded from benefits and protection and are subject to forms of exploitation, including long hours and unsafe working conditions, making migrant workers one of the most 'at risk' segments of the workforce (Connell & Burgess, 2013). In summary, Singapore needs to do more regarding migrant labour when addressing SDG8.

Bridging the Skills Gap

Given the challenges to progress outlined earlier, the question for policymakers turns on whether the country has the infrastructure and political will to bridge these skill gaps. Singapore boasts a world-class education system with a strong focus on skill development. To promote skills and competency development and identify deficits, the Singapore government has adopted a skills framework known as the workforce skills and qualifications (WSQ), designed on principles of open access, competency-based training and assessment (Bound & Lin, 2011).

Each framework has an 'Industry Skills and Training Council' representing employers, unions, industry associations, and training organisations. Each Industry Skills and Training Council is responsible for developing an 'industry competency map' to chart the employability skills, occupational skills, and industry knowledge required for that particular industry.

In addition to this strong tripartite approach, Singapore launched in 2014 a 'whole-of-government' policy focused on skills, known as *SkillsFuture*. SkillsFuture maintains four key thrusts—helping individuals make well-informed choices in training and education; ensuring a responsive and integrated high-quality system of education and training is in place; promoting career development based on skill mastery and employer recognition; and encouraging lifelong learning (SkillsFuture, 2017). To support this direction, the Singapore government has restructured its machinery of policy-making and implementation with the creation of an agency known as *SkillsFuture Singapore* (SSG), which operates under the imprimatur of the Ministry of Education. Additionally, every Singapore citizen is provided with SkillsFuture credit, which they can use to upgrade their skills through paid training courses.

This skills-centric government infrastructure is unquestionably first class, but it may be insufficient to overcome the twin challenges of demographic change and foreign worker dependency: Singapore's ageing population and low birth rate compound skills shortages. Government policy and economic incentives are in place to extend older workers' participation in the labour market and encourage Singaporeans to have more children. However, there are deep cultural and social factors that blunt their effectiveness. Similarly, the country's dependency on low-wage migrant labour disincentivises employers to invest in the skill development of foreign workers, who are also largely excluded from the SkillsFuture infrastructure. Without tackling these admittedly complex problems, critical skill deficits will continue to plague further progress towards achieving the SDGs.

Conclusion

In this chapter, we examine the challenge of critical skill shortages with respect to two SDGs of primary importance to the city-state—these are decent work (SDG 8) and climate action (SDG 13). Since embracing the SDGs, Singapore has made steady progress with respect to climate change action. Its continuous improvement reflects not only the particular vulnerability of the low-lying city-state but also the significant economic opportunity it savours by developing into a regional, if not global, hub for sustainable finance.

There is a recognition that a key enabler of future climate change success will be the reskilling and upskilling of the labour force. New green economy jobs that did not exist until a few years before Singapore's 2023 National Voluntary Review (such as Carbon Accountant and Sustainability Engineer, to name just a few) are emerging rapidly. Some government training initiatives are underway to address the skills deficit, but at this stage, there is little evidence that these efforts will be sufficiently scaled to support the transformation of the Singaporean economy. Skilled migration might be an obvious solution to such a skills deficit, but for the reasons already articulated, the Singapore government has been tightening these pathways. Without policy change, a critical skills shortage across 'green economy' jobs is likely to emerge, hampering further progress to a low-carbon economy.

While targets towards SDG 13 (climate action) are progressing with more to be done to address the necessary, critical skills that will meet the actions outlined in Singapore's green plan, targets towards SDG 8 highlight a segment of the workforce that has been largely overlooked in Singapore, that of migration management. The SDG 8 sub-goal 8.8 is problematic; specifically, it is to 'protect labour rights and promote safe and secure working environments for all workers, including migrant workers, in particular women migrants, and those in precarious employment'. If the concept of decent work is to be achieved, Singapore needs to address all aspects of sustainability including the migrant workforce system. Although improved workplace safety is a step in the right direction, the TWCT (2023, p. 15) authors point out that '[g]reater financial and employment security would increase compliance with SDG 8 while also effectively reducing the psychological stress many face'. Clearly, a more productive, less injury-prone, and ethically sound working environment for migrants would help to ensure an economically sustainable Singapore (TWCT, 2023).

Note

* Corresponding author: p.waring@murdoch.edu.au.

References

Bal, C. (2017). *Myths and facts: Migrant workers in Singapore*. Retrieved 24 September 2023, from https://newnaratif.com/myths-and-facts-migrant-workers-in-singapore/

Bound, H., & Lin, M. (2011). *Singapore Workforce Skills Qualification (WSQ), workplace learning and assessment (Stage One)* (Research Paper). Institute for Adult Learning Singapore.

British Broadcasting Company (BBC). (2018). *Singapore country profile*. Retrieved 23 September 2023, from www.bbc.com/news/world-asia-15961759

Chen, H. (2023). In a rare move, a migrant worker sued his bosses in Singapore. And won. *CNN*. Retrieved 24 September 2023. https://edition.cnn.com/2023/08/26/asia/singapore-migrant-worker-sues-company-lorry-safety-intl-hnk/index.html

Committee of the Future Economy. (2017). *Report of the committee on the future economy: Pioneers of the next generation*. Singapore Government.

Connell, J., & Burgess, J. (2013). Vulnerable workers in an emerging Middle Eastern economy: What are the implications for HRM? *The International Journal of Human Resource Management*, *24*(22), 4166–4184.

ILO (International Labour Organisation). (2020). *Public attitudes towards Migrant Labour in Singapore* (ILO Research Brief). Retrieved 24 September 2023, from www.ilo.org/asia/publications/issue-briefs/WCMS_766633/lang--en/index.htm

IPCC (Intergovernmental Panel on Climate Change). (2023). *The sixth assessment report*. Retrieved 6 July 2023, from www.ipcc.ch

Khan, K. S., Kunz, R., Kleijnen, J., & Antes, G. (2003). Five steps to conducting a systematic review. *Journal of the Royal Society of Medicine*, *96*(3), 118–121.

Lee, K. Y. (1967). Singapore to become beautiful clean city within three years. *The Straits Times*, p. 4. Retrieved September 5, 2023.

Lee, K. Y. (1995, October 20). Speech at the Launch of the National Orchid Garden. Retrieved September 4, 2023, from www.rembering.sg.gov

MFA (Ministry of Foreign Affairs). (2018) *Towards a sustainable and resilient Singapore, Singapore's Voluntary National review report to the 2018 UN high-level political forum on sustainable devlopment*. Retrieved May 31, 2023, from www.mfa.gov.sg

MFA (Ministry of Foreign Affairs). (2023). *Building a sustainable, resilient & inclusive Singapore, Singapore's voluntary national review report to the 2023 UN high-level political forum on sustainable development*. Retrieved 10 July 2023, from www.mfa.gov.sg

Ministry of Manpower. (2022a). *Foreign workforce numbers*. Singapore Government. Retrieved 24 September 2023, from www.mom.gov.sg/documents-and-publications/foreign-workforce-numbers

Ministry of Manpower. (2022b) *Workplace safety and health reports and statistics*. Retrieved 24 September 2023, from www.mom.gov.sg/workplace-safety-and-health/wsh-reports-and-statistics

Ministry of Manpower. (2023). *Labour force in Singapore 2022*. Singapore Government. Retrieved 6 July 2023, from www.stats.mom.gov.sg

Ministry of the Environment and Water Resources. (2016). *Singapore's climate action plan: A climate-resilient Singapore, for a sustainable future*. Retrieved May 31, 2023, from www.mewr.gov.sg

NSC (National Skills Commission). (2023). Skills shortages and labour market tightness: A global perspective. Retrieved 7 July 2023, from www.nationalskillscommission.gov.au

O'Neill, A. (2022). *Employment in Singapore 2023*. Retrieved 24 September 2023, www.statista.com/statistics/795438/employment-in-singapore/

Sachs, J., Lafortune, G., Fuller, G., & Drumm, E. (2023). *Sustainable development report, implementing the SDG stimulus*. Sustainable Development Solutions Network, A Global Initiative for the United Nations.

Singapore Green Plan. (2022). *The Singapore green plan 2030*. Retrieved 30 November 2022, from www.greenplan.gov.sg
SkillsFuture. (2017). *About SkillsFuture*. Retrieved December 7, 2017, from www.skillsfuture.sg/AboutSkillsFuture#section4
SkillsFuture. (2022a). *The green economy explained: Trends, skills and jobs you need to know about*. Retrieved 30 November 2022, from www.myskillsfuture.gov.sg
SkillsFuture. (2022b). *Skills demand for the future economy*. Retrieved 30 November 2022, from www.myskillsfuture.gov.sg
Sustainable Development Report. (2022). *From crisis to sustainable development: The SDGs as a roadmap to 2030 and beyond*. Retrieved 20 September 2022, from https://dashboards.sdgindex.org/
Trading Economics. (2022). *Ease of doing business in Singapore*. Retrieved 21 September 2022, from http://EaseofDoingBusinessSingapore
TWCT (Transient Workers Count Too). (2023). *Lost in the garden city: Singapore's migrant worker system in the age of the sustainable development goals*. Retrieved 24 September 2023, from lost_in_the_garden_city_feb2023_96558.pdf
World Bank. (2022a). *The World Bank in Singapore*. Retrieved 24 September 2023, www.worldbank.org/en/country/singapore
World Bank. (2022b). *Human Capital Index (HCI) Scale 0–1 Singapore*. Retrieved 22 September 2023, https://data.worldbank.org/indicator/HD.HCI.OVRL?locations=SG

10 Local Tourism Businesses in the Digital Era

Implications for Bridging the Critical Skills Gap in Indonesia

Subas P. Dhakal and Saskia Tjokro*

Introduction

Like many other Asian Pacific countries, Indonesia faces critical shortages of skilled labour due to the out-migration of skilled workers, an ageing workforce, and a lack of capacity to upskill or reskill the workforce (ILO, n.d.). In 2018, the Indonesian government developed the Critical Occupations List (COL) to overcome the deficiency in the labour market based on two criteria: (a) it must be in shortage and (b) it must be strategic for the Indonesian economy (Coordinating Ministry for Economic Affairs of the Republic of Indonesia (CMEARI), 2020). For example, jobs related to the accommodation and food services sector (AFS) are included in the COL (p. vii). This study focuses on the country's travel and tourism industry (TTI), including the AFS and the transport, postal, and warehousing (TPW) sectors—considered one of the main drivers for achieving the sustainable development goals (SDGs) as a part of the United Nations' (UN) 2030 Agenda. Despite the impact of the COVID-19 pandemic, the TTI collectively contributed around 6% of the GDP and 8% of total employment in Indonesia in 2021 (WTTC, 2022a). One of the significant global issues associated with the TTI relevant in an Indonesian context is the impact of innovation and digitisation associated with the Fourth Industrial Revolution (4IR) or Industry 4.0. Nankervis et al. (2021) state that 'the impending Fourth Industrial Revolution (FIR), encompassing artificial intelligence (AI), robotics and machine learning, is predicted to have both positive and negative effects on society as a whole, and on many workplaces, jobs, employee skills, and competencies' (p. 4). Although the literature on the 4IR and TTI nexus is still emerging, the potential for technologies to catalyse economic growth in the digital era (Armoo et al., 2020; Gatti et al., 2018; Wyman, 2020) has been increasingly recognised.

There is a growing consensus on the role of digital technologies in becoming 'game-changers' for local tourism businesses (LTBs) (Dhakal, 2021; OECD, 2020; Ollivaud & Haxton, 2019; Prasetyo et al., 2020). For example, several studies have considered wide-ranging digital innovations, such as robots, automated kiosks, chatbots, augmented realities, voice-controlled technologies, and generative AI in the TTI (Alam et al., 2022; Buhalis & Moldavska,

DOI: 10.4324/9781003379065-12

2021; Osei et al., 2020). These technological advances are relevant for LTBs as they play a vital role in achieving SDG #8—which promotes sustained, inclusive, and sustainable economic growth, full and productive employment, and decent work for all. In particular, the third target under SDG #8: 'promote development-oriented policies that support productive activities, decent job creation, entrepreneurship, creativity, and innovation, and encourage the formalisation and growth of micro, small, and medium-sized enterprises, including through access to financial services' (Global Goals, 2023, para 4), priorities the viability of LTBs. However, LTBs will increasingly find it challenging to thrive in the current highly competitive business environment without external support, as they have traditionally struggled with technology adoption (access) and lacked skills to harness technologies (utilisation) to benefit from them (Dhakal & Tjokro, 2022; O'Connor, 2023). According to Levesque (2019), the notion of a skills gap 'captures a mismatch between the skills that businesses rely upon in their workers' (para 4). For example, Korn Ferry (2015) estimated that the skills gap cost for Indonesia by 2030 could be over AU$500 billion (p. 5). Although the inability to bridge the skills gaps can adversely impact LTBs in the 4IR era, the unfolding workforce implications of the 4IR remain underexplored. This chapter addresses this gap and draws on the Strategic Human Resources Management (SHRM) perspective (Nankervis et al., 2021).

SHRM emphasises the importance of workforce readiness, namely the ability to adopt and utilise digital technologies with the support of owners or managers and informed employees to help thrive in the digital economy and has the potential to reveal meaningful insights for overcoming the critical skills gap (CSG). For the purpose of this chapter, we consider CSG to be a difference between the skills needed to fulfil job responsibilities and the actual skills possessed by employees within the TTI. The main assumption is that the 4IR will improve human-technology interactions in the workplace if employers and employees can harness digital opportunities by bridging the CSG. Unlike the digital divide perspective that focuses on have-nots in terms of access and use (Dhakal & Tjokro, 2022), the SHRM perspective focuses on skills and willingness of employees to adapt and reskill/upskill in accordance with the changing circumstances and needs in the workplace.

Country Background

Indonesia has a population of nearly 273.8 million and is the largest Southeast Asian nation. The Indonesian workforce is approximately 138 million (World Bank, 2021), and the pre-pandemic data showed the labour force participation rate of age 15+ at 65.9% (World Bank, 2021). According to the National Statistics Bureau (BPS), the unemployment rate stood at 6.3% (World Bank, 2021), and over half (59.6%) of the workforce is employed in the informal sector (BPS, 2021). The number of informal workers in Indonesia continues to increase in size, although the proportion has decreased (BPS,

2021). For example, the number of informal workers reached 78.14 million in February 2021, an increase of 2.64 million compared to 2020 of 77.68 million people (BPS, 2021). However, the proportion of informal workers decreased from 60.47% to 59.62% in 2021, at least partially due to a slight increase in formal workers from 39.53% to 40.38% (BPS, 2021). According to the World Bank (2021), the unemployment rate of the youth segment (15–24 years old, comprising 28% of the total population) was 14%, with females accounting for 4%. Within the context of the United Nations' (UN) 2030 Agenda and 17 SDGs, Indonesia has been prioritising four systematic reforms: (a) social protection, (b) national health system, (c) disaster resilience, and (d) recovery of the tourism sector and investment towards the green economy, supported by low-carbon development (Government of Indonesia, 2021). The focus on the recovery of the TTI provides an interesting case for two reasons: (a) despite the collapse of international visitors due to travel restrictions, the TTI is expected to expand as much as twice the rate of overall economic growth over the next decade (WTTC, 2022b) and (b) the government announced the overarching policy of Making Indonesia 4.0 in 2018 as an integrated roadmap for exploiting the economic potential of the 4IR (Nur et al., 2021).

First, the UNWTO (2021) data indicated that about 2.6 million people are employed within the TTI, 55% of which are held by women and 17% by youth. The TTI was undoubtedly one of the worst-impacted industries in employment (ILO, 2021, p. iv). Nonetheless, the TTI has often been linked with the achievements of the SDGs in Indonesia. For instance, the Deputy Minister of Tourism and Creative Economy (MoTCE) recently said: 'We have been able to achieve the SDGs through the development of ecotourism, strengthening cultural identity, and strengthening local communities' (Antara News, 2022, para 2). In addition, the recovery of TTI has become a national priority. For instance, the MoTCE recently announced the five 'super-priority tourist destinations (DSP) in Indonesia (Lake Toba in North Sumatera, Borobudur in Central Java, Mandalika in West Nusa Tenggara, Labuan Bajo in East Nusa Tenggara, and Likupang in North Sulawesi)' as a way to not only empower local communities but also build a creative economy ecosystem and contribute to the SDGs (see Sunil, 2021, paras 2–6). The primary focus of this new initiative is to support the TTI in terms of (a) cleanliness, health, safety, and environmental sustainability and (b) digitalisation strategies and big-data utilisation. According to the current minister, Sandiaga Salahuddin Uno, these initiatives are designed to overcome the CSG and prepare the human resources to facilitate the 'future of world-class tourism in Indonesia' (Sunil, 2021, para 8).

Second, the Making Indonesia 4.0 roadmap is aimed at the digital economy, with a clear focus on boosting local human resources and education to support the development of the 4IR. For example, Nugraha (2018) indicated that attention to overcoming CSG is warranted for Indonesia to benefit from the 4IR instead of being a mere spectator. The roadmap focuses on five different sectors—automotive, chemicals, electronics, food and beverage, and textiles—of which the food and beverage sector directly relates to the AFS within the TTI. Dhakal et al. (2020) pointed out two possible outcomes concerning the 4IR: one in which the socio-technical divide between developing and developed economies is narrowed in terms of skills and capabilities, and the other in which the divide is widened. Consequently, overcoming the CSG is a priority for Indonesia because adequate investment in the diffusion of and preparedness in the appropriate use of digital technologies could foster the TTI. In contrast, the absence of this investment is likely to accentuate pre-existing inequalities and hinder its socio-economic development. This chapter concurs with a growing consensus on the need for skilled labour for businesses to thrive in the digital era and to catalyse sustainable development (Armoo et al., 2020; Gatti et al., 2018).

Data Collection and Analysis

This study utilised a sequential multi-method approach with three objectives: (a) to explore the 4IR readiness and resistance of LTBs and (b) to gauge the 4IR-related skills gap between LTBs in the AFS and TPW sub-sectors. First, an online survey was distributed via the Indonesian Tour & Travel Agencies and Hotel & Restaurant Association Indonesia members in 2019. A total of 147 usable responses were received from LTBs within the AFS (n = 85) and the TPW (n = 62) sectors. Descriptive statistical analyses (i.e. mean score, two-by-two cross-tabulations, chi-square, and Kruskal—Wallis (K—W) statistical tests) were conducted. Second, 11 interviews with willing managers of LTBs (who responded to the survey) were conducted using a purposive sampling technique between April and July 2020 (Subawa et al., 2021). The interviews allowed the in-depth examination of managerial views on CSG and the readiness for and resistance to digital technologies associated with the 4IR. Due to the pandemic-related constraints, interviews were sent out via email for written responses (see Fritz & Vandermause, 2018).

Findings

Attributes of LTBs

Over half (57%) of the respondents were male, and one-third (35%) were female. Less than one-tenth (8%) did not reveal their gender. An overwhelming majority (97%) were between 18 and 55, and nearly two-thirds (61%) had undergraduate or postgraduate-level qualifications. Although all the responding LTBs employed fewer than 200 people, over two-thirds (67%) of the responding AFS-LTBs and over three-fourths (82%) of TPW-LTBs employed between 1 and 99 people respectively. This difference was statistically significant [$\chi 2$ (n = 147) = 4.249, df = 1, $p \leq 0.005$]. Although the recent classification of small and medium enterprises (SMEs) in Indonesia focuses on capital and sales figures (see BCA, 2022) rather than the number of people employed, these findings are consistent with Tambunan's (2008) observation that SMEs with fewer than 100 workers are the dominant feature of the TTI landscape in Indonesia.

Self-Assessment of Four Stages of the Industrial Revolution

Drawing on Schwab (2017), Dhakal and Tjokro (2022) summarised the four evolutionary stages of the Industrial Revolution (IR) as (a) steam power to mechanise production (1IR), (b) electric power to create mass production (2IR), (c) information technologies to automate production (3IR), and (d) digital technologies with fuzzy boundaries between the physical, digital, and biological spheres. In aggregate, 41.5% and 24.5% of the responding LTBs indicated they were in the 3IR and 2IR stages respectively. Only 3.5% of the AFS-LTBs (total responses = 57) and two-fifths (21%) of the TPW-LTBs (total responses = 61) were perceived to be in the 4IR stage. This difference was statistically significant [$\chi 2$ (n = 147) = 29.515, df = 4, $p < 0.001$]. These findings concur with Halim's et al. (2022) observations that LTBs in Indonesia have generally struggled with the access-related digital divide, such as unstable or inadequate broadband connections.

Perceived Benefits of AI/Digital Applications

Most LTBs agreed that AI/digital applications have the potential to benefit their organisations. Although no statistical differences were detected between LTBs in the two sectors, aligning business strategy and allocating adequate resources towards AI/digital applications were the critical challenges across the board (Table 10.1). In addition, most respondents were uncertain about their current jobs and feared redundancy.

Table 10.1 The mean score of LTB's expectations related to AI/digital applications

Disagree (1); Neutral (2); Agree (3)					
Variables (business-oriented)	*Obs*	*Mean*	*SD*	*Min*	*Max*
Business strategy aligns with AI/digital applications	147	2.204	0.681	1	3
Business enthusiastic about AI/digital applications	147	2.53	0.664	1	3
Business has allocated adequate resources for AI/digital applications	147	1.877	0.681	1	3
Business expects to increase profit from AI/digital applications	147	2.431	0.597	1	3
Variables (employees-oriented)					
AI/digital applications expected to enhance employee satisfaction	147	2.333	0.705	1	3
AI/digital applications expected to enhance job performance	147	2.564	0.641	1	3
Employees confident of keeping their jobs despite AI/digital applications	147	1.979	0.687	1	3
Employees fear redundancy due to increased adoption of AI/digital applications	147	2.6871	0.582	1	3

Fear about redundancy featured during the interviews. For example, one of the interviewees [ID #7: AFS] indicated:

> [N]ot only the jobs like reservation specialists and housekeeping might drastically disappear due to the increasing automation extinct in the future due to the rapid technological advancement . . . the evolving technologies will be, in fact, a threat to my own role—especially if I am unable to adapt to the new technological environment.

This sentiment around fear of job loss and the need to reskill and/or upskill to remain employable is consistent with media reporting that up to 23 million jobs are predicted to be displaced in Indonesia because of automation (Shofa, 2022).

4IR Readiness and Resistance of LTBs

In order to compare the 4IR readiness and resistance between the two sectors, the survey asked the following two questions:

- To what extent is your organisation prepared for the forthcoming changes in AI/robotics technologies? (Readiness)
- Based on your knowledge concerning your organisation, do you anticipate resistance to the forthcoming changes in AI/robotics technologies? (Resistance)

Significant differences existed in how LTBs in the AFS and TPW sectors perceived the 4IR readiness and resistance (Table 10.2). Two-thirds of respondents (66%) indicated that the LTBs were moderately prepared for the 4IR, and half (50%) anticipated moderate resistance towards 4IR. The 4IR readiness between the AFS and TPW sectors was statistically significant ($p \leq 0.05$). One of the interviewees (ID #1-TPW) stated: 'I don't see any jobs disappearing, only shifting into the "online version" of those jobs. People just need to learn

Table 10.2 4IR Readiness versus resistance of LTBs

Variables		*AFS*	*TPW*	*Total*
4IR readiness	Low	26 (30.6%)	7 (11.3%)	33 (22.4%)
$\chi 2$ (n = 147) = 12.763,	Mod	46 (54.1%)	51 (82.3%)	97 (66.0%)
df = 2, $p \leq 0.005$**	High	13 (15.3%)	4 (6.5%)	17 (11.6%)
	Total	85 (100%)	62 (100%)	147 (100%)
4IR resistance	Low	21 (24.7%)	15 (24.2%)	36 (24.5%)
$\chi 2$ (n = 147) = 5.343,	Mod	37 (43.5%)	37 (59.7%)	74 (50.3%)
df = 2, $p \leq 0.069$*	High	27 (31.8%)	10 (16.1%)	37 (25.2%)
	Total	85 (100%)	62 (100%)	147 (100%)

Source: ** Significant at 0.05 probability level; * Significant at 0.1 probability level

how to be agile and flexible.' This view shows that the uptake of digital technologies associated with the 4IR is needs-based in a country where less than 15% of SMEs in Indonesia use digital platforms for marketing their products/services (Syafrian, 2022).

4IR-Related Skills Gap Between LTBs in the AFS and TPW Sub-sectors

The survey collected data on specific skills (Table 10.3) to assess LTB's digital needs for the future. K-W tests were conducted to compare the two sectors' digital skills needs. There were significant differences in the mean ranks. For instance, LTBs in the TPW sector identified a greater need for skills in data analytics, application development, and non-technical soft skills than those in the AFS sector [$p \leq 0.001$]. The need for reskilling/upskilling digital capabilities for the future was featured during the interviews.

On the one hand, one interviewee (ID # 8: TPW) stated: 'I don't think we have labour shortages but definitely skills-related issues. Future investment in digital skills should be equally on technology and education so that we can be skilled to partner with machines in the future rather than compete with them.' Conversely, the interviewee (ID # 11: AFS) stated:

> I think tourists are looking for cultural interaction . . . we need knowledgeable tourist guides, not robots or other technologies. I don't see the reason why a local business like mine needs to spend money to digitise and invest in digital skills.

These contradictory sentiments echo the readiness versus resistance debate, as mentioned earlier, and concur with a recent media report which suggests that 'digital literacy in Indonesia has remained suboptimal . . . despite the accelerated adoption of technology across a wide range of industries' (see Harsono, 2022).

Table 10.3 K-W test on skills need between AFS and TPW sectors

Variables	*Mean Ranks of*			
Critical skills needed in the next five years	*AFS (n = 85)*	*TPW (n = 62)*	X^2	*P value*
Data analytics	67.12	83.43	6.679	0.01
Data security	70.75	78.45	1.566	0.211
App development	65.41	85.78	10.537	0.001
Collaborative software	67.57	82.81	5.776	0.016
Non-technical skills	73.59	74.56	0.023	0.878

Source: ** Significant at 0.05 probability level; * Significant at 0.1 probability level

Discussion and Conclusion

The COVID-19 pandemic had a devastating impact on the Indonesian TTI and either hindered or halted the country's progress towards SDG8. As the AFS subsector is deemed to be facing skills shortages at the country level (CMEARI, 2020), the TTI-specific policy responses so far have assumed that the post-pandemic recovery of the sector hinges on promoting the digital transition and reimagining tourism for the future as well as the future of tourism. In this context, the findings on the CSG and the divide between AFS and TPW sectors regarding digital readiness highlight LTBs specific digitalisation challenges in Indonesia. The fact that LTBs in the AFS sector are yet to prioritise the need for digital skills should be understood as a needs-driven mindset. For example, an AFS-related workforce may not immediately need advanced AI/Digital Applications to run hotels or restaurants compared to a TPW-related workforce dependent on digital technologies to provide logistics and services expeditiously.

In a recently edited volume titled *Industry 4.0 for SMEs: Challenges, Opportunities, and Requirements*, Matt and Rauch (2020) contend from a techno-centric perspective that 'a significant opportunity for the future lies in the transfer of Industry 4.0 expertise and technologies in SMEs' (p. viii). Nonetheless, the findings above raise the question of how this transfer is happening or is likely to happen among SMEs like LTBs in Indonesia, that is, dealing with socio-economic inequalities, for example, lack of digital infrastructure. The contributions of this chapter are twofold. First, it highlights the challenges associated with the uptake of digital technologies. Second, it demonstrates the need for TTI-specific initiatives to bridge the CSG among SMEs like LTBs.

Nonetheless, this research is not free from limitations. Because of the sample size, the extent of digital resistance and readiness of LTBs, and the associated CSG may differ from what is reported here. Future studies might build on the findings of a single-point pre-pandemic data and longitudinally investigate the CSG among LTBs across Indonesia. It is in this context that CSG-related implications will be discussed next.

First, it is clear from the extent of LTB's responses that if disruptive digital technologies are to be a vehicle for strengthening the Indonesian TTI sector, the national digital agenda needs a strong and tourism-specific policy focus. Policy priorities on digital spheres will only occur when technological advances have straightforward utility in productivity and political opportunities. For example, the Indonesian government's intention to exploit digital tourism opportunities beyond popular destinations like Bali (Ministry of Investment, n.d.) is evident from the five super-priority tourist destinations initiative. However, unlike other countries in the region, the Indonesian agenda is broad and not necessarily backed up with specific digitisation mechanisms and targets for the TTI. In contrast, the Thailand 4.0 initiative specifically targets medical and wellness segments under health tourism (Kohpaiboon, 2020). The fact that Indonesia is behind its regional counterparts in terms of digital readiness (EIU, 2018), coupled with the country's tourism sector's lacklustre standing in digitalisation (WEF, 2019), presents an opportunity for the non-governmental and tourism sectors to engage in collaborative efforts to learn from other emerging economies in the region to develop TTI-specific digital priorities within the 'Making Indonesia 4.0' strategy. For example, in a recent Asia-Pacific-wide survey, respondents perceived employers as responsible for upskilling the workforce (Bhandari, 2023). Consequently, there is growing evidence that influential non-governmental actors, for example, the Angel Investment Network Indonesia (ANGIN), are engaged in developing and implementing interventions to overcome CSG that match the digital needs of the labour market (Dhakal et al., 2021).

Second, although it has been posited that digital technologies have a critical role to play in the revival of tourism in the post-pandemic era (Sharma et al., 2021), LTBs are unlikely to make workforce-related changes that focus on digitalisation without government investment and business interest in digital infrastructure in terms of access, as well as a push toward reskilling/upskilling the workforce for the future (see Stylos et al., 2021; Dhakal & Tjorko, 2020). The lack of capacity or willingness to invest and strategically overcome digital CSG among many LTBs in this study reflects a ground-level reality despite policy-level ambitions at a national level (see OECD, 2020). If the digital era is to enable the adoption of new digital systems among LTBs to foster innovative organisational solutions (see Bissola & Imperatori, 2020), TTI-specific initiatives within the 'Making Indonesia 4.0' to guide and support LTBs to gradually develop a digital-ready workforce are a prerequisite for overcoming CSG.

Disclosure Statement

No potential conflict of interest was reported by the author(s).

Note

* Corresponding author: subas.dhakal@une.edu.au.

References

Alam, S. S., Masukujjaman, M., Susmit, S., Susmit, S., & Abd Aziz, H. (2022). Augmented reality adoption intention among travel and tour operators in Malaysia: Mediation effect of value alignment. *Journal of Tourism Futures*. https://doi.org/10.1108/JTF-03-2021-0072

Antara News. (2022, 15 June). Tourism sector plays vital role in achieving Indonesia's SDGs. https://en.antaranews.com/news/234269/tourism-sector-plays-vital-role-in-achieving-indonesias-sdgs

Armoo, A. K., Franklyn-Green, L. G., & Braham, A. J. (2020). The fourth industrial revolution: A game-changer for the tourism and maritime industries. *Worldwide Hospitality and Tourism Themes*, *12*(1), 13–23.

Badan Pusat Statistik (BPS). (2021). *Number of accommodation, average worker, and visitor per day by province 2009–2018*. Government of Indonesia. www.bps.go.id/subject/6/tenaga-kerja.html),%20and%20most%20of%20them%20are%20private%20domestic%20companies

BCA. (2022). *MSMEs: Definitions, types and criteria*. https://www.bca.co.id/en/informasi/Edukatips/2022/02/10/03/15/kenali-pengertian-umkm-jenis-dan-kriteria-bisnis-di-dalamnya

Bhandari, R. (2023). *Bridging the skills gap: Fuelling careers and the economy in Indonesia*. https://impact.economist.com/perspectives/economic-development/bridging-skills-gap-fuelling-careers-and-economy-indonesia

Bissola, R., & Imperatori, B. (2020). *HRM in the industry 4.0 era: Are workers still in the center? HRM 4.0 for human-centered organisations*. Emerald Publishing Limited.

Buhalis, D., & Moldavska, I. (2021). In-room voice-based AI digital assistants transforming on-site hotel services and guests' experiences. In W. Wörndl, C. Koo, & J. L. Steinmetz (Eds.), *Information and communication technologies in tourism 2021 proceedings of the ENTER 2021 eTourism conference* (pp. 30–44). Springer.

Coordinating Ministry for Economic Affairs of the Republic of Indonesia (CMEARI). (2020). *Indonesia's critical occupations list 2018*. Author.

Dhakal, S. P. (2021). Accommodation & food services. In A. Nankervis, J. Connell, A. Montague, & J. Burgess (Eds.), *The fourth industrial revolution what does it mean for Australian industry?* (Chapter 5). Springer.

Dhakal, S. P., Dahal, D., & Dahal, S. (2020). Nepal. In A. Nankervis, J. Connell, & J. Burgess (Eds.), *The future of work in Asia and beyond: A technological revolution or evolution?* (Chapter 11, pp. 167–183). Routledge.

Dhakal, S. P., Karamina, K., Tjorko, S. P., Burgess, J., & Cameron, R. (2021, 11 November). *Entrepreneurship & SDGs in Indonesia*. Paper presented at the SEAANZ Symposium: SMEs and COVID-19: Just Surviving or Thriving? Sorting Rhetoric from the Realities of COVID-19 for SMEs.

Dhakal, S. P., & Tjorko, S. P. (2020). Travel and tourism workforce planning and development for sustainable development in Indonesia. In K. Dayaram, L. Lambey, J. Burgess, & T. W. Afrianty (Eds.), *Developing the workforce in an emerging economy: The case of Indonesia* (Chapter 13, pp. 165–176). Routledge.

Dhakal, S. P., & Tjokro, S. P. (2022). Tourism enterprises in Indonesia and the fourth industrial revolution—are they ready? *Tourism Recreation Research*. https://doi.org/10.1080/02508281.2021.1996687

Economist Intelligence Unit (EIU). (2018). *The automation readiness index: Who is ready for the coming wave of automation?* www.automationreadiness.eiu.com/static/download/PDF.pdf

Fritz, R. L., & Vandermause, R. (2018). Data collection via in-depth email interviewing: Lessons from the field. *Qualitative Health Research*, *28*(10), 1640–1649.

Government of Indonesia. (2021). *Indonesia's Voluntary National Review (VNR) 2021*. Government of Indonesia. https://sustainabledevelopment.un.org/content/documents/280892021_VNR_Report_Indonesia.pdf

Gatti, C., Aquilani, B., & Piccarrozi, M. (2018). Special issue call for papers: Industry 4.0 and the Internet of things: Changes in business model, strategy formulation and implementation, firm operations towards sustainable development and sustainability. *Sustainability, MDPI*. www.mdpi.com/journal/sustainability/special_issues/Industry_4.0#info

Global Goals. (2023). *8. Promote sustained, inclusive, and sustainable economic growth, full and productive employment, and decent work*. www.globalgoals.org/goals/8-decent-work-and-economic-growth/

Halim, D., Johnson, H. C., & Perova, E. (2022). Preschool availability and women's employment: Evidence from Indonesia. *Economic Development and Cultural Change*, *71*(1), 39–61.

Harsono, N. (2022). Despite improvements, Indonesia's digital literacy remains low. https://www.thejakartapost.com/business/2022/01/20/despite-improvements-indonesias-digital-literacy-remains-low.html.
ILO. (n.d.). *Skills and employability in Asia and the Pacific*. International Labour Organisation. https://www.ilo.org/regions-and-countries/asia-and-pacific-deprecated/ilo-asia-and-pacific/areas-work/skills-and-employability-asia-and-pacific
ILO. (2021). *Modelling and comparing the employment impacts of COVID-19 crisis and recovery policies in Indonesia*. www.ilo.org/wcmsp5/groups/public/—ed_emp/—emp_ent/documents/publication/wcms_866943.pdf
Kohpaiboon, A. (2020). *Industry 4.0 policies in Thailand*. Yusof Ishak Institute. http://hdl.handle.net/11540/11693
Korn Ferry. (2015). *The global talent crunch: Country perspective: Indonesia*. https://focus.kornferry.com/wp-content/uploads/2015/02/KF-Talent-Crunch-Country-Report-Indonesia-Digital-2.pdf
Levesque, E. M. (2019). *Understanding the skills gap—and what employers can do about it*. www.brookings.edu/articles/understanding-the-skills-gap-and-what-employers-can-do-about-it/
Matt, D. T., & Rauch, E. (2020). SME 4.0: The role of small-and medium-sized enterprises in the digital transformation. Industry 4.0 for SMEs. In D. T. Matt, V. Modrák, & H. Zsifkovits (Eds.), *Industry 4.0 for SMEs challenges, opportunities and requirements*. Palgrave Macmillan.
Ministry of Investment. (n.d.). *Indonesian tourism investment: How is it looking?* https://www9.investindonesia.go.id/en/article-investment/detail/indonesian-tourism-investment-how-is-it-looking
Nankervis, A., Connell, J., Cameron, R., Montague, A., & Prikshat, V. (2021). 'Are we there yet?' Australian HR professionals and the Fourth Industrial Revolution. *Asia Pacific Journal of Human Resources*, *59*(1), 3–19.
Nugraha, E. (2018). *Making Indonesia's Industry 4.0*. The Australia-Indonesia Centre. Retrieved 1 October 2019, from http://australiaindonesia.com/digital-economy/making-indonesias-industry-4-0/
Nur, A. C., Burhanuddin, B., Niswaty, R., Cante, S. R., & Akib, H. (2021). Opportunity to develop tourism potential based on entrepreneurial outbreaks of endemic covid-19 in South Sulawesi Indonesia. *Journal of Entrepreneurship & Organization Management*, *10*(7), 1–5.
O'Connor, P. (2023). Small-and medium-sized tourism enterprises and smart tourism: Tourism agenda 2030 perspective article. *Tourism Review*, *78*(2), 339–343.
OECD. (2020). *OECD tourism trends and policies*. https://doi.org/10.1787/6b47b985-en
Ollivaud, P., & Haxton, P. (2019). *Making the most of tourism in Indonesia to promote sustainable regional development*. OECD Publishing.
Osei, B. A., Ragavan, N. A., Mensah, H. K., & Kandappan, B. (2020). Hospitality revolution 4.0: A literature review on a unified typology of IR 4.0 technologies for the tourism and hospitality industry in the era of COVID-19. *Asia-Pacific Journal of Innovation in Hospitality and Tourism*, *9*(1), 25–45.
Prasetyo, B. D., Kurniadi, R., & Setyowati, R. (2020, August). Industry 4.0 and the future challenges for the local community to manage ecotourism (a case study of the participatory ecotourism management in Menipo Island, West Timor, Indonesia). In *IOP Conference Series: Earth and Environmental Science* (Vol. 533, No. 1, p. 012002). IOP Publishing.
Schwab, K. (2017). *The fourth industrial revolution*. World Economic Forum.
Sharma, G. D., Thomas, A., & Paul, J. (2021). Reviving tourism industry post-COVID-19: A resilience-based framework. *Tourism Management Perspectives*, *37*, 100786.

Shofa, N. J. (2022, 14 July). Tech to displace 23m jobs, but it can create more. *Jakarta Globe*. https://jakartaglobe.id/tech/tech-to-displace-23m-jobs-but-it-can-create-more
Stylos, N., Fotiadis, A. K., Shin, D. D., & Huan, T. C. T. (2021). Beyond smart systems adoption: Enabling diffusion and assimilation of smartness in hospitality. *International Journal of Hospitality Management*, *98*, 103042.
Subawa, N. S., Widhiasthini, N. W., Astawa, I. P., Dwiatmadja, C., & Permatasari, N. P. I. (2021). The practices of virtual reality marketing in the tourism sector, a case study of Bali, Indonesia. *Current Issues in Tourism*, *24*(23), 3284–3295.
Sunil, P. (2021). *Indonesia's plans to boost human resources in five 'super-priority' tourist destinations.* www.humanresourcesonline.net/indonesia-s-plans-to-boost-human-resources-in-five-super-priority-tourist-destinations
Syafrian, D. (2022, 15 August). Improving digital access and utilisation for SMEs. *Jakarta Globe*. https://jakartaglobe.id/opinion/improving-digital-access-and-utilization-for-smes
Tambunan, T. (2008, August 11). *SME development in Indonesia: Do economic growth and government supports matter?* SSRN: https://ssrn.com/abstract=1218922 or http://dx.doi.org/10.2139/ssrn.1218922
UNWTO. (2021). International tourism highlights. https://www.e-unwto.org/doi/pdf/10.18111/9789284422456
The World Bank. (2021). *Unemployment.* https://data.worldbank.org/indicator/SL.UEM.1524.ZS?locations=ID
The World Economic Forum (WEF). (2019). *The global competitiveness report.* Author.
World Travel and Tourism Centre (WTTC). (2022a). *Indonesia 2022 annual research: Key highlights.* Author. https://wttc.org/DesktopModules/MVC/FactSheets/pdf/704/131_20220613162338_Indonesia2022_.pdf
World Travel and Tourism Centre (WTTC). (2022b). *More than five million new travel & tourism jobs to be created in Indonesia within the next decade.* https://wttc.org/news-article/more-than-five-million-new-travel-and-tourism-jobs-to-be-created-in-indonesia-within-the-next-decade
Wyman, O. (2020). *The future of travel & tourism in the wake of COVID-19.* World Travel and Tourism Centre (WTTC). https://wttc.org/initiatives/to-recovery-beyond

11 Digital Transformation and Its Impact on the Malaysian Labour Market

Skill Shortages and the Future of Work

Jason J. Turner, Nadiah Suki, and Nan Jiang*

Introduction

Digital transformation is frequently referred to in the academic and practitioner literature as a phrase that characterises business change. Although no one definitional size fits all as digital transformation is context-specific, the phrase is arguably perceived as the latest revolutionary cycle or transition where businesses engage with technology to make operational improvements to performance and efficiency, and afford employees the opportunity to upskill and reskill themselves, enhancing their digital engagement and literacy (Chan et al., 2021). While sharing similarities to previous transformational or change-related evolutions, digital transformation is arguably different, stimulating a degree of attitudinal and behavioural change among the labour force, particularly the youth. Many current and prospective employees have not simply accepted the need for digital upskilling as inevitable to remain employed; rather, some have engaged in digital self-improvement to transition to the gig economy, become entrepreneurial, and/or pursue a better work-life balance, which has created a skill gap and, in some sectors, a skill shortage. Digital transformation has been transitional for both businesses and employees, being associated with labour trends such as the 'great attrition', 'digital fatigue', and 'work worship', as well as contributing to the sustainable development goal (SDG) 8—decent work and economic growth.

For those employees who felt that their employment relationship was more transactional, lacking the antecedents of employer recognition for their labour (Thapa, 2022), digital transformation has opened up socio-economic choices in the labour market, which has, in part, facilitated the great attrition, a phenomenon felt across Asia, although arguably not as severely as in Western countries. For those employees who chose to remain with their employer, many have exhibited digital fatigue and inertia, demonstrating resistance towards enhancing their skills set as employers drive initiatives to 'optimise' the use and usefulness of technology and embed digital culture into the business (Schmid, 2019; Haskamp et al., 2021; McKinsey Digital, 2022). This resistance, underpinned by the notion that transformation is designed to improve efficiencies and reduce costs rather than enhancing the workplace

DOI: 10.4324/9781003379065-13

and easing the human capital burden, has arguably contributed to a lack of alignment between skill development and market needs, with only 20–30% of businesses in Malaysia considering their 'transition' successful (Walker, 2020). A lack of employee consultation in the digital transformation process has been argued to create a disenfranchised workforce (Tabrizi et al., 2019; Salmeron, 2020; Trenerry et al., 2021) and would appear to drive employees further and prospective employees to re-evaluate their career choices and skills relative to the labour market. This chapter investigates the relationship between digital transformation, the labour market in Malaysia, its role in skill development and shortages, and the links to SDG #8.

Although skill development and shortages in the Malaysian labour market have previously been explored in government-led policy and practitioner literature, there still appears to be a lack of an accepted solution on how best to address skill shortages across industry sectors and even less discussion on the role that digital transformation has played and will play in tackling skill development and shortages in Malaysia. This chapter, incorporating a literature review, methodology, analysis, discussion, and conclusion sections, explores the growing importance of transitional digital skills, and by reflecting on the perceptions of identified stakeholders, it assesses whether such skill shortages can be effectively resolved so that the workforce can be better prepared for the future challenges of work.

Literature Review

Digital Transformation

Digital disruption has impacted business and society globally in relatively equal measure, in part precipitating and driving digital transformation within organisations. There are various definitions of 'digital transformation' (Gartner, 2021; Wessel et al., 2021), with differing motivations and approaches to implementation. However, it is generally agreed that digital transformation is an integrated approach that involves a series of processes (Gurbaxani & Dunkle, 2019), aligning with the objectives of the business (Peter et al., 2020; Verhoef et al., 2021) and an 'end-goal' of digital maturity and the creation of value (Gudergan et al., 2019; Kutnjak et al., 2019; Gökalp & Martinez, 2021). The narrative of technological adoption over the years has largely been met with employee scepticism because of the resultant job uncertainty and potential unemployment (Mills, 2018; Plis & Schislyaeva, 2020; Sima et al., 2020), where organisations tend to focus on operational efficiencies and less on employee consultation or an assessment of their digital skills preparedness (Tabrizi et al., 2019; Salmeron, 2020; Trenerry et al., 2021).

In the context of digital transformation, the organisational perspective has evolved, in theory, from perceiving employees as a resource or unit of production to achieve organisational goals towards 'human capital', where there is training and employee support, towards a reciprocal employer-employee relationship with mutual benefit (Nicolás-Agustín et al., 2021). Such training is likely to be personalised to the needs of the individual employee, encouraging an understanding of the working relationship with digital learning rather than being threatened by it (Bresciani et al., 2021; Delfanti & Frey, 2021). This role evolution is expected to be increasingly important to develop digital talent and to retain employees as well as to prevent the attrition (de Smet et al., 2021), of those employees who prefer the flexibility of the gig economy (Kuhn et al., 2021). The preference of young people and the new generation of workers is often towards flexibility and the gig economy (Kuhn et al., 2021), which has the potential to create gaps in the skills portfolio of the organisation. The demands of work have changed in a post-pandemic environment, with workers preferring work flexibility and better work-life balance, rather than engaging with additional work and re- and upskilling (Saul, 2022).

Malaysian Labour Market

Malaysia is a country comprising 13 states and 3 Federal territories with a population of circa 34 million in 2023. The labour market, in contrast to the population trend, has observed declining unemployment figures to around 3.5% in 2023, with a return to pre-pandemic figures of 3.3% anticipated in 2024 (Department of Statistics Malaysia, 2023; Sofiah, 2023a). In line with declining unemployment, the number of job vacancies has also shown a downward trend since the pandemic, with the number of vacancies in 2023 standing at around 200,000, which is its lowest figure since August 2021 (Sofiah, 2023a). Overall, the number of individuals considered employed has increased to 16.06 million (Department of Statistics Malaysia, 2023), with a labour force participation rate of 69.8% (Department of Statistics Malaysia, 2023). These figures present a relatively positive outlook for the labour market, but there is an underlying issue concerning the growing digital talent and an identified skills gap (Ismail, 2023; Ling et al., 2023).

Digital Skills in Malaysia

The Malaysian government has introduced a series of policy initiatives to address an identified skills gap and better engage with the $14.5 trillion ICT sector (Mohammad, 2023) and the resultant job opportunities (Ling et al., 2023), which include the National Digital Skills Strategy, the Digital Economy Blueprint (MyDIGITAL), and the MADANI policy framework (JAC Recruitment, 2023; Khairun, 2023; Mohammad, 2023). The Ministry of Human Resources, which is responsible for skill development, employment, labour unions, and occupational health and safety, and the Malaysian Critical Occupations List (MyCOL) have identified several areas which are required to be addressed if SDG 8—decent work and economic growth—is to be achieved. The first to emerge, supported by human capital reports from government-led and professional bodies, was that the ICT, construction, manufacturing, and aerospace industries were identified as sectors experiencing skill shortages and mismatches (Mohammad, 2023; Sofiah, 2023b). The theme of graduate work readiness (GWR) is revealed here, with the 'skills and competencies of the workforce, particularly amongst fresh graduates, do not meet the requirements of industry employers' (Sofiah, 2023b, p. 5). A mixture of graduates leaving Malaysia to pursue opportunities overseas (Jaafar, 2022) and lacking the necessary skills to compete in a specialised industry has created a skill shortage in the market overall and in these sectors in particular. The second issue which also impacts on graduates is the challenge of underemployment, where the employment position secured by a graduate does not align with their skills set and/or educational background (Poo, 2022; Sofiah, 2023b). The third issue is talent retention, where the advent of digital transformation has disrupted the labour market, encouraging individuals to engage with the gig economy, become self-employed, and/or pursue employment which offers better work/life balance. This has led to a gap between the demand for certain skilled workers in Malaysia and a lack of supply of these skills, such as soft skills and digital skills including digital literacy, data analysis, coding, cybersecurity, digital marketing, and cloud computing (JAC Recruitment, 2023; Mohammad, 2023; Sofiah, 2023b). The labour force is argued by organisations to be 'slow' technology adopters, resisting upskilling in these areas, which is considered a consequence of digital disruption (Naeem, 2022).

Skills and Competencies

When businesses digitalise, their key resources are information technology, employee skills, and digital strategy (Eller et al., 2020). The process of digital transformation is not all about technology but competence (Anderson et al., 2021): the willingness to evolve via digital cultural shifts (Berges & Kon, 2019) and organisations' adaptive capability (Rangaswamy, 2021). The employee skills gap is one of the major obstacles to digital transformation in business (Dhasarathy, 2020). There is worker commoditisation in the lower-skilled labour category, whereby employees' work processes are controlled by machinic algorithms (Delfanti & Frey, 2021), and employees are more easily replaceable (Gilbert, 2021). Higher digital skills are currently required of employees: employees with improved digital skills earn more income than their less-skilled counterparts, and employees are encouraged to 'upskill' to fit their job descriptions and remain relevant in the workplace (Varshney, 2020). In a digital workplace, employees collaborate and connect, and businesses face human capital hurdles such as employee engagement and leading their employees (Haddud & McAllen, 2018). It is considered optimal for organisations to have employees rated high on the 'digital affordance actualisation' scale as they are more likely to support the organisation's digital transformation initiative (Kozanoglu & Abedin, 2020). Low-skilled or unskilled employees experience digital transformation differently: the former are more at risk unless they upgrade their skills (Delfanti & Frey, 2021; Gilbert, 2021). Labour-intensive and lower-skilled workers tend to be at risk, or more skilled workers are put under pressure to upskill when work is reorganised around technology infrastructure, such as automation, artificial intelligence, and machine learning (Günsel & Yamen, 2020).

More digitally savvy employees may be more suited to adapt to this change, leaving lower-skilled labour at risk of higher churn in 'digital capitalism'. Compared to their more skilled counterparts, unskilled workers face a greater turnover threat (Delfanti & Frey, 2021). During the pandemic, digital workspaces became the default position as organisations adapted to a new way of working in various states of readiness. The Internet connectivity and virtual network enabled these workspaces to exploit and manage information (White, 2012), drive work processes by digital data and analytics (Ozcan, 2019), and are mobilised via the use of remote teams (Walsh, 2019). By leveraging on IR5.0, industries achieve increased efficiency, enhanced productivity, and reduced labour costs; however, the disadvantages are rising unemployment and the reduction of human capital creativity (Sima et al., 2020).

Employee Disengagement

Employees are arguably interested in participating in digital transformation, but many do not know how or where they can contribute (Newman et al., 2020). This lack of engagement has caused many related issues, such as the expectation (stress) on employees to upskill/improve their digital literacy (Kozanoglu & Abedin, 2020; Chan et al., 2021). In some cases, this leads to employee attrition when employees feel that they are part of a 'transactional' instead of an 'interactional' relationship with the employers and their jobs (Thapa, 2022). Among employees who remained in the organisation, digital inertia, fatigue, and resistance (towards technology adoption) set in, and employers struggled in their 'push' to achieve the 'optimisation' of technology (Schmid, 2019; Haskamp et al., 2021; McKinsey Digital, 2022).

Disengaged employees were found to be more influential in discouraging other employees' participation in the digital transformation process compared to engaged co-workers (Mitra et al., 2017), underlining the importance of re-training disengaged employees to reduce resistance, boost participation, and prevent employee burnout (Alexander et al., 2021). Nicolás-Agustín et al., 2021) argued that the mediating role of human resources is to ensure 'strategic alignment' and 'digital transformation' and enable the workforce to adapt to the new digital environment. Moving forward to the future of decentralised data models and open/collaborative environments, empowering employees in key skills will enable businesses to experiment with customised solutions for each organisation (Bechtel et al., 2021). If implemented correctly, digital transformation will motivate employees to participate, reduce turnover, retain talent (Gilbert, 2021), and create an environment to engage with digital talent growth better.

Methodology

The research for this chapter used a qualitative, semi-structured interview approach with 12 Malaysian managers and 13 employees from 5 businesses in the information and communication technology (ICT) industry. It was considered relevant to focus on the ICT industry in particular because of its importance to the Malaysian economy, contributing 22.6% to Malaysian GDP (International Trade Association, 2022), and the fact that businesses in this industry have exhibited a significant degree of digital transformation. The research interviewed managers and employees to gain a comparative perspective on the relationships between digital transformation, the labour market in Malaysia, and its role in skill development and shortages, which informs SDG 8: decent work and economic growth. Using a convenience sample of businesses known to the research team and representative of the sector, five businesses agreed to participate in the research.

In line with the ethical process approved by the educational institution to which two of the researchers belong, the researchers contacted respondents via telephone in April 2023. Potential respondents were provided with an overview of the research, and the voluntary nature of engaging with the interview: 20 managers and 15 employees provided an initial response, with eight managers and two employees eventually 'opting out' of the interview process, leaving 25 respondents willing and able to participate in the interviews. The interviews were carried out with those 25 respondents face-to-face over four months. The number of respondents was considered valid and in line with the literature, which advises between 5 and 20 respondents to be a valid sample for qualitative research (Cresswell & Cresswell, 2018), with the adequacy of the sample underlined by reaching saturation (Hennink & Kaiser, 2021). The questions were derived from the literature and pilot-tested for understandability and clarity. The responses were analysed using content analysis, which allowed for a better understanding of respondents' experiences from their individual and collective perspectives, and the underlying impact of digital transformation on human capital, skill development, and shortages. The approach allowed for the interpretation and deriving of meaning (Denzin & Lincoln, 2017), with coding used to assign meaning to statements and interpret the data (Strauss & Corbin, 2008).

Results and Discussion

The respondents' demographic information is summarised in Table 11.1, where it is revealed that most respondents were male. This was not considered a limitation of the research, given that the focus was not on gender; however, it did reveal an interesting perspective relating to length of service, with males observed to have a shorter working relationship with the company than their female counterparts. As indicated earlier, the composition of the industry background was focused on ICT services, representative of the fact that ICT is a popular industry

Table 11.1 Respondent demographics

Respondent	*Gender*	*Business*	*Working engagement*
Employ1	Male	1	Less than 5 years
Employ2	Male	1	More than 10 years
Employ3	Female	1	Less than 5 years
Employ4	Male	2	Between 5 and 10 years
Employ5	Male	2	Less than 5 years
Employ6	Male	3	Less than 5 years
Employ7	Female	3	More than 10 years
Employ8	Male	4	Less than 5 years
Employ9	Male	4	Less than 5 years
Employ10	Male	5	Less than 5 years
Employ11	Female	5	Between 5 and 10 years
Employ12	Female	5	Between 5 and 10 years
Employee1	Female	1	Between 5 and 10 years
Employee2	Female	1	Between 5 and 10 years
Employee3	Female	1	Between 5 and 10 years
Employee4	Female	2	More than 10 years
Employee5	Female	2	Less than 5 years
Employee6	Male	2	Less than 5 years
Employee7	Male	3	Less than 5 years
Employee8	Male	3	Less than 5 years
Employee9	Male	4	Less than 5 years
Employee10	Female	4	Less than 5 years
Employee11	Female	5	Less than 5 years
Employee12	Male	5	Between 5 and 10 years
Employee13	Female	5	Between 5 and 10 years

(*Note:* 'Employ' refers to managers)

in Malaysia, exhibiting a significant degree of digital transformation. In terms of ethnic background, most respondents were Chinese and Malay (Bumiputera), which does not necessarily represent the current population, with 62.5% considered Bumiputera, 20.6% Chinese, 6.2% Indian, 0.9% considered 'other', and 9.8% considered non-citizens (Statista, 2023). This was not considered a limitation of the study, given that the research was not exploring the relationship between ethnicity, digital transformation, and skill shortages.

To address the objectives of this research, the qualitative responses from both managers and employees were grouped around three main themes: digital transformation and skills; sector skill gap; and digital transformation and the future of work. After gathering the insights from each group of respondents, there were commonalities and new discoveries. Throughout the analysis of the qualitative data, representative quotes from respondents are used to evidence the themes that emerged from the interviews.

Digital Transformation

All respondents, regardless of length of service, business, gender, or whether they were employees or managers, understood the concept of digital transformation, identifying that it is a process that requires implementing digital input to enhance business operations. A typical response was 'It is a process of adopting and implementing digital technology to improve the business', which aligns with the literature (Gökalp & Martinez, 2021). The fact that all respondents understood the concept of digital transformation suggests that all subsequent responses were founded on informed opinion.

There was a degree of variation in responses concerning how involved respondents felt in the digital transformation process and what they perceived as its purpose relative to the business. Most managers felt they were involved in the process and understood the purpose of digital transformation to improve operational efficiency, with a typical response being 'I, and the rest of the senior management, were very much involved in the roll-out. It was to improve operational efficiency and processes.' A minority of managers referred to 'improved financial performance and customer satisfaction' as the purpose of digital transformation, but no employer mentioned the opportunities for the workforce to upskill themselves or improve their digital literacy, which is argued to be one of the consequences of digital transformation (Kozanoglu & Abedin, 2020; Chan et al., 2021). In contrast, all employees felt that they were not involved in the digital transformation process but understood its purpose, with a typical response being 'I was not really involved in the implementation, but I know that it is to improve the business and its operations.' A minority of employees from across three businesses added, 'digital transformation is meant to improve the operations and all those in the business', alluding to the human capital impact of digital transformation. It is this perceived lack of employee engagement and its consequences on the disenfranchised employee that link to potential skill gaps and shortages, which are discussed in the next section of the chapter.

Skill Training and Digital Transformation

Respondents were asked to assess the role of digital transformation in developing skills and what skills were developed as an outcome in their respective businesses. All management respondents indicated that digital transformation necessitated employee upskilling for an identified skill gap across all businesses. The identified skills varied across responses but included all skills reported by managers: 'leadership; digital analytics; digital marketing; communications; governance and ethics; remote working and the ability to work independently'. Most managers indicated the importance of digital literacy, which, although a broad concept, meant that 'digital transformation has revealed areas where there were skills gaps in digital literacy, communications, digital analytics, digital marketing, and governance'. The responses from managers also reflect the literature (Chan et al., 2021; Ismail, 2023), but what was perhaps more interesting was that most managers indicated that there was a degree of resistance among some employees towards upskilling and enhancing digital literacy. A typical response was 'We identified gaps in the skill set of our staff and introduced training which they attended, but we did not see an upturn in skills development.' Another manager from the same business indicated that 'staff feel more comfortable doing what they do and not in adding to their skill set'. Resistance to digital transformation has been identified in the literature (Al-Haddad & Kotnour, 2015), with reasons for that resistance in part revealed by the employees interviewed in this research.

The majority of employees indicated that digital transformation had led to an identified need in their skill set, having to adapt to new ways of working and develop new skills. The identified skills were common across responses, with a typical response being 'We had to learn new digital skills, data analytics, automation, and learning'. These identified themes echo those cited by employers and the literature (Poo, 2022; Ismail, 2023; Sofiah, 2023b) and link to identified skill gaps in the Malaysian labour market. In a partial response to managers' identification of resistance, the majority of employees indicated that the motivation to learn digital skills and to enhance their digital literacy was, in part, the fear of losing their jobs and, in part, to enhance their employment prospects. Typical responses were 'You worry you are going to be replaced by AI, so you learn new skills' and 'Learning new technical or digital skills helps your career, whether you want to stay in this job or get another.' A minority of employees felt anxious with regard to the constant training, and although not resistant to upskilling and reskilling, they felt the incessant nature of the training was leading to burnout. A typical response was 'I am tired of the additional training which I have to do at night or weekends. You still have to do your job plus more work, it leaves you tired and anxious, not knowing what training is coming next.' Two respondents added that they are considering leaving their current job within the next six months to 'have a better work/life balance'. It is interesting to see the contrast between management and employee perspectives, where employers identify resistance to digital skilling but not necessarily the reasons for this resistance. There appears to be a gap between the stakeholders which must be addressed if these organisations and the Malaysian economy more broadly are to realise SDG 8: decent work and economic growth.

The Sector Skill Gap

Respondents were asked if there was a skill gap in their sector and what measures could be taken to address this identified gap. Most managers felt that there was a shortage of skilled graduates and, more broadly, potential employees lacking communication, leadership, and digital analytics skills. A typical response was 'In our sector, new graduates lack soft skills and analytical skills. They need to be able to use the industry software.' A minority of managers indicated that if skilled employees leave the industry and graduates continue to lack the necessary digital skills, there will be a critical skill shortage. A typical response was 'Although we have only lost two staff in the past six months, if we start to lose more and cannot replace them, we will have a staff shortage, which will impact the business.'

In contrast, managers did not identify the onboarding of graduates as an issue, but rather that the depth and breadth of skills required to do the job were the main issue. The majority of employees indicated that there was a skill gap in communication, leadership, project management and analytics, and a minority of respondents indicated that they knew this because 'we get training on leadership, communication and project management, so these must be the areas where there is a lack of skills'. The majority of respondents indicated that they themselves identified skill gaps in the sector but that employers should provide more time and incentives for training.

A typical response was 'There are skill gaps in the business; project management, communication, and analytical skills are lacking, particularly among younger employees. Businesses should give more time to do the training otherwise we are going to burnout.' A minority of employees indicated that younger staff may resist the dual nature of the job, which would leave businesses with additional recruitment problems: 'the new generation might not be so happy doing two jobs, training at night. Yes, there is a skills gap, but they might not see it like that and leave'.

The Role of Digital Transformation in the Future of Work

As has been alluded to earlier, digital transformation will continue to impact the ICT sector, other sectors, and employees. The majority of both managers and employees in our study indicated that they saw no end to change in the sector, with managers in particular identifying a widening gap between the needs of the business and the skills set of new employees. Typical responses were 'digital transformation is driving change so much that there is an increasing gap in knowledge between what the future employee is being taught and what is needed in industry' and, 'the gap between what graduates know and need to know is getting bigger'. A minority of managers also touched on the fragile nature of 'new' employees who possessed a different mindset towards work and life and having to multi-task at the same time as multi-skilling themselves. A typical response was 'new employees to the business, I mean younger employees maybe don't want to take on so much which means they won't have the skills to do the job in the future'. Most employees acknowledged the skill gap, with a minority indicating that they planned on leaving the business they are currently in and the sector to do, as five respondents referred to it as 'something different'. The majority of respondents indicated that the sector would be 'a difficult place to work if the pace of digital change continues'. A minority of respondents were optimistic, indicating that 'continued automation will make the job easier in the future, we can then focus on the project management'.

Conclusion

In an increasingly disruptive labour market, it is the responsibility of identified stakeholders to ensure a suitably prepared workforce for the future. These stakeholders include the government, organisations, education providers, and employees, both current and prospective (Khairun, 2023), who collectively must engender a framework that can position Malaysia at the forefront of digital talent development. The research revealed three main themes from the interviews with managers and employees: digital transformation and skills, ICT sector skill gap, and digital transformation and the future of work. All respondents understood the concept of digital transformation and its impact on the labour market as well as the economy but disagreed on the motivation behind its implementation and the level of engagement they had with its introduction and continued use in their respective organisations. This was an underlying theme in this research: a contrast in opinion on the relationship between digital transformation and skill development. Both managers and employees did, however, agree that there was a digital skill gap in the sector, with identified shortages in part due to employee resistance to digital transformation, perceiving upskilling and reskilling as additional work rather than an opportunity to future-proof their career aspirations. The research revealed that specific skills were lacking in the industry, and attempts to upskill and reskill employees had mixed success, with some employees pursuing alternative employment as a result, which in turn created unfilled vacancies in the organisation.

The research consolidates existing research in the area of GWR and the future of work, taking research forward in the area of employee readiness for digital transformation and the necessary skills development associated with this organisational change. With regard to the practical implications, a skill gap has been identified in the ICT sector, which can readily be applied to other sectors where skill shortages and a gap have been acknowledged by government-led policy. The research indicates that for the policy initiatives to prove successful, they have to be appropriately implemented by organisations to avoid being perceived as a top-down strategy that benefits the business and not the workforce, and in turn the Malaysian economy.

With regard to the limitations of this research, it is acknowledged that the methodological approach, although appropriate for this research, would benefit from adding a quantitative dimension and expanding across the construction, manufacturing, and aerospace sectors, which have also been identified as labour markets experiencing skills shortages (Sofiah, 2023b). Such limitations are being addressed by a larger empirical study across Malaysia, which will take the identified research themes forward regarding skill shortages and digital talents. Other areas of further research include gaining additional insight into soft skills development, which have been previously identified as important variables in a disruptive economy, and GWR and future talent engagement with digital transformative organisations. It would also be interesting to understand further the perspectives of different stakeholders, specifically migrant workers, expatriates, and Gen Z employees, with the former groups impacted by Malaysia's work immigration policies, and the latter perceived to have different views on the world of work. A final area for further research would be to conduct a comparative investigation of the generational perspectives related to new technology, particularly AI, which would add further insight into digital literacy and the digital skill gap.

Note

* Corresponding author: jasonturner@apu.edu.my.

References

Al-Haddad, S., & Kotnour, T. (2015). Integrating the organizational change literature: A model for successful change. *Journal of Organizational Change Management*, *28*(2), 234–262. https://doi.org/10.1108/JOCM-11-2013-0215

Alexander, A., De Smet, A., Langstaff, M., & Ravid, D. (2021). *Organization practice: What employees are saying about the future of remote work*. www.mckinsey.com/featured-insights/coronavirus-leading-through-the-crisis/charting-the-path-to-the-next-normal/employee-burnout-is-ubiquitous-alarming-and-still-underreported

Anderson, C., Bieck, C., & Marshall, A. (2021). How business is adapting to COVID-19: Executive insights reveal post-pandemic opportunities. *Strategy and Leadership*, *49*(1), 38–47. https://doi.org/10.1108/SL-11-2020-0140

Bechtel, M., Buscaino, R., Erb, L., Golem, A., & Hickin, R. (2021). Technology futures: Projecting the possible, navigating what's next. *World Economic Forum—Insight Report*.

Berges, R. P., & Kon, F. (2019). "We want change", but who's we? How to transition cultural change in the digital era as a team. *Strategic HR Review*, *18*(5), 210–214. https://doi.org/10.1108/shr-07-2019-0054

Bresciani, S., Ferraris, A., Romano, M., & Santoro, G. (2021). Digital leadership. *Digital Transformation Management for Agile Organizations: A Compass to Sail the Digital World*, *2020*, 97–115. https://doi.org/10.1108/978-1-80043-171-320211006

Chan, A. J., Hooi, L. W., & Ngui, K. S. (2021). Do digital literacies matter in employee engagement in digitalised workplace? *Journal of Asia Business Studies*, *15*(3), 523–540. https://doi.org/10.1108/JABS-08-2020-0318

Cresswell, J. W., & Cresswell, J. D. (2018). *Research design: Qualitative, quantitative and mixed methods approaches* (5th ed.). SAGE.

Delfanti, A., & Frey, B. (2021). Humanly extended automation or the future of work seen through Amazon patents. *Science Technology and Human Values*, *46*(3), 655–682. https://doi.org/10.1177/0162243920943665

Denzin, N. K., & Lincoln, Y. S. (2017). *The SAGE handbook of qualitative research*. SAGE.

Department of Statistics Malaysia. (2023). *Quarterly principal statistics of labour force, Malaysia*. Department of Statistics Malaysia.

De Smet, A., Dowling, B., Mugayar-Baldocchi, M., & Schaninger, B. (2021). "Great attraction" or "great attrition"? The choice is yours. *McKinsey Quarterly*. www.mckinsey.com/business-functions/people-and-organizational-performance/our-insights/great-attrition-or-great-attraction-the-choice-is-yours

Dhasarathy, A. (2020). *Managing the fallout from technology transformations*. www.mckinsey.com/business-functions/mckinsey-digital/our-insights/managing-the-fallout-from-technology-transformations#

Eller, R., Alford, P., Kallmünzer, A., & Peters, M. (2020). Antecedents, consequences, and challenges of small and medium-sized enterprise digitalization. *Journal of Business Research*, *112*(March), 119–127. https://doi.org/10.1016/j.jbusres.2020.03.004

Gartner. (2021). Gartner forecasts worldwide IT spending to reach $4 trillion in 2021. *Gartner.com*. Press Release. www.gartner.com/en/newsroom/press-releases/2021-04-07-gartner-forecasts-worldwide-it-spending-to-reach-4-trillion-in-2021
Gilbert, B. (2021). Amazon burns through workers so quickly that executives are worried they'll run out of people to employ, according to a new report. *Insider*. www.businessinsider.com/amazon-warehouse-turnover-worker-shortage-2021-6
Gökalp, E., & Martinez, V. (2021). Digital transformation capability maturity model enabling the assessment of industrial manufacturers. *Computers in Industry*, *132*. https://doi.org/10.1016/j.compind.2021.103522
Gudergan, G., Mugge, P., Kwiatkowski, A., Abbu, H., Michaelis, T. L., & Krechting, D. (2019). Patterns of digitization—What differentiates digitally mature organizations? *Proceedings—2019 IEEE International Conference on Engineering, Technology and Innovation, ICE/ITMC 2019*. https://doi.org/10.1109/ICE.2019.8792585
Günsel, A., & Yamen, M. (2020). Digital Taylorism as an answer to the requirements of the new era. *Agile Business Leadership Methods for Industry*, *4*, 103–119. https://doi.org/10.1108/978-1-80043-380-920201007
Gurbaxani, V., & Dunkle, D. (2019). Gearing up for successful digital transformation. *MIS Quarterly Executive*, *18*(3), 209–220. https://doi.org/10.17705/2msqe.00017
Haddud, A., & McAllen, D. (2018). *Digital workplace management: Exploring aspects related to culture, innovation, and leadership*. PICMET 2018 — Portland International Conference on Management of Engineering and Technology: Managing Technological Entrepreneurship: The Engine for Economic Growth, Proceedings, 1–6. https://doi.org/10.23919/PICMET.2018.8481807
Haskamp, T., Dremel, C., Marx, C., & Uebernickel, F. (2021). *Understanding inertia in digital transformation: A literature review and multilevel research framework*. Proceedings on the International Conference on Information Systems (ICIS), 2020.
Hennink, M., & Kaiser, B. N. (2021). Sample sizes for saturation in qualitative research: A systematic review of empirical tests. *Social Science & Medicine*, *292*(6), 114523.
International Trade Association. (2022). *Information & communications technology*. www.trade.gov/country-commercial-guides/malaysia-information-communications-technology#:~:text=The%20Information%20and%20Communication%20Technology,a%20country%2Dwide%20digital%20transformation
Ismail, I. (2023). Digital skills in demand for Malaysian companies. *New Straits Times*. www.nst.com.my/lifestyle/bots/2023/07/928058/digital-skills-demand-malaysian-companies
Jaafar, F. (2022). FMM warns of possible skilled workers shortage due to Malaysia-Japan MoC. *The Malaysian Reserve*. https://themalaysianreserve.com/2022/05/31/fmm-warns-of-possible-skilled-workers-shortage-due-to-malaysia-japan-moc/#:~:text=FMM%20said%20the%20government's%20decision,the%20details%20of%20the%20agreement
JAC Recruitment. (2023). The evolving landscape of Malaysia's digital sector and high-demand skills. *JAC Recruitment Blog*. www.jac-recruitment.my/blog/2023/06/the-evolving-landscape-of-malaysias-digital-sector-and-high-demand-skills
Khairun, I. (2023). How Malaysia is developing successful digital talents for the future? *Linkedin*. www.linkedin.com/pulse/how-malaysia-developing-successful-digital-talents-future-khairun/?trk=public_post
Kozanoglu, D. C., & Abedin, B. (2020). Understanding the role of employees in digital transformation: Conceptualization of digital literacy of employees as a multi-dimensional organizational affordance. *Journal of Enterprise Information Management*, *34*(6), 1649–1672. https://doi.org/10.1108/JEIM-01-2020-0010
Kuhn, K. M., Meijerink, J., & Keegan, A. (2021). Human resource management and the gig economy: Challenges and opportunities at the intersection between organizational HR decision-makers and digital labour platforms. *Research in Personnel and Human Resources Management*, *39*(1), 1–46. https://doi.org/10.1108/S0742-730120210000039001

Kutnjak, A., Pihir, I., & Furjan, M. T. (2019). *Digital transformation case studies across industries—Literature review*. 2019 42nd International Convention on Information and Communication Technology, Electronics and Microelectronics, MIPRO 2019—Proceedings, 1293–1298. https://doi.org/10.23919/MIPRO.2019.8756911

Ling, K. C., Cheng, M. L. S., Ling, A. Y. M., Sin, C. K., & Li, Z. (2023). Readiness of digital transformation among Malaysian digital talents. *International Journal of Business and Management*, *18*(4), 161–181.

McKinsey Digital. (2022, January). CEO lessons from digital transformation. *McKinsey & Company*. www.mckinsey.com/business-functions/mckinsey-digital/our-insights/ceo-lessons-from-digital-transformation?cid=other-eml-alt-mip-mck&hdpid=d1306630-e862-471f-b4cd-b1bb9eee0306&hctky=13106356&hlkid=de77608996304eac96bbf8d1fe31446f

Mills, M. P. (2018). *Work in the age of robots*. Encounter Books. https://web-p-ebscohost-com.ezproxy.apiit.edu.my/ehost/ebookviewer/ebook/ZTAwMHh3d19fMTgxMjEzMl9fQU41?sid=cba5815c-6ea7-4ae5-b761-6146d7fbad05@redis&vid=1&format=EK

Mitra, T., Muller, M., Shami, N. S., Golestani, A., & Masli, M. (2017). Spread of employee engagement in a large organizational network: A longitudinal analysis. *Proceedings of the ACM on Human-Computer Interaction*, *1*(CSCW). https://doi.org/10.1145/3134716

Mohammad, H. (2023). Malaysia's tech industry: Addressing the skills gap. *DSA Editorial*. https://datastorageasean.com/expert-opinions-opinion-byline/malaysia%E2%80%99s-tech-industry-addressing-skills-gap

Naeem, F. (2022). Malaysia's labour market still lacks skilled talent. *Leadereconomics*. www.leadereconomics.com/articles/functional/malaysia-labour-lacks-skilled-talent

Nicolás-Agustín, Á., Jiménez-Jiménez, D., & Maeso-Fernandez, F. (2021). The role of human resource practices in the implementation of digital transformation. *International Journal of Manpower*, *43*(2), 395–410. https://doi.org/10.1108/IJM-03-2021-0176

Newman, D., Kramer, S., & Mcclimans, F. (2020). *Four insights on the culture of digital transformation today*. https://futurumresearch.com/wp-content/uploads/2020/12/Pega.Four-Insights-on-the-Culture-of-Digital-Transformation-Today.pdf?dm_i=4R13,FRES,4TPDPI,1UUYT,1

Ozcan, C. (2019). Technology trends, education 4.0 and beyond. *Contemporary Educational Researches Journal*, *9*(3), 39–49.

Peter, M. K., Kraft, C., & Lindeque, J. (2020). Strategic action fields of digital transformation: An exploration of the strategic action fields of Swiss SMEs and large enterprises. *Journal of Strategy and Management*, *13*(1), 160–180. https://doi.org/10.1108/JSMA-05-2019-0070

Plis, K., & Schislyaeva, E. (2020). Digital transformation in business in the modern world—A new approach to the development of human capital. *ACM International Conference Proceeding Series*, 18–23. https://doi.org/10.1145/3446434.3446454

Poo, C. (2022). Shortage of skilled and TVET talents hampering pandemic recovery. *Edge Weekly*. www.pwc.com/my/en/assets/media/pwc-in-the-news/2022/220725-theedge-shortage-of-skilled-and-tvet-talents-hampering-pandemic-recovery-kartina.pdf

Rangaswamy, U. S. (2021). Industry 4.0 disruption: Assessing the need for adaptive capability. *Development and Learning in Organizations*, *35*(6), 7–10. https://doi.org/10.1108/DLO-01-2021-0003

Salmeron, A. (2020, January). How employee experience can drive digital transformation. *IDC Market Spotlight*, 1–9.

Saul, D. (2022). Return to office: Here's where tech giants stand after apple employees protest mandate. *Forbes*. www.forbes.com/sites/dereksaul/2022/08/22/return-to-office-heres-where-tech-giants-stand-after-apple-employees-protest-mandate/?sh=3d57cf0872ce

Schmid, A. M. (2019). *Beyond resistance: Toward a multilevel perspective on socio-technical inertia in digital transformation.* 27th European Conference on Information Systems—Information Systems for a Sharing Society, ECIS 2019, 1–19.
Sima, V., Gheorghe, I. G., Subić, J., & Nancu, D. (2020). Influences of the industry 4.0 revolution on the human capital development and consumer behavior: A systematic review. *Sustainability (Switzerland)*, *12*(10). https://doi.org/10.3390/SU12104035
Sofiah, A. (2023a). Malaysia's labour force in May 2023: Employment, unemployment rate and more. *Human Resources.* www.humanresourcesonline.net/malaysia-s-labour-force-in-may-2023-employment-unemployment-rate-and-more
Sofiah, A. (2023b). List of Malaysia's most critical occupations in 2022/2023. *Human Resources.* www.humanresourcesonline.net/list-of-malaysia-s-most-critical-occupations-in-2022-2023
Statista. (2023). Share of population in Malaysia from 2019 to 2023, by ethnicity. *Statista.* www.statista.com/statistics/1017372/malaysia-breakdown-of-population-by-ethnicity/
Strauss, A., & Corbin, J. (2008). *Basics of qualitative research* (3rd ed.). SAGE.
Tabrizi, B., Lam, E., Girard, K., & Irvin, V. (2019). Digital transformation is not about technology. *Harvard Business Review.* https://hbr.org/2019/03/digital-transformation-is-not-about-technology
Thapa, A. (2022). How "quiet quitting" became the next phase of the great resignation. *CNBC Economy.* www.cnbc.com/2022/09/02/how-quiet-quitting-became-the-next-phase-of-the-great-resignation.html
Trenerry, B., Chng, S., Wang, Y., Suhaila, Z. S., Lim, S. S., Lu, H. Y., & Oh, P. H. (2021). Preparing workplaces for digital transformation: An integrative review and framework of multi-level factors. *Frontiers in Psychology*, *12*, 620766. https://doi.org/10.3389/fpsyg.2021.620766
Varshney, D. (2020). Digital transformation and creation of an agile workforce: Exploring company initiatives and employee attitudes. In M. A. Turkmenoglu & B. Cicek (Eds.), *Contemporary global issues in human resource management* (pp. 89–105). Emerald Publishing. https://doi.org/10.1108/978-1-80043-392-220201009
Verhoef, P. C., Broekhuizen, T., Bart, Y., Bhattacharya, A., Qi Dong, J., Fabian, N., & Haenlein, M. (2021). Digital transformation: A multidisciplinary reflection and research agenda. *Journal of Business Research*, *122*, 889–901. https://doi.org/10.1016/j.jbusres.2019.09.022
Walker, M. (2020). Rethinking digital transformation—New data examines the culture and process change imperative in 2020. *Harvard Business Review, Pulse Survey, 16.*
Walsh, T. (2019). Chapter 9 virtual team success with the power of technology advancements. In *Advances in the technology of managing people: Contemporary issues in business* (pp. 99–107). https://doi.org/10.1108/978-1-78973-073-920191009
Wessel, L., Baiyere, A., Ologeanu-Taddei, R., Cha, J., & Jensen, T. B. (2021). Unpacking the difference between digital transformation and it-enabled organizational transformation. *Journal of the Association for Information Systems*, *22*(1), 102–129. https://doi.org/10.17705/1jais.00655
White, M. (2012). Digital workplaces: Vision and reality. *Business Information Review*, *29*(4), 205–214. https://doi.org/10.1177/0266382112470412
Wong, D. J. (2022). KL, S'pore, and Bangkok among the worst 10 cities for work-life balance. *Mashable SE Asia.* https://sea.mashable.com/life/20457/kuala-lumpur-singapore-and-bangkok-rank-among-worlds-most-overworked-cities

12 Critical Skills Shortages in the Mauritian Information Technology Sector

Vikash Rowtho, Sarita Hardin-Ramanan, and Shafiiq Gopee*

Introduction

The Republic of Mauritius has a population of nearly 1.3 million (Statistics Mauritius, 2023) and occupies an area of 2040 square kilometres. Despite its small land mass, this island nation, situated 2,200 kilometres off the south-eastern coast of Africa in the Indian Ocean, has an Exclusive Economic Zone of 2.3 million square kilometres. Mauritius was a French colony between 1735 and 1810 when the British took over the island which they administered until it became independent in 1968. Since the early days of colonisation, Mauritius has been a mono-crop economy highly dependent on sugar exports. This economic model started to change shortly after Mauritius achieved independence when it started to diversify its economic base by attracting foreign investment to develop (a) an export processing zone (EPZ) manufacturing sector and (b) a tourism sector. More recently, two new pillars, namely financial services and information and communications technology, were added to the economy. This facilitated the shift from a low-income to a high-income economy in July 2020. However, due to the pandemic, Mauritius reverted to an upper middle-income status in 2021 (World Bank, 2021).

As one of the pillars of the Mauritian economy, the information and communication technology (ICT) sector has the support of the Ministry of Information Technology, Communication and Innovation which has put forward several policies and strategies such as the Open Source Policy, Open Data Policy, Digital Government Transformation Strategy, Digital Mauritius Strategy and the Artificial Intelligence Strategy as tools to transform the country into a high-income, inclusive, and green economy well before 2030 (Ministry of Information Technology, Communication and Innovation, 2022). Several parastatal bodies—which are established under Acts of Parliament to serve as instruments of national policies—and private companies falling under the ministry, for example, the National Computer Board (NCB) and the Mauritius Research & Innovation Council (MRIC) but also Mauritius Telecom Ltd (MT), Mauritius Post Ltd (MP) and State Informatics Ltd (SIL)—have been assigned the responsibility of implementing the strategies mentioned earlier together with the accompanying measures to achieve the Vision 2030

DOI: 10.4324/9781003379065-14

(Ministry of Information Technology, Communication and Innovation, 2022).

While the IT sector has contributed to the Mauritian economy for over 20 years, its 5.8% of GDP share remained stable between 2010 and 2019 (ICT Info—NCB, 2020). In 2021, while the contributions of the textile and sugar sectors saw a decline, the 850 enterprises providing ICT-BPO services employed 30,000 people and contributed 7.4% to the GDP of Mauritius (EDB Mauritius, 2022). Although the sector has shown resilience during the pandemic, sustaining its development in the post-pandemic world is crucial. In a recent strategic planning exercise conducted by the Mauritius Research and Innovation Council, the ICT workgroup identified skills shortage as one of the sector's main challenges (MRIC, 2022). Navigating difficult and uncertain times while steering the economy in the right direction will be crucial to sustainable economic development.

Context

COVID-19 reminded nations of the power of technological innovation in supporting economic resilience. Countries with strong infrastructure, such as fast and reliable internet connectivity, and industries with higher innovative technology adoption proved to be more resilient during the pandemic (United Nations, 2022). As a Small Island Development State, Mauritius fully accepts its limitations and strong dependence on technology and innovation to drive its development. One of its strategies is to build a digital economy that rests on innovations in ICT while nurturing a highly skilled workforce capable of matching international standards.

Thus, businesses are encouraged to embrace technology and transform smartly for increased efficiency and productivity, propelling SDG 9—innovation—high on the Mauritian agenda (United Nations Sustainable Development Goals Knowledge Platform, 2019). Aligning with SDG 8, sustainable job creation in these areas is also key to reaching the targeted economic growth. Additionally, quality education largely underpins the successful achievement of SDGs 8 and 9. Without a suitably skilled and trained workforce, the adoption of innovative practices and technology and the success of the island's economic diversification strategy are likely to remain elusive. Despite an encouraging decrease in graduate unemployment from 22% in the fourth quarter of 2021 to 16.6% in the first quarter of 2022 (Statistics Mauritius, 2022), a severe shortage of high-end skills in key areas such as STEM, banking, and finance hinder progress (United Nations Mauritius, 2019). The Mauritian education and training system struggles to meet the demand for industry-sought and relevant skills vital for the knowledge-based, digital economy aspired by Mauritius (United Nations Mauritius, 2019). As the skills gap between workforce capabilities and industry requirements widens to a chasm, education and training providers face the increasing challenge of producing industry-ready labour. The achievement of SDG 4 is, therefore, critical for the economic growth and well-being of the country.

Mauritius Vision (2030) (2017) is clear. The island's ascent from an upper-middle-income to a higher-income economy can only happen if the island focuses on technology and innovation while successfully securing all underlying skills. The Mauritius Artificial Intelligence Strategy (2018) emerged from this vision and identified artificial intelligence (AI) and innovative technologies such as blockchain and the internet of things (IoT) as critical tools to not only revitalise longstanding economic pillars such as manufacturing and agriculture but also boost other sectors such as finance. SDGs 8, 9, and 4 are thus key objectives in the island's economic mission.

With a host of intelligent technologies born from Industry 4.0 and the emergence of Industry 5.0, Mauritius can only aim for a truly competitive digital economy if it is at the forefront of technological knowledge and infrastructure. Businesses investing or contemplating investment in cloud computing, IoT, AI, big data analytics and robotics and blockchain, among others, rely on a strong IT infrastructural backbone along with a skilled Mauritian labour force to not only implement and/or set up innovative systems but also maintain and use them. With the world being at the cusp of Industry 5.0, humans and machines must collaborate harmoniously for smart, energy-efficient and green production (Noble et al., 2022). This warrants another set of new skills, and consequently, many new entrants to the job market will require cutting-edge technological capabilities, while a section of the existing workforce will need upskilling or even reskilling.

According to the Human Resource Development Council (HRDC) survey on automation, robotics and industrial internet of things (IIOT) skills in the Mauritian manufacturing sector (HRDC, 2022), the industry is yet to adopt advanced technologies such as virtual reality, augmented reality, digital twins, and big data to align with the island's vision of a digital economy. While the manufacturing sector acknowledges the benefits of such technology, it deplores the scarcity of skills in these areas. The selection of appropriate technology is often left to the company CEO or IT engineers, who might not be sufficiently knowledgeable to shoulder such decisions. As automation takes over routine and repetitive tasks, a greater shift towards high-value jobs is expected. More than ever, these would require the new and existing workforce to demonstrate critical thinking, people management, flexibility, continuous learning, and the ability to make sound decisions under pressure. Other soft skills such as crisis management, problem analysis, and communication will be even more prominent to strike the best balance between human and machine resources. Despite a comprehensive overview of the lack of skills essential for technological innovation, the HRDC study (2022) is limited to the Mauritian manufacturing sector. Its findings do, however, raise an important research question: Is Mauritius ready to embrace technological innovations (SDG 9) to support its strategy for sustainable economic growth and work (SDG 8) based on quality education (SDG 4)?

SDGs 4, 8, and 9 thus provide a salient lens for this study to gauge further the skills shortages and challenges inhibiting Mauritius's economic strategy.

The research will focus on the IT industry since it is a strong pillar of the Mauritian economy and a key enabler for innovation and sustainable growth.

A joint initiative by the Mauritian government and the United Nations, the Strategic Partnership Framework (SPF) 2019–2023 (United Nations Mauritius, 2019) defines collaborative outcomes to address the island's main strategic concerns and their associated SDGs. Out of the six SPF outcomes, two (outcomes 1 and 4) are directly related to SDGs 4, 8, and 9. In line with the national vision for a strong economy, outcome 1 focuses on transformed business and aims at reinforcing a policy and regulatory environment conducive to business innovation, productivity, and sustained diversification in selected old (e.g. textile) and newer sectors such as IT. SPF outcome 4 covers quality education and skills for increased employability and links to the achievement of SDGs 8 and 9 while fully aligning with SDG 4.

As mentioned in its national vision, the Mauritian government is strongly committed to investing in the success of its youth. The SPF thus advocates for the provision of specialised and high-standard education instrumental in producing the appropriately skilled, current, and employable workforce needed to fuel a growing digital economy. Strong emphasis is also placed on quality technical and vocational training to bridge the skills gap. The main outputs of outcome 4 include revamped teaching and learning practices to optimise student experiences and strengthened curricula for world-standard, industry-relevant content. Through outcomes 1 and 4, the SPF envisions working towards a supportive regulatory framework coupled with quality, targeted education, and a strong ICT infrastructural backbone to drive innovation and value-added technology investment.

This mission is nonetheless riddled with challenges. For example, the Mauritian education system faces constant criticism for its inability to produce industry-relevant experts to champion digital transformation and power a knowledge economy. Primary and secondary curricula do not present sufficient opportunities to develop cognitive skills such as critical and analytical thinking and problem-solving. Teachers continue to use traditional approaches and are not always exposed to more engaging methods that encourage students to understand, apply, and transfer knowledge to different scenarios instead of rote learning (United Nations Mauritius, 2019). Universities are accused of being overly academic and graduates are often criticised for their lack of valuable industry exposure, as graduate work readiness features high on the government agenda (Hardin-Ramanan et al., 2020). The private sector repeatedly deplores the lack of industry-ready graduates and the shortage of technical skills on the job market, as the quality and relevance of education and training are often questioned. Additionally, the island's ageing population, decreasing demography due to low birth rates, and declining number of university students add further pressure to an already shrinking pool of human resources. As the need for local skills to shape the Mauritian economy becomes more pressing, Mauritius remains largely dependent on foreign workers to fill critical skill requirements in key areas such as ICT (United Nations Mauritius, 2019).

In light of the central role of the ICT sector as a driving force in the Mauritian economy and considering the pressing human capital challenges impeding its progress, the research presented in this chapter is both timely and essential. It sets out to gain a thorough understanding of the complexities inherent in the issue of critical skills shortages in the Mauritian IT sector and formulate targeted, actionable, and sustainable recommendations.

Methodology

This research embraced an exploratory approach centred on stakeholder analysis to achieve these objectives. Brugha and Varvasovszky (2000, p. 239) argue that 'stakeholder analysis can be used to generate knowledge about the relevant actors to understand their behaviour, intentions, interrelations, agendas, interests, and the influence or resources they have brought—or could bring—to bear on the decision-making processes'. In line with this paradigm, this research used a two-staged approach to first gather relevant information by analysing publicly available documents. Second, the research used qualitative methods to engage with the various stakeholders to gain insights on the issue from their respective standpoints.

The most crucial step in any stakeholder analysis approach is identifying the most appropriate stakeholders. It sets the foundation for the research but also ensures that the insights gathered will be a true and valid reflection of the perceptions and interests influencing the issue at hand and, in this case, the critical skills shortages in the IT sector in Mauritius. Therefore, in line with the literature and after several brainstorming sessions and iterations, the stakeholders more likely to provide candid and meaningful insights were the government and governmental bodies (e.g. HRDC), the IT industry, and universities offering IT courses and IT graduates.

While an extensive range of qualitative data-gathering tools can be used to gather insights from stakeholders (Yang, 2014), it was imperative to carefully select the best approach that would provide a safe space to maximise stakeholder engagement. Specifically, it was deemed most appropriate to conduct a focus group with IT graduates and run semi-structured interviews with government, IT industry, and university representatives.

Considering the scope and limited resources available, a purposive sampling method was used to identify and curate the list of representatives from the government, the IT industry, and universities. For the government category, a high-ranking official from the Ministry of Information Technology, Communication and Innovation and a representative from the Human Resource Development Council—the government body responsible for training and development – were interviewed. For the IT industry group, executives from five leading IT companies were selected. Finally, three main IT course providers were selected for academia: two private institutions and one public university. A total of ten interviews were thus conducted. Table 12.1 summarises the various stakeholders used.

Table 12.1 Table of data collection tools used for each stakeholder

Category	*Data collection tool*
Graduate	Focus group
Government	Semi-structured interviews
IT industry	Semi-structured interviews
Higher education institution	Semi-structured interviews

For each of the three categories of interviews (government, IT industry and university), guiding questions were prepared to ensure a smooth running of the sessions. While there were specific questions for each category, for example, regarding the number of people employed and the number of vacancies still needed to be filled for IT organisations, the discussions revolved around the following themes.

1 Understanding the causes of the IT skills shortages in Mauritius
2 Understanding the areas of IT skills shortages
3 Understanding the current actions/initiatives being done to curb the shortages
4 Identifying potential solutions to address the skills shortage on the island.

All ethical clearances, be it at the institutional level or national level, were sought before the data-gathering process, and for each interaction with stakeholders, prior written consent was provided. Each participant received a comprehensive information pack and consent form to read and sign.

While every effort has been made to ensure the validity and reliability of the methods used and, consequently, the findings, it is critical to acknowledge the limitations of this research. While the research uses an exploratory approach, it does not, unfortunately, allow for a larger generalisation of the results for the industry. Nonetheless, it opens avenues for further exploration, especially within various stakeholder groups.

Findings and Discussion

Focus Group

Three themes emerged when asked about the key skills required to be employable in the IT industry. The first one, technological currency, emphasised the dynamic nature of IT and its resulting need to adopt a continuous learning mindset towards new and evolving technology. As stated by one of the participants:

> *I joined as a BI developer, but I'm required to know about quantum mechanics, machine learning, AI, and other emerging technologies. This is important to align employees with business goals and objectives.*

The second theme, versatility, highlighted evolving technology as a prominent reason for being flexible and adaptable. Participants also emphasised the third theme, collaboration, and problem-solving skills, deemed critical for people to work effectively as a team, demonstrate good leadership and management skills, and successfully resolve problems.

In the second part of the conversation, graduates compared their university-acquired knowledge and skills to their work requirements. Diverse views were discussed under the first emerging theme: university curriculum and learning experience. While some participants praised their university curriculum for providing a strong foundation to build on at work, many condemned the predominantly theoretical nature of their studies. A few graduates extended the discussion to the vastness of IT and the impossibility of universities to cover every possible area and technology. As quoted next, to them, it was more important for students to graduate with good employability skills and a sound knowledge base to support continuous learning at work.

> *I think that the IT field is very large, with vastly different companies having different needs and technologies. Academia will never be able to train a student to be skilful across the whole industry. But if a student comes out of university as a good programmer with good soft skills, the student would easily be able to learn and fill any gaps in industry.*

Under the second theme, personal and professional development, participants applauded those universities that offered project-based or authentic capstone modules and extracurricular activities to develop leadership, interpersonal, teamwork, and presentation skills.

> *During Capstone Computing, we needed to solve a real business problem. The advantage of having an industry mentor helped me dive deep into project sprints before eventually stepping out into the real world.*

The third part of the discussion focused on suggestions for career-readiness initiatives. To address technological gaps, some participants proposed industry support for professional certifications. Others advocated for more internships and bridging programmes run jointly by companies and academia to shape employable graduates. Participants also recommended an increased focus on soft skills through workshops and leadership opportunities at the university. A review of course curricula for increased practical sessions and exposure to a wider range of current technologies was also suggested. Regular conferences uniting universities, industry, and the government could also fuel three-way conversations about critical skills required in the IT workplace.

In their study of employability in the Korean ICT sector, Ahn et al. (2023) identified interpersonal or team-working skills, communication, problem-solving, technical competency in the application and practice of modern ICT tools, and knowledge of contemporary issues (or continuous learning) as the top five skills sought by the industry. Similarly, Ohei and

Evangelos Mantzaris (2023) highlight technical currency and durable (soft) skills such as problem-solving, interpersonal communication, and teamwork as key enablers for ICT employability in South Africa. These findings align with the outcomes of the IT alumni focus group, where the same technical and soft skills emerged as a priority across the ICT industry. According to the IT graduates, not all universities in Mauritius equip their students to be employable despite an expectation for technical and durable (soft) skills to be embedded in intra and extra-curricular learning experiences. While there is an understanding that universities cannot package every single technology into one course, higher education institutions have a crucial role to play in collaborating with industry and the government to generate lifelong learners with the capacity to keep pace with fast-changing technology and the dynamic nature of the IT industry (Naik, 2023). Students should therefore be exposed to experiential and hands-on learning in real-world settings, as well as challenged in different situations to develop their adaptability, problem-solving, and ability to innovate while nurturing a growth mindset.

University Interviews

The interviews conducted with representatives from both public and private universities in Mauritius have highlighted several critical themes related to the significant IT skills shortage in the country. The shortage is attributed to the unique demographic challenges facing the nation, including a shrinking population and an aging workforce. As a result, there is a consensus that the existing number of IT specialists in the workforce is inadequate to meet the growing demands of the industry.

This skills shortage goes beyond just the number of IT professionals and encompasses a lack of diverse and specialised IT skills required by the industry. Recognising the importance of addressing this issue, there is a collective realisation that bridging the IT skills gap is vital for Mauritius's continued economic development and competitiveness on the global stage. One key theme that emerged from the interviews is the necessity of establishing a comprehensive educational ecosystem that spans from primary education to tertiary levels. This ecosystem should be designed to adequately prepare future IT employees, incorporating formal education as well as initiatives related to reskilling and upskilling in the IT sector. At the same time, it was emphasised that while reskilling can address beginner-level skills, it may not fully meet the demand for specialised IT expertise.

The respondents were unanimous in highlighting the ongoing debate around the balance between soft skills and technical skills in university education. Soft skills, such as communication and client interaction, have gained significance in response to industry requirements which also have started putting more emphasis on creativity. Universities have introduced modules to enhance these skills. However, the industry's demands in the technical skills landscape are diverse, and there is a mismatch between what the industry requires in terms of specific technical competencies and what universities are currently producing. This challenge is partly attributed to the difficulty of covering the entirety of the industry's technological demands in a standard undergraduate curriculum. Universities aim to strike a balance between industry relevance and providing a versatile degree that equips students with various possibilities upon graduation. Since there is agreement on the need to align university curricula with the evolving needs of the IT industry, universities have taken steps to conduct consultative meetings with the ICT industry to obtain feedback on technology trends and industry requirements and to set up advisory boards comprising industry leaders in the ICT sector as they play a crucial role in integrating industry perspectives into curriculum development. Additionally, internships are being organised as they expose students to the practical realities of the IT industry, bridging the gap between theory and application.

To attract students to IT careers, it was suggested that industry engagement start from the secondary school level. The ICT industry should participate in schools to explain job profiles, career prospects, and clear misconceptions about IT jobs. Early sensitisation through activities like hackathons and coding competitions can inspire students to pursue IT careers. Universities are encouraged to collaborate with the ICT industry, where ICT companies provide access to the latest versions of software or related technologies to ensure education remains relevant and up to date.

In Mauritius, the shortage of IT skills is not limited to traditional areas but extends to emerging technologies like AI, blockchain, fintech, virtual reality, and content production. Collaboration between universities, the ICT industry, and the government is crucial to bridge the gap. Universities are taking steps to ensure curriculum alignment and industry engagement, which can take various forms, including sponsoring research initiatives. Government intervention is vital in creating synergy between academia, industry, and government. Measures such as extending support for reskilling and upskilling in IT, funding for AI competencies, and incentives for science, technology, engineering, and mathematics (STEM) students can help address the shortage. Introducing a technological education path at the secondary level is also recommended.

Government Interviews

The scarcity of IT skills is not a localised issue, but rather a global phenomenon, impacting nations worldwide, Mauritius included. This trend was confirmed by interviews with the government representatives who describe the origins of this scarcity as multifaceted, encompassing individual factors, such as personal ambitions and motivations, as well as broader aspects, including government policies and strategies or ageing and shrinking population. Frequently, the spotlight is cast upon specific IT job roles, like software developers, while the importance of the current and future skill set required is sometimes overlooked.

> *The ever-shifting landscape of technology, like a moving target, further complicates the prediction of future demands.*

This situation significantly contributes to the persistent shortage of IT professionals. In some cases, the educational system often falls short in evolving to provide students with a robust foundation for the skills required in the future job market. In the pursuit of high grades, students and parents may inadvertently neglect the imperative of skill acquisition.

There was a consensus that the education system should provide opportunities for engagement with STEM subjects as early as possible. Teachers have been identified as having a crucial role to play in sensitisation and awareness about STEM subjects and career opportunities. However, this task proves to be quite challenging as teachers in both the primary and secondary schools have limited or no access to the latest developments in the IT industry. This issue can be addressed by providing teachers with training and industry exposure during school holidays, enabling them to stay updated on the latest technological advancements.

While policies have been formulated to address the skills shortage, effective implementation in a coherent and integrated manner is essential to avoid a fragmented approach. Conversion programmes, which aim to provide graduates from non-IT backgrounds with IT degrees, have proven successful, with most participants finding employment. Notably, these programmes are jointly developed by public universities and the industry, with candidates having STEM backgrounds showing higher success rates. However, the practice of implementing conversion programmes after the first year of non-IT programmes is considered wasteful, and a thorough restructuring is required to encourage more students to pursue STEM modules.

The industry often raises concerns about the quality and quantity of IT graduates, underscoring the significance of creativity and analytical skills for success in the IT sector. Recognising that universities cannot prepare graduates for all industry requirements, there should be a shift towards cultivating the right mindset. Mauritius' small size offers an advantage, which can be leveraged by facilitating direct interactions between the industry and students, providing insights on interviews, the role of IT in various sectors, and fostering engagement with representatives from diverse industries, such as banking and logistics.

Lecturers also share the responsibility of staying attuned to the latest industry developments. Efforts should be made to actively involve them in the industry. Additionally, a more responsive approach involving curriculum changes at higher frequencies, while considering regulatory and compliance aspects, could help address the persistent skills gap. The cultivation of critical thinking skills is paramount, as some individuals resist adopting new technologies due to entrenched mindsets.

Based on the interviews with government representatives, the question about whether Mauritius is ready to embrace technological innovations (SDG 9) for sustainable economic growth and work (SGD 8) based on quality education (SDG 4) resulted in a consensus that scarcity of skills indeed affects Mauritius while at the same time acknowledging that it is a global phenomenon. The fact that an awareness campaign on the range of job opportunities in the IT field was considered imperative as there is the misconception that the top professions are limited only to doctors, engineers, and lawyers. This can be addressed by having a well-thought strategy of introducing STEM to pupils in schools so that their choice of subjects can lead towards a career in IT.

Industry Interviews

All the industry representatives were in accord with the critical skills shortage in the IT in the Mauritian market. All of those interviewed reported that their companies were functioning below the optimum required manpower with some requiring up to 60% more of their current workforce, and they were to various degrees finding it hard to recruit skilled workers. They associated this skills shortage to four key problems namely (a) increased competition, (b) brain drain and retention, (c) lack of awareness, and (d) skill set mismatch.

The boom in the IT sector over the past decades has led to a fiercely competitive landscape. The sector not only has attracted local entrepreneurs or business ventures but has been the playground for major international players seeking to explore favourable sites to delocalise some of their processes. Indeed, over the past years, companies in the IT BPO sector have mushroomed. As quoted by one of the interviewees:

> *It's a very competitive market in Mauritius, and it is becoming increasingly difficult to attract what we call top talent. There's so much competition now, not just between the global companies but also with local players on the market—all looking for similar talent.*

This increased competition puts additional pressure on the labour market as these companies source their manpower within the same, already limited, pool of local talents. With global companies offering more attractive compensation packages. This situation is exacerbated by the limited scope of IT activities in Mauritius, making it challenging for local companies to compete effectively.

While not a specific problem to the IT sector, industry representatives outlined the issue of brain drain as a possible cause of the IT skills shortages in Mauritius and pinpointed two such facilitators. First, the fact that many students fly abroad for further studies after their undergraduate course and tend to remain abroad due to better career prospects. Second, interviewees commented that the local IT sector is rather restricted to the services sector and customisation of already existing packages. While there are few companies involved in the latest high-end development and latest technologies, the scope is rather limited. As a result, companies are either resorting to hiring talent from abroad to work in Mauritius or setting up branches in other countries such as India, where there is a much larger pool of IT professionals to carry out some of their activities.

The issue is further compounded by high turnover and the difficulty in retaining staff. IT companies are therefore compelled to find innovative and creative ways to retain staff. One of the representatives commented that the company has introduced a non-financial incentive of a compressed work week (CWW) where employees work for four days every second week and catch up during the two-week time period. Such incentives are proving to be quite successful with the new generation for whom work-life balance is a concept they strongly uphold.

According to an interviewee, the lack of awareness of the IT industry and the career possibilities might also be a possible cause of the shortage and suggested that the image of the IT career needs to be improved not just among potential students but also among their parents. According to an interviewee, the traditional preference for careers like engineering and medicine is still very much prominent in Mauritian society, making it challenging to attract talent to IT.

The interviews highlighted that while all participating companies faced critical skills shortages, there were no consensus as to the specific skills required due to the varying nature of the companies represented. Interestingly, while lack of technical skills is a major concern, employers are equally worried about the lack of soft skills and work attitude. In terms of technical expertise, the interviews revealed a huge need for specialised skills in Java, Oracle, SQL, and cybersecurity. The need is across the board with demand for both freshers joining the company and experienced professionals.

However, technical skills are not the only critical shortage faced by companies. The interviews revealed that since the Mauritian IT landscape is more geared towards the service industry, the ability to communicate effectively with customers is equally crucial. This involves not just language proficiency and being fully bilingual but also the confidence to engage in meaningful dialogue. Moreover, the interviews shed light on another crucial aspect: the importance of having the right attitude in the workplace.

> *It's not just about possessing the right technical skills; employees must also have the right mindset and approach to their work especially as the workplace etiquette is evolving with flexitime and work-at-home programmes.*

Attitude has been identified as a significant factor affecting both employee performance and long-term retention. This observation is consistent with a broader theme that has emerged from the discussions namely that soft skills are not secondary or optional. Rather, they are integral to technical roles, complementing technical skills to create a well-rounded, effective employees.

Based on the interviews with industry representatives, the question about whether Mauritius is ready to embrace technological innovations (SDG 9) for sustainable economic growth and work (SGD 8) based on quality education (SDG 4) resulted in a range of opinions, but all very much hopeful and optimistic on the future of the IT industry in Mauritius. This aligns well with the goals of fostering innovation and economic growth. However, the sector is hampered by a skills gap, particularly in fundamental technical skills and soft skills like communication and work attitude. However, there is much to be done in terms of quality of education and training (SDG 4) being provided, as well as the sustainability of economic growth (SDG 8) if these gaps are not addressed.

Conclusion

From the focus group findings, the question about whether Mauritius is ready to embrace technological innovations (SDG 9) for sustainable economic growth and work (SGD 8) based on quality education (SDG 4) resulted in mixed feelings. While the graduates identified technological currency, versatility, collaboration, and problem solving as essential skills required to thrive in the IT industry, not all of them felt sufficiently prepared for work. Many criticised their university learning experience for being too academic with insufficient opportunities to put theory to practice, learn about emerging technologies, and shape soft skills. Some solutions proposed included more practical-oriented and technological-current curricula, industry-supported professional certifications, employability workshops, and regular conferences uniting industry, universities, and government for a common understanding of critical skills. Nonetheless, it was acknowledged that a university course cannot prepare graduates for the entire range of present and future IT-related areas and technologies. Continuous learning is key, and as long as all universities provide a strong foundation to build on through experiential and authentic learning opportunities (Hutson et al., 2023), IT graduates should be equipped to apply theory to practice, learn new technologies smartly, and contribute to the growth of the IT industry.

Government intervention was acknowledged as vital in addressing the IT skills shortage. Proposed initiatives included extending support for reskilling and upskilling in IT, providing funding for emerging technologies, and introducing incentives for STEM students. Early sensitisation at the secondary school level to attract students to IT careers was emphasised, along with the importance of involving the ICT industry in schools to educate students about job prospects. Digitising government services and enhancing connectivity were viewed as essential components of government initiatives to support technological innovation.

Industry representatives confirmed a critical skills shortage in the IT sector, attributing it to factors like increased competition, brain drain, lack of awareness, and skill set mismatch. The need for specialised technical skills, such as Java, Oracle, SQL, and cybersecurity, was highlighted, alongside the challenge of sourcing experienced professionals. Soft skills, including effective communication and the right attitude in the workplace, were considered crucial for employee performance and retention. A recurring theme was the need to strike a balance between soft and technical skills in university education.

While soft skills are important, universities also face the challenge of providing a broad technical foundation to equip students for various IT specialties. The importance of cultivating the right mindset for continuous learning and adaptability was underscored. The rapidly evolving nature of the IT sector requires professionals to embrace new technologies and approaches.

In conclusion, all the stakeholders, namely universities, industry and the government should collaborate towards the creation of an appropriate ecosystem with suitable initiatives that will lead to quality education in Mauritius to supply the industry with work ready graduates which will ultimately contribute to sustainable economic growth.

Note

* Corresponding author: vrowtho@curtinmauritius.ac.mu.

References

Ahn, J., Jeong, S., & Lee, D. (2023). Research on the items of importance and satisfaction for employability in the Korean Information Communication Technology sector. *Sustainability (Switzerland)*, *15*(16). https://doi.org/10.3390/su151612338

Brugha, R., & Varvasovszky, Z. (2000). Stakeholder analysis: A review. *Health Policy and Planning*, *15*(3), 239–246.

EDB Mauritius. (2022). *Annual report*. https://edbmauritius.org/wp-content/uploads/2022/10/EDB-Annual-Report-2020-2021.pdf

Hardin-Ramanan, S., Gopee, S., Rowtho, V., & Charoux, O. (2020). Graduate work-readiness in mauritius : A multi-stakeholder approach. *The Journal of Teaching and Learning for Graduate Employability*, *11*(1), 93–109.

HRDC. (2022). *Fostering automation, robotics and IIOT in the manufacturing sector: A skills perspective*. www.hrdc.mu/index.php/projects/sectoral-projects/351-fostering-automation-robotics-and-iiot-in-the-manufacturing-sector

Hutson, J., Valenzuela, M., Hosto-Marti, B., & Wright, S. (2023). The role of higher education in developing durable skills: Reframing general education. *Journal of Higher Education Theory and Practice*, *23*(3), 1–12. https://doi.org/10.33423/jhetp.v23i3.5836

ICT Info—NCB. (2020). *Information society outlook*. https://ncb.govmu.org/ncb/reports/NCB%20Information%20Society%20Outlook%20-%20Aug%202020.pdf

Mauritius Artificial Intelligence Strategy. (2018). https://ncb.govmu.org/ncb/strategicplans/MauritiusAIStrategy2018.pdf.

Mauritius Vision 2030. (2017). *Foreign Affairs*. www.foreignaffairs.com/mauritius 2017.

Ministry of Information Technology, Communication and Innovation. (2022). ICT sector. https://mitci.govmu.org/Pages/MITCI/ICTSector.aspx

MRIC. (2022). *National roadmap for research and innovation 2023–2027*. www.mric.mu/_files/ugd/f94712_c1b1a364bd284fa8ac9273fe423211a3.pdf

Naik, B. M. (2023). Is the role of universities and colleges vital in employment generation? Can Indian universities afford to ignore? At what cost? Who pays? *I-Manager's Journal on Management*, *17*(4), 35. https://doi.org/10.26634/jmgt.17.4.19774

Noble, S. M., Mende, M., Grewal, D., & Parasuraman, A. (2022). The fifth industrial revolution: How harmonious human—Machine collabouration is triggering a retail and service [r]evolution. *Journal of Retailing*, *98*(2), 199–208. https://doi.org/10.1016/j.jretai.2022.04.003

Ohei, K., & Mantzaris, E. (2023). Investigating ICT skills as enablers for sustainable youth employability in South Africa: A literature review. *International Journal of Research in Business and Social Science (2147–4478)*, *12*(6), 228–238. https://doi.org/10.20525/ijrbs.v12i6.2714

Statistics Mauritius. (2022). *Labour force, employment and unemployment—1st quarter 2022.* https://statsmauritius.govmu.org/Pages/Statistics/ESI/Labour/Labour/LF_Emp_Unemp_1Qtr22.aspx#:~:text=The unemployment rate for the,3

Statistics Mauritius. (2023). *Population and vital statistics - Republic of Mauritius.* https://statsmauritius.govmu.org/Pages/Statistics/ESI/Population/Pop_Vital_Stats_Yr23.aspx

United Nations. (2022). *Goal 9—SDG indicators.* https://unstats.un.org/sdgs/report/2022/goal-09/

United Nations Mauritius. (2019). *Strategic partnership framework (SPF) 2019–2023.* www.undp.org/sites/g/files/zskgke326/files/2022-05/mauritius-UNSCDF-strategic-partnership-framework-2019-2023.pdf

United Nations Sustainable Development Goals Knowledge Platform. (2019). *Mauritius—Voluntary national review 2019.* https://sustainabledevelopment.un.org/memberstates/mauritius

World Bank. (2021). *Mauritius.* https://thedocs.worldbank.org/en/doc/bae48ff2fefc5a869546775b3f010735-0500062021/related/mpo-mus.pdf

Yang, R. J. (2014). An investigation of stakeholder analysis in urban development projects: Empirical or rationalistic perspectives. *International Journal of Project Management*, *32*(5), 838–849. https://doi.org/10.1016/j.ijproman.2013.10.011

13 Decent Work, the Critical Skills Shortage in the Health Sector, and the Role of the State

A Case Study of the Philippine Exported Labour Policy and Sustainable Development

Jonathan Sale and Arlene Sale*

Introduction

The Philippines has been a labour-exporting country with a web of statutory regulations detailed in the country's Labour Code and Migrant Workers and Overseas Filipinos Act 1995 as amended (Sale, 2021). Labour export as a policy was started by the first Marcos regime during the Martial Law period as a temporary measure to address unemployment and to improve the economy. Remittances from Overseas Filipino Workers (OFWs) strongly contribute to the country's economy and GDP growth. Amendments have been introduced to the Labour Code, enhancing the exported labour policy, to protect the welfare of migrant workers and their families by ensuring that OWFs are deployed to host countries with labour and social legislation protecting worker rights (Republic Act 10022; Sale, 2021).

Like other labour-exporting countries, the Philippines also experiences labour shortages. For instance, in 2020, the Philippines recorded a shortage of 290,000 health workers during the COVID-19 pandemic (POEA, 2020). On average, 13,000 health care professionals were leaving the country annually (POEA, 2020). That same year, the nursing profession was listed as one of the mission critical skills (MCS), that is, internally developed skills that require extensive training and are not easily replaceable (POEA, 2020). Deployment of this and other healthcare professionals was temporarily suspended (POEA, 2020).

What is the Philippines' exported labour policy? What is the role of the state in developing and implementing this policy? Has the exported labour policy contributed to decent work (SDG 8) and sustainable development? Is decent work among the push-pull factors influencing the movement of OFWs, specifically nurse labour? Are there links between the exported labour policy and critical skills shortages, particularly in terms of the nursing profession, in the country? This case study explores these research questions.

Documents related to the exported labour policy and its outcomes are analysed through the lens of decent work, its indicators, and patterns as key aspects of the country's decent work performance under the Sustainable Development

DOI: 10.4324/9781003379065-15

Goal (SDG) 8. In terms of structure, this chapter is divided into five sections. The country's background, including topography, cultural heritage, education system, policy framework and labour market, decent work and economic development, are reviewed in the first section. The following section outlines the research questions and methodology. Findings on exported labour policy, the role of the state in policy development and implementation, decent work and sustainable development as push and pull factors influencing the movement of OFWs, specifically nurse labour, and links between policy and critical skills shortages, particularly within the country's nurse profession, are tackled in the third section. The last section outlines the discussions before the conclusions are offered in the final part of the chapter.

Country Background

The Philippines is an archipelago of over 7,000 islands in coastal and mountainous areas (Licuanan et al., 2019). It is prone to environmental disasters such as typhoons, earthquakes, and volcanic eruptions (Wingard & Brändlin, 2013). It is a nation 'of Malay origin' (Milner & Drakard, 2009, p. 2; Sale, 2021, p. 208) with a mixture of influences from the Spanish, Americans, and other Eastern countries through colonisation and trading (Britannica, n.d.). Having been colonised by Spain, for a period lasting more than 300 years, 80% of the population are Catholic (Gregorio, 2023; USAID, 2022; BBC, n.d.).

The Philippines recorded a consistent average gross domestic product (GDP) growth of 6.3% from 2010 to 2014 (PG, 2015a), and the country's GDP growth was recorded at 9.6% in 2020, 5.6% in 2021, 7.6% in 2022, and 6.4% during the first quarter of 2023, with a population of more than 112 million (IMF, 2023a, 2023b; ARIC, 2022). In 2021, the biggest contributor to GDP growth was the services sector, which increased by 5.3% (ARIC, 2022). In the same year, remittances from OFWs grew by 5.1%, reaching $34.9 billion or 8.9% of GDP (ARIC, 2022). Broadly and historically, the growth of the services sector coincided with the Labour Code and exported labour policy, as well as export-oriented industrialisation (EOI); from the 1970s, employment expanded in services and as at August 2023, the share of employment in services reached 57.3%, while that in agriculture and industry stood at 24.5% and 18.2%, respectively, of total employment (PSA, 2023a).

In an early 2023 survey, 51% of Filipino families (around 14 million people) considered themselves poor or within the national median self-rated poverty threshold of ₱15,000 or about US$260 (CNN Philippines, 2023; Pinlac, 2023). The national poverty threshold for a family of five is set at a monthly average of ₱12,030, slightly higher than the average monthly minimum wage of ₱8,902 (IBON Foundation, 2023a). Poverty is one of the factors that tend to limit a Filipino family's access to education. One government approach that aims to address this situation is the conditional cash transfer program, through which the poorest families receive money in exchange for the regular attendance of their children in basic education classes (PG, 2015b).

The national unemployment rate stood at 4.4% in August 2023 (PSA, 2023b), while the proportion of youth (15–24 years) not in education, training, or employment was 14.7% in July 2023 (PSA, 2023c). Of those unemployed, 38.8% had secondary education, and 38.1% had tertiary education qualifications (PSA, 2023c). The shortage of appropriate skills has been cited as a key reason for unfilled vacancies (Barr et al., 2017). These also show that 'unemployment tends to affect disproportionately youth and the well-educated' (Barr et al., 2017, p. 16). As noted earlier, employment in the services sector outstripped that in the agriculture and industry sectors. In August 2023, wage and salary workers accounted for 62.6% of the total employed, followed by self-employed individuals without any paid employee (27.3%), unpaid family workers (8.0%), and employers in own family-operated farm or business (2.1%) (PSA, 2023b). The biggest proportion of OFWs came from a region in the country (CALABARZON), where the unemployment rate was among the highest (5.9%) (PSA, 2023a, 2023d; Ofreneo & Sale, 2014). Moreover, the labour force participation rate (LFPR) was 64.7%, with male and female LFPR reaching 76.3% and 52.9%, respectively, while the national underemployment rate stood at 11.7% (PSA, 2023b). About 1.96 million Filipinos were working abroad as of 2022 (PSA, 2023a), contributing to the national economy through their dollar remittances. The majority of OFWs (60.2%) have been women with four in every ten OFWs performing elementary occupations or jobs relating to 'simple and routine tasks using hand-held tools, in the areas of cleaning, maintenance, food preparation, delivery, luggage handling, and others' (Eugenio, 2023, para. 2). The top OFW destination was Asia at 78.3%—about 24.4% worked in Saudi Arabia and 14.4% in the United Arab Emirates; other Asian countries with big numbers of OFWs include Hong Kong at 6.7%, Kuwait at 5.9%, Singapore at 5.8%, and Qatar at 4.8% (PSA, 2022).

Policy Framework and Labour Market

Considering its unemployment, underemployment, and poverty situation, the Philippines has been a labour-exporting country with a web of statutory regulations set out under the country's Labour Code 1974 (Presidential Decree 442) and Migrant Workers and Overseas Filipinos Act (MWOFA) 1995 (Republic Act 8042) as amended (Sale, 2021). Labour export was originally intended as a transitory action to reduce unemployment while the national economy had not yet expanded under the EOI approach during the 1970s (Ofreneo & Sale, 2014). However, the anticipated economic growth based on EOI did not materialise, and the government, in time, shifted to 'managing migration' as the preferred policy approach (Ofreneo & Sale, 2014, pp. 179–182).

The Labour Code has tended to encourage 'growth of employment in the services sector, where low-productivity and low-paying jobs are abundant, and the quality of employment is doubtful' (Congress of the Philippines, 2001; Sale, 2021, p. 106). It is worth noting that the pre-employment policy in the

Labour Code is aimed to 'promote and maintain a state of full employment through improved manpower training, allocation and utilisation' and to 'facilitate and regulate the movement of workers in conformity with the national interest' (Presidential Decree 442, art. 12, 1974). Moreover, the code sets forth the rule requiring 'all Filipino workers abroad to remit a portion of their foreign exchange earnings to their families, dependents, and/or beneficiaries in the country' (Presidential Decree 442, art. 22, 1974). Ironically, the Labour Code was part of the developmentalist agenda under the first Marcos regime that has been embraced by subsequent governments and eventually contributed to the expansion of the services sector pursuant to the EOI strategy (Thompson, 2014; Sale, 2021).

Amendments have been introduced to the Labour Code to enhance the exported labour policy, which regulates the recruitment and placement of workers for overseas work (Presidential Decree 442, 1974). Republic Acts 8042, 9422, and 10022 were enacted by the state to bolster the protections to and foster the welfare of migrant workers and their families through rules regarding reciprocity that make sure these workers are deployed to host countries that have extant labour and social legislation protecting worker rights (Republic Act 10022; Sale, 2021).

Under the Philippine Overseas Employment Administration (POEA) Governing Board Resolution No 01 Series of 2006, mission-critical skills (MCS) are defined as 'skills that reflect the primary function of the organisation without which mission-critical work cannot be completed and which skills are internally developed and require extensive training, thus, not easily replaceable'.

In 2020, POEA issued another resolution under this framework, that is, Governing Board Resolution No 09, which indicated a shortage of 290,000 health workers in the country even before the onset of the COVID-19 pandemic. This was aggravated by the annual outward migration of about 13,000 healthcare professionals (POEA, 2020). Based on the same document, 14 occupations were listed as new MCS, including medical doctor/physician, nurse, microbiologist, molecular biologist, medical technologist, clinical analyst, respiratory therapist, pharmacist, laboratory technician, X-ray/radiology technician, nursing assistant/aid, operator of medical equipment, supervisor of health services and personal care and repairman of medical-hospital equipment (POEA, 2020). Deployment of these professions was temporarily suspended until the national state of emergency, and COVID-19-related travel restrictions were lifted (POEA, 2020). Recently, the second Marcos government that ascended to power after winning the 2022 election, approved the Philippine Development Plan for 2023–2028, which aims to create jobs and reduce poverty while tackling the problems generated by COVID-19 (Galvez, 2023). However, the Plan still relies on the same EOI framework (IBON Foundation, 2023b).

In 2021, a new agency in the executive arm or branch of the State was created—the Department of Migrant Workers—to protect the rights and promote the welfare of OFWs (Republic Act 11641).

Decent Work and Economic Growth

The United Nations reported that the Philippines' overall rank in terms of sustainable development was 92, with a score of 67.47% (UN, n.d.). SDG 8 is about inclusive and sustainable economic growth, full and productive employment, and decent work, and the report shows that major challenges exist in the Philippines (UN, n.d.). Unemployment is improving, but fundamental labour rights guarantees are stagnating (UN, n.d.). ILO conventions thus play an important role because they lay down a set of global social minimum requirements that member states of the ILO are expected to respect, promote, and realise (ILO, 1998) as part of the Decent Work Agenda. The Philippines has been able to ratify all eight fundamental conventions that are regarded as the global social minimum (Table 13.1).

How Are These Conventions Respected, Promoted, and Recognised in the Philippines? In Short, How Are They Being Enforced?

Regular courts are granted the power to prosecute unfair labour practice as a criminal offence as it interferes with, restrains, or coerces workers in exercising their rights to self-organisation and collective bargaining (Labour Code art 258–260). However, no person has been prosecuted and found guilty so far despite final judgments that unfair labour practices have been committed (Disini, 1992). Declining trade union density and collective bargaining

Table 13.1 Philippines' ratification of fundamental ILO conventions

Fundamental ILO convention	*Date*	*Status*
C29—Forced Labour Convention, 1930 (No. 29)	15 July 2005	In force
C87—Freedom of Association and Protection of the Right to Organise Convention, 1948 (No. 87)	29 December 1953	In force
C98—Right to Organise and Collective Bargaining Convention, 1949 (No. 98)	29 December 1953	In force
C100—Equal Remuneration Convention, 1951 (No. 100)	29 December 1953	In force
C105—Abolition of Forced Labour Convention, 1957 (No. 105)	17 November 1960	In force
C111—Discrimination (Employment and Occupation) Convention, 1958 (No. 111)	17 November 1960	In force
C138—Minimum Age Convention, 1973 (No. 138) Minimum age specified: 15 years	4 June 1998	In force
C182—Worst Forms of Child Labour Convention, 1999 (No. 182)	28 November 2000	In force

Source: derived from NORMLEX Ratifications for the Philippines (ILO, n.d.-b). See Sale (2021)

coverage also contribute to the overall weakness of implementation (Sale, 2021). Union membership fell from nearly 3.8 million in 1999 to around 1.54 million in 2017, while CBA coverage dropped from about 530,000 workers in 1999 to nearly 191,000 in 2015 (Sale, 2021). While slavery is prohibited under the 1987 Constitution, still precarious and vulnerable work abounds, especially in the informal economy (Sale, 2021). The Labour Code recognises the employment of minors, but youth unemployment remains high. Discrimination against women is proscribed under the Labour Code. However, the participation rate of women in the labour force is much lower than that of men.

These 'decent work deficits' (ILO, n.d.-a) disclose the 'law/practice gap' that permeates the Philippine labour law system (Sale, 2021). ILO (n.d.-a) defines 'decent work deficit' as 'the absence of sufficient employment opportunities, inadequate social protection, the denial of rights at work and shortcomings in social dialogue' and identifies four types, that is, 'employment gap' (which includes 'underemployment'), 'rights gap' (such as 'denial of freedom of association', the occurrence of 'forced labour', 'discrimination'), 'social protection gap' (presence of 'income insecurity', for instance), and 'social dialogue gap' ('representational gap' owing to the absence of voice) (para. 3–6).

Method

As a migrant-sending country, the Philippines is the world's leading exporter of nursing labour (Brush & Sochalski, 2007; Lorenzo et al., 2007; Cabanda, 2017). Focusing on nursing labour as the critical skill in shortage, this chapter aims to answer the following questions:

1 What is the exported labour policy of the Philippines?
2 What is the role of the State in the development and implementation of this policy?
3 Has the exported labour policy contributed to decent work (SDG 8) and sustainable development?

    a. Is decent work among the push and pull factors influencing the movement of OFWs, specifically nurse labour?

4 Are there links between the exported labour policy and critical skills shortages within the nurse profession in the country?

More broadly, what do these portend for future work in the country?

A case study of the exported labour policy and outcomes in the Philippines as they pertain to nursing labour is employed in this chapter. The said policy and outcomes, as well as indicators and patterns of decent work performance (see Ghai, 2006; PSA, 2019; ILO, 2020), are studied through the analysis of documents, such as the Philippines constitution, legislative acts, policies, implementing rules or regulations like POEA resolutions, reports, and other documents. Rights at work, employment, social security or protection, and social dialogue are elements of decent work (Ghai, 2006; Dhakal & Burgess, 2020). Document sources include the government, state agencies, international bodies, and other researchers (Dhakal & Burgess, 2020).

Findings

Exported Labour Policy of the Philippines

Presidential Decree 442 of 1974 was aimed at 'instituting a Labour Code' and 'revising and consolidating labour and social laws to afford protection to labour, promote employment and human resources development and ensure industrial peace based on social justice' (Presidential Decree 442, 1974). It declared the basic policy to 'afford protection to labour, promote full employment, ensure equal work opportunities regardless of sex, race or creed and regulate the relations between workers and employers' and to 'assure the rights of workers to self-organisation, collective bargaining, security of tenure, and just and humane conditions of work' (Presidential Decree 442, art.3, 1974).

The regulation of recruitment and placement of workers for local and overseas work was among the significant rules codified (Labour Code Book 1 Title 1). The Labour Code laid down the rule, inter alia, requiring 'all Filipino workers abroad to remit a portion of their foreign exchange earnings to their families, dependents, and/or beneficiaries in the country' (Presidential Decree 442, art. 22, 1974). These rules entrenched the country's 'exported labour' (Cooney & Mitchell, 2003) strategy and set its pathway to remittance dependency. The remittances reached around 10% of the country's GDP (Boquet, 2017; Sale, 2021). This policy, initiated by the first Marcos regime, 'became critical in addressing the problems of employment and generating income for a rapidly expanding population' and developed into 'a permanent institution that was upheld by the administrations that succeeded the dictatorship' (Bello et al., 2005; Sale, 2021, p. 96).

The exported labour policy has been aptly described as a 'new' form 'of unilateralism' that creates 'a "Magna Carta of rights" for Filipinos working overseas'—a 'developing practice' of extending 'country-of-origin protection to national workers employed abroad' (Ortiz et al., 2014; Olivier, 2017; Sale, 2021, p. 221). Under Section 4 of the MWOFA, as amended in 2009, the Philippines allows the deployment of OFWs only to countries that protect their rights.

Role of the State in the Development and Implementation of This Policy

When the Labour Code was enacted in the 1970s, the autocratic regime of the first Marcos government began to undertake the outward-looking EOI approach (Felker, 2004; Wie, n.d.). EOI was labour-intensive and part of the division of labour at the international level, which lowered the cost of labour (Sale, 2021). The exported labour strategy became institutionalised. That is why the pre-employment policy in the 1974 Labour Code was (and still is) aimed to, inter alia, 'promote and maintain a state of full employment through improved manpower training, allocation and utilisation' and to 'facilitate and regulate the movement of workers in conformity with the national interest' (Presidential Decree 442, art. 12, 1974).

Moreover, legislative amendments have been introduced to the 1974 Labour Code to enhance the exported labour policy, which regulates the recruitment and placement of workers for overseas work. The policy, which was put in place initially as a stop-gap measure to mitigate the impact on the domestic economy of the oil crisis during the 1970s, requires, as aforementioned, 'all Filipino workers abroad to remit a portion of their foreign exchange earnings to their families, dependents, and/or beneficiaries in the country' (Presidential Decree 442, art. 22, 1974).

The Department of Migrant Workers (DMW) was created through legislation by the Philippine Congress in 2021. This new Department absorbed all powers, functions, and mandates of the POEA and the other entities named in the law and is the primary state agency tasked to protect and promote OFW rights and welfare, regardless of status and of means of entry into countries of destination (Republic Act 11641). It formulates, plans, coordinates, promotes, administers, and implements policies and undertakes systems for regulating, managing, and monitoring the overseas employment and reintegration of OFWs, taking into consideration the national development programmes formulated by the National Economic and Development Authority (NEDA) (Republic Act 11641). DMW also promotes the empowerment and protection of Filipinos working overseas by empowering and training them to gain appropriate skills and ensuring access to continuous training and knowledge development (Republic Act 11641).

Exported Labour Policy, Decent Work, and Sustainable Development: Push and Pull Factors Influencing the Movement of OFWs, Specifically Nurses

Since 1999, 20,000 graduates have been produced annually by 233 nursing schools in the Philippines (Elmaco, 2022). The country's aim is to train 'a surplus of registered nurses' to provide for labour markets abroad, as evidenced by the growth in nursing schools over time (Elmaco, 2022, p. 215). However, push and pull factors influence labour mobility (Ofreneo & Sale, 2014). Push factors are linked to the area of origin, while pull factors are connected to the destination area (Lee, 1966; Ofreneo & Sale, 2014). In a 2007 Philippine case study, it was pointed out that a big majority (around 85%) of employed nurses (193,223) worked abroad (Lorenzo et al., 2007). The focus group discussions that were part of the study disclosed the following push and pull factors (Table 13.2):

Table 13.2 Nurse mobility: push and pull factors

Push factors	*Pull factors*
Economic: low salary at home, no overtime or hazard pay, poor health insurance coverage	Economic: higher income, better benefits, and compensation package
Job-related: work overload or stressful working environment, slow promotion	Job-related: lower nurse-to-patient ratio, more options in working hours, chance to upgrade nursing skills
Socio-political and economic environment: limited opportunities for employment, decreased health budget, socio-political and economic instability in the Philippines	Personal/family related: an opportunity for the family to migrate, the opportunity to travel and learn other cultures, influence from peers and relatives
	Socio-political and economic environment: advanced technology, better socio-political and economic stability

Source: derived from Lorenzo et al. (2007)

More recently, the Commission on Filipinos Overseas (CFO) and POEA reported that a total of 350,361 doctors, nurses, and midwives left the Philippines to work overseas from 1990 to 2017, of which 95% were nurses (HRH2030 Program, 2020). In this 2020 study, the following push and pull factors were identified:

Table 13.3 Medical professionals migration: push and pull factors

Push factors	*Pull factors*
Poor working conditions in the Philippines which include low salaries, insecure jobs without tenured positions, unsafe and inadequate working environments, outdated healthcare technologies, and lack of employment and career opportunities	Prospect of better social, economic, and professional opportunities abroad and the presence of relatives in the destination country
Poor health infrastructure, job insecurity, inconsistencies in practice, outdated or inappropriate curricula, institutional politics, and inadequate opportunities for specialty training	Higher salaries, higher quality working conditions and technologies, and job vacancies with available positions due to local shortages
Human rights abuses, peace, and order issues especially in rural areas	Policy and institutional support currently in place, such as the destination countries' visa provisions allowing family members to join the migrating health worker to facilitate family reunification

Source: derived from HRH2030 Program (2020)

Tables 13.2 and 13.3 tend to suggest that decent work is among the push and pull factors influencing the movement of OFWs, specifically nursing labour. The salary differential offered internationally is a particularly strong pull factor (HRH2030 Program, 2020). For instance, mid-level public hospital nurses in Vietnam earn 57% higher than their Filipino counterparts, while entry-level and private hospital nurses in the Philippines receive less (Robredo et al., 2022). Thus, around 17,000 Filipino nurses had overseas contracts in 2019 (Robredo et al., 2022).

Links Between the Exported Labour Policy and Critical Skills Shortages Within the Nursing Profession

Mass nurse resignations and consequent migration occurred at the height of the COVID-19 pandemic because of unfair compensation, unreceived benefits and hazard pay, and delays in insurance reimbursements (Robredo et al., 2022). The POEA developed a definition of mission-critical skills (MCS). It also created a framework for projecting the shortage of MCS due to outward migration, considering MCS local demand, inventory of qualified workers, number of MCS deployed out of the country, and prospective MCS entrants over a given time period (POEA, 2020).

This framework allowed the POEA to declare in 2020 that 'there was a shortage of about 290,000 health workers in the country, and that an average annual migration of 13,000 care professionals aggravates the deficiency in the national supply' (POEA, 2020). The nurse occupation was included in the roster of existing MCS under the POEA declaration, which meant that nurse deployment overseas was temporarily suspended (POEA, 2020). In 2021, the Philippines raised the number of nurses and healthcare workers that could be deployed overseas to 6,500 every year (Morales, 2021).

Discussions

Nurse migration to the United States originated from the US colonial period through the American education system as Filipino nurses were American trained, so when the demand for nurses increased after World War II, the Philippines became an important supplier of nursing labour to the United States (Ladrido, 2020). More broadly, the demand for labour in the Gulf countries in the area of construction was high during the 1970s, which created an opportunity for the Philippines to supply labour in the context of a domestic situation characterised by high unemployment, the poor economy, political instability, and low wages (Cai, 2011). These suggest that decent work deficits in the Philippines are push factors while decent work surpluses (which are the opposite of deficits) in countries of destination are pull factors, especially in terms of better and more decent pay and work conditions. Overall, these also reflect the weak position of employees, workers and/or unions as societal actors and institutions (Sale, 2021). 'As "sources of agency" "outside the state", employees, workers and/or unions have hardly influenced "society-centered", "bottom-up" rulemaking' except in a few situations like the passage of the MWOFA in 1995, which was advocated by civil society (Sellers, 2011, pp. 129–135; Sale, 2021, p. 225).

This legislation laid down state policies on overseas employment and higher standards of welfare protection and promotion for migrant workers, their families, and overseas Filipinos in distress (Lorenzo et al., 2007). The law also required the Overseas Workers Welfare Administration (OWWA) to provide assistance to OFWs and their families in the enforcement of the contractual obligations of recruitment and placement agencies and/or their principals, as well as in the repatriation of OFWs (Ofreneo & Sale, 2014). Predeparture orientation seminars about laws, customs, and practices in destination countries, model employment contracts that ensure the welfare of OFWs, a foreign employer accreditation system, and the creation of overseas labour offices have been among the approaches under the law (Lorenzo et al., 2007). The POEA, OWWA, Department of Foreign Affairs, and Department of Labour and Employment administered interweaving programmes of protection and regulation, even while the number of undocumented overseas Filipinos remained large, and social protection for those documented varied (Ofreneo & Sale, 2014). The DMW was created by the Philippine government in 2021 to bring these programmes and institutions together (Ang & Tiongson, 2023).

Consolidating disparate state agencies involved in enforcing the exported labour policy into the DMW appears to be a step in the right direction. In a presentation to the United Nations Committee on Migrant Workers, former DMW Secretary Maria Susana Ople reported, in relation to the Department's function of regulating private recruitment and manning agencies involved in OFW deployment abroad, that

> *[a] strict licensing system existed, and out of 452 license applicants, only 104 were granted between 2018 and 2022. Licensed recruitment agencies were required to adhere to strict rules, and any violation would result in the cancellation of the license. In 2022, 124 recruitment agencies were suspended, and 59 licenses were cancelled for various offences, including excessive collection of fees. Annual and surprise inspections of these agencies were also carried out.*
>
> *(UN, 2023a, para. 6)*

The DMW secretary also discussed state actions in regard to a recent death abroad—that of domestic worker Juleebee Ranara—and highlighted the importance of engaging civil society, upholding the rights of migrants, and protecting the family members left behind, particularly children, from social costs associated with labour migration (UN, 2023a).

For the future of work in the country, this also means a stronger national coordination of efforts to fulfil the objectives of the United Nations Global Compact for Safe, Orderly and Regular Migration (GCM) (Ang & Tiongson, 2023). In the policy declaration of the law that created DMW, Section 2 of Republic Act 11641, the Philippines is committed to increasingly aligning state programmes and policies to achieve the GMC objectives, including decent work under GMC Objective 6, which overlaps with SDG 8. What this means is attaining Target 8.8 under SDG 8, which is about protecting 'labour rights' and promoting 'safe and secure working environments for all workers, including migrant workers, in particular women migrants, and those in precarious employment' (UN, 2023b, para. 8), is among the actions that DMW will need to enforce or implement under state programmes and policies. At a fundamental level, such rights at work include freedom *of* association and collective bargaining as well as freedom *from* forced and child labour, including the worst forms of child labour and discrimination at work (ILO, 1998), which are deemed 'so basic that their acceptance is regarded as a prerequisite' to membership in the International Labour Organization (Ghai, 2006, pp. 9–10).

The same policy declaration mentions that the Philippine state 'does not promote overseas employment as a means to economic growth and national development and shall continuously aim to make it a choice not a necessity' and will 'institute measures that will strengthen the domestic labour market for the effective reintegration of' OFWs (Republic Act 11641). This suggests that 'marketing Filipino migrant workers as desirable labour in gendered occupations, such as domestic work, nursing and care work for women, and construction and production work for men' (Liao, 2023, p. 3) may no longer be actively pursued by state actors.

Around 15 years ago, the policy debates about labour migration within the nursing sector revolved around the themes of *regulation versus deregulation of recruitment services* and *managing versus promoting labour migration* (Lorenzo et al., 2007). The first theme was about liberalising the 'migration services of recruitment entities' and whether that would benefit the country and/or individual OFWs, while the second theme delved into whether the policy should shift from a 'reactive' approach to overseas demand that was limited to 'managing' migration flows to a 'proactive' stance of 'promoting' migration that meant 'actively seeking out international markets and marketing Filipino human resources in selected markets' (Lorenzo et al, 2007, p. 1415). The enactment of Republic Act 11641 seems to have resolved both issues in favour of more regulation of recruitment services and stronger management of labour migration.

Conclusions

The process of migration, from the overseas deployment to the return of OFWs, including nursing labour, entails a slew of 'actors, policies and structures', which means 'the sending state is not a unitary actor' (Liao, 2023, p. 2). State and non-state actors are involved in the Philippines' exported labour policy. The Philippine legislature passed some laws to strengthen the protections and promote the welfare of migrant workers and their families through rules around reciprocity that ensure these workers are deployed to host countries that have existing labour and social legislation protecting worker rights (Republic Act 10022; Sale, 2021). These were enhanced with the creation through Republic Act 11641 of a new Department in the executive arm of the state—the Department of Migrant Workers—aimed at providing tougher regulation of private recruitment and manning agencies and more effective management of overseas labour migration. These are consistent with the goal or objective of decent work articulated under the United Nations SDG and GCM frameworks. However, for the Philippines' nursing sector in particular, decent work deficits are push factors, while decent work surpluses in countries of destination are pull factors, especially in terms of better and more decent pay and work conditions. The confluence of the exported labour policy, the COVID-19 pandemic and decent work deficits contributed to the critical skills shortage of nurses and healthcare workers in 2020, which required the temporary banning of their overseas deployment. The new department needs to be able to exercise its vast powers and functions under the law to address decent work deficits (whether in the form of employment gap, rights gap, social protection gap, or social dialogue gap), and critical skills shortages over time, and help achieve sustainable development in the Philippines.

Note

* Corresponding author: Jonathan.Sale@unisa.edu.au.

References

Ang, A., & Tiongson, E. R. (2023). *Philippine migration journey: Processes and programs in the migration life cycle.* Background paper prepared for the World Development Report. https://thedocs.worldbank.org/en/doc/10c897a073055768 2d8b1d67a5a65adc-0050062023/original/Philippine-Migration-Experience-and-Cases-FORMATTED.pdf

Asia Regional Integration Center (ARIC). (2022). *Philippines: Asian development outlook 2022.* https://aric.adb.org/philippines

Barr, J., Sale, J., & Nigaus, S. (2017). *Employment and skills strategies in the Philippines.* OECD. www.oecd-ilibrary.org/employment/employment-and-skills-strategies-in-the-philippines_9789264273436-en

Bello, W., De Guzman, M., Lou Malig, M., & Docena, H. (2005). *The anti-development state: The political economy of permanent crisis in the Philippines.* Zed Books.

Boquet, Y. (2017). *The Philippine archipelago.* Springer International Publishing.

Britannica. (n.d.). *Philippines.* www.britannica.com/place/Philippines/The-19th-century

British Broadcasting Corporation (BBC). (n.d.). *Philippines: Country profile.* www.bbc.com/news/world-asia-15521300

Brush, B. L., & Sochalski, J. (2007). International nurse migration: Lessons from the Philippines. *Policy, Politics, & Nursing Practice*, *8*(1), 37–46.

Cabanda, E. (2017). Higher education, migration and policy design of the Philippine Nursing Act of 2002. *Higher Education Policy*, *30*, 555–575.

Cable News Network (CNN) Philippines. (2023, May 8). *SWS: 51% of Filipino families still consider themselves poor.* www.cnnphilippines.com/news/2023/5/8/SWS-self-rated-poverty-March-2023.html

Cai, F. (2011). *The labour export policy: A case study of the Philippines.* Institut Barcelona d'Estudis Internacionals (IBEI).
Congress of the Philippines. (2001). *Report and recommendations of the Congressional Commission on Labour: Human capital in the emerging economy.* The Congressional Commission on Labour.
Cooney, S., & Mitchell, R. (2003). What is labour law doing in East Asia? In S. Cooney, T. Lindsey, R. Mitchell, & Y. Zhu (Eds.), *Law and labour market regulation in East Asia* (pp. 246–274). Routledge.
Dhakal, S. P., & Burgess, J. (2020). Decent work for sustainable development in post-crisis Nepal: Social policy challenges and a way forward. *Social Policy & Administration, 55*, 128–142. https://doi.org/10.1111/spol.12619
Disini, D. (1992). Analytical survey of 1991 Supreme Court decisions on the law on labour standards and labour relations. *Philippine Law Journal, 67*, 53–119.
Elmaco, J. L. (2022). Philippine nurse migration: Assessing vulnerabilities and accessing opportunities during the COVID-19 pandemic. In D. E. Degila & V. M. Valle (Eds.), *Governing migration for development from the global souths: Challenges and opportunities* (pp. 208–233). Brill. https://journals.openedition.org/poldev/4853?lang=de#tocto2n1
Eugenio, L. J. (2023, 11 August). Overseas Filipino workers: The modern-day heroes of the Philippines. *Harvard International Review.* https://hir.harvard.edu/overseas-filipino-workers-the-modern-day-heroes-of-the-philippines
Felker, G. (2004). Southeast Asian development in regional and historical perspective. In M. Beeson (Ed.), *Contemporary Southeast Asia: Regional dynamics, national differences* (pp. 61–63). Palgrave Macmillan.
Galvez, D. (2023, 30 January). Marcos Jr. signs Philippine development plan for 2023–2028. *INQUIRER.net.* https://newsinfo.inquirer.net/1722904/marcos-signs-philippine-development-plan-for-2023-2028
Ghai, D. (2006). Decent work: Universality and diversity. In D. Ghai (Ed.), *Decent work: Objectives and strategies* (pp. 7–31). International Labour Organization.
Gregorio, X. (2023, February 22). Philippines still overwhelmingly Catholic. *The Philippine Star.* www.philstar.com/headlines/2023/02/22/2246855/philippines-still-overwhelmingly-catholic
Human Resources for Health Migration. (2020). *HRH2030 program.* https://hrh2030program.org/wp-content/uploads/2020/08/x12.8_HRH2030PH_Migration-policy-brief.pdf
IBON Foundation. (2023a, April 28). *PH minimum wages are family poverty wages.* www.ibon.org/ph-minimum-wages-are-family-poverty-wages-ibon/
IBON Foundation. (2023b, 30 January). *IBON: PDP 2023–2028 non-solution to PH economic crisis.* www.ibon.org/ibon-pdp-2023-2028-non-solution-to-ph-economic-crisis/
International Labour Organization (ILO). (1998, 18 June). *ILO declaration on fundamental principles and rights at work and its follow-up.* International Labour Conference 86th Session. www.ilo.org/declaration/thedeclaration/textdeclaration/lang--en/index.htm
International Labour Organization (ILO). (2020). *State of skills—Philippines.* www.ilo.org/wcmsp5
International Labour Organization (ILO). (n.d.-a). *Decent work deficit.* www.ilo.org/global/about-the-ilo/newsroom/news/WCMS_007843/lang--en/index.htm
International Labour Organization (ILO). (n.d.-b). *NORMLEX ratifications for Philippines.* www.ilo.org/dyn/normlex/en/f?p=1000:11200:0::NO:11200:P11200_COUNTRY_ID:102970
International Monetary Fund (IMF). (2023a, May 12). *IMF staff concludes visit to the Philippines.* www.imf.org/en/News/Articles/2023/05/12/pr23148-philippines-imf-staff-concludes-visit

International Monetary Fund (IMF). (2023b, April). *World economic outlook*. www.imf.org/external/datamapper/LP@WEO/PHL?zoom=PHL&highlight=PHL

Ladrido, P. (2020, May 6). How the Philippines became the biggest supplier of nurses worldwide. *CNN Philippines*. www.cnnphilippines.com/life/culture/2020/5/6/ofw-nurses.html

Lee, E. S. (1966). A theory of migration. *Demography*, *3*(1), 47–57. https://doi.org/10.2307/2060063

Liao, K. A. S. (2023). Infrastructuring repatriation: The Philippine sending state and the return of migrant workers caught in disruptions. *International Migration*. https://doi.org/10.1111/imig.13155

Licuanan, W. Y., Cabreira, R. W., & Aliño, P. M. (2019). Chapter 23 — The Philippines. In C. Shappard (Ed.), *World seas: An environmental evaluation* (2nd ed., pp. 515–537). Academic Press.

Lorenzo, F., Galvez-Tan, J., Icamina, K., & Javier, L. (2007). Nurse migration from a source country perspective: Philippine country case study. *Health Services Research*, *42*, 1406–1418. https://doi.org/10.1111/j.1475-6773.2007.00716.x

Milner, A., & Drakard, J. (2009). *The Malays*. John Wiley & Sons. https://ebookcentral-proquest-com.ezproxy.newcastle.edu.au/lib/newcastle/reader.action?docID=427981&query=

Morales, N. (2021, 18 June). *Philippines raises cap on health professionals going abroad*. Reuters. www.reuters.com/world/asia-pacific/philippines-raises-cap-health-professionals-going-abroad-2021-06-18/

Ofreneo, R., & Sale, J. (2014). Social security and migrant workers in the Philippines: Social protection for the country's economic protectors. In R. Blanpain, P. A. Ortiz, M. Olivier, & G. Vonk (Eds.), *Social security law and migrant workers: Selected studies of cross-border social security mechanisms* (pp. 167–186). Kluwer Law International.

Olivier, M. (2017). Social protection for migrant workers abroad: Addressing the deficit via country-of-origin unilateral measures? In M. McAuliffe & M. Klein Solomon (Conveners), *Ideas to inform international cooperation on safe, orderly and regular migration*. International Organization for Migration. https://publications.iom.int/system/files/pdf/social_protection.pdf

Ortiz, P. A., Olivier, M., & Vonk, G. (2014). Labour migration and social security rights: New solutions in a globalizing world. In R. Blanpain, P. A. Ortiz, M. Olivier, & G. Vonk (Eds.), *Social security law and migrant workers: Selected studies of cross-border social security mechanisms* (pp. 1–5). Kluwer Law International.

Philippine Government (PG). (2015a). *Gross domestic product*. www.officialgazette.gov.ph/report/gdp/

Philippine Government (PG). (2015b). *The Philippine education and training system*. https://pqf.gov.ph/Home/Details/16

Philippine Overseas Employment Administration (POEA) Governing Board Resolution No 01 Series of 2006.

Philippine Overseas Employment Administration (POEA) Governing Board Resolution No 09 Series of 2020.

Philippine Statistics Authority (PSA). (2019). *Decent work statistics*. https://openstat.psa.gov.ph/Featured/Decent-Work-Statistics-Philippines/Decent-Work-Statistics

Philippine Statistics Authority (PSA). (2022, 2 December). *2021 overseas Filipino workers (final results)*. https://psa.gov.ph/statistics/survey/labour-and-employment/survey-overseas-filipinos

Philippine Statistics Authority (PSA). (2023a, 11 October). *2022 survey on Overseas Filipinos (final result)*. https://psa.gov.ph/statistics/survey/labour-and-employment/survey-overseas-filipinos

Philippine Statistics Authority (PSA). (2023b, 6 October). *Labour force survey*. https://psa.gov.ph/statistics/labour-force-survey

Philippine Statistics Authority (PSA). (2023c, 8 September). *Labour force survey.* https://psa.gov.ph/statistics/labour-force-survey

Philippine Statistics Authority (PSA). (2023d, 9 March). *Unemployment rate in January 2023 is estimated at 4.8 percent.* https://psa.gov.ph/content/unemployment-rate-january-2023-estimated-48-percent

Pinlac, B. (2023, May 8). 14 million Filipino families consider themselves poor—SWS. *Inquirer.* https://newsinfo.inquirer.net/1766165/14-million-filipino-families-consider-themselves-poor-sws

Robredo, J. P., Ong, B., Eala, M. A., & Naguit, R. J. (2022). Outmigration and unequal distribution of Filipino physicians and nurses: An urgent call for investment in health human resource and systemic reform. *The Lancet Regional Health. Western Pacific, 25*, 100512. https://doi.org/10.1016/j.lanwpc.2022.100512

Sale, J. (2021). *Harmonisation of ASEAN labour laws on disputes settlement: The Philippines and Malaysia as case studies* [PhD thesis, The University of Newcastle]. NOVA open access repository. http://hdl.handle.net/1959.13/1430275

Sellers, J. (2011). State-society relations. In M. Bevir (Ed.), *The SAGE handbook of governance* (pp. 124–141). SAGE.

Thompson, M. (2014). The politics Philippine presidents make: Presidential-style, patronage-based, or regime relational? *Critical Asian Studies, 46*(3), 433–460. https://doi.org/10.1080/14672715.2014.935135

United Nations (UN). (2023a, 31 March). *Raise issues concerning exploitation by recruitment agencies and the alleged murder of a Filipina domestic worker abroad.* In Dialogue with the Philippines, experts of the Committee on Migrant Workers commend ratification of key labour conventions. www.ohchr.org/en/news/2023/03/dialogue-philippines-experts-committee-migrant-workers-commend-ratification-key-labour

United Nations (UN). (2023b). *Goal 8: Promote inclusive and sustainable economic growth, employment and decent work for all.* https://unric.org/en/sdg-8/

United Nations (UN). (n.d.). *Sustainable development report 2024.* https://dashboards.sdgindex.org/profiles/philippines

United States Agency for International Development (USAID). (2022). *Philippines: Country profile.* www.usaid.gov/sites/default/files/2022-05/Philippines_Country_Profile_0.pdf

Wie, T. K. (n.d.). *Export-oriented industrialisation and foreign direct investment in the ASEAN countries.* Old United Nations University. http://archive.unu.edu/hq/academic/Pg_area4/Thee.html

Wingard, J., & Brändlin, A. (2013, 10 November). *Philippines prone to natural disasters.* www.dw.com/en/philippines-a-country-prone-to-natural-disasters/a-17217404

14 Critical Labour Shortages in the Nepalese Tourism and Hospitality Sector

Strategic Implications

Subas P. Dhakal and Kerry Brown*

Introduction

According to the United Nations (UN) (2015), 'the 2030 Agenda with 17 Sustainable Development Goals (SDGs) provides a shared blueprint for peace and prosperity for people and the planet, now and into the future' (para 1). The literature has increasingly recognised the tourism and hospitality sector's (THS) role in supporting SDG achievement (see Jones et al., 2017; Dhakal & Tjokro, 2022). Although contested (see Sharpley, 2022), one of the ways to contextualise the role of the THS towards SDGs is through the employment lens. The UN World Trade Organisation (UNWTO) highlights this contribution: 'Tourism as an economic powerhouse . . . representing 10% of world GDP, 30% of services exports and 1 out of every ten jobs in the world. Tourism has the potential to contribute, directly or indirectly, to all the goals' (UNWTO, n.d., para 3). Aspects of labour and skills shortages are of relevance to the THS-related strategies (see Dhakal & Tjorko, 2020), mainly when the sector is considered a vehicle to achieve SDGs in developing economies like Nepal (National Planning Commission (NPC), 2020).

Nepal is an interesting case to examine for a couple of reasons. First, the country is recovering from three major crises in the last three decades: a decade-long (1996–2006) armed conflict that claimed the lives of at least 13,000 people (UNOHCR, 2012), the 2015 earthquake with over 9,000 casualties and 22,000 injuries (Dhakal, 2018a), and the COVID-19 pandemic that killed over 12,000 people (JHCRC, 2023). The pandemic led to the first economic contraction in 30 years and de-escalated the speed of ongoing socio-economic recovery from the two earlier crises by significantly hurting the services sector (World Bank, 2020a). Second, with the collapse of international visitor numbers due to travel restrictions, the THS was undoubtedly one of the worst-hit sectors in Nepal impacted by the pandemic in terms of employment (ILO, 2021, p. iv; ILO, n.d.). Tourism has been the backbone of the Nepalese economy for decades. The sector accounted for one in eight direct jobs and contributed nearly 7.5% to the GDP before the pandemic (WTTC, 2022). In the National Review of Sustainable Development Goals Report (NPC, 2020), Nepal's apex planning entity—NPC, considers

DOI: 10.4324/9781003379065-16

the sector a strategic priority to achieve the country's sustainable development aspirations. This emphasis is consistent with the position that tourism-related opportunities to improve socio-economic conditions in developing economies should not be overlooked in the post-pandemic context. For example, although the country has been exporting skilled and semi-skilled labour to the Middle East and Asia-Pacific for over three decades, the outbound migration rate has significantly spiked in the post-pandemic era. So much so that some observers have raised alarms, stating: '*the relentless outflow of Nepali youths has raised the possibility of a labour shortage and consequent economic slowdown*' (Prasai, 2023, para 1), signifying the urgent need for strategic interventions to retain human resources within the country.

The inability to overcome labour and skills shortages can adversely impact the THS in developed economies (see Liu-Lastres et al., 2023) nonetheless, it remains an underexplored topic. More importantly, the paradox of labour shortages in labour-exporting developing economies like Nepal has received little attention. This chapter responds to this gap and utilises SDG#8 as an appropriate lens to advance a critical understanding of labour and skills shortages within the Nepalese THS. There are three specific targets associated with SDG#4: a) '*Target 8.3—promote policies to support job creation and growing enterprises, b) Target 8.6—promote youth employment, education and training, and c) Target 8.9—promote beneficial and sustainable tourism*' (Global Goals, 2023, paras 2–8) that are relevant in the context of THS-related labour shortages. Veneri (1999) states:

> [L]abour shortages occur in a market economy when the demand for workers for a particular occupation is greater than the supply of workers who are qualified, available, and willing to do that job. Jobs remain vacant as employers seek to hire more workers than are willing to work at the prevailing wage or salary.
>
> (p. 15)

In the absence of official recognition and description of labour and skills shortages in Nepal, for the purpose of this research, we consider critical labour shortages (CLS) to be acute and/or chronic difficulties in overcoming the difference between the demand for fitting workers and the supply of available workers. Since Bajracharya and Regmi (2023) posit the THS as a '*mainstay of the Nepalese economy and one of the priority sectors for the government*' (para 1), this chapter contends that a granulated understanding of the causes and effects associated with the CLS can inform the revitalisation of the THS in post-pandemic Nepal.

This chapter is organised in five parts, with the next section providing a brief overview of the Nepalese THS in the broader South Asian context, followed by a section on data collection and analysis. The following sections present key findings and discuss strategic implications before making concluding remarks.

Nepalese THS in the Broader South Asian Context

Nepal, with a population of nearly 30 million (CBS, 2021), is a South Asian nation sandwiched between China and India. Although the South Asian region comprising eight nations—Afghanistan, Bangladesh, Bhutan, India, Maldives, Nepal, Pakistan, and Sri Lanka (see SAARC Secretariat, 2020)—is collectively transforming into middle-income economies, the state of socio-economic development remains varied (Dhakal et al., 2020). For instance, a recent World Bank (2022) report states that '*[d]espite progress in reducing poverty, the most recent international poverty estimates remain double-digit in India and Bangladesh*' (p. 49). Notwithstanding the challenges associated with human resources and digital and physical infrastructure (Rasul et al., 2020), South Asia has become an attractive destination for international visitors because of socio-cultural and environmental attractions and price competitiveness. Manzoor et al.'s (2019) position that the THS is an engine of economic development in South Asia is supported by the World Travel and Tourism Centre' (WTTC) data, which show that the sector contributed to almost 7% of the GDP and employed nearly 50 million people (WTTC, 2022, p. 1) prior to the COVID-19 pandemic. For example, the Maldives and Sri Lanka are not only two of the nations in the region that perform well in terms of the human development index (HDI)—ranked 90th and 73rd out of 160 nations respectively but these two countries also rely on tourism the most, with tourism's GDP contribution amounting to 50% and 10% respectively. Not surprisingly, the most populous country in the world—India, tops the list of tourism-related employment, with over 40 million people employed in the sector.

The size of Nepal's workforce is approximately 21 million people. Pre-pandemic labour force participation rate and unemployment were 83% and 11.4% respectively (Central Bureau of Statistics (CBS), 2021). The informal sector employs nearly two-thirds (62%) of the workforce (MoLE, 2018). However, the unemployment rate in the youth segment (15–29 years old) that makes up over a quarter (28%) of the total population) is 19% (Serrière & CEDA, 2014, p. 2). More importantly, more than half (52.5%) of youth in the workforce hold '*vulnerable short-term, seasonal jobs*' (Sparreboom & Staneva, 2014, p. 48) in the informal economy. While the lack of appropriate employment opportunities means that nearly one-tenth of the workforce is gainfully employed outside the country (MoLE, 2018), Nepal faces THS-related skilled and semi-skilled labour shortages. The Asian Development Bank's (ADB) pandemic-related data indicates that between 2019 and 2020, the outflow of migrant workers from Nepal declined the least (19%) across South Asia when compared to India, which saw a 74% decline (ADB, 2020, p. 2), exacerbating the CLS challenge in a recovery phase. For example, the president of the Hotel Association of Nepal recently said: '*[H]ospitality industry is severely understaffed . . . all over Nepal . . . currently, the hotel industry demands about 15,000 skilled workers, but there are only 5,000 available*' (Nepal Traveller, 2022, para 3). While the government is yet to recognise CLS as a policy issue officially, Lemma et al. (2017) projected labour shortages in four main economic sectors (THS, Information and Communication Technologies (ICT), Agro-processing, and Manufacturing) as a critical challenge for achieving the country's socio-economic aspirations. Although the literature has examined some aspects of the tourism and sustainable development nexus in Nepal, such as digital tourism development and sustainability (Tan et al., 2019), tourism industry's role in addressing the SDGs (Birendra et al., 2021), the social responsibility of corporate endeavours (Joshi et al., 2022); and the importance of holistic planning and development (Dangi et al., 2021), the CLS aspect has been overlooked. Under the assumption that there are fertile opportunities to bridge SDG#8 and the strategic priorities of THS, the central question that this chapter asks is: 'What policy insights can be generated from stakeholders' perspectives on the current state of the CLS?'

Data Collection and Analysis

This study utilises a case study approach to answer the research question with three specific objectives to explore (a) the trend of international tourists' arrival in the country amidst three significant crises, (b) the magnitude and scope of the employment supported by the THS, and (c) stakeholder's perspectives on the THS related CLS. An exploratory multi-method research design (see Grinnell & Unrau, 2010) was adopted to fulfil the aforementioned research objectives. First, analysing the trend in international tourists' arrival relied on publicly available secondary data from the Ministry of Culture, Tourism and Civil Aviation's (MoCTCA) website. Second, the magnitude of enterprises and employment within the THS was assessed based on publicly available secondary data at the Central Bureau of Statistics (CBS) website. Third, the literature on stakeholders' theory informed the identification and classification of various stakeholders based on their interests and influence.

Freeman et al. (2004) defined stakeholders as 'any group or individual who can affect or is affected by the achievement of the purpose and objectives' as 'committed value-chain partners to create outstanding performance and customer service' (p. 365). More importantly, Mitchell et al. (1997) suggested the notion of relative saliency—the comparative prominence of diverse stakeholders at various timeframes, such as urgency, legitimacy, power, etcetera. According to Reed (2008), the interest-influence matrix of stakeholder identification, which assumes stakeholder categories based on the degree of their interest and/or influence, is particularly helpful in strategic decision-making. The power versus influence matrix was adopted to classify stakeholders based on Nankervis et al.'s (2019, p. 34) interpretation of Mendelow's power-interest framework.

In order to identify stakeholders and capture their perspectives on CLS, a Google search (5 September 2023) of six keywords—'Nepal + Tourism + Hospitality + Skills + Labour + Manpower'—yielded a total of 54 relevant online media reports published between 2018 (pre-COVID-19) and 2023 (post-COVID-19). This purposeful sampling method (Palinkas et al., 2015) identified 30 key stakeholder organisations that had been consulted, interviewed, or quoted in online media reports. Finally, a thematic content analysis (Krippendorff, 2018) was instigated to organise stakeholders' perspectives (see Sutcliffe & Dhakal, 2018) on the THS-related CLS.

The Trend of International Tourists' Arrival in Nepal Amidst Three Major Crises

The long-term trend (Figure 14.1) of international visitors arriving in Nepal between 2000 and 2022 can be contextualised to three major crises. First, 2002 was the peak of the armed Maoist conflict between 1996 and 2006 (UNOHCR, 2012), which triggered a substantial dip in the number of foreigners visiting the country. As the sector started rebounding after the peace accord was signed in 2006, the arrivals increased more than three times (compared to the low of 2002) by 2014. Second, the 2015 earthquake significantly affected the economy and the tourism sector, as nearly 12% of tourism-related GDP was wiped out (Rijal, 2016). Figure 14.1 shows that the tourist arrivals took two years after the earthquake to return to the 2014 level. Third, right before the pandemic, a record number of nearly 1.2 million international tourists visited Nepal in 2019 (MoCTCA, 2020). However, the number of visitors drastically declined by almost 90% in 2021 because of the pandemic-related restrictions on international travel. The recent evidence indicates an encouraging pattern where the arrivals have rebounded by as much as four times in 2022 compared to the low of 2021 (MoCTCA, 2023).

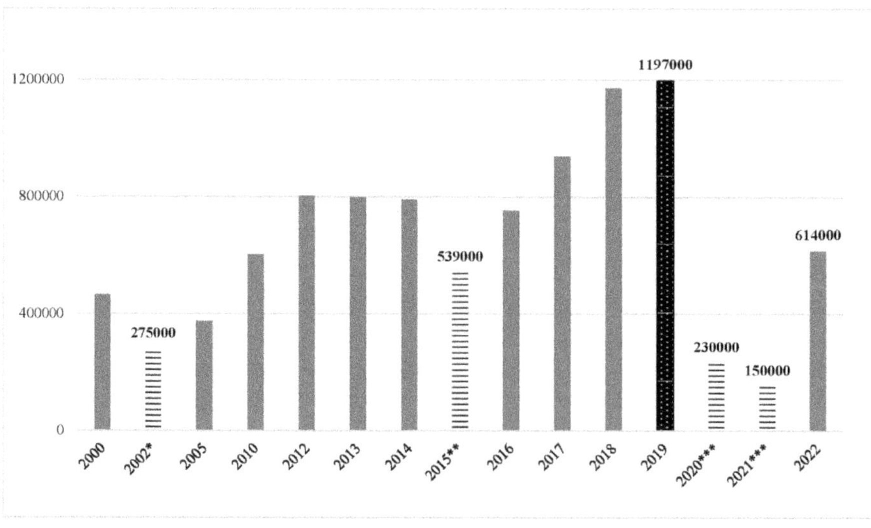

Figure 14.1 International tourists arrival in Nepal

Source: www.tourism.gov.np/publications/

The Magnitude of the THS and Associated Employment Outlook

The Nepalese tourism sector has five main sub-sectors: (a) freight and passenger transport, (b) accommodation, (c) food services, (d) travel and tour operation, and (e) miscellaneous inclusive of the museum and nature/culture-related services (CBS, 2018, 2021). A total of 134,832 enterprises were operating within the tourism sector, accounting for nearly 15% of all businesses in the country (p. 13). With nearly 400,000 people engaged in the industry, tourism is the fourth largest sector after the wholesale and retail (nearly one million engaged persons) and the manufacturing and education sectors, with slightly more than half a million engaged persons in both (CBS, 2021, p. 40). A breakdown of the THS sub-sectors indicates that accommodation and food services are two prominent components, with a collective share of 93% of all businesses within the THS. The sector received attention to reverse the trend of jobs lost due to the pandemic and to explore ways to generate employment. For example, the then minister stated: '*[T]he government was at work to make rules making it compulsory for tourists visiting Nepal to have a Nepali guide, which would require a big manpower in the country*' (Khabar Hub, 2020, para 3). However, Nepal's overall environment for establishing and running businesses remains poor, adversely impacting the potential THS-related job prospects in the private sector-dominated industry. For example, the labour market survey carried out by the Nepalese Council for Technical Education and Vocational Training (CTEVT) found that most THS entrepreneurs in the country were not optimistic about the future of their businesses (CTEVT, 2016, p. 65). The World Bank's (2020a) Doing Business report, at least, partially explains this pessimism because starting a business in Nepal has become more complex and property registration more expensive (p. 113) in recent years.

THS-Related Stakeholders

A total of 30 stakeholder organisations were extracted from the online media reports (Figure 14.2). These stakeholders are grouped into four categories according to their influence and interest. For example, two high-influence and high-interest stakeholders are the Ministry of Culture, Tourism, and Civil Aviation (MoCTCA), the authority responsible for developing and implementing THS-related acts, legislation, and policies and the Nepal Tourism Board (NTB)—an independent body '*established in 1998 by an Act of Parliament in the form of partnership between the Government of Nepal and private sector tourism industry to develop and market Nepal as an attractive tourist destination*' (NTB, 2024, para 12).

Stakeholders' Perspectives on the Cause and Effect of the CLS

The thematic analysis of stakeholders' perspectives based on online media reports revealed three main areas related to the root causes of CLS: limited employment opportunities, inadequate education and training, and increasing outbound migration.

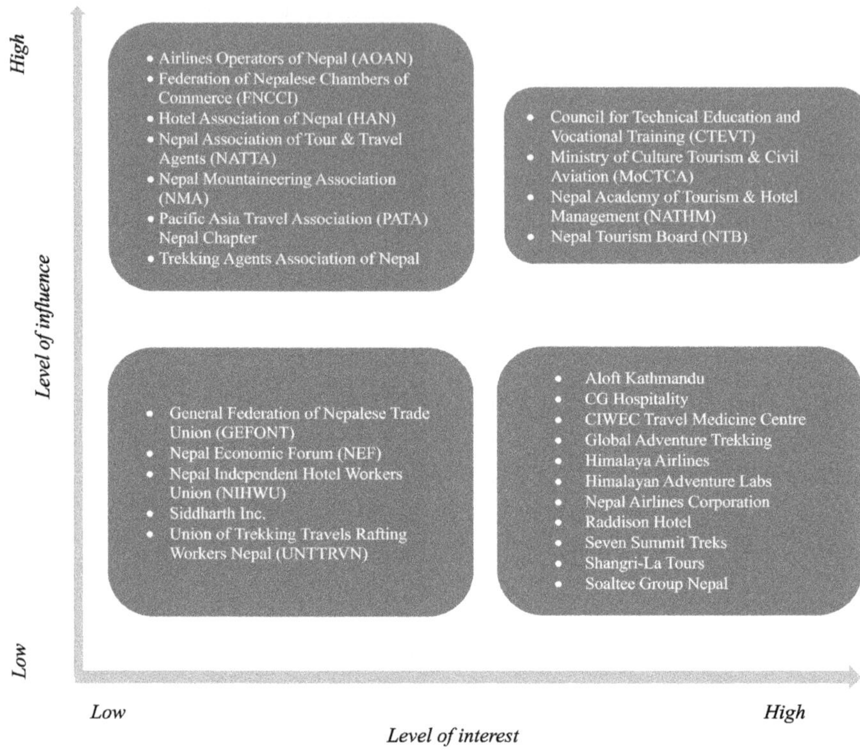

Figure 14.2 Stakeholders' classification based on the level of power/interest

Source: Compiled by authors

Limited Employment Opportunities

Online media reports indicate that although key stakeholders have been keen on generating job opportunities within the THS, these efforts have been inadequate. For instance, the NTB has recently revised the provision for trekking, making it compulsory to hire a guide to ensure safety and well-being with dual objectives: (a) to create additional tourism-related jobs and (b) to deter unauthorised trekking operations (NTB, 2023). This policy instrument of embedding social outcomes into tourism activities uses a mandatory approach to ensure policy prescriptions to generate employment by relying on the ability of the sector to absorb the additional costs. Nonetheless, auxiliary initiatives to support or train guides and generate employment have been inadequate. For example, the CEO of NTB was quoted as saying: '*We aim to provide short-term employment to 1,600 tourism workers*' (IANS, 2021, para 4) affected by the pandemic. Although a laudable effort, with nearly two-thirds of the entire workforce being laid off during the pandemic (UNDP, 2020), the president of UNITRAV, Suma Parajuli, indicated that '*there are altogether around 100,000 people working in the trekking sector expected to lose their jobs*' (Menge & Paudel, 2020), the job creation initiatives by NTB is insignificant in terms of volume. Ghimire (2021) assessed the impact of COVID-19 on the labour market and reported, '*[T]here is almost no help at all for tour guides and other tourism workers from any organisations or the government . . . and there will be an insufficient labour force once the tourism sector picks up again*' (para 2). These stakeholders' perspectives concur with the view that the country's struggle to generate decent employment opportunities for most youths in the workforce (ILO, 2016) was exacerbated by the pandemic and lacklustre response.

Inadequate Education and Training

Multiple stakeholders highlighted the critical role of education and training related to the upskilling of the THS workforce. The then Minister for Culture, Tourism, and Civil Aviation stated: '*Tourism sector is a main base for the economic development of the country. We have expanded a branch of Nepal Academy of Tourism and Hotel Management (NATHM) to produce a qualified workforce*' (Khabar Hub, 2020, para 1). Some influential stakeholders have focused on the educational initiatives. For example, the executive director of the NATHM stated that '*NATHM has produced 45,000 qualified human resources through training and classes, of which 90 per cent is in employment*' (Khabar Hub, 2020, para 5). Meanwhile, stakeholders viewed the lack of quality education and training opportunities available at the country level as a critical impediment to THS revival. The HR manager of a five-star establishment (Soaltee Kathmandu) said:

> Fresh college graduates are not job-ready when they enter the market. A few organisations are working towards it in regard to graduate skills. It is a major responsibility of colleges and universities to provide their students with adequate skills (technical and soft), and mentoring is required.
>
> (Adhikari, 2022, para 9)

This sentiment was reinforced by the CEO of GATE Vocational-FAB School—*The service sector needs and deserves highly competent and committed human capital that needs to be continually renewed as younger people join jobs* (*Nepali Times*, 2021, para 2). More importantly, the need to upskill and reskill the youth workforce for the digital tourism era has become a priority only very recently. For example, NATTA posits emerging technologies as significant for digital tourism and has undertaken initiatives to equip travel agents with crucial digital skills such as online marketing, social media strategies, and digital customer engagement (NATTA, 2023). These stakeholders' perspectives suggest that the potential to fast-track high-quality THS-related contemporary education and training needs strategic attention.

Increasing Outbound Migration

This theme was echoed by various stakeholders represented in the online media analysis. Rural-to-urban migration within the country and overseas migration have adversely impacted several sectors, including agriculture (Kapri & Ghimire, 2020), construction (Adhikari et al., 2023) and tourism (Lemma et al., 2017). For example, the president of the HAN said: '*[M]any of our youth are leaving the country for better opportunities. HAN, in collabouration with other associations, is working our level best to ensure we can retain the local talents.*' In the same vein, the CEO of NTB was cited as saying:

> [W]e are facing skilled manpower shortage. During the pandemic, many people migrated to their villages from Kathmandu or tourist areas and started new occupations. So, NTB is focusing on giving training to different people to serve different parts of the tourism industries.
>
> (Murarka, 2022, para 8)

In addition, the president of HAN said:

> [P]eople involved in the hospitality industry were unable to sustain themselves during the COVID-19 pandemic, so some changed their profession, while others went abroad for foreign employment . . . many of our youth are leaving the country for better opportunities. In collaboration with other associations, HAN is working our level best to ensure we can retain the local talents.
>
> (Nepal Traveller, 2022, para 3)

These excerpts indicate that retaining workers coupled with attracting and retaining youth and millennials in the workforce (see Sutcliffe & Dhakal, 2018) to lessen the outflow of labour requires strategic focus.

Next, three themes that emerged from the analysis of stakeholder perspectives and their strategic implications are discussed in the context of SDG#8 and the aforementioned three targets.

Discussion

This study relied on publicly available secondary data and utilised multi-pronged techniques to explore the trend of international tourists' arrival in the country amidst three significant crises, the magnitude and scope of employment within the THS, and stakeholder perspectives on the cause and effects of THS-related labour and skills shortages. The findings reported earlier indicate that Nepalese THS is rebounding. However, despite the potential of the THS to serve as a main engine for economic growth and opportunities, stakeholders perceived the absence of adequate job opportunities at the country level, inadequate education and training, and rapid rate of outbound migration as the three root causes of the CLS. Three specific implications of the analysis are discussed in the broader context of three targets associated with SDG#8 were highlighted earlier.

The THS is Nepal's fourth most significant sector in terms of the volume of enterprises and employees. Although job creation has garnered interest in strengthening pull factors, poor employment conditions within the THS have not received the attention they deserve. For example, dismal employment conditions in mountaineering, one of the economically significant sub-sectors, are a policy concern. Mathema (2018) reported that '*while the number of Everest climbers has more than doubled in two decades, the Sherpa supply has not kept pace*' (para 4). One of the main reasons is that Sherpa guides make up more than one-third of deaths as they work in dangerous conditions such as frostbite, hypothermia, and other extreme condition injuries (see Rai, 2022), amidst meagre pay that culminated in a revolt in 2014 (see Draven, 2019). Such working conditions suggest that push factors leading to the CLS are yet to receive policy attention. Foreign mountaineers and tourism operators' inability or reluctance to pay living wages impedes new entrants into the labour market and has long-term consequences, creating a shallow pool of potential Sherpas and the exodus of labour to foreign countries.

On the one hand, Nepal's growth policy instruments relying on strategies to support business growth remain weak, as indicated by its poor ranking in terms of doing business (World Bank, 2020). On the other, the Ministry of Education's spokesperson was recently cited as saying that the government was issuing between 1,000 and 1,200 permits/day for students seeking to pursue higher and vocational education abroad (Online Khabar, 2022, para 2)—which translates into a conservative estimate of over 405,000 students a year. In addition, about 400,000 youth seek foreign employment each year on average (Dhakal, 2018b). However, actual number of job seekers and students leaving the country is much higher on both fronts. For example, outbound migrants bypassing the cumbersome labour permits (see Khadka, 2021) and students avoiding the bureaucratic hassle of obtaining permits to study abroad, that is, no objection letters (Dhakal, 2022), are frequently reported in the media. Nepal's current situation has been framed as a conundrum between surplus labour and shortages (see Adhikari, 2022), the mass exodus of nearly one million young people as students and labour migrants per annum has ramifications for the THS not only in terms of the decent work agenda associated with SDG#8 (see Dhakal & Burgess, 2021) but also in the context of country's SDGs aspirations (Dhakal et al., 2020). One of the remedial strategies could be to focus on migrant workers and migrants overseas—who are not only a significant base for the country's non-resident Nepalese tourism market but also a source of skilled and experienced talent. The potential utility of returnee migrants in resolving the CLS crisis deserves strategic attention. For example, UNDP (2022) initiated job-oriented skills training for 1,500 returnee migrants who lost their jobs overseas during the pandemic.

Reversing the trend of labour outflow as one of the ways to address the CLS necessitates strategic attention to aspects of youth employment, education, and training. For example, according to the president of the European Association of Hotel Schools Directors (EUHOFA), there are nearly 40 institutions running THS-related programmes in Nepal, of which five are EUHOFA members that provide excellent education and training initiatives (see RepublicaNepal, 2018). Internationally accredited vocational training and higher education programmes for the youth with guaranteed employment within the THS could be developed in close consultation with relevant stakeholders to slow down outbound migration and enhance socio-economic well-being. For example, the NTB has focused on education and training opportunities specifically aimed at empowering women. The CEO of NTB was cited as saying,

> [W]e realised that training given to women is going to be more sustainable because they are going to live in the villages while male members of the family look for new occupations. So, providing training to women will also help to keep them sustainable. Our focus is to empower women.
>
> (Murarka, 2022, para 6)

Based on the findings reported earlier and the discussions earlier, this chapter recommends three SDG #8 related evidence-based strategic priorities to address CLS.

First, there is a need to develop a list of labour and skills in demand, similar to the critical occupations list in countries like Indonesia (Dhakal & Tjokro, in this volume) and to monitor and continuously update the list. Second, in order to overcome the paucity of tourism-related employment data (Sigdel, 2020), socio-economic evidence gathered from the work-in-progress Tourism Satellite Account, needs to be exploited to shape relevant initiatives such as promoting digital readiness skills (see Dhakal, 2021), enabling gender employment and empowerment (see Dhakal, 2018c) and relying on sustainability-driven employment policies in countries like Bhutan (see Planning & Research Tourism Council of Bhutan, 2022). Third, since the Tourism Decade 2023–2032 Plan in development aims to attract 3.5 million international tourists to Nepal (The Annapurna Express, 2023), designing short to medium-term education and training schemes in close consultation with the stakeholders to not only advance Nepalese tourism in the digital era but also spur opportunities for the youth and attract migrants to return.

Limitations

As with any scholarly research, there are limitations to this study. First, this is exploratory research, and the nature of secondary data analysis is primarily descriptive in nature. Second, stakeholder perspectives were extracted from online media reports in English, and hence, the media reports in the local language were not a part of the analysis. Future studies need to consider these limitations, build on the current analysis, and investigate the issue of CLS going forward.

Conclusion

This chapter began by highlighting how the THS has become more critical in the context of progress towards SDGs of South Asian nations like Nepal, which is recovering from three major crises in the past two decades. Although it is generally suggested that labour shortages will translate to increased wage growth when demand for labour exceeds supply, the main contribution of this study is the granulated understanding of complex root causes and evidence-based stakeholder-centric strategic responses. Following the gradual lifting of travel restrictions worldwide, recent evidence indicates that although tourist arrivals have rebounded, the THS's sustained revival in Nepal will likely be hindered if CLS is not urgently addressed. As UNWTO (n.d.) advocates that the tourism-related opportunities to push SDGs aspirations of developing and emerging economies should not be overlooked, this study contends that steering the revitalisation of the Nepalese THS in the post-pandemic digital era will be challenging without concerted efforts to make SDG#8 a strategic priority.

Disclosure Statement

No potential conflict of interest was reported by the author(s).

Note

* Corresponding author: subas.dhakal@une.edu.au.

References

Adhikari, I. (2022). The conundrum of labour shortage in a labour surplus economy: An investigation of Nepal. *Journal of Social and Economic Development*, *24*(2), 404–435.

Adhikari, J., Rai, M. K., Baral, C., & Subedi, M. (2023). Labour migration from Nepal: Trends and explanations. In *Migration in South Asia: IMISCOE regional reader* (pp. 67–81). Springer International Publishing.

The Annapurna Express. (2023). Nepal tourism decade 2023–2032: Government comes up with yet another grand plan. https://theannapurnaexpress.com/news/nepal-tourism-decade-2023-2032-government-comes-up-with-yet-another-grand-plan-36102/

Asian Development Bank (ADB). (2020). *Labour migration in Asia COVID-19 impacts, challenges, and policy responses.* Author. www.adb.org/sites/default/files/publication/797536/labour-migration-asia.pdf

Bajracharya, S., & Regmi, D. (2023). *Post-COVID tourism recovery: Can nature-based tourism power Nepal's green recovery?* www.undp.org/nepal/post-covid-tourism-recovery-can-nature-based-tourism-power-nepal%E2%80%99s-green-recovery

Birendra, K. C., Dhungana, A., & Dangi, T. B. (2021). Tourism and the sustainable development goals: Stakeholders' perspectives from Nepal. *Tourism Management Perspectives*, *38*, 100822.

Central Bureau of Statistics (CBS). (2018). *National economic census 2018. Analytical report tourism.* Author.

Central Bureau of Statistics (CBS). (2021). *The National population and housing census.* Central Bureau of Statistics. https://censusnepal.cbs.gov.np/Home/Index/EN

Council for Technical Education and Vocational Training (CTEVT). (2016). *Labour market survey*. http://ctevt.org.np/files/2073%20Publication%20LABOUR%20MARKET%20SURVEY%20(1).pdf
Dangi, M. B., Schoenberger, E., Boland, J. J., & Chaudhary, R. P. (2021). Quest for development: An examination of more than a half-century of national planning and foreign aid practice in Nepal. *Sustainable Futures*, *3*, 100051.
Dhakal, M. (2022). *Govt has no record of students going abroad for higher education*. www.risingnepaldaily.com/news/15036
Dhakal, S. P. (2018a). Analysing news media coverage of the 2015 Nepal earthquake with the lens of community capitals: Implications for disaster resilience. *Disasters*, *42*(2), 294–313.
Dhakal, S. P. (2018b). Cooperative enterprises and sustainable development in post-crisis Nepal: A social responsibility perspective on women's employment and empowerment. In N. Apostolopoulos, H. Al-Dajani, & D. Holt (Eds.), *Contemporary issues in entrepreneurship research* (Chapter 8). Emerald Publishing.
Dhakal, S. P. (2018c). The state of higher education and vocational education and training sectors in Nepal: Implications for graduate work-readiness and sustainable development. In R. Cameron, S. Dhakal, & J. Burgess (Eds.), *Transitions from Education to Work: Workforce ready challenges in the Asia Pacific*. Routledge.
Dhakal, S. P. (2021). Accommodation & food services sector. In A. Nankervis, J. Connell, A. Montague, & J. Burgess (Eds.), *The fourth industrial revolution what does it mean for Australian industry?* (Chapter 5). Springer Nature.
Dhakal, S. P., & Burgess, J. (2021). Decent work for sustainable development in post-crisis Nepal: Social policy challenges and a way forward. *Social Policy & Administration*, *55*(1), 128–142.
Dhakal, S. P., Dahal, D., & Dahal, S. (2020). Nepal. In A. Nankervis, J. Connell, & J. Burgess (Eds.), *The future of work in Asia and beyond: A technological revolution or evolution?* Routledge.
Dhakal, S. P., & Tjorko, S. P. (2020). Travel and tourism workforce planning and development for sustainable development in Indonesia. In K. Dayaram, L. Lambey, J. Burgess, & T. W. Afrianty (Eds.), *Developing the workforce in an emerging economy: The case of Indonesia*. Routledge.
Dhakal, S. P., & Tjokro, S. P. (2022). Tourism enterprises in Indonesia and the fourth industrial revolution—Are they ready? *Tourism Recreation Research*. https://doi.org/10.1080/02508281.2021.1996687
Draven, J. (2019, 8 April). Sherpas and the ethics of Everest. *National Geographic*. www.nationalgeographic.co.uk/travel/2018/08/sherpas-and-the-ethics-of-everest
Freeman, R. E., Wicks, A. C., & Parmar, B. (2004). Stakeholder theory and "the corporate objective revisited." *Organisation Science*, *15*(3), 364–369.
Ghimire, R. (2021). *Nepal must support its tourism sector or face losing a critical workforce*. Friedrich-Ebert-Stiftung. https://asia.fes.de/news/nepal-tourism.html
Global Goals. (2023). Decent work and economic growth. https://www.globalgoals.org/goals/8-decent-work-and-economic-growth/
Grinnell Jr, R. M., & Unrau, Y. A. (2010). *Social work research and evaluation: Foundations of evidence-based practice*. Oxford University Press.
IANS. (2021). *Nepal creates short-term jobs for tourism workers amid Covid*. https://travel.economictimes.indiatimes.com/news/destination/international/nepal-creates-short-term-jobs-for-tourism-workers-amid-covid/84615215
International Labour Organization. (2016). *50 Years of work in Nepal together for social justice: 1966–2016*. ILO.
International Labour Organization (ILO). (2021). *Rapid assessment of the impact of COVID-19 on private recruitment agencies in Nepal*. www.ilo.org/wcmsp5/groups/public/—asia/—ro-bangkok/—ilo-kathmandu/documents/publication/wcms_800103.pdf

International Labour Organization (ILO). (n.d.). *COVID-19 labour market impact in Nepal.* www.ilo.org/wcmsp5/groups/public/—asia/—ro-bangkok/—ilo-kathmandu/documents/briefingnote/wcms_745439.pdf

John Hopkins Coronavirus Resource Centre (JHCRC). (2023). *Nepal.* Author.

Jones, P., Hillier, D., & Comfort, D. (2017). The sustainable development goals and the tourism and hospitality industry. *Athens Journal of Tourism*, *4*(1), 7–18.

Joshi, A., Franco, I. B., & Thorley, R. (2022). Ensuring sustainable post-pandemic tourism in Nepal: The role of corporate agencies. In *Corporate approaches to sustainable development: international experiences and insights* (pp. 199–210). Springer Nature Singapore.

Kapri, K., & Ghimire, S. (2020). Migration, remittance, and agricultural productivity: Evidence from the Nepal Living Standard Survey. *World Development Perspectives*, *19*, 100198.

Khadka, U. (2021). *History of female (im)mobility in Nepal.* https://nepalitimes.com/here-now/history-of-female-im-mobility-in-nepal

Khabar Hub. (2020). *Govt prioritizes tourism development: Minister Bhattarai.* 18 November 2020. https://english.khabarhub.com/2020/18/142890/

Krippendorff, K. (2018). *Content analysis: An introduction to its methodology.* Sage Publications.

Lemma, A., Henley, G., Hoque, S., & te Velde, D. W. (2017). *The Nepal labour market. A four sector case study.* Overseas Development Institute. https://set.odi.org/wp-content/uploads/2017/10/2.-SET-Nepal-The-Labour-Market-4-sector-case-study_Oct-2017-1.pdf

Liu-Lastres, B., Wen, H., & Huang, W. J. (2023). A reflection on the Great Resignation in the hospitality and tourism industry. *International Journal of Contemporary Hospitality Management*, *35*(1), 235–249.

Manzoor, F., Wei, L., Asif, M., Haq, M. Z. U., & Rehman, H. U. (2019). The contribution of sustainable tourism to economic growth and employment in Pakistan. *International Journal of Environmental Research and Public Health*, *16*(19), 3785.

Mathema, P. (2018). A shortage of Sherpa guides as more climbers head to Mt Everest. https://www.hindustantimes.com/photos/world-news/photos-a-shortage-of-sherpa-guides-as-more-climbers-head-to-mt-everest/photo-XswsPS7AmJx1zemn0bK0rI-2.html

Menge, J., & Paudel, S. (2020). *Nepal: Tourism sector workers lose livelihoods.* https://asia.fes.de/news/nepal-tourism-sector-workers-lose-livelihoods

Ministry of Culture, Tourism, and Civil Aviation. (2020). *Tourism statistics.* Kathmandu, Government of Nepal.

Ministry of Culture, Tourism, and Civil Aviation. (2023). *Tourism statistics.* Kathmandu, Government of Nepal.

Ministry of Labour and Employment (2018). Labour Migration for Employment: A Status Report for Nepal: 2015/2016–2016/2017. Ministry of Labour and Employment (MoLE), Kathmandu.

Mitchell, R. K., Agle, B. R., & Wood, D. J. (1997). Toward a theory of stakeholder identification and salience: Defining the principle of who and what really counts. *Academy of Management Review*, *22*(4), 853–886.

Murarka, S. (2022, July 19). *Nepal reviving its tourism sector through women's participation.* WION. https://www.wionews.com/south-asia/nepal-reviving-its-tourism-sector-through-womens-participation-498899

Nankervis, A., Prikshat, V., & Dhakal, S. (2019). Mapping stakeholders of graduate work-readiness (GWR). In *The transition from graduation to work: Challenges and strategies in the twenty-first century Asia Pacific and beyond* (pp. 31–42). Springer.

National Planning Commission (NPC). (2020). *National review of sustainable development goals*. Author. https://sustainabledevelopment.un.org/content/documents/26539VNR_2020_Nepal_Report.pdf
NATTA. (2023). *Digital capacity building training Gandaki Province*. https://natta.org.np/news_event/digital-capacity-building-training-gandaki-province-7th-11th-december-2023/
Nepali Times. (2021, February 13). Pokhara, the education hub. *Nepali Times*. https://nepalitimes.com/business/pokhara-the-education-hub
Nepal Traveller. (2022). The hospitality industry is severely understaffed. *Laxman Subedi*. https://nepaltraveller.com/sidetrack/the-hospitality-industry-is-severely-understaffed-laxman-subedi#:~:text=The%20hospitality%20industry%20is%20severely%20understaffed%2C%20not%20just%20here%20in,there%20are%20only%205%2C000%20available
NTB. (2023). *New provision for trekking in Nepal*. Nepal Tourism Board. https://ntb.gov.np/latest-travel-updates#:~:text=The%20new%20rule%20will%20come,similar%20treks%20in%20mountain%20bikes%3F
NTB. (2024). About us. Nepal Tourism Board. https://ntb.gov.np/about-us
Online Khabar. (2022). Over 1,000 Nepali students receive permits to go abroad for studies every day. https://english.onlinekhabar.com/over-1000-nepali-students-abroad-day.html
Palinkas, L. A., Horwitz, S. M., Green, C. A., Wisdom, J. P., Duan, N., & Hoagwood, K. (2015). Purposeful sampling for qualitative data collection and analysis in mixed method implementation research. *Administration and Policy in Mental Health and Mental Health Services Research*, *42*, 533–544.
Planning & Research Tourism Council of Bhutan. (2022). *2019 tourism satellite account*. www.tourism.gov.bt/uploads/attachment_files/tcb_jP2NfOiM_Bhutan%20Tourism%20Satellite%20Account.pdf
Prasain, S. (2023, 9 June). Everyone seems to be leaving the country. *Kathmandu Post*. https://kathmandupost.com/money/2023/06/09/everyone-seems-to-be-leaving-the-country
Rai, D. (2020). *The ethics of summit: The commodification of the Sherpa People*. https://protocolmag.com/2022/03/14/ethics-and-the-himalayas-the-commodification-of-the-sherpa-people/
Rasul, T., Zaman, U., & Hoque, M. R. (2020). Examining the pulse of the tourism industry in the Asia-Pacific region: A systematic review of social media. *Tourism and Hospitality Management*, *26*(1), 173–193.
Reed, M. S. (2008). Stakeholder participation for environmental management: A literature review. *Biological Conservation*, *141*(10), 2417–2431.
Republica Nepal. (2018). *Nepal hosting global meet of hospitality schools in 2019*. https://myrepublica.nagariknetwork.com/news/nepal-hosting-global-meet-of-hospitality-schools-in-2019/
Rijal, S. P. (2016). Impact of earthquake on tourism sector in Nepal. *Tribhuvan University Journal*, *30*(2), 183–194.
Serrière, N., & Centre for Economic Development and Administration. (2014). Labour market transitions of young women and men in Nepal. Work4Youth Publication Series No. 12. ILO, Geneva.
Sharpley, R. (2022). Tourism and development theory: Which way now? *Tourism Planning & Development*, *19*(1), 1–12.
Sigdel, R. R. (2020). Compilation of Nepal tourism satellite accounts: Opportunities and challenges. https://www.unescap.org/sites/default/files/APS2020/44_Compilation_of_Nepal_Tourism_Satellite_Accounts_Opportunities_and_Challenges.pdf
South Asian Association for Regional Cooperation (SAARC). (2020). *About SAARC*. www.saarc-sec.org/index.php/about-saarc/about-saarc
Sparreboom, T., & Staneva, A. (2014). Is education the solution to decent work for youth in developing economies? Identifying qualifications mismatch from 28

school-to-work transition surveys. Work4Youth Publication Series No. 23. ILO, Geneva.

Sutcliffe, J. E., & Dhakal, S. P. (2018). Youth unemployment amidst aged care workers shortages in Australia: Why care about the millennials? *Equality, Diversity and Inclusion: An International Journal, 37*(2), 182–198.

Tan, W., Shrestha, D., & Jeong, S. (2019) Digital tourism development and sustainability model for Nepal. In W. Shen, H. Paredes, J. Luo, & J. Barthes (Eds.), *2019 IEEE 23rd International Conference on Computer Supported Cooperative Work in Design (CSCWD)* (pp. 182–187). IEEE.

UNDP. (2020). *Three in five employees lost their jobs due to COVID-19 in Nepal.* www.undp.org/nepal/news/three-five-employees-lost-their-jobs-due-covid-19-nepal

UNDP. (2022). *Job oriented skills training for returnee migrants commences in Madhesh Province.* www.undp.org/nepal/news/job-oriented-skills-training-returnee-migrants-commences-madhesh-province

United Nations (UN). (2015). *Transforming our world: The 2030 agenda for sustainable development* (A/RES/70/1). https://sustainabledevelopment.un.org/post2015/transformingourworld

United Nations Office of the High Commissioner for Human Rights (UNOHCR). (2012). *Nepal conflict report.* Author.

UNWTO. (n.d.). *Tourism and SDGs.* https://tourism4sdgs.org/tourism-for-sdgs/tourism-and-sdgs/

Veneri, C. M. (1999). Can occupational labour shortages be identified using available data. *Monthly Labour Review, 122*, 15.

World Bank. (2020a). *COVID-19 impact on Nepal's economy hits hardest informal sector.* www.worldbank.org/en/news/press-release/2020/10/08/covid-19-impact-on-nepals-economy-hits-hardest-informal-sector

World Bank. (2020b). *Doing business 2020.* https://documents1.worldbank.org/curated/en/688761571934946384/pdf/Doing-Business-2020-Comparing-Business-Regulation-in-190-Economies.pdf

World Bank. (2022). *Harnessing tourism to enhance the value of biodiversity and promote conservation in Nepal.* www.worldbank.org/en/news/feature/2022/06/03/harnessing-tourism-to-enhance-the-value-of-biodiversity-and-promote-conservation-in-nepal

World Travel and Tourism Council (WTTC). (2022). *Nepal economic impact report 2022.* https://researchhub.wttc.org/factsheets/nepal

15 Labour Skills Shortages in the Construction Industry of Bangladesh

*Muhammad Nateque Mahmood,**
Glenn P. Costin, and Azmeri Rahman

Introduction

A skilled labour force is crucial to sustainable economic growth and social progress. Like other developing countries, the Bangladesh government's 8th Five-Year Plan (2020–2025) (Bangladesh Planning Commission [BPC], 2020) stresses the development of skilled labour and improved employment conditions. According to reports from the Ministry of Finance (MoF), the skill level of Bangladeshi employees does not match the country's present economic ambitions (MoF, 2017b). Further, the industry sector's GDP contribution is steadily rising, with the Bangladesh Bureau of Statistics (BBS) 2018 labour force report showing the Broad Industrial Sector's (BIS) GDP contribution as 32.42% in FY2016–2017, up from 31.54% in FY2015–2016 (BBS, 2018). The BIS contains four of the 15 sectors for calculating national income: mining and quarrying; manufacturing; electricity, gas and water supply; and construction (MoF, 2017a). Such data support, in part, the government's intent to ensure comprehensive reporting on all industrial and service sector development and growth, including those of information and communication technology, agriculture and forestry, tourism and services, mineral extraction and processing, manufacturing, the fuel industry, health services, as well as construction, the primary focus of this chapter (MoF, 2022).

Bangladesh's initial industrial policy was released by the government of Bangladesh (GoB) in the 1980s. The current rendition, Industrial Policy 2016, was developed to further expedite national industrialisation with a greater emphasis on sustainable and inclusive growth. The essential underlying goals of Industrial Policy 2016 include productive employment contexts that encourage entrepreneurship, the integration of women into the industrialisation process, and international market linkages (MoF, 2021).

As per the BBS (2020), the construction sector accounted for 8.13% of the country's gross domestic product (GDP) in the fiscal year 2019–2020. This positions it as the fourth-largest sector, following agriculture, manufacturing, and services. Consequently, the construction industry holds significant importance in Bangladesh for economic growth and social development. Unfortunately, the progress of Bangladesh's construction industry is hampered by skills

DOI: 10.4324/9781003379065-17

shortages (ADB, 2015; Rahman & Islam, 2013), something this chapter seeks to investigate. A shortage of skills occurs when there is a disparity between the demand and supply of workers possessing particular skills or qualifications in a labour market (OECD, 2014).

The construction sector contributes, directly and indirectly, to almost all of the United Nations (UN) sustainable development goals (SDGs) but most directly to SDG 7—affordable and clean energy; SDG 8—sustained, inclusive, and sustainable economic development, full and productive employment, and decent work for everyone; SDG 9—inclusive and sustainable industrialisation and the fostering of innovation; and SDG 11—inclusive, safe, resilient and sustainable cities and human settlements (UN, 2015). Notably, both the 8th Five Year Plan (8FYP) (BPC, 2020) and the 7th Five Year Plan (7FYP) (BPC, 2015) have included policies targeted towards achieving these specific SDGs. However, both documents recognise industrial skill shortages, particularly in the construction industry, as stated clearly in the 7FYP: 'As Bangladesh continues to industrialise and undergo structural change, it has been observed that the skill level of workers was not aligned with the stage of growth. Industries in the private sector consistently identify low skill levels among the labour force as a fundamental constraint to Bangladesh's growth' (BPC, 2015, p. 4). Hence, comprehending the cause(s) of skill shortages in the construction industry in Bangladesh is essential for addressing this concern. There has been some research undertaken on the skill shortages in the Bangladesh industrial sector, such as that focusing on skilled worker parameters (Ahmed et al., 2020), general labour market skills gaps (MoF, 2017b), and road mapping skill development (ADB, 2015), to date, no research has focused on the cause(s) of skill shortages in the construction sector. Aiming to bridge this research gap, the chapter explores the key causes through a comprehensive literature review and seeks mitigation strategies.

Country Background and Labour Market

According to the most recent labour force survey from 2016–2017, the growth rate between 2010 and 2017 was 1.6% per year, compared to the 7FYP prediction of 2.9% per year (BBS, 2018). Thus, the number of workers entering the employment market annually was significantly lower than the 7FYP's projection of 2 million (BPC, 2020). This outcome is partially explained by a static female participation rate approximating 36%. It also indicates that the anticipated proportional rise in the available worker population to the overall population did not occur. Several factors may account for this: more potential workers in the age group 15–24 remaining in education; an increasing proportion of displaced youth, youth neither in employment, education, nor training (NEET); and an increasingly aging (64+) population (Mondal, 2022).

The outlook is also poor when the overall number of new domestic jobs is compared to the marginal increase in available labour. Severe underemployment and the fact that 10% of all Bangladeshi employment is unpaid family work demonstrates that domestic job creation during the 7FYP fell significantly short of expectations (MoF, 2022). The workforce outflowing from a restructured agricultural sector has persisted, decreasing that sector's employment. However, employment in manufacturing and construction failed to increase as anticipated despite the presumed increased labour availability (BBS, 2021). Further, irrespective of the construction sector's growth accelerating to 11.1% per year between 2010 and 2017 (the highest of all industries), construction employment rose only 4.5% yearly. Notably, the construction industry's employment elasticity for this period also plummeted to a low of 0.4%. However, in the manufacturing and services industries, it was 4% and 6.8% respectively (BPC, 2020), that is, the increased workforce deriving from a retracting agricultural sector tended to align with manufacturing and services, not construction.

The Construction Sector

The 2021 BBS report notes that Bangladesh's construction sector increased at an annual rate of 8.69% in FY06, declining to 6.95% in FY11 (BBS, 2021). Through large infrastructure expenditures and a spike in housing demand, FY12 saw it rise to 8.42%, then consistently around 8% for some years (MoF, 2017b). The same report identified that the sector grew again in FY18 to 9.92% and 10.25% in FY19, the highest level since FY06. Employment in the sector, however, did not replicate this growth pattern. Between 1999 and 2000, the total employment in the construction industry stood at approximately 1.13 million, experiencing a subsequent increase to 2.60 million in FY10. This expansion declined to 2.4 million in FY17, accounting for only 5.6% of the employed population (MoF, 2017a). However, recent statistics reveal that the construction industry provides employment opportunities for about 3.6 million people, which would account for 7.8% of Bangladesh's total labour force (BBS, 2019; World Bank, 2019).

Beyond employment, construction sectors hold significance in developing infrastructure, industrialisation, housing, urbanisation, and disaster resilience (Fei et al., 2021). Nevertheless, despite the importance of its role, Bangladesh's construction industry remains under-supported. It continues to face multiple challenges affecting performance and quality. One of the significant challenges is the identified shortage of skilled workers adapted to construction (MoF, 2017b). Skills shortages negatively impact an industry's productivity, efficiency, competitiveness, and innovation (Durdyev et al., 2018). In Bangladesh, skills shortages seriously hamper the development and sustainability of the construction sector and impact the achievement of targeted UN SDGs (Fei et al., 2021). A further issue arising from skill shortages, in construction mainly, is the impact on building and infrastructure quality (Hoque et al., 2023). Without a skilled workforce, ensuring that buildings and infrastructure are constructed safely and to appropriate standards and durability becomes problematic (Ahmed, 2019; Islam & Suhariadi, 2018). In turn, this can negatively impact contexts beyond the construction process, both temporally and geographically, including the natural environment and the desired or planned-for built environment, to public safety and life quality more generally.

The importance of skills shortages goes beyond simple economics and infrastructure. The earlier discussion shows that a shortage of skilled labour also affects the affordability and accessibility of housing and infrastructure. Such issues arise from delays in the construction process, increased wastage, insurance costs, and the tendency to restrict construction to locations of available labour (Alshahrani et al., 2023). In turn, affordable housing availability diminishes, and public funds for infrastructure projects are less productive (Calderón & Servén, 2014). It follows that people in lower socio-economic contexts will find it difficult to access safe and decent housing. Yet the availability of housing plays a crucial role in realising the objectives of SDGs 9 and 11, striving to create inclusive, safe, resilient, and sustainable cities and human settlements. Additionally, this poses a challenge to the attainment of SDG 8, which aims to foster sustained, inclusive, and sustainable economic growth, along with promoting full and productive employment and ensuring decent work for all, that is, improving the conditions of those lower-income earners now being excluded by rising house prices (Parisotto, 2015). Although incidental, it follows that a shortage of skilled labour impacts the environment, and hence the ability to achieve SDG 7, doing so through problematising affordable and clean energy projects. Skilled labour is needed to design, construct, and maintain energy-efficient buildings and infrastructure; likewise, it is needed to implement renewable energy source programmes and reduce the nation's greenhouse gas emissions (Iqbal et al., 2021).

The chapter's focus is on identifying skills shortages. However, it is clear from the earlier discussion that the implications of skill labour shortages in the construction industry ripple through a country's socio-economic fabric in ways not always easily discerned. Hence, though scoped to identify and offer mitigation strategies to skills shortages, the importance of this chapter goes to the core of Bangladesh's socio-economic development, including its responsibilities to UN SDGs.

Data Collection and Analysis

Understanding policy issues related to skill shortages in the contemporary Bangladeshi construction industry necessitated assessing pertinent national policies and statistical data sets. Therefore, document analysis was adopted in this study. Through a review of the policies, the context, and the execution of such policies, as well as their consequences, the challenges associated with promoting productive employment may become less opaque. Taking a qualitative approach to get behind the numbers and asking 'why', a systematic assessment and analysis of existing academic and grey literature was duly undertaken; the knowledge convergence from such diverse pieces of evidence and reputable data sources enabled a keen understanding of the topic. Document analysis is a research method widely used to examine and interpret various textual sources. It involves systematically examining written, printed, or electronic documents to extract valuable insights and generate knowledge. According to Bowen (2009), document analysis allows researchers to explore historical records, policy documents, organisational reports, and other textual sources to uncover hidden patterns, understand social phenomena, and gain a deeper understanding of the context under investigation.

Further, Davie and Wyatt (2021) suggest that document analysis allows researchers to analyse primary and secondary sources, including multimedia materials, providing a rich, diverse range of research data. Document analysis's methodological rigour and flexibility make it a valuable tool for researchers in history, education, social sciences, the built environment, and public policy (Bowen, 2009; Davie & Wyatt, 2021). Such analysis allowed the researchers to identify the context in which skill shortages in the Bangladeshi construction sector have developed over time and the policies planned and or implemented to address the issue. All key policy documents were obtained online from government websites and the websites of active Bangladeshi building industry stakeholders. Table 15.1 lists the key grey and academic literature used for the document analysis.

Table 15.1 Document analysis for skills shortages in the construction industry of Bangladesh

Year	*Author*	*Title*
2020	Ahmed, S., Islam, H., Hoque, I., & Hossain, M.	Reality check against skilled worker parameters and parameters failure effect on the construction industry in Bangladesh
2019	Ahmed, S.	Causes and effects of accident at construction site: A study for the construction industry in Bangladesh
2004	Alwi, S.	Training field personnel for small to medium construction companies: An alternative tool to increase productivity
2015	Asian Development Bank (ADB)	Roadmap for skill development in Bangladesh
2022	Assafi, M. N., Hoque, M. I., & Hossain, M. M.	Investigating the causes of construction delay from the perspective of organisation sectors involved in the construction industry of Bangladesh
2018	Bangladesh Bureau of Statistics (BBS)	Report on labour force survey
2016	Braňka, J.	Understanding the potential impact of skills recognition systems on labour markets
2017	Ministry of Finance	BIDS study report: Labour market and skill gap in Bangladesh

(*Continued*)

Table 15.1 (Continued)

Year	*Author*	*Title*
2018	Mella, A., & Savage, M.	Construction sector employment in low-income countries
2012	Hajela, R.	Shortage of skilled workers: A paradox of the Indian economy
2016	Hearle, C.	Skills, employment and productivity in the garments and construction sectors in Bangladesh and elsewhere
2016	International Labour Organization (ILO)	Enhancing the skills of workers in the construction industry in Bangladesh
2013	Rahman, R.I. and Islam, R.	Female labour force participation in Bangladesh, trends, drivers and barriers

Source: Compiled by authors

The examination of the literature mentioned earlier led to an expansion of the reviewed material, bringing into focus a brief overview of other countries. This expansion was derived from the search for strategies that may mitigate key factors influencing skill shortages in Bangladesh.

Labour Skill Shortage in the Bangladeshi Construction Industry

As identified previously, the construction industry in Bangladesh has been proliferating in recent years, driven by an increasing demand for infrastructure development, housing, and commercial buildings. However, the lack of skilled labour remains a significant bottleneck for the sector's growth. Using the information derived through documentary analysis, the key drivers behind Bangladesh's construction skill shortages were identified as lack of formal training and education, poor working conditions, lack of regulations and standards, cultural and social factors, migration of skilled workers, and low proportion of female workers The findings are described in following sections.

Lack of Formal Training and Education

A key contributor to Bangladesh's skill shortage in the construction industry is the lack of formal training and education for workers. The current situation reveals that 37.5% of construction employees are skilled experientially, with only 12.6% having advanced skills (MoF, 2017b). In addition, only 7.8% of the construction sector's workforce is female: the majority engaged in low-skilled employment confined to few occupations. Training is vital for developing workforce capability. However, just 6.45% of construction employees have obtained vocational training, with the remaining 93.55 % having none (Ahmed et al., 2020). This poorly trained workforce affects the performance of construction projects through reworking of errors, wastage, time delays, and injuries (Ahmed et al., 2018, 2020; MoF, 2017b). So, while Bangladesh's construction industry has grown dramatically over the last decade, the shortage of locally available, trained workers remains a crucial challenge for the sector.

The reviewed material offers several reasons construction workers' limited formal training and education persists in Bangladesh. First, construction in Bangladesh is traditionally seen as a low-skilled and lowly-paid field of human endeavour. As a result, it is not prioritised for investment in training and education programmes, leaving the field underfunded and poorly resourced (MoF, 2017b). This leads to a lack of opportunities for workers to acquire the necessary skills, knowledge, and identifiable qualifications to work safely and effectively in the industry. High unemployment and youth unemployment typically translate to construction firms having access to labour pools, whether low-skilled or skilled, often originating from the restructured agricultural sector. However, the challenge lies in obtaining workers with the specific skills required for the ongoing projects. This depresses wages and encourages ongoing reliance on inefficient and dangerous construction practices. The alternative is to invest in increased mechanisation and/or pre-fabrication, to which contemporary Bangladeshi construction firms are historically adversely or economically ill-prepared due to their capital-intensive nature (Mella & Savage, 2018).

Furthermore, in Bangladesh and India, most construction workers are hired on employer-favouring 'employment agreements'. Such agreements include no provisions on specific duration, working hours, leave, or holiday pay, and termination may occur anytime without severance pay. With such a transient workforce, construction-based enterprises lack the motivation to allocate resources for training. Receiving daily wages only, rather than holding permanent positions, workers are likewise disincentivised to self-fund (Hajela, 2012). Further, many vocational schools and institutions lack the necessary funding and resources to provide high-quality training and education programmes for construction workers, even if there was a desire for such from either party.

The lack of incentives for workers to acquire and improve their skills exacerbates the issue. Given low wage rates, the uncertainty of tenure, and the typically high fees associated with training programmes, it is unsurprising that workers find it challenging to participate in training initiatives when available. It is evident from the documentation that neither governments nor construction firms provide financial support for formal worker training, again, primarily due to the prevalence of generally hiring workers solely for specific projects (Hearle, 2016). Given this dominant paradigm, the lack of awareness and understanding among workers and employers of the importance of formal training and education to the sector remains prevalent, with neither party seeing the long-term benefits of such skill and knowledge development to the individual, the company, the industry, nor the country at large (ILO, 2016).

Poor Working Conditions

The low wages, poor working conditions, and high risks have resulted in many semi-skilled and skilled workers leaving the industry to search for better opportunities. According to a report by the International Labour Organization (ILO), many workers in the construction industry in Bangladesh leave their jobs within a few months due to this issue and the lack of career advancement opportunities (ILO, 2016). The Ministry of Finance (MoF, 2017b) identifies construction workers as having higher average wages than agricultural labourers. However, they earn less than those employed in the manufacturing sector. As a result, skilled construction workers tend to transition to better-paying jobs in manufacturing.

The construction industry is known to be high-risk globally. Bangladesh has been plagued with safety issues exacerbated by these poor working conditions and lack of training. This further discourages skilled workers from either joining or staying in the industry. According to Ahmed (2019) and Assafi et al. (2022), inadequate safety measures, such as a lack of protective equipment and training, have resulted in severe accidents and fatalities in Bangladesh's construction sector. Low wages have led to a high turnover of skilled workers, further lowering working conditions, reducing the safety of untrained day-hire labourers, and impacting project quality.

Lack of Regulation and Standards

The lack of regulations, standards, and a certificated qualification framework is notable within the reviewed documentation. This makes it difficult for construction workers to prove their developed skills and knowledge in applying for positions and lowers the construction industry's perceived need for hiring formally trained workers. This is exacerbated by governments not enforcing labour laws and building codes, making it difficult for workers to demonstrate the value of their qualifications and skills on-site to employers who, having no firm standard to judge by, do not see the importance (Mella & Savage, 2018). Furthermore, no regulations require workers to undergo training programmes before commencing construction projects. regulations mandate workers to participate in training programmes before engaging in construction projects. Employers, therefore, seldom acknowledge skills developed through formal training, diminishing the motivation for skill enhancement through this approach (Hearle, 2016; Alwi, 2004).

Mella and Savage's (2018) study revealed substantial variations in economy-wide collective bargaining coverage across five distinct developing nations. Collective bargaining coverage denotes the proportion of total employees whose compensation and employment terms are established through one or more collective agreements. The researchers noted that in Sierra Leone, South Africa, and Malawi, approximately 46.8%, 32.6%, and 18.1% of the workforce benefit from at least one collective agreement. In contrast, only 0.8% and 5% of employees in Ethiopia and Bangladesh benefit from such collective agreements. In addition, Bangladesh, like many developing countries, has a large informal employment sector, with the vast majority of the construction workers employed in this unorganised space, where any labour laws or regulations do not cover the workers and remain open to manipulation, persecution, and discrimination.

Cultural and Social Factors

Given the earlier discussion, it is unsurprising that the documentation also demonstrates a lack of awareness among young people (aged 18–35 years) in Bangladesh about career opportunities in the construction sector, furthering the skills shortage issue (Braňka, 2016). Young people see construction as a poor career option due to the identifiably low social status, poor working conditions, and wages mentioned earlier. Moreover, many workers who join the industry come from low socio-economic and marginalised communities, where access to education and training opportunities is limited (ADB, 2015). Moreover, as noted previously, such training is generally outside their capacity to afford.

Migration of Skilled Workers

One of the most significant issues the documentation identifies is migration and the associated skill loss or 'brain drain'. Many skilled and or experienced workers in the construction industry migrate to other countries in search of better-paying jobs, thus generating a skill shortage in Bangladesh (MoF, 2017b). Middle Eastern nations such as Oman, Qatar, and the United Arab Emirates, as well as Singapore and Malaysia, are the primary destinations for Bangladeshi migrants—collectively absorbing around 95% of the nation's total construction-based emigration. Of the more than 20.49 million registered migrant workers departing Bangladesh between 1976 and 2016, 10.45 million or 51% were classified as 'less-skilled', 15.2% as 'semi-skilled', and 32.5% as 'skilled'. Only 2% of this migrating workforce comprised professionals (MoF, 2017b). Emigrant skilled workers often possess specialised expertise and knowledge in construction trades, the loss of which deprives the nation of valuable technical know-how, innovation capacity, and operant best practices, all of which are crucial to the quality and efficiency of construction projects. Emigration thereby worsens skills shortages, creating upward pressure on the construction industry. Notable is the Ministry of Finance's (MoF, 2017b) position on construction worker emigration: positioning it as an opportunity for Bangladeshi foreign exchange earnings as occurs in other regional countries such as the Philippines and Nepal.

Low Proportion of Female Workers

The representation of female workers within the total construction workforce is minimal. Merely 1.3% of workers in the surveyed project sites were female

(MoF, 2017b). However, this is notably lower than the broader construction sector, which the BBS (2018) suggests has 7.8% female workers. Within this female workforce, 43% are categorised as unskilled, with only 19% and 38% holding skilled or semi-skilled positions respectively. Equally noteworthy is that all employed female workers held roles described as either helpers or labourers. Hence, Bangladeshi women undertake the most arduous and physically taxing tasks in a challenging context. Such tasks include cleaning, producing and transporting bricks, shovelling gravel, or excavating trenches for sewage systems: duties assigned to women potentially because of their comparatively lower wages (Mella & Savage, 2018; Rahman & Islam, 2013).

Looking Abroad: The Experience of Other Countries

Investing in education and training is crucial for bridging the skills gap among neighbouring economies. This not only enhances productivity but also contributes to improved conditions on construction sites and ensures compliance with safety standards. However, it may have little or no impact on the issue of migration. Over time, emigration is the biggest issue confronting countries such as Bangladesh as they attempt to improve productivity and development, doing so when worker access to a more powerful neighbouring economy is viable. It also shows that no lasting achievement in economic security or labour stability will be achieved unless structurally attended to through social policies. Thus, where countries like Bangladesh, India, Pakistan, Malawi, and Zambia have addressed skills development through Community Technical Colleges teaching vocational occupations (carpentry and the like) and improved apprenticeship schemes, in themselves do not necessarily reduce emigration flows (DBEI, 2018). This is not to suggest that educational funding is unimportant to economic success. Instead, such policies can mitigate emigration when it transitions to developing safer work environments, improved life quality and higher wages (FitzGerald, 2022). The issue, however, is time—what may occur as this transition plays out and whether such changes are sufficient to overcome other emigration drivers. It also depends upon a nation's perception of emigration—as a threat or boon. Hence, discussing migration drivers will be valuable before reflecting upon particular interventions.

What drives emigration is a complex issue deriving much from the connections between nations (Brennan et al., 2023). But not necessarily the closest neighbour. Even when wages and conditions are demonstrably superior in the potential host country, cross-border flows may be minimal (FitzGerald, 2022). This supports the understanding that workers and families move for reasons other than just wages. Improving their societal conditions is just as, or more, important.

The global history of cyclic labour and 'brain drain' offers some significant inferences for Bangladesh. Notably, the perception of progressive government action is as important as the actions undertaken. The government must be seen to be acting in the broader interest of workers, particularly young workers. Workers must feel that progress is taking place and that remaining or returning to Bangladesh is in their long-term interests. This may be played out through equity and consistency in the policies that are applied. Likewise, skill standards and accreditation are consistently set across the construction industry and the nation.

Equally important are governmental perceptions of the implications of migration. Emigration should not be seen as lowering unemployment or importing foreign currency (O'Connell, 1999; MoF, 2017b; FitzGerald, 2022; Walsh, 2023). Nor should it be seen as a means of developing skills that will somehow 'naturally' return to Bangladesh. All too frequently, history has shown that this is seldom the case (the joint nations of Northern Ireland and the Irish Republic being a case in point—see Humphries (2023), FitzGerald (2022) and Brennan et al. (2023)).

An enlightening study undertaken in Northern Ireland by Pivotal in 2021 offers some potential solutions relevant to any nation undergoing significant workforce emigration: doing so through young and old voices. These cohorts say much of the importance of local and central government actions, particularly the desire to let go of past divisions and demonstrable movement towards shared futures. Other key proposals include youth involvement in policy development; services that link overseas students and workers with employers in the home country; free or low-cost education and skill development provided with equity; incentives for attracting skilled and senior workers back to the home nation; business hubs connecting expatriate companies/workers with those in-country for knowledge exchange; and easy relocation services including spousal visas (Pivotal, 2021).

Further, nations like Indonesia (and other more developed economies) have created critical occupation lists based on criteria such as significant occupational shortages and their strategic importance to the national economy (CMEARI, 2020). Bangladesh could employ this strategy to its ongoing socio-economic advantage.

Discussion

Global examples offer relevant, experiential insights into Bangladesh's skills shortages issue, but only regarding migration drivers and inhibitors, that is, those factors that drive people away and those that reduce their desire to return. However, other factors identified in the broader literature need to be addressed.

One of these is the necessity of structuring training centres, vocational schools, and universities as the first level of a national certification system. It is evident that much reliance on construction skills training is placed on Bangladesh-based foreign training facilities (MoF, 2017b). Such agencies are designed to draw graduates to their parent nation, training them on their standards and not necessarily improving the host nation's skill capital. Preference should be placed upon nationally funded centres using national standards that are audited regularly. Certification, the assessment process to recognise a worker's skill and knowledge, should also be developed and met through regulated performance evaluation practices. The certification aims to reliably enhance skill, quality, and worker ability, enabling greater surety of construction products to meet established quality standards safely, on time, and budget (Adi & Ni'am, 2012). Tailoring training to meet specific industry needs proves more beneficial than generic training initiatives (Alwi, 2004; Hajela, 2012). Ideally, these programmes should be responsive to the actual demand for training, avoiding a sole focus on supplying pre-packaged courses in predetermined areas. In other words, the training should align closely with tradespeople's current tasks or future plans (Alwi et al., 2006).

Establishing vocational training is but one level of industry support. Sectors such as construction also require accreditation schemes through universities to standardise higher-level workers and professional roles such as construction managers, building supervisors and surveyors, architects, and engineers (EIU, 2015). Incentives for students to study such disciplines should be provided through accommodation grants, fee waivers, zero-interest loans, and scholarships for prospective low-income students. Establishing apprenticeship and internship programmes is crucial to thoroughly prepare graduates for the workforce (UNDP, 2014). Implementing such initiatives would align Bangladesh with many Southern Asian countries, which have promoted trade schools providing updated theoretical knowledge, accredited apprenticeships, industry incentives, and student financial support (EIU, 2015). Alwi (2003) and Ahn et al. (2013) also recommend regular, incentivised training programmes for workers at all levels to ensure that new concepts around waste reduction and greener construction practices are understood. This is backed by a study of 26 small to medium enterprises (SMEs) in the construction industry that found contractors reduced direct wastage costs by up to 90% after relevant on-site worker training (Alwi, 2004). Structured on-the-job training has likewise been shown to increase productivity and improve work quality while reducing wastage and accidents (Alwi, 2004; Padasalkar & Admane, 2015).

Conclusion

The labour skill shortage in Bangladesh's construction industry is a major bottleneck for its growth. This chapter aimed to identify the leading causes of labour skills shortages and recommend potential solutions drawn from an analysis of the literature and international examples. Based on the document analysis, skills shortages derive from a combination of factors, including insufficient formal training and education, low governmental and industry prioritising of investment in training and education, lack of awareness of the value of such training, poor understanding of the implications of a lowly skilled workforce, a large informal sector, societal issues, low wages and poor conditions, and vastly under-utilised female workforce. Thus, it becomes clear that the implications of construction skill labour shortages influence Bangladesh's entire socio-economic fabric. In identifying and offering mitigation strategies to skills shortages, this chapter's importance goes beyond the construction industry, articulating pathways towards enhanced societal conditions, including national UN SDG responsibilities.

Since construction industry skill shortages can significantly impact the achievement of the UN's SDGs, addressing the identified issues through targeted investment and considering societal change is paramount. Creating incentives for workers to acquire and improve their skills, enforcing labour laws, and building codes will all help create a more skilled and competent workforce. This, in turn, contributes to the growth and development of not just the construction industry but of the environment and the overall quality of Bangladeshi life through enhanced living conditions, pollution reduction, and national productivity. This can be done through government and private sector industry partnerships, highly developed vocational training, and university-based programmes. Such initiatives should be backed by worker incentives promoting skill and knowledge development, such as higher wages and benefits and improved working conditions. The government is playing its role by equitably enforcing labour laws and building codes and incentivising industries to employ and develop a more skilled and competent workforce.

Note

* Corresponding author: n.mahmood@deakin.edu.au.

References

Adi, R. P., & Ni'am, M. F. (2012). Improving skill's strategies of Indonesian construction labours to have global competitiveness. *International Journal of Civil & Structural Engineering*, *3*(1), 150–157.

Ahmed, S. (2019). Causes and effects of accident at construction site: A study for the construction industry in Bangladesh. *International Journal of Sustainable Construction Engineering and Technology*, *10*(2), 18–40.

Ahmed, S., Islam, H., Hoque, I., & Hossain, M. (2020). Reality check against skilled worker parameters and parameters failure effect on the construction industry for Bangladesh. *International Journal of Construction Management*, *20*(5), 480–489.

Ahmed, S., Hoque, M. I., Islam, M. H., & Hossain, M. (2018). A reality check of status level of worker against skilled worker parameters for Bangladeshi Construction Industry. *Journal of Civil Engineering and Construction*, *7*(3), 132–140.

Ahn, Y. H., Pearce, A. R., Wang, Y., & Wang, G. (2013). Drivers and barriers of sustainable design and construction: The perception of green building experience. *International Journal of Sustainable Building Technology and Urban Development*, *4*(1), 35–45.

Alshahrani, A., Alaboud, N., Leje, M. I., Karban, A., & Altowerqi, Z. (2023). Rating the significance of the factors influencing shortage of skilled labours for sustainable construction: A perception of Makkah construction practitioner. *Journal of Umm Al-Qura University for Engineering and Architecture*, *14*(1), 13–25.

Alwi, S. (2003, 29 October – 1 November). *Factors influencing construction productivity in the Indonesian context*. The 5th EASTS conference, Fukuoka.

Alwi, S. (2004, 3–6 August). *Training field personnel for small to medium construction companies: An alternative tool to increase productivity*. 12th of the International Group of Lean Construction Conference, Copenhagen.

Alwi, S., Kajewski, S. L., & Hampson, K. D. (2006, May 23–26). *Investigation into the relationship between Just-in-time (JIT) training and productivity in building construction in Indonesia.* 1st International Construction Speciality Conference, Calgary.

Asian Development Bank (ADB). (2015). *Roadmap for skill development in Bangladesh.* Author. Retrieved 10 August 2023, from www.adb.org/sites/default/files/linked-documents/42466-014-ssa.pdf

Assafi, M. N., Hoque, M. I., & Hossain, M. M. (2022). Investigating the causes of construction delay on the perspective of organisation-sectors involved in the construction industry of Bangladesh. *International Journal of Building Pathology and Adaptation.* https://doi.org/10.1108/IJBPA-10-2021-0137

Bangladesh Bureau of Statistics (BBS). (2018). *Report on labour force survey.* Government of Bangladesh. Retrieved 11 August 2023, from http://data.bbs.gov.bd/index.php/catalog/200

Bangladesh Bureau of Statistics (BBS). (2019). *Statistical yearbook of Bangladesh.* Retrieved 11 August 2023, from https://bbs.portal.gov.bd/sites/default/files/files/bbs.portal.gov.bd/page/a1d32f13_8553_44f1_92e6_8ff80a4ff82e/2020-05-15-09-25-dccb5193f34eb8e9ed1780511e55c2cf.pdf

Bangladesh Bureau of Statistics (BBS). (2020). *Statistical yearbook of Bangladesh.* Retrieved 11 August 2023, from https://bbs.portal.gov.bd/sites/default/files/files/bbs.portal.gov.bd/page/b2db8758_8497_412c_a9ec_6bb299f8b3ab/2021-08-11-04-54-154c14988ce53f65700592b03e05a0f8.pdf

Bangladesh Bureau of Statistics (BBS). (2021). *Statistical yearbook of Bangladesh.* Retrieved 11 August 2023, from https://bbs.portal.gov.bd/sites/default/files/files/bbs.portal.gov.bd/page/b2db8758_8497_412c_a9ec_6bb299f8b3ab/2022-06-15-10-49-3cf641425dd693f9e954de5ae9470775.pdf

Bangladesh Planning Commission (BPC). (2020). *Eight five year plan (2020–2025): Promoting prosperity and fostering inclusiveness.* Government of People's Republic of Bangladesh. Retrieved 12 August 2023, from https://plancomm.gov.bd/sites/default/files/files/plancomm.portal.gov.bd/files/68e32f08_13b8_4192_ab9b_abd5a0a62a33/2021-02-03-17-04-ec95e78e452a813808a483b3b22e14a1.pdf

Bangladesh Planning Commission (BPC). (2015). *Seventh five year plan (2015–2020): Accelerating growth and reducing poverty.* Government of People's Republic of Bangladesh. Retrieved 12 August 2023, from https://erd.portal.gov.bd/sites/default/files/files/erd.portal.gov.bd/page/2f97258a_6f25_479a_8545_a498c65783f2/Development%20Planning%207FYP%20%26%20SDG.pdf

Bowen, G. A. (2009). Document analysis as a qualitative research method. *Qualitative Research Journal, 9*(2), 27–40.

Braňka, J. (2016). *Understanding the potential impact of skills recognition systems on labour markets.* International Labour Organization (ILO). Retrieved 12 August 2023, from www.ilo.org/wcmsp5/groups/public/—ed_emp/—ifp_skills/documents/publication/wcms_532417.pdf

Brennan, N., Langdon, N., Bryce, M., Burns, L., Humphries, N., Knapton, A., & Gale, T. (2023). Drivers and barriers of international migration of doctors to and from the United Kingdom: A scoping review. *Human Resources for Health, 21*(1), 11.

Calderón, C., & Servén, L. (2014). Infrastructure, growth, and inequality: An overview. *World Bank Policy Research Working Paper* (7034). Retrieved 13 August 2023, from http://hdl.handle.net/10986/20365

Coordinating Ministry for Economic Affairs of the Republic of Indonesia (CMEARI). (2020). *Indonesia's critical occupations list 2018* (Technical report). Retrieved 16 October 2023, from https://documents1.worldbank.org/curated/en/763611585857010121/pdf/Indonesias-Critical-Occupations-List-2018-Technical-Report.pdf

Davie, G., & Wyatt, D. (2021). Document analysis. In *The Routledge handbook of research methods in the study of religion* (pp. 245–255). Routledge.

Department of Business, Enterprise and Innovation (DBEI). (2018). *Review of economic migration policy report of the inter-departmental group*. Government of Ireland, Dublin. Retrieved 21 August 2023, from https://enterprise.gov.ie/en/publications/publication-files/review-of-economic-migration-policy.pdf

Durdyev, S., Ismail, S., & Kandymov, N. (2018). Structural equation model of the factors affecting construction labour productivity. *Journal of Construction Engineering and Management*, *144*(4), 04018007.

Economist Intelligence Unit (EIU). (2015). *Skills needed: Addressing South Asia's deficit of technical and soft skills: Analysing the gap in Afghanistan, Bangladesh, India, Nepal, Pakistan and Sri Lanka*. Author. Retrieved 21 August 2023, from www.britishcouncil.org/sites/default/files/skills_gap_jan2015_print.pdf

Fei, W., Opoku, A., Agyekum, K., Oppon, J. A., Ahmed, V., Chen, C., & Lok, K. L. (2021). The critical role of the construction industry in achieving the sustainable development goals (SDGs): Delivering projects for the common good. *Sustainability*, *13*(16), 9112.

FitzGerald, J. (2022). One Island, two labour markets, Irish studies in international affairs. *Analysing and Researching Ireland, North and South*, *33*(2), 316–372.

Hajela, R. (2012). *Shortage of skilled workers: A paradox of the Indian economy* (SKOPE Research Paper No. 111, COMPAS). University of Oxford. Retrieved 15 August 2023, from https://skope.ox.ac.uk/wp-content/uploads/2020/07/WP111.pdf

Hearle, C. (2016). *Skills, employment and productivity in the garments and construction sectors in Bangladesh and elsewhere*. London: OPM. Retrieved 15 August 2023, from https://assets.publishing.service.gov.uk/media/5977616f40f0b649a7000022/Skills_productivity_and_employment.pdf

Hoque, M. I., Safayet, M. A., Rana, M. J., Bhuiyan, A. Y., & Quraishy, G. S. (2023). Analysis of construction delay for delivering quality project in Bangladesh. *International Journal of Building Pathology and Adaptation*, *41*(2), 401–421.

Humphries, N. (2023, February 25). Doctors are leaving Ireland and heading for Australia in droves—Here's why. *The Conversation*. Retrieved 21 August 2023, from https://theconversation.com/doctors-are-leaving-ireland-and-heading-for-australia-in-droves-heres-why-199998

International Labour Organization (ILO). (2016). *Enhancing the skills of workers in the construction industry in Bangladesh*. Retrieved 14 August 2023, from www.ilo.org/wcmsp5/groups/public/—asia/—ro-bangkok/documents/publication/wcms_513843.pdf

Iqbal, M., Ma, J., Ahmad, N., Hussain, K., & Usmani, M. S. (2021). Promoting sustainable construction through energy-efficient technologies: An analysis of promotional strategies using interpretive structural modeling. *International Journal of Environmental Science and Technology*, 1–24.

Islam, M. S., & Suhariadi, B. T. (2018). Construction delays in privately funded large building projects in Bangladesh. *Asian Journal of Civil Engineering*, *19*, 415–429.

Mella, A., & Savage, M. (2018). *Construction sector employment in low income countries*. ICED and DFID. Retrieved 15 August 2023, from www. academia.edu/36965702/Construction_Sector_Employment_in_Low_Income_Countries_Construction_Sector_Employment_in_Low_Income_Countries

Ministry of Finance (MoF). (2022). *Bangladesh economic review*. Government of Bangladesh. Retrieved 10 August 2023, from https://mof.portal.gov.bd/sites/default/files/files/mof.portal.gov.bd/page/f2d8fabb_29c1_423a_9d37_cdb500260002/02_BER_22_En_Inner.pdf

Ministry of Finance (MoF). (2021). *Bangladesh economic review*. Government of Bangladesh. Retrieved 10 August 2023, from https://mof.portal.gov.bd/sites/default/files/files/mof.portal.gov.bd/page/f2d8fabb_29c1_423a_9d37_cdb500260002/02.%20Inner%20Cover%20Eng-21.pdf

Ministry of Finance (MoF). (2017a). *Bangladesh economic review*. Government of Bangladesh. Retrieved 10 August 2023, from https://mof.portal.gov.bd/sites/default/files/files/mof.portal.gov.bd/page/e8bc0eaa_463d_4cf9_b3be_26ab70a32a47/D.%20Appendices_%28English-2017%29_Final.pdf

Ministry of Finance (MoF). (2017b). *BIDS study report: Labour market and skill gap in Bangladesh*. Government of Bangladesh. Retrieved 10 August 2023, from www.researchgate.net/publication/330441508_LABOUR_MARKET_AND_SKILL_GAP_IN_BANGLADESH

Mondal, A. H. (2022). *Tracer study on the graduates of technical and vocational education and training in Bangladesh*. BIDS. Retrieved 10 August 2023, from https://seip-fd.gov.bd/wp-content/uploads/2023/03/Stocktaking-of-Technical-and-Vocational-Education.pdf

O'Connell, P. J. (1999). *Astonishing success: Economic growth and the labour market in Ireland* (Employment and Training Papers 44). Employment and Training Department. Retrieved 24 August 2023, from www.ilo.org/wcmsp5/groups/public/@ed_emp/documents/publication/wcms_120374.pdf

Organisation for Economic Co-operation and Development (OECD). (2014). *Is migration good for the economy? Migrant Policy Debates*. OECD Publishing. Retrieved 27 August 2023, from www.oecd.org/migration/OECD%20Migration%20Policy%20Debates%20Numero%202.pdf

Padasalkar, P. P., & Admane, S. V. (2015). Skill gap and training- need analysis of construction sector. *International Journal on Recent and Innovation Trends in Computing and Communication*, *3*(5), 2712–2715.

Parisotto, A. (2015). Promote sustained, inclusive and sustainable economic growth, full and productive employment and decent work for all. *UN Chronicle*, *51*(4), 19–20.

Pivotal. (2021). *Should I stay or should I go? Reasons for leaving Northern Ireland for study or work*. Pivotal Public Policy Forum Northern Ireland. Retrieved 30 August 2023, from www.pivotalppf.org/cmsfiles//Stay-or-go-final.pdf

Rahman, R. I., & Islam, R. (2013). *Female labour force participation in Bangladesh, trends, drivers and barrier* (Asia-Pacific Working Paper). ILO. Retrieved 12 August 2023, from www.ilo.org/wcmsp5/groups/public/—asia/—ro-bangkok/—sro-new_delhi/documents/publication/wcms_250112.pdf

United Nations (UN). (2015). *Transforming our world: The 2030 agenda for sustainable development* (A/RES/70/1). Author. https://sustainabledevelopment.un.org/post2015/transformingourworld

United Nations Development Programme (UNDP). (2014). *Employment generating sector and skill development program for urban poor: Report on identifying employment-generating sector of Bangladesh based on secondary data research*. Author. Retrieved 20 August 2023, from https://urbanpovertybd.org/wp-content/uploads/2021/01/Employment-Generating-Sector-and-Skill.pdf

Walsh, B. (2023). *When unemployment disappears: Ireland in the 1990s*. CESifo Working Paper No. 856, Category 4: Labour Markets, Conference on Unemployment in Europe: Reasons and Remedies, December 2002. Retrieved 23 August 2020, from www.ifo.de/DocDL/cesifo_wp856.pdf

World Bank. (2019). *Bangladesh economic update, October 2019: Creating more and better jobs*. Retrieved 10 August 2023, from https://openknowledge.worldbank.org/handle/10986/32530

16 Capitalising Resourcefulness of the Seasoned

Insights from India on Building a Skilled Workforce

Lata Dyaram, Apoorva Goel, Nabila Khan, and Samina Yasmin*

Rise of Ageing Workforce

As much as we like to talk about Millennials, the future of work is much older.
—Roy Bahat (Head, Bloomberg)

Contemporary workplaces are being influenced by two significant themes, both of which are contributing to their dynamic and developing nature. The primary trend concerns the aging of the global workforce and the growing diversity of its members (Truxillo et al., 2015). In contrast, the second trend pertains to the continuous advancements in technology, which alters the ways in which we undertake our job activities (Landers & Marin, 2021). When juxtaposed, these two trends present distinct challenges for companies. The swift progress of technology leads to the quick obsolescence of knowledge within a short span of time, often referred to as the 'half-life of knowledge' (Helmrich & Leppelmeier, 2020). In contrast, an individual's professional career often spans four decades and shows a consistent rising trend (Eurostat, 2020). To remain employable, it is essential for workers, particularly senior and older workers, to stay updated on their knowledge and skills, including digital and technological skills, and actively engage in continuous learning programmes. Therefore, the main aim of this chapter is to examine the critical skills that may be lacking in the ageing labour force yet are indispensable in the contemporary work environment.

Despite having the world's highest youth population, India's workforce is rapidly ageing (United Nations, 2023). In the last few years, there has been a change in the age structure of the Indian population. The proportion of young people in the entire workforce has fallen from 25% in 2016–2017 to 17% in 2022–2023. The statistics show that there has been a steady increase in the share of older people in total employment in India in recent times. From around 37% in 2016–2017, the share of older people in total employment has increased (OECD, 2019). According to CMIE (2022), the upward trend is anticipated to continue, leading firms to increasingly rely on older workers as a valuable talent pool to recruit from.

DOI: 10.4324/9781003379065-18

Compared to their younger counterparts, senior workers typically have advanced career progressions and longer durations of employment with their respective organisations. Additionally, they tend to command a wider range of knowledge and skills, often holding prominent positions of authority in a professional environment (North, 2019). Nevertheless, many older employees experience forms of age-based intimidation, including negative stereotypes and attributions predicated on the perception of declining abilities (Allen et al., 2021). Workforce plans often disregard the significance of actively involving senior personnel because of the presumed inverse correlation between age and performance or potential (Earl et al., 2018). As a result, this might engender adverse attitudes and biases against older workers, hence exerting a detrimental influence on their physical and mental health. This may manifest in diminished decision-making skills and suboptimal performance, eventually resulting in decreased employee retention rates (Fasbender & Gerpott, 2022). Talent acquisition is becoming increasingly challenging due to a limited talent pool, frequently marked by a scarcity of available positions, intensifying rivalry for qualified employees, and the growing demand for advanced technological expertise in all employment positions. The increasing number of organisations in various industries, including manufacturing, along with the changing skill requirements resulting from technological improvements, has caused a decrease in the pool of competent applicants. Industries and organisations should create inclusive work environments that prioritise talent acquisition. This can be achieved by actively involving senior staff in meaningful opportunities to develop and improve critical and potential skills. By doing so, organisations can embrace employees of all age groups and help espouse SDG 4 and SDG 3.

Sustainable Development Goals in Focus

The 17 sustainable development goals (SDGs) for 2030 are set to promote global peace and prosperity. Sustainable development relies on learning and skill development to address the evolving demands of the labour market (ILO, 2017). We analyse the resourcefulness of senior workers through the lens of SDG 4, 'quality education/lifelong learning opportunities', which can, in turn, reinforce and uphold SDG 3, 'good health and well-being' (United Nations, 2015). While SDGs are interconnected and can explain well-being (De Neve & Sachs, 2020), we demonstrate how SDG 4 translates to SDG 3 with a focus on an understudied domain—upskilling/reskilling an ageing workforce (Dhakal et al., 2022). We emphasise the organisation's imperative to invest in and leverage senior personnel to address and fill in skill gaps and overall talent crunch. Given the current socio-political and economic instability, we analyse the essential skill requirements to extend the purposeful working lives of older workers.

Literature Analysis

Businesses can derive significant advantages from employing older individuals due to their extensive experience, demonstrated competence, continuous learning, and exceptional work ethic (Finkelstein et al., 2020). Previous studies have demonstrated that older individuals exhibit superior social and interpersonal abilities compared to their younger counterparts (Karpinska et al., 2013). The phenomenon of an ageing workforce necessitates an increased dependence on individuals in the mid and late stages of their careers to meet the growing requirements for specific skills (Parker & Andrei, 2020). Nevertheless, with shifts in work approaches, older employees are more prone to encountering skill obsolescence in contrast to their younger colleagues. This underscores the need to provide older employees with improved opportunities to acquire new skills and adapt to existing ones (SDG 4). By planning for senior workers' potential growth and development, firms may reduce the risk of their skill obsolescence and show their commitment to their employees (Kooij, 2015). Hence, it is imperative to allocate resources towards developing expertise among senior personnel. The process of reskilling and upskilling ensures that experienced employees have the requisite skills to effectively perform their job responsibilities and seamlessly adjust to changing work requirements. Consequently, this improves their employability prospects.

Research demonstrates the effects of ageism, age discrimination, and stereotypes on individual and organisational outcomes among senior employees in India (Maurya et al., 2022). Studies examining the phenomenon of ageing in the workplace have emphasised the significance of the active engagement of older employees (Bal et al., 2015). Nevertheless, senior personnel often face challenges that hinder their continued participation in the labour market, such as negative age-related prejudices (Allen et al., 2021). One implication of this phenomenon is that workforce plans often overlook the importance of retaining and effectively managing older personnel, as they tend to assume a negative relationship between age and both potential and performance (Earl et al., 2018). To continue to mitigate social and employment disparities related to age (Kluge & Krings, 2008) as well as leverage the valuable contributions of individuals across all age cohorts (Kooij & Van De Voorde, 2014), it is crucial for organisations to foster collaborations and facilitate knowledge exchange among diverse age groups. Undoubtedly, one of the major challenges encountered by human resource managers revolves around the task of identifying effective solutions that can promote sustained engagement and active involvement of older employees over extended periods of time (Kadefors et al., 2020). Given the evolving nature of work and employment, it becomes imperative to leverage the core and unique skills of elderly personnel.

Research Setting and Data Collection

The manufacturing sector is anticipated to experience a shortage of approximately 2.1 million job opportunities by the year 2030 (Egan, 2021). While there are multiple university courses available to address this issue and equip the younger workers for the future, it will require a significant amount of time for them to become effective and self-sufficient. The 'manufacturing skills gap', as it is better known, highlights the important role of senior employees in this context. However, it is worth noting that only a limited number of firms have implemented specific efforts with the purpose of supporting the knowledge and skills of their older/senior employees (Vasconcelos, 2018).

To this end, the present chapter focuses on the older/senior workforce within the manufacturing sector in India. The manufacturing sector confronts constant transformations owing to the emergence of new technologies, often resulting in the phenomenon of skill gaps. This becomes evident when the skill requirements of employers do not align with the skills of workers (Chenoy et al., 2019). The development of well-established skill sets among older workers in the Indian manufacturing industry is of paramount importance for their personal and professional growth and for the expansion and sustenance of this dynamic sector. This chapter responds to this concern by exploring senior workers' valued skills and skill shortages. The investigation focuses on identifying skills shortages among senior staff members, specifically those between the ages of 40 and 60, aiming to determine how these employees may be efficiently utilised to address skills shortages.

The investigation employed the interactive qualitative analysis (IQA) technique, developed by Northcutt and McCoy in 2004. This methodology is designed to provide a systematic, thorough, and clear framework for doing qualitative investigations. The unique interactive protocol of this system allows study participants to actively contribute to the development, gathering, and analysis of data. The researcher's function is limited to that of a facilitator in this process (Bargate, 2014).

We included two focus groups (FG1 and FG2), each comprising participants from different cohorts: older and junior employees. Comprehensive interviews with several participant groups were also undertaken to get diverse perspectives. The focus group themes led to individual interviews during data collection and analysis. Interviews clarified focus group results (Northcutt & McCoy, 2004) and helped the study reach data saturation by revealing participant perspectives into the collective pool (Fusch & Ness, 2015; Guest et al., 2006). Participants were employees in managerial positions in manufacturing firms in India. The two groups had 20 participants with work experience ranging from 4 to 10 years for FG1 and above ten years for FG2. The ratio of men to women participants for FG1 and FG2 was 11:8 and 16:5 respectively. This was followed by 15 in-depth interviews with a mix of older and young employees working in senior and mid-managerial roles in the manufacturing firms. The participants had an average work experience of 14 years and an age range of 25 to 60 years.

The data were collected in two distinct phases, following the established protocol of IQA as outlined by Northcutt and McCoy (2004). The first phase included focus group discussions and the development of a *visual representation* of the discussion points and perspectives, which subsequently served as a tool for the second phase in conducting individual semi-structured interviews. To operationalise the investigation, the groups were presented with a question to actively engage with and critically examine: '*What are the critical skill shortages among senior colleagues aged 40 to 60 years in your unit or firm?*' Participants were instructed to write down one idea (skill/s), thought, or reflection per index card without any imposed restrictions on the number of thoughts they could produce. They were then asked to place these cards on the whiteboard. Consequently, participants combined and created clusters of themes with similar reflections. All index cards were prominently displayed, allowing all members of the group a gallery walk of the themes. This facilitated the development of a socially constructed and mutually understood interpretation of each response among group members. Additionally, this process aimed to mitigate any potential vagueness or ambiguity pertaining to the intended meaning of the words or phrases depicted on the cards.

The individual interviews entailed two parts; in the first part, participants shared their thoughts and experiences on the dearth of each of the 11 skills among older employees as emerged from the FGDs. This was followed by the second part, which involved responding to the affinity relationship table (ART). The ART aimed to elicit the relationships and causal effects between pairs of the 11 skills under investigation, along with a rationale for each of the stated effects.

Analysis

The participants were instructed to discern themes or affinities in their responses after understanding the skills/words being sought—subsequently, inductive coding aided in clustering and categorising the cards (Northcutt & McCoy, 2004). The group discussion process was adopted to describe, refine, and narrow down affinities until all participants reached a consensus regarding the accurate representation of the affinity's meaning. Successively, the group proceeded to generate titles that accurately encapsulated the essence of each affinity, employing a method commonly referred to as deductive coding. A concise paragraph description was documented to represent the overall content and significance of each affinity based on the cards and affinities created by the group (Northcutt & McCoy, 2004). The two focus groups generated 11 affinities described in Table 16.1.

Theoretical Coding

Data for FGl indicated that power reached a maximum (35.76) at 38 relationships, which accounted for 50% of the system's variance. The first 38 affinity pair relationships were, therefore, included in the inter relational diagram (IRD). Similarly, for FG2, power reached a maximum (28.57) at 26 relationships, which accounted for 50% of the system's variance. The first 26 affinity pair relationships were, therefore, included in the Inter relational diagram (IRD).

Table 16.1 Affinities generated by the focus groups

Number	*Affinity*	*Affinity definition*
1	Digital skills	Knowledge and ability to implement basics—such as computers and smartphones, as well as advanced digital and technological tools, such as robotics and machine learning for work-related purposes
2	Analytical skills	Ability to break large chunks of information into smaller categories so that conclusions can be drawn for work-related solutions
3	Business acumen	Having a business sense to effectively contribute to the goals of the company in terms of economic or financial value
4	Communication skills	Speaking as well as listening to convey ideas and thoughts from others effectively
5	Cognitive skills	Which is how people learn, remember and solve problems, such as critical thinking/processing any data
6	Technical skills	Specialised knowledge/expertise required to perform any task
7	Strategic orientation	Having a long-term vision and future forecasting for the company gains
8	People management	People skills involve communicating and leading your team for maximum results, and they include networking skills, conflict management, and collaboration
9	Agility	Capability to work in an ever-evolving setting, recognising and taking opportunities, and reacting quickly to change
10	Leadership skills	Ability to delegate, inspire, and communicate effectively to reach a shared goal
11	Task management	Organising work to complete tasks on time and efficiently, such as project management and allocation of work

The constructs were subsequently categorised to identify the relative drivers (causes) and outcomes (effects) in the system (Human-Vogel & Van Petegem, 2008). The primary driver, a significant causal factor, exerts influence on numerous other affinities while remaining unaffected by others, whereas the secondary driver contributes to or influences affinities within the system. The primary outcome, which demonstrates a statistically significant impact, is often influenced by various affinities but does not have an effect on certain others. The secondary outcomes indicate a relative effect (Northcutt & McCoy, 2004).

System Influence Diagram

In the final stage of the analysis of focus group data, a system influence diagram (SID) was created to visually represent the comprehensive system of affinities and their interrelationships (Northcutt & McCoy, 2004). Due to the inherent complexity of the SID, a simpler representation was sought by identifying and eliminating redundant links, a process known as rationalisation. The uncluttered SID serves as a visual representation of a mind map, encompassing only the essential links necessary to fully depict the underlying logic of the IRD (Northcutt & McCoy, 2004). The uncluttered SID was modified more linearly, which was utilised for phase 2 of the IQA procedure, the individual semi-structured interviews. SID for FG1 is depicted in Figure 16.1 and for FG2 is in Figure 16.2.

Interviews

The interview was framed by drawing on the affinities determined in the focus group sessions. To provide an independent view of the affinities, interviews were conducted with 15 participants who did not partake in the focus group sessions. The focus group participants' affinity descriptions were shared with the interviewees, and their understanding/experiences with the affinities were inquired. To reduce order bias, participants were shown shuffled affinities. The interview responses were categorised similarly to the focus group discussions to construct an interrelationship diagram (IRD). The IRD was then

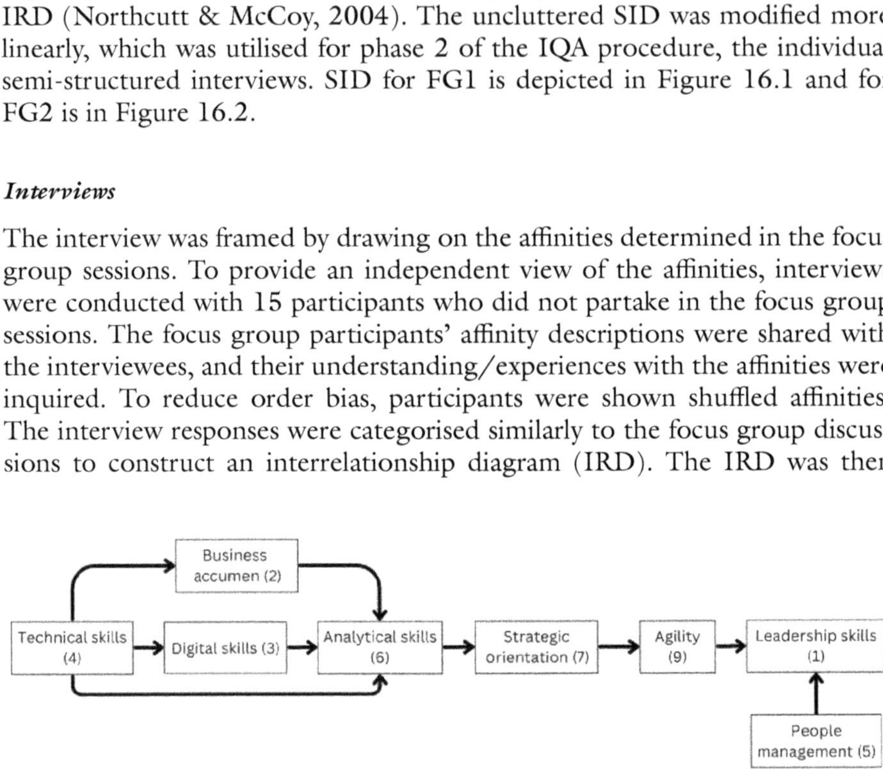

Figure 16.1 System influence diagram—FG1

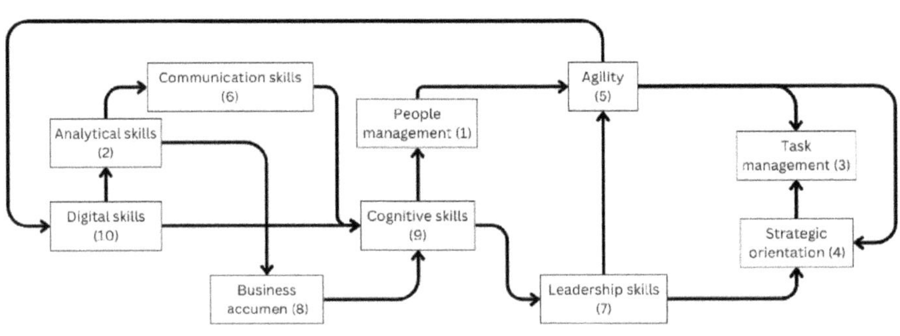

Figure 16.2 System influence diagram—FG2

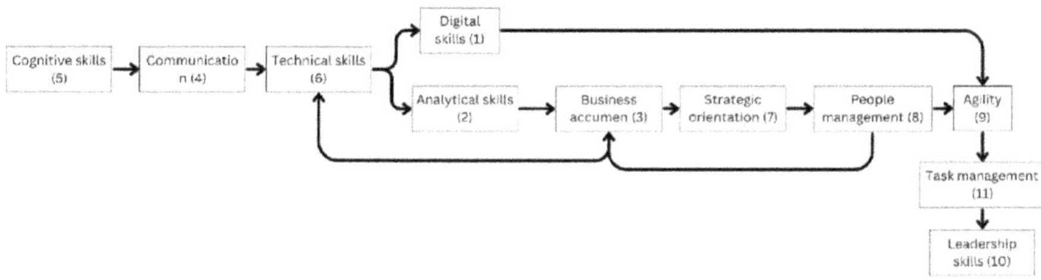

Figure 16.3 System influence diagram—Interviews

transformed into a composite interview mind map known as systems influence diagram (SID). This offered perspective on the system's unified individual reality and aided in the clarification of affinities. The mind map or SID of the interview participants is indicated in Figure 16.3.

Interview Results

1 *Cognitive skills*

The interview participants expressed their views and observations on senior workers' cognitive skills and performance in different roles within a professional setting and provided perspectives on senior employees in the capacity of team leader versus their performance as an individual contributor.

> *[T]heir knowledge processing of any data or their critical thinking is good if they are leading a team, but yes, it is not up to the mark when they are individual contributors or when they are executing on their own.*
>
> (Participant 4)

2 *Communication skills*

The participants presented their experiences working with some of the senior managers. It was reported that senior managers often delegate tasks without adequately elucidating the larger context or big picture of the project.

> *[T]hey would just give you a task and not really explain on what the project is about and why and where we are in the big scheme of things. . . . So, they are more like can you do this work and get this done? Why not really give you an understanding of why we are doing this? What is going to happen after five months? How and where everything lined up? So those communication skills, and how to inspire, how to keep your subordinates motivated to work towards something is important. That is probably one thing which is lacking in some of the senior managers.*
>
> (Participant 1)

The communication challenges within a multigenerational workforce were attributed to the existence of a generational divide, as noted by the participants.

> *[P]eople generally dislike senior guys as their managers because of what values they bring to the table perhaps. It's the communication, not even the communication gap! The generational gap has become humongous.*
>
> (Participant 8)

3 *Technical skills*
The participants articulated a rationale for the necessity of enhancing technical skills, indicating that a multitude of factors undergo constant change, particularly advancements in technology, market dynamics, and other important socio-political influences and that these changes create a dynamic and evolving landscape that businesses and their employees need to adapt to.

> *[T]his is a must . . . for me these skills needs to improve because the technology is rapidly changing, So, this is the company's responsibility to train their manpower accordingly and, you know, emphasize on their development in terms of technological upgradation, which is very critical for business.*
>
> (Participant 4)

4 *Analytical skills*
The significance of analytical skills within the purview of senior managerial positions in an organisation was reaffirmed by the participants.

> *[W]e need more of analytical skills than we actually know, the shop floor mind-set is mostly based on, you know if there is some small problem, you just solve it immediately and go ahead, but when you work from a strategic mind-set, you look at a longer horizon and you need more strong analytical skills to judge what problems might occur. So, lack of diagnostic and analytical skills in senior managers is one of the problems that we faced.*
>
> (Participant 3)

5 *Digital skills*
The responses highlighted that the senior managers who were usually identified as 'hardcore manufacturing sector managers' are the ones who have extensive knowledge and expertise in conventional manufacturing methodologies. The persons in question presumably dedicated a substantial amount of their professional lives to labouring on the shop floor, a term denoting the tangible site where manufacturing or production operations are conducted. It was noted that there may be a need for shop floor supervisors to undergo regular upskilling in digital approaches.

[S]ome of the managers that we had were pure hardcore manufacturing sector managers who used to work on the shop floor, so there was a lot of gap between us and them. So, we are well verse with computers, cloud based competencies, and other digital project management, but those guys typically are good at shop floor- capabilities be it assembling heavy machines, fabricating, to safety. So, there was a gap. Considering the advancements in our industry, it was not easy to convince them of the challenges that we were facing and push them for these skills in any particular task.

(Participant 3)

6 *Business acumen*

The participants indicated that senior employees occupying top managerial roles exhibit a robust understanding of business practices, acquired via either formal education or innate aptitude, hence justifying their appointment to such positions.

[W]hat happened is that they fired some of the senior people, these are the guys who knew how the business was running, like how the business grows, how retail is managed etc. they were discharged and replaced. but after losing them, revenue margins which they used to manage, or how the business was functioning actually went down.

(Participant 2)

Far from being an area of improvement, business acumen was noted as being among the key strengths of senior employees.

[T]ypically these top and senior executives are fairly old, but they are either born with business intelligence or develop it over the course of a long career, as I have witnessed in more than three companies where I have worked.

(Participant 8)

7 *Strategic orientation*

The participants saw that senior-level personnel exhibited a strategic orientation, indicating their ability to engage in strategic thinking and make judgments that include long-term implications. However, the participants expressed the view that the middle-level managers, who were responsible for implementing tasks and overseeing daily operations, were deficient in possessing this strategic mindset. In essence, the middle-level managers exhibited a greater inclination towards fulfilling immediate objectives, rather than taking into account the overarching strategic objectives of the firm.

In my experience, senior and high-level managers have a strategic mindset and an eye for what is important, but the middle-level managers remain heavily involved in day-to-day operations and generally lack this outlook.

(Participant 6)

8 *People management*
The participants highlighted the viewpoint that there is a need for continuous upgrading and adaptation of people management skills and abilities at regular intervals. The rationale behind this phenomenon can be attributed to the shifting dynamics resulting from the influx of new generations into the labour force, each characterised by distinct mindsets and attitudes. The existence of generational disparities can pose difficulties in fostering amicable collaboration between younger individuals and more seasoned employees.

> *[P]eople management skills is the key . . . they need to be upgraded every few years because with every new generation, the attitude and mindset is quite different. And that becomes a little difficult for the younger generation as well as you know, the senior folks to work together with no reservations. . . . So, yeah, I mean, I feel that they need to upgrade their people management skills.*
>
> (Participant 5)

Participants asserted that with the entry of each successive generation into the labour force, there may be variations in their expectations, communication methods, work styles and habits, and preferences compared to the preceding generation and that this has the potential to give rise to misinterpretations, disputes, or challenges in the process of team collaboration.

9 *Agility*
The participants noted that senior employees generally exhibit reduced levels of flexibility in response to tough or unclear circumstances. It has been proposed that older workers prefer to rely on known and validated conceptions of work rather than experiment with novel ways.

> *I would say senior people are less agile and less flexible in testing times . . . they rather try to, you know, stick to the tested classic theories of work, so that they have something to blame on if things do not go in the right direction. So, they become averse to new ideas or to try new things, and are inflexible . . . so they stick to SOPs and so-called 'guidelines'.*
>
> (Participant 4)

10 *Task management*
The participants expressed that some senior managers, potentially belonging to an older cohort, may adhere to a work ethic characterised by extended periods of work, potentially spanning from 10 to 12 hours per day. It is plausible that they were raised within a professional environment wherein dedicating substantial amounts of time was perceived as customary or important for the successful completion of assignments. Nevertheless, the younger cohort, which places a premium on achieving an optimal

balance between professional and personal spheres, may exhibit a preference for engaging in employment activities for a more moderate duration of time, often ranging from 6–8 hours per day effectively managing their time and avoiding excessive workloads that may have adverse effects on their personal lives.

> *Yeah, so it is because some senior managers think that probably we will work like 12 hours a day, like probably the way their generation works, and there is no concept of a work-life balance for them. So, say if, according to them, a project can be completed in four months. So that will work like 10 to 12 hours a day. And we would like to work maybe six hours or eight hrs a day, right? So that way, I think there is this expectation of allocation of time, right?*
>
> (Participant 1)

Variations in work methodologies and expectations can pose difficulties in effectively managing and fostering collaboration within a workforce comprising employees from different generations. Achieving a work-life balance while effectively meeting work schedules may necessitate the establishment of open channels of communication and the fostering of mutual understanding between organisational members.

11 *Leadership skills*
The participants noted that a specific cohort of senior guys is adept at task delegation and allocating work assignments to their team members and subordinates. However, they noted that these senior employees may actually lack the capacity to inspire and motivate their younger colleagues effectively.

> *They can and they delegate left, right and centre, but you know . . . I am not sure why but they find it super hard to inspire the team. They aren't inspirational, nor do they communicate effectively . . . it's just delegation.*
>
> (Participant 8)

12 *Overview of skills—Importance and shortages*
Figure 16.4 depicts two significant factors pertaining to senior employees: the scarcity of skills and the level of priority attributed to these skills, which have been sorted in ascending order. The identification of shortages originates from the data collected through focus group discussions and interviews. The importance and significance of skills, as assessed using IRD tables with a focus on the primary driver, focuses on fundamental skills crucial for diverse professional achievements. Respondents stress the primacy of primary driver abilities as the starting point from which to instil outcome themes. Prioritising helps senior staff members focus on developing the most important abilities that will have the greatest impact on their work.

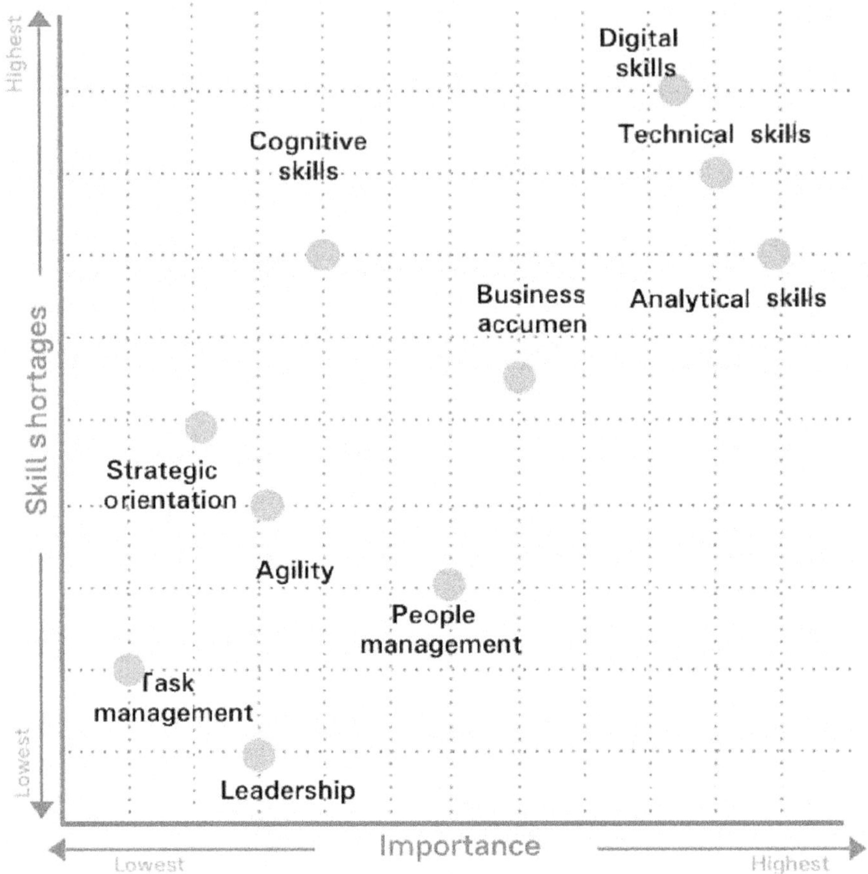

Figure 16.4 Skill matrix for older employees

Discussion and Conclusion

The multi-method approach delineated skill shortages and strengths that can be leveraged among ageing employees. In the contemporary dynamic technological environment, individuals across different age groups are required to effectively assimilate digital tools and technologies to sustain their relevance and enhance their productivity. The results underscored a shortage of digital and technological competencies among older workers. Competencies pertaining to people management, communication, strategic direction, and task management are commonly refined over a long-drawn spell within the workplace and may have evolved into an essential element of the professional personas of experienced professionals. In addition, their strategic orientation and effective task management can be seen as drawn from their prior expertise in effectively overseeing complex projects and navigating organisational challenges (Sheng et al., 2022). Any upskilling requires ongoing learning and perseverance, which a growth mindset can help promote. Older workers with a growth attitude tend to gain new skills and maintain existing skill growth, making it easier to self-learn and aid in their professional success. Nevertheless, the need for experienced individuals to possess effective people management skills can lead to difficulties due to generational differences and varying communication approaches. Acquiring new skills can be challenging at any stage of life, but it becomes even more difficult due to ageism and other forms of exclusion that older individuals face. This will substantially impact shaping the global framework for sustainable development goals (SDGs).

Preconceptions against older people may have influenced the perceived skill shortages of senior workers. Ageism is becoming an increasingly prevalent worldwide problem (World Health Organization, 2021). Preconceived beliefs about the skill set of older employees can impede the effectiveness of managing a staff that consists of multiple generations. Businesses can enhance their likelihood of success by acknowledging and harnessing the varied skill sets that personnel from different age cohorts possess. Hence, it is imperative to combat ageism in the workplace in order to cultivate a fair and inclusive work environment that recognises and appreciates the abilities and contributions of all employees, irrespective of their age.

Ageism exacerbates critical skills shortages, hampering progress towards several SDGs. Organisations fail to capitalise on the valuable knowledge, expertise, and mentorship potential of experienced elderly workers when marginalising them. This results in skill gaps that impede sustainable development, productivity, and innovation. SDGs pertaining to quality education/lifelong learning (SDG 4) and good health/well-being (SDG 3) are hindered by this exclusion, which restricts opportunities for intergenerational knowledge exchange. Ageism must be addressed to achieve SDGs, build inclusive workplaces, and use the diverse capacities of all age groups, which drives holistic societal progress.

Implications

For Organisations

Key implications align with SDGs for businesses wanting to leverage seasoned resourcefulness. First, lifelong learning promotes a culture of learning and skill development. It encourages senior staff to learn and adapt. Second, developing senior staff shows an organisation's commitment to their advancement and well-being. This helps improve employee engagement, job satisfaction, and retention, lowering turnover, and preserving organisational knowledge and expertise. Third, an age-inclusive workplace that acknowledges senior employees' contributions and experience boosts employees' sense of belonging and well-being.

For Society and Policy

Organisations and governments can support senior employees' well-being, employability, and societal growth by implementing SDGs 4 and 3 policies that encourage continuous learning, skill development, and personal development.

Future Research

The senior personnel of Indian firms face several complex issues. The challenges linked to the process of aging in India are multidimensional, often involving a wide array of socio-economic health and well-being-related problems. Further investigation is required to examine workplace characteristics such as age-neutral work and HR policies, intergenerational co-worker dynamics and differences in status, motivations, and affective evaluations to identify the factors that promote the resilience of older employees and those that impede it. Hence, it may be necessary to thoroughly comprehend the influence of age-related preconceptions in India on several aspects of employment, including hiring, training, career advancement, and other elements related to the later phases of one's professional life.

Note

* Corresponding author: lata.dyaram@iitm.ac.in.

References

Allen, J., Alpass, F. M., Szabó, Á., & Stephens, C. V. (2021). Impact of flexible work arrangements on key challenges to work engagement among older workers. *Work, Aging and Retirement*, *7*(4), 404–417.

Bal, P. M., Kooij, D. T. A. M., & Rousseau, D. M. (2015). Aging workers and the employee-employer relationship. In *Aging workers and the employee-employer relationship* (pp. 1–268). Springer International Publishing.

Bargate, K. (2014). Interactive qualitative analysis—a novel methodology for qualitative research. *Mediterranean Journal of Social Sciences*, *5*(20), 11–19.

Chenoy, D., Ghosh, S. M., & Shukla, S. K. (2019). Skill development for accelerating the manufacturing sector: The role of 'new-age' skills for 'Make in India'. *International Journal of Training Research*, *17*(Suppl. 1), 112–130.

CMIE. (2022). www.cmie.com/kommon/bin/sr.php?kall=warticle&dt=20220912145132&msec=900

De Neve, J. E., & Sachs, J. D. (2020). The SDGs and human well-being: A global analysis of synergies, trade-offs, and regional differences. *Scientific Reports*, *10*(1), 1–12.

Dhakal, S. P., Burgess, J., & Nankervis, A. (2022). Population ageing: Challenges in the Asia Pacific and beyond. In *Ageing Asia and the pacific in changing times* (pp. 3–15). Springer.

Earl, C., Taylor, P., & Cannizzo, F. (2018). "Regardless of age": Australian University managers' attitudes and practices towards older academics. *Work, Aging and Retirement*, *4*(3), 300–313.

Egan, M. (2021). American factories are desperate for workers. It's a $1 trillion problem. *CNN Business*. https://edition.cnn.com/2021/05/04/economy/manufacturing-jobs-economy/index.html

Eurostat. (2020). Duration of working life—Statistics. https://ec.europa.eu/eurostat/statistics-explained/index.php/Duration_of_working_life_-_statistics

Fasbender, U., & Gerpott, F. H. (2022). Knowledge transfer between younger and older employees: A temporal social comparison model. *Work, Aging and Retirement*, *8*(2), 146–162.

Finkelstein, L. M., Voyles, E. C., Thomas, C. L., & Zacher, H. (2020). A daily diary study of responses to age meta-stereotypes. *Work, Aging and Retirement*, *6*(1), 28–45.

Fusch, P. I., & Ness, L. R. (2015). Are we there yet? Data saturation in qualitative research. *The Qualitative Report*, *20*(9), 1408–1416.

Guest, G., Bunce, A., & Johnson, L. (2006). How many interviews are enough? An experiment with data saturation and variability. *Field Methods*, *18*(1), 59–82.

Helmrich, I., & Leppelmeier, R. (2020). *Sinkt die Halbwertszeit von Wissen? [Is the half-life of knowledge falling?]* (pp. 1–20). Bundesinstitut Für Berufsbildung.

Human-Vogel, S., & Van Petegem, P. (2008). Causal judgments of positive mood in relation to self-regulation: A case study with Flemish students. *Contemporary Educational Psychology*, *33*(4), 451–485.

International Labour Organisation. (2017, August 1). SDG note: Skills for employment. http://www.ilo.org/global/topics/sdg-2030/notes-series/lang–en/index.htm

Kadefors, R., Wikström, E., & Arman, R. (2020). The capability of organizations to manage delayed retirement. *Journal of Organizational Effectiveness*, *7*(1), 38–51.

Karpinska, K., Henkens, K., & Schippers, J. (2013). Retention of older workers: Impact of managers' age norms and stereotypes. *European Sociological Review*, *29*, 1323–1335.

Kluge, A., & Krings, F. (2008). Attitudes toward older workers and human resource practices. *Swiss Journal of Psychology*, *67*(1), 61–64.

Kooij, D. T. (2015). Successful aging at work: The active role of employees. *Work, Aging and Retirement*, *1*(4), 309–319.

Kooij, D. T., & Van De Voorde, K. (2014). Strategic HRM for older workers. In *Aging workers and the employee-employer relationship* (pp. 57–72). Springer International Publishing.

Landers, R. N., & Marin, S. (2021). Theory and technology in organizational psychology: A review of technology integration paradigms and their effects on the validity of theory. *Annual Review of Organizational Psychology and Organizational Behavior*, *8*, 235–258.

Maurya, P., Sharma, P., & Muhammad, T. (2022). Prevalence and correlates of perceived age-related discrimination among older adults in India. *BMC Public Health*, *22*(1), 1–10.

North, M. S. (2019). A gate to understanding "older" workers: Generation, age, tenure, experience. *Academy of Management Annals*, *13*(2), 414–443.

Northcutt, N., & McCoy, D. (2004). *Interactive qualitative analysis: A systems method for qualitative research*. SAGE.

OECD. (2019). *An OECD learning framework 2030* (pp. 23–35). Springer International Publishing.

Parker, S. K., & Andrei, D. M. (2020). Include, individualize, and integrate: Organizational meta-strategies for mature workers. *Work, Aging and Retirement*, *6*(1), 1–7.

Sheng, N., Fang, Y., Shao, Y., Alterman, V., & Wang, M. (2022). The impacts of digital technologies on successful aging in non-work and work domains: An organizing taxonomy. *Work, Aging and Retirement*, *8*(2), 198–207.

Truxillo, D. M., Cadiz, D. M., & Hammer, L. B. (2015). Supporting the aging workforce: A review and recommendations for workplace intervention research. *Annual Review of Organizational Psychology and Organizational Behavior*, *2*, 351–381.

United Nations. (2015, 18 September). General assembly resolution A/RES/70/1. Transforming our world: The 2030 agenda for sustainable development. *Seventieth United Nations General Assembly, New York*, *25*, 86–97.

United Nations. (2023). *UN DESA policy brief No. 153: India overtakes China as the world's most populous country.* Retrieved May 2, 2023, from www.un.org/development/desa/dpad/publication/undesa-policy-brief-no-153-india-overtakes-china-as-the-worldsmost-populous-country/

Vasconcelos, A. F. (2018). Older workers as a source of wisdom capital: Broadening perspectives. *Revista de Gestão, 25*(1), 102–118.

World Health Organization. (2021). *Global report on ageism.* www.who.int/publications/i/item/9789240016866.

17 Valuing Unpaid Care, Labour Rights, and Decent Work for All—an Analysis of Tonga's Participation in the Pacific Labour Mobility Schemes as a Sustainable Development Strategy

*Julie I. Cunningham**

Introduction

The United Nations (2021) sustainable development goals (SDGs) have established international targets in the valuing of unpaid care, decent work, skill development, and labour rights. Preceding these goals has been the promotion of the development possibilities of temporary migration schemes (World Bank, 2006), and the implementation of the SDGs is occurring within this context. For example, in 2007, New Zealand launched the Recognised Seasonal Employer (RSE) Scheme. Following in their footsteps, Australia launched the Pacific Seasonal Worker Pilot Scheme in 2008, which, after several iterations and expansions, is now known as the Pacific Australia Labour Mobility (PALM) Scheme. While the Australian government recently signalled that some exemptions will soon be applied to enable family accompaniment in principle (Department of Foreign Affairs and Trade, 2022), the situation remains that workers participating in Pacific Labour Mobility Schemes (PLMS) do not attract any corresponding visa entitlements to enable family accompaniment.

These PLMS are promoted as remittance-as-development models that facilitate a 'triple win': a win for the sending country, the destination country, and the migrant worker. As the World Bank (2017) outlined, the 'triple win' benefits for the receiving countries and employers appear obvious: reliable access to flexible, cheap labour on demand to mitigate reported skill shortages, with minimal exposure to the usual financial costs of supporting citizens through the life-course. Albeit, these reported skill shortages are contested, with minimal transparency provided in countries such as Australia, meaning such claims of labour shortages are inadequately scrutinised (Campbell, 2019).

At the same time, sending countries, such as Tonga, are also said to enjoy the *triple win*, with improved economies from the inflow of remitted wages, and reductions in unemployment. The migrant worker benefits from increased income and the opportunity to return home with new skills and savings that can benefit households as well as trade and investment (World Bank, 2017).

DOI: 10.4324/9781003379065-19

Reflecting the coalescence of interests between labour-sending and receiving countries described by Piper and Withers (2018), maximising labour mobility and remittances has become a national strategic focus in Tonga (Tonga Ministry of Finance & National Planning, 2015; IOM, 2021). The cash and goods transfers sent by migrants to Tonga, known as remittances, have ballooned in recent decades. At least 72% of households receive overseas remittances (Tonga Statistics Department, 2022c). Since 2015, Tonga has dominated as the top remittance-receiving country globally as a proportion of gross domestic product (GDP), with remittances equating to 46.1% in 2021 (World Bank, 2023). Australia and New Zealand's labour mobility schemes can offer earning potential five times higher than for equivalent local work (MBI&E, 2016; World Bank, 2018a). Additional factors such as limited formal employment opportunities in Tonga, a persistent youth demographic bulge, and a remittance-dependent economy, induce the government of Tonga's support for temporary labour migration schemes.

PLMS are described as 'crucial for increasing access to decent and productive work for Tongan men and women' (IOM, 2022, p. 8), with remittances regarded as holding 'tremendous potential for small business investment' (IOM, 2021, p. 28). In 2018/19, 12.9% of the workforce migrated to work in these schemes; this is projected to increase to 31.5% by 2024–25 (Kingdom of Tonga, 2023). Indeed, consistent with the SDG target 1.4 to increase access to basic services and property ownership, PLM scheme remittances have been found to increase household savings, household improvements expenditure on education and basic consumption (World Bank, 2018a; Maeda & Edwards, 2023). They have also positively impacted cash cropping, plantation expansions, and post-disaster recovery (Bedford et al., 2020), indicating their role in progressing SDG targets 2.3, 2.4, and 1.5 to increase agricultural productivity and sustainable food production systems and reduce vulnerability to disasters.

However, these remittance gains have also been described as 'speeding up' the commodification of labour in PICs, as waged labour replaces social relations, communal work, and traditional subsistence practices, triggering changes to the organisation of family and society (Petrou & Connell, 2023). Thus, as the Kingdom of Tonga continues to expand its involvement in Pacific labour mobility schemes in both Australia and New Zealand, concerns persist regarding the social impacts of participation for the nation (IOM, 2021). Drawing on available studies and government publications, this chapter will evaluate the social impacts of Tonga's focused labour mobility approach and their alignment with the SDGs targets: to recognise and value unpaid care and domestic work, the promotion of shared responsibility within the household and family (5.4); full employment and decent work for all women and men and of equal value (8.5); to increase relevant skills for employment, decent jobs, and entrepreneurship (4.4); and to protect labour rights and promote safe and secure working environments for all workers (8.8). Castles (2010) suggested that migration be conceptualised as embedded within social transformation processes, and this lens will be utilised to contextualise findings and emerging themes.

First, to situate Tonga's participation in temporary labour mobility schemes, this chapter will provide a brief overview with regard to coloniality and current political infrastructure, extreme vulnerability, and the uneven development of education, economic, and labour markets. The framework for the literature review will then be provided. Following this, the analyses of available studies and government policy and literature will be ordered through the emerging themes: the impact on social reproduction; unequal access to full and productive employment; limited opportunity for skill development and transference; and the depreciation of labour rights. Following this, findings will be summarised and further contextualised utilising social transformation theory to demonstrate the exploitative and extractive nature of PLMS that perpetuate uneven development.

Country Background

The Kingdom of Tonga has a total land area of 748 square kilometres stretched across an archipelago of 170 islands in western Polynesia. First understood to be inhabited in 900 BCE, Tonga has a long history of agricultural production, maritime trade, and migration (Burley, 1998). 'Respect, humility, reciprocation and patriotism are the four core values that underpin' the Kingdom of Tonga (Parliament of Tonga, 2016).

In 1900, Tonga became a British Protectorate before being declared (once again) independent in 1970. This maintenance of sovereignty is highly valued in Tonga, enabling some preservation of the monarchy and chiefly leadership. However, this has not disrupted the coloniality progressed through Western imports of governing structures, definitions of political legitimacy, education, economic, and employment practices (Tecun & Ata Siu'ulua, 2023). Now a constitutional monarchy, the current Head of State, King Tupou VI, operates within a parliamentary system.

Tonga is ranked among the most vulnerable countries in the world to natural disasters (Kirch et al., 2021). This extreme vulnerability, combined with Tonga's remoteness, small population, scant profitable natural resources, plus high transport and energy costs, inhibits the development of infrastructure, business, and the labour market. Due to these 'deep structural impediments' to sustainable economic development, the United Nations classifies Tonga as a small island developing state (SIDS) with special needs (ESCAP, 2019, p. 2). Countries with special needs are defined as the 'least developed countries, landlocked developing countries and small island developing States' (ESCAP, 2019, p. xvi).

Census data from Tonga shows that following the tripling of the population in the last century, while recent decades have seen the population growth rate decline and then stall to 100,179 (Tonga Statistics Department, 2022c). The male-to-female ratio also continues to decline within the population, with 95 males to 100 females in 2021. Following intensive urbanisation over the past century, the main island, Nuku'alofa, is home to 74% of the population. With 37% of the population being school-age, the provision of education remains a national challenge (Government of Tonga, 2019; Tonga Statistics Department, 2022c). Girls enjoy greater access to secondary school, while boys experience almost double the drop-out and repetition rate of girls. Loss of interest in education, family problems, school exclusion, and exam failure rates inhibit school completion (Fonua, 2017; Tonga Statistics Department, 2022c). Household expenditure on education has also declined since 2015, equating to 1% of household expenditure in 2021 (Menaouer & Sharp, 2023). A World Bank (2022) project to enhance secondary school retention from the 48-month baseline to 60 months reported only a one-month increase on the baseline at the mid-point review. Despite these obstacles, around 14% of the population have attained technical or vocational qualifications such as a certificate or a diploma, and 4% have completed a tertiary degree (Tonga Statistics Department, 2022c).

While Tongan practices of complex exchange networks, reciprocity, and subsistence agriculture persist, Tonga is increasingly a monetised economy of consumption rather than production. Imports primarily consist of mineral products, food and beverages, machinery, appliances, and vehicles (Tonga Statistics Department, 2022a). Vegetables and animal products account for 92% of exports. However, personal remittances persist as the major inflow for foreign receipts, exceeding exports by a ratio of 11 to 1 (National Reserve Bank of Tonga, 2022).

Unsurprisingly, given the significant trading imbalance, where imports now exceed exports by around 13 to one, the country has long run a sizeable deficit (Tonga Statistics Department, 2022b). In addition, the Tongan government's continued reliance on overseas aid to address the economic situation and debt burdens remains an area of national concern (IMF, 2020). The service sector now dominates the market, accounting for half of GDP; agriculture and fishing contribute 18% and manufacturing only 5%. This is all within the context of declining GDP since 2019 (Tonga Statistics Department, 2022d). Added to this is the increasing prevalence of national disasters, such as the volcanic eruption and tsunami in 2022 and cyclone Gita in 2019, both of which incurred significant costs and substantial loss of tourism infrastructure.

Like many Pacific neighbours, Tonga has limited formal employment opportunities, and youth unemployment remains a major challenge (IOM, 2022). At the same time, Tonga experiences widespread high and semi-skilled shortages. These range from qualified engineers, teachers, nurses, trade and maintenance skills, chefs, retail and service workers, with almost half of the jobs advertised in 2022 requiring a bachelor's degree or higher (Kingdom of Tonga, 2023). Around half of people of working-age labour are in the informal sector (Tonga Statistics Department, 2018), while almost all households (88%) report income from primary activities such as agriculture, livestock, fishing, and handicraft activities (Menaouer & Sharp, 2023).

In the absence of earnings from labour mobility schemes, families can struggle to generate alternative incomes to meet their needs. This has resulted in decreased consumption, disrupted health care, school withdrawal, sale of land, premature harvesting, depleted savings, and deferred debt (World Bank,

2021). Thus, participation in PLMS can provide a satisficing approach, enabling households to 'mitigate *existing* conditions of precarity at home' (Piper et al., 2017, p. 1093).

Temporary Labour Mobility as Contributing to Sustainable Development?

The 'triple win' narratives extolling temporary labour mobility schemes generally 'emphasise increased income as a primary logic for assessing benefit' (Stead & Petrou, 2023). Given the claims of the 'triple win', the recent expansion of labour mobility schemes in Australia, alongside Tonga's commitment to these labour mobility schemes, this chapter will examine the contributions of labour mobility schemes to sustainable development outcomes for people in Tonga. This chapter will evaluate the social impacts of Tonga's focused temporary labour mobility approach according to its alignment with the SDGs targets as previously outlined: to recognise and value unpaid care and domestic work, the promotion of shared responsibility within the household and family (5.4); full employment and decent work for all women and men and of equal value (8.5); to increase relevant skills for employment, decent jobs and entrepreneurship (4.4); and to protect labour rights and promote safe and secure working environments for all workers (8.8).

Method

Several primary search terms were utilised to source data for this analysis (see Figure 17.1) with search parameters restricted from 2007 to June 2023. Results were reviewed for inclusion in this analysis. Those that contained

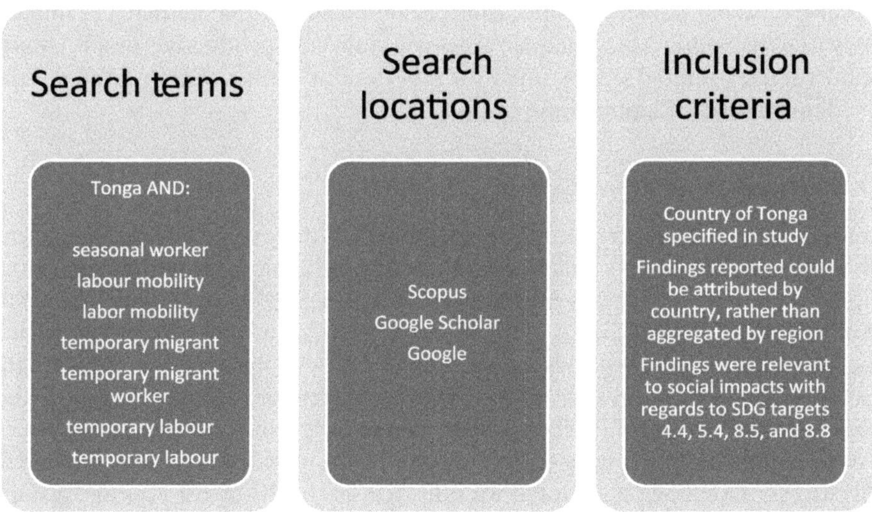

Figure 17.1 Search terms, locations, and inclusion criteria for analysis

original study data specified Tonga as a nation of study with findings attributed to Tonga and relevant to the social impacts of the defined SDG targets were included. Whereas studies that were solely literature reviews, or not relevant to the social impact on SDG targets, were excluded. In addition, in recognition that PICs are not culturally homogenous, that is to say, findings in one nation are not necessarily readily transferable to another, studies that reported for the Pacific as a whole, rather than being attributed specifically to Tonga, were excluded. Following this search, government policy documents, reports, and news articles were also reviewed to provide context to this analysis. The bibliographies of included studies were also reviewed for additional studies of relevance that had not been identified within the search parameters. All findings were then reviewed against the SDG targets outlined.

Findings from the Literature Analysis

Castles (2013) explained how workers, as a consequence of human insecurity arising through the global class hierarchy, become obliged to migrate to ensure satisfactory provision for themselves and their families. Wealthy nations impose restrictions on migration to maintain frameworks of accumulation (that minimise cost and maximise profit) enacted through existing global power imbalances. Previous exploitative practices such as colonialism and dispossession established these economic, political, and racialised power imbalances. Continued migration restrictions institutionalise this inequality, structuring the continuation of unfree labour practices through the denial of rights and imposition of conditions that maintain the vulnerability, subordination, and exploitation of the migrant worker while exporting these costs to the labour-sending country.

On reviewing available publications utilising Castles' (2010) theoretical framing of social transformation, four key themes emerged: namely the impact on social reproduction, unequal access to full and productive employment opportunities, limited opportunity for skill development and transference, and the depreciation of labour rights.

The Impact on Social Reproduction

Tonga's Labour Mobility Supply Management Strategy (LMSMS) (Kingdom of Tonga, 2023) asserts that there is no demographic labour shortage, noting 'the population age 20–59 years in 2021 (44,579) was virtually the same as it was in 2006 (44,371)'. This in itself raises questions regarding where the youth bulge of 2006 has gone. Nonetheless, analysis of the census data for 2006 and 2021 shows a marked change in gender representation for the population who remain in Tonga within this age group. In 2006, the productive population age group were evenly split: 50% male, 50% female. By 2021, this had shifted: males accounted for only 46% of the 20-to-59-year age group, while females had increased to 54%.

Therefore, obscured in these migration figures are the demographic and gendered distortions induced by PLMS and the corresponding care deficits and systemic care depletion that remittances do not resolve (Withers & Hill, 2023). While acknowledging the indirect emotional and financial care performed transnationally by temporary migrant workers, this hollowing out of productive citizens impacts reproductive availability for cultural and community activities, subsistence agricultural production, domestic work, and care. This has triggered concerns about the erosion of culture, social cohesion, and traditional social protection mechanisms, as community activities, such as the church and village leadership, are negatively impacted (Moala-Tupou, 2016; Bedford et al., 2020).

Consequently, family and household members who remain undertake additional responsibilities to maintain care, domestic, agricultural, and community responsibilities (Moala-Tupou, 2016; Cunningham, 2022). As males continue to dominate PLM scheme participation, women, in particular, are required to perform the 'double shift' where they carry out increased household duties plus 'the traditional roles and communal commitments of the husband' (Rohorua et al., 2009; Chattier, 2019, p. 60). In contrast, when females migrate, males undertake some additional responsibilities while also enlisting other female family members to perform this extra work (Chattier, 2019). This reliance on females to maintain domestic and community responsibilities further entrenches traditional gender norms, thus undermining progression towards the SDG target for shared responsibility between genders within the household and the family.

This amplified work burden for females also curtails their capacity to participate in employment and economic activities, thus impeding their own ability to participate in PLMS (Chattier, 2019). Not that increased female participation would resolve these care deficits. Rather, an increased supply of either gender to PLMS would further distort and deplete the population available to perform direct and indirect reproductive care in the domestic, community, cultural, and environmental domains.

At times, traditional gender roles can be renegotiated, suggesting the potential of PLM scheme participation to promote shared responsibilities in households and families (Cunningham, 2022). For example, participation in PLMS can increase women's roles in decision-making and managing finances; however, such changes have been found to be short-lived (Chattier, 2019).

In addition, PLM scheme participation has been observed to impact intimate and family relationships negatively. Issues raised have included extra-marital affairs, disagreement regarding remittances, savings and expenditure (particularly on alcohol), inadequate communication, and the failure of migrant workers' to return (World Bank, 2018b; Chattier, 2019). Younger generations are reported to prioritise 'fast money', 'social freedom', and 'individualism' above cultural practices of respect, constraint, and reciprocity (Bedford et al., 2020). At the same time, young people speak of being subject to increased discipline and struggling in the absence of usual parental support and guidance

(Moala-Tupou, 2016; Cunningham, 2022). These all create additional stressors for families and households of PLM scheme workers to navigate. In some instances, marital and family breakdown occurs, and the PLMS scheme worker does not return (Moala-Tupou, 2016; Chattier, 2019).

Supporting Equal Employment Opportunities

Consistent with the development aims of PLMS and SDG target 8.8 to achieve full and productive employment, in Tonga, most workers who participated were unemployed for at least six months before departure (World Bank, 2018a). However, the opportunity to participate in these schemes has not been accessible to all in Tonga. Instead, direct employer recruitment approaches have favoured particular workers, families, or villages, thus reinforcing systems of patronage and inequality (Bedford et al., 2020).

Age and racial biases have also been widespread within PLMS. The upper age limit of 45 years in Australia was only removed in 2021 (Government of Australia, 2021). While in New Zealand, despite there being no upper age limit for inclusion, over 90% of workers were below the age of 50 (Bedford et al., 2020). Community leaders have also expressed concern that selection processes discriminate against people with a disability (World Bank, 2018b). This seems likely given the 'fit and healthy' medical clearances required (Government of Australia and Government of Tonga, 2017). Racialised depictions of the favourability of migrant workers are also common (Nishitani et al., 2023). One example is the Australian government's (2021) recommendation to choose Tongan workers as 'Tongans are physically strong.'

PLMS are regarded to have the potential to increase empowerment and agency by enabling access to job opportunities for females (World Bank, 2018b). However, gender disparity persists in these schemes. Employer bias, segregated accommodation sites, local selection processes, and gendered perceptions of women's roles and caring responsibilities in Tonga all inhibit women's access (World Bank, 2018b; Bedford et al., 2020).

Should Tonga seek to establish more inclusive access, their capacity to resolve any of these selection biases is somewhat limited, as 'employers have the final say on workers recruited' (Kingdom of Tonga, 2023, p. 25). Notably, such employer preferencing of male employees for physically demanding duties would be an illegal recruitment practice if recruiting locally in Australia and New Zealand. This under-utilisation of the female workforce contributes to further entrenching caring, employment, educational, financial, and social inequalities. The PALM scheme expansion of employment sectors to include traditionally more feminised employment sectors, such as aged and disability care, may begin to address this gender imbalance, which is also likely to intensify the social reproductive burden for women who remain in Tonga.

Bedford et al. (2020) observed that labour mobility flows could generate the employment of farm workers to replace the migrant worker's labour, contributing to a wider distribution of employment and remittances. Albeit, also noting that monetising traditional exchange items further fuels the need to attain cash incomes. Yet labour mobility schemes can also divert the focus of sending countries from creating decent, sustainable employment. Thus, within this context of continued influxes of remittances, the relative earnings available for wages in the usual occupations of agriculture and fishing are further diminished. Compounding this is the risk that any national wage adjustments to address these wage gaps could jeopardise the competitiveness of Tonga's agricultural export market (IOM, 2022).

While households increase savings during PLM scheme participation, these do not necessarily translate to long-term gains for the migrant worker or their household (World Bank, 2018a). Remittance incomes have been found to have a negligible effect on investments (World Bank, 2018a; Maeda & Edwards, 2023). For example, only 7.1% of households utilised earnings to start a business (World Bank, 2018a). In addition to these spending trends, it remains unclear how remittance investment could overcome the persistent structural factors that inhibit economic development (and impel workers to migrate in the first place) to unlock the 'tremendous potential' for small business investment (IOM, 2021, p. 28).

Limited Skill Development and Skill Transfers

The government of Tonga does not assess the labour market to ascertain either the effect of emigration or the demand for migrant labour (IOM, 2022). However, the Labour Mobility Supply Management Strategy (Kingdom of Tonga, 2023) reports that there is no absolute shortage of labour nor concern that PLMS participation will deplete Tonga's labour force. Rather, the perceived challenge remains 'to enhance the economic development of labour mobility . . . whilst not undermining the supply of labour required domestically' (Kingdom of Tonga, 2023, p. 20). Given the projection that almost one-third of the available workforce will be engaged in PLMS by 2024, these assertions appear somewhat optimistic.

The exodus of workers has already been reported to generate labour shortages (Fonua, 2019; IMF, 2023). Due to direct recruitment approaches, these shortages disproportionately impact some villages and regions more than others. Consequently, traditional skills in crop production are reportedly disappearing, threatening traditional subsistence practices that can sustain food security (IOM, 2021, 2022). Illustrating the burden that falls on labour-sending countries to resolve this labour imbalance, a key strategic objective includes the retention of essential workers, yet the imposition of any limit or targets to cap participation in PLMS has been ruled out as unacceptable (Kingdom of Tonga, 2023). Nonetheless, with the expectation that the expansion of PALM employment to four years will intensify the challenge of skill exodus, Tonga has signalled there is the intention to 'refine worker selection criteria to mitigate brain drain risks' and ensure a 'pro-poor approach' by excluding high-skilled workers from PLM scheme participation (Strategic

Action 2.2 Kingdom of Tonga, 2023). Such proposals raise questions regarding the freedom of mobility—limiting who can depart a country is highly unusual but is perhaps indicative of the constrained ability of small nations such as Tonga to influence these bilateral arrangements.

This proposed limit is also likely to exacerbate rather than resolve the issue of an under-skilled labour force. First, excluding high-skilled workers from participation creates a perverse incentive. People and their potential may divert from pursuing skill acquisition pathways to preserve their PLM scheme eligibility. Second, this proposal does not resolve the PLM scheme market-induced distortions that disincentivise upskilling. Tonga is unable to compete with the high minimum wages available in New Zealand and Australia (Kingdom of Tonga, 2023). Thus, participation in PLMS can provide higher wages than high-skill professions in Tonga, without the deferred wages, investment of time or funds required for training to attain professional qualifications.

Consistent with the SDG target 4.4 to increase relevant skills for employment, decent jobs, and entrepreneurship, the transfer of skills and knowledge is an anticipated benefit of PLMS (IOM, 2017, 2021). Yet only one quarter of workers reported accessing formal training, primarily due to insufficient time available for study on their only day off each week (World Bank, 2018a). Still, most who undertook training felt the skills obtained were transferable to work in Tonga (Bedford et al., 2020). However, picking, packing, sorting, and pruning were the predominant on-the-job skills acquired for most, which are not always readily transferable to the informal labour market and small-scale agricultural practices of Tonga (World Bank, 2018a).

Eroded Labour Rights

Demonstrating the demand and perceived benefits, PLM scheme workers overwhelmingly indicate their satisfaction with participating in these schemes (World Bank, 2018a, 2021). This is well illustrated by the high return rate for additional seasons—70% of Tongan workers returned for additional seasons with the RSE scheme (Bedford et al., 2020).

Yet a persistent premise of these schemes is the notion of circulation, enabling workers the flexibility to opt in and out to suit their life circumstances, needs, and goals. Such high repeat migration rates suggest that the triple-win premise of reintegration with accompanying skill acquisitions in Tonga is not being actualised. This continued reliance on labour mobility schemes as a long-term employment option is evident. For example, most PLM scheme workers do not intend to work during their period at home as they instead plan to utilise their savings and return to participate in PLMS for as long as possible (World Bank, 2018a). This high return rate, alongside recent expansions of the PALM scheme that enables workers multiple entries or to remain in Australia for up to four years, means workers and their families will experience repeated and significant periods of separation.

Alternately, those who chose to cease engagement in PLMS cited parental and home responsibilities as inhibiting repeat engagements (Gibson &

McKenzie, 2014), thus illustrating the iterative negotiations and tensions as transnational families choose between remaining together as a family or transnational householding as a family survival strategy.

With no legitimate pathway to residency, workers and their families are captive in regulated protracted precariousness and compliance to the employer with whom they are indentured and often indebted, as they compete with other migrant workers to secure their return for another season (Piper et al., 2017). As PLM scheme employers are often under no requirement to recognise the experience or skills of returned workers acquired from previous migrations, the employer can persist in paying return migrant workers at the minimum hourly or piece rate. Workers can also endure poor work conditions, underpayment, unsafe, intense work requirements, and the threat of deportation if they raise concerns (Fair Work Ombudsman, 2018; Unions NSW & MWC, 2021)

Employers well understand this precarity. For example, Petrou and Connell (2018) outlined workers' experience of threats of deportation being utilised and actioned by the employer to ensure workers' acceptance of unfavourable conditions. Yet, within this known precarity, more than half of PLM workers regarded their participation as important to progress a pathway to permanent residency, despite no such pathway being available to them (World Bank, 2018a). Workers can also be required to abide by arbitrary rules (including in their personal time) imposed by their employer. Examples include curfews, restrictions on freedom of circulation and association, prohibitions on sexual relationships (including between married spouses), limitations on heating and showering, plus bans on alcohol, kava, and tobacco use (New Zealand Human Rights Commission, 2022). Failure to adhere to the conditions set by employers can result in fines or the worker being sent home, with sanctions applied against future labour mobility that can extend to their family and village (Nishitani et al., 2023). Thus, with regard to SDG target 8.8 to protect labour rights for migrant workers, it is as Piper and Withers (2018, p. 569) discerned: 'labour markets are inherently transnational yet labour rights, it seems, are not'.

While anticipated higher gross wages may be realised, these diminish once costs are deducted. In the absence of any clear framework for reasonable wage deductions, exploitation by recruiters or employers can extend to enforced and inflated living costs of varying but too frequently, poor quality (Unions NSW & MWC, 2021). For example, the New Zealand Human Rights Commission (2022) found that it was standard practice for between two to seven workers to share one bedroom, accruing an average NZD $1000 income per bedroom per week for the accommodation provider. Between 40% to 52% of earnings are utilised to oblige necessary clearances, travel costs, health insurance, taxation, living, and contract costs for PLM scheme workers (MBI&E, 2016; World Bank, 2018a). Further to this, as detailed in the World Bank (2021) report, during the COVID-19 pandemic, workers whose work was cancelled before departure had already incurred non-refundable costs of over USD $600 per person. One-third had financed these costs through debt. Nonetheless (or perhaps in the hope of resolving this debt), these workers indicated their continued desire to work in labour mobility schemes.

Negative pay balances can also occur when the worker is stood down due to illness, unfavourable weather or crop conditions, or work is reduced or delayed (Petrou & Connell, 2018). Regardless, deductions for living costs continue to be incurred through this downtime. As PLM workers are largely ineligible for government assistance, to manage these losses, workers resort to decreasing savings, personal consumption, and remittances (Petrou et al., 2021; World Bank, 2021). Recent Australian government changes are phasing in a minimum of 30 hours of work each week. This has provoked ire from horticultural employer groups, arguing this would be unsustainable and impractical for the industry (Askew, 2023; Halter & Buchanan, 2023). Evidently, lost in this argument is how sustainable or practical it is for PLM scheme workers to subsist in the absence of a minimum wage or welfare safety net.

Discussion

Utilising Castles (2013) theoretical framing of social transformation, the shortfalls of PLMS to progress the SDG targets previously outlined could be surmised as follows.

Tongan participants in PLMS experience 'forced transnationalism' to secure a family survival strategy due to local precarity induced and reproduced by neoliberal globalisation and uneven global development (Piper & Withers, 2018). Empowered by previous colonial dominance, continued coloniality, and the resulting advantage established, nations such as Australia and New Zealand seek to minimise the costs (and maximise the profit) of importing people to perform labour through the design of systems that legitimise the diminishing of the PLM scheme worker to simply a labour component. In doing so, wealthy and powerful nations can prioritise profits above all else, while simultaneously depleting Tonga of its productive citizens, and therefore devaluing family stability, care, community, cultural and agricultural reproduction. These schemes serve to further institutionalise and maximise inequalities through the dehumanisation and demeaning of PLM scheme workers and the creation of new forms of social differentiation. Examples discussed include gender, racial and disability recruitment biases that would be illegal if applied to citizens of the labour-receiving nations. Exploitative labour practices and minimal rights include being indentured to employers with the threat of deportation. At the same time, unregulated wage deductions satisfy frameworks of accumulation for periphery profiteers rather than a decent wage proportional to the skill and experience of the worker.

To expand further on Castles' framework, all of this is undertaken while the boundaries of the nation-state are enacted to preclude any visibility of the subordination experienced by the families who remain in Tonga. To facilitate this concealment, these arrangements are packaged as temporary and circular despite the repeated evidence to indicate they are not. Withers (2019, p. 432) observations provide a useful summary:

> [T]he assumptions behind the promotion of temporary labour migration as a *'triple win'* scenario amount to an unequal distribution of 'wins' that benefit the developed before the developing, and migrant workers least of all.

Within this imbalanced context, it remains unclear how countries such as Tonga can exert influence to secure desired objectives to 'maximize migration benefits for Tonga's sustainable development planning' (IOM, 2021, p. 34). Instead, SIDs such as Tonga remain compelled to depend on the social cooperation of wealthier and more powerful nations in negotiating bilateral labour mobility agreements.

Conclusion

In summary, while providing much-needed access to employment and income opportunities, PLMS largely ignore and deplete unpaid care, domestic work, and shared responsibility within households and families. Inducing demographic distortions by age and gender, PLMS amplify the domestic and community work burdens that usually fall to women while also impeding their ability to participate. Income injections enable increased household consumption but do not resolve the additional stresses for relationships as families are separated.

Gender, age, and racial biases permitted within the governance of PLMS result in unequal access. Limited employment protections, such as for minimum hours, and workers' likely unemployment between repeat seasons, diminish notions of full employment. The structural factors that impelled PLM scheme participation persist, hindering job creation, entrepreneurship, and opportunities for skill transfer. At the same time, significant skill shortages are incurred in Tonga, yet skill development is disincentivised as local wages in Tonga cannot compete with PLM scheme offerings. The majority who participate in PLMS are unable to prioritise formal training within their work schedule or are unlikely to transfer mass production skills to Tonga, resulting in unrealised skill dividends.

Indentured and often indebted to their employer, with no permanent visa pathways, permanent employment, or welfare safety net, workers persist in precariousness. Navigating arbitrary rules set by their employer, while accepting substandard conditions that consume around half of their earnings, workers compete to be selected for return for the next season. Therefore, on reviewing the available information regarding the social impacts of Pacific labour mobility schemes, their contribution to progress sustainable development remains questionable and is yet to be demonstrated in Tonga. Instead, PLMS are discordant with recognising and valuing unpaid care and domestic work and the promotion of shared responsibility within the household and family. Promises of full employment and decent work for all women and men being of equal value are not being realised as access remains biased and uneven. Opportunities to increase relevant skills for employment, decent jobs, or entrepreneurship are largely unavailable and insufficient to address the structural constraints that inhibit the Tongan market. With regard to the protection of labour rights and promotion of secure working environments for all workers, in addition to the exploitation and erosion of labour rights occurring, the very establishment of restrictive exclusionary temporary migration systems evidences the system of global inequality being perpetuated rather than alleviated. Instead, in the steadfast effort to be divisible to support these unfair labour arrangements as a survival strategy, temporary migrant workers and their families have been rendered invisible, as the needs and prerogatives of the wealthy elite dominate.

Note

* Corresponding author: Julie.Cunningham@anu.edu.au.

References

Askew, Z. (2023, 14 August). PALM pain with reforms. *Gippsland Times.*

Australian Government. (2021). *Pacific labour scheme seasonal worker programme: An Australian Government Initiative (Tonga).* Retrieved 29 June 2021, from http://pacificlabour.siteindev.com.au/about/countries/tonga/

Bedford, C., Bedford, R., & Nunns, H. (2020). *RSE impact study: Pacific stream report.* New Zealand Government.

Burley, D. V. (1998). Tongan archaeology and the Tongan past, 2850–150 B.P. *Journal of World Prehistory, 12*(3), 337–392.

Campbell, I. (2019). Harvest labour markets in Australia: Alleged labour shortages and employer demand for temporary migrant workers. *Journal of Australian Political Economy*, (84), 46–88.

Castles, S. (2010). Understanding global migration: A social transformation perspective. *Journal of Ethnic and Migration Studies, 36*(10), 1565–1586.

Castles, S. (2013). The forces driving global migration. *Journal of Intercultural Studies, 34*(2), 122–140.

Chattier, P. (2019). Beyond development impact: Gender and care in the Pacific Seasonal Worker Programme. *Gender and Development, 27*(1), 49–65. https://doi.org/10.1080/13552074.2019.1570733

Cunningham, J. I. (2022). *International labour migration and the children left behind: Hearing the voices of young people traversing transnational parenting in Tonga* [Doctor of Philosophy, University of Wollongong].

Department of Foreign Affairs and Trade. (2022). *Family accompaniment frequently asked questions.* Government of Australia. Retrieved 5 September 2023, from www.palmscheme.gov.au/sites/default/files/2022-12/Family%20accompaniment%20frequently%20asked%20questions%20-%20221222.pdf

Fair Work Ombudsman. (2018). *Harvest trail inquiry report.* Commonwealth of Australia.

Fonua, P. (2017, 5 February). Hundreds of secondary school students fail end of year exam, parliament told. *Matangi Tonga Online.*

Fonua, P. (2019, 27 July). Local business can't compete with seasonal worker pay rates. *Matangi Tonga.*

Gibson, J., & McKenzie, D. (2014). The development impact of a best practice seasonal worker policy. *The Review of Economics and Statistics*, *96*(2), 229–243.

Government of Australia. (2021). *A new era for Pacific Australia labour mobility, Australian Government Department of Foreign Affairs and Trade.* Retrieved 18 August 2023, from www.foreignminister.gov.au/minister/marise-payne/media-release/new-era-pacific-australia-labour-mobility

Government of Australia and Government of Tonga. (2017). *Memorandum of understanding between the Australian Government and the Government of the Kingdom of Tonga in support of Australia's Seasonal Worker Programme (SWP).* Author.

Government of Tonga. (2019). *Ministry of education and training: Corporate plan & budget for 2019/2020–2021/2022.* Author.

Halter, A., & Buchanan, K. (2023, 10 August). Changes to Pacific Islander labour mobility scheme lack seasonal flexibility, growers say. *ABC News.*

International Monetary Fund (IMF). (2020). *IMF country report: Tonga debt sustainability analysis* (21/26). Author.

International Monetary Fund (IMF). (2023). *Tonga: Staff concluding statement of the 2023 article IV mission.* Author.

International Organization for Migration (IOM). (2017). *Harnessing the contributions of transnational communities and diasporas.* Author.

International Organization for Migration (IOM). (2021). *Migration and sustainable development policy.* International Organization for Migration: Migration Technical Working Group of Tonga.

International Organization for Migration (IOM). (2022). *The Kingdom of Tonga national voluntary GCM review: Implementing the global compact for safe, orderly and regular migration.* Author.

Kingdom of Tonga. (2023). *Tonga labour mobility supply management strategy* (Online). PACER Plus.

Kirch, L., Prütz, R., & Bündnis Entwicklung, H. (2021). *WorldRiskReport 2021: Social protection.* Bündnis Entwicklung Hilft Ruhr University Bochum—Institute for International Law of Peace and Armed Conflict (IFHV).

Maeda, H., & Edwards, R. (2023, 2 February). Seasonal work supports everyday expenses in Tonga. *Devpolicy Blog from the Development Policy Centre.* Retrieved 6 September 2023, from https://devpolicy.org/seasonal-work-supports-everyday-expenses-in-tonga-20230203/

Ministry of Business Innovation & Employment (MBI&E). (2016). *The remittance pilot project—The economic benefits of the recognised seasonal employer work policy and its role in assisting development in Samoa and Tonga.* Author.

Menaouer, O., & Sharp, M. (2023). *Tonga 2021 household income and expenditure survey report.* Tonga Statistics Department.

Moala-Tupou, L. (2016). *The social impacts of seasonal migration on left-behind children: An exploratory study from Lifuka, Tonga* [Masters, The University of Waikato].

National Reserve Bank of Tonga. (2022). *Economic releases: Remittances.* Government of Tonga.

New Zealand Human Rights Commission. (2022). *The RSE scheme in Aotearoa New Zealand: A human rights review.* Author.

Nishitani, M., Boese, M., & Lee, H. (2023). The production of precariousness and the racialisation of Pacific Islanders in an Australian horticultural region. *Journal of Ethnic and Migration Studies*, 1–20.

Parliament of Tonga. (2016). *Crown prince calls POCC meeting to embrace Tonga's 4 golden values.* Legislative Assembly of Tonga. www.parliament.gov.to/~parliam1/media-centre/latest-news/latest-news-in-english/525-crown-prince-calls-pocc-meeting-to-embrace-tonga-s-4-golden-values

Petrou, K., & Connell, J. (2018). "We don't feel free at all": Temporary ni-Vanuatu workers in the Riverina, Australia. *Rural Society*, *27*(1), 66–79.

Petrou, K., & Connell, J. (2023). *Pacific Islands guestworkers in Australia: The new blackbirds?* Palgrave Macmillan.
Petrou, K., Dun, O., Farbotko, C., & Kitara, T. (2021). *Pacific labour mobility on pause: Consequences of temporary immobility during the pandemic* (pp. 299–319). Springer Nature.
Piper, N., Rosewarne, S., & Withers, M. (2017). Migrant precarity in Asia: "Networks of labour activism" for a rights-based Governance of Migration: Debate: Addressing Migrant precarity in Asia. *Development and Change*, *48*(5), 1089–1110.
Piper, N., & Withers, M. (2018). Forced transnationalism and temporary labour migration: Implications for understanding migrant rights. *Identities*, *25*(5), 558–575.
Rohorua, H., Gibson, J., McKenzie, D., & Garcia Martinez, P. (2009). How do Pacific Island households and communities cope with seasonally absent members?. *Pacific Economic Bulletin*, *24*(3), 19–38.
Stead, V., & Petrou, K. (2023). Beyond the "triple win": Pacific Islander farmworkers' use of social media to navigate labour mobility costs and possibilities through the COVID-19 pandemic. *Journal of Ethnic and Migration Studies*, *49*(9), 2194–2212.
Tecun, A., & Ata Siu'ulua, S. (2023). Tongan coloniality: Contesting the "never colonized" narrative. *Postcolonial Studies*. Advance online publication. https://doi.org/10.1080/13688790.2022.2162353
Tonga Ministry of Finance & National Planning. (2015). *Tonga strategic development framework (TSDFII): 2015–2025*. Author.
Tonga Statistics Department. (2018). *Tonga Labour Force Survey (TLFS 2018) analytical report*. Tonga Statistics Department, International Labour Organisation and Pacific Community.
Tonga Statistics Department. (2022a). *Balance of payments*. Author.
Tonga Statistics Department. (2022b). *International merchandise trade statistics annual report 2021*. Author.
Tonga Statistics Department. (2022c). *Tonga census of population and housing 2021*. Author.
Tonga Statistics Department. (2022d). *Tonga national accounts statistics*. Author.
Unions NSW & MWC. (2021). *Working for $9 a day: Wage theft & human rights abuses on Australian farms* (Online). Unions NSW.
United Nations. (2021). *Global indicator framework for the Sustainable Development Goals and targets of the 2030 Agenda for Sustainable Development*. Retrieved 25 August, 2023, from https://unstats.un.org/sdgs/indicators/Global%20Indicator%20Framework%20after%202023%20refinement_Eng.pdf
United Nations: Economic and Social Commission for Asia and the Pacific (ESCAP). (2019). *Structural transformation and its role in reducing poverty: Asia-Pacific countries with special needs development report 2019*. Author.
Withers, M. (2019). Temporary labour migration and underdevelopment in Sri Lanka: The limits of remittance capital. *Migration and Development*, *8*(3), 418–436.
Withers, M., & Hill, E. (2023). Migration and development, without care? Locating transnational care practices in the migration-development debate. *Population Space and Place*, *29*(3).
World Bank. (2006). *Pacific Island at home & away: Expanding job opportunities for Pacific Islanders through labour mobility (English)*. Author.
World Bank. (2017). *Pacific possible: Long-term economic opportunities and challenges for Pacific Island countries*. Author.
World Bank. (2018a). *Maximizing the development impacts from temporary migration*. Author.
World Bank. (2018b). *The social impacts of seasonal migration: Lessons from Australia's seasonal worker programme for Pacific Islanders*. Author.
World Bank. (2021). *Pacific labour mobility, migration and remittances in times of COVID-19*. Author.

World Bank. (2022). *Skills and employment for Tongans, the World Bank: What we do/ projects & operations.* https://projects.worldbank.org/en/projects-operations/ project-detail/P161541?lang=en

World Bank. (2023). *Personal remittances received (% of GDP)—Tonga.* Retrieved 17 August, 2023, from https://data.worldbank.org/indicator/BX.TRF.PWKR.DT.GD.ZS?locations=TO

Part 3

Conclusion

18 A Comparative Analysis of Critical Skill Shortages and Sustainable Development Nexus

Concluding Remarks

Alan Nankervis, Subas P. Dhakal, and John Burgess*

Introduction

As set out in the first chapter, the book aimed to examine the nature, scope, and implications of the challenges associated with critical skills shortages (CSS) in the Asia-Pacific and beyond within the context of meeting the UN Sustainable Development Goals (SDGs). In relation to the broad findings, labour, skills, and talent shortages are recognised in all countries represented in the volume. We use the term 'CSS' as an umbrella term to encapsulate labour and skill shortages in the short and longer term. The European Labour Authority (ELA) has identified broader drivers of labour market challenges that are equally relevant in the context of this volume. For example, ELA (2022) stated: '[T]he rapid diffusion of new digital technologies to every sector of the European economy, the ageing of the European population, the transition to a climate-neutral economy and the working conditions associated with being employed in different occupations' (p. 9) as three of the main drivers of CSS. In the Asian context, Suwannarat (2022) highlights countries' reliance on foreign labour and the labour shortages in the post-pandemic era, adversely impacting sectors such as agriculture, construction, tourism, and manufacturing. This chapter summarises the key CSS-related similarities and differences across countries represented in this volume with respect to specific SDGs.

The State of CSS in the Asia-Pacific and Beyond

The Asia-Pacific region contains nearly 60% of the global population (UNFPA, 2021), including two population giants—India and China. The region has made significant socio-economic progress in the past few decades, but the countries that are represented in this book are at varying stages of socio-economic development (Dhakal et al., 2022). As the region is expected to be home to almost 3.5 billion middle-class people by 2030 (DFAT, 2017), the divide between developed and developing economies remains wide. For example, the recent country rankings based on the UN SDG Rankings[1] (UNDP, 2023a, 2023b) show that New Zealand (27th) and South Korea (31st) are ranked at

DOI: 10.4324/9781003379065-21

the top, whereas Bangladesh (101st) and India (112th) are at the bottom in terms of the countries included in this book. It is evident that although the SDGs addressed varied across the countries, SDGs 4 and 8 were two of the most recurring goals. For example, SDG 4 is a commitment to 'ensure inclusive and equitable quality education and promote lifelong learning opportunities for all' (Global Goals, 2024a, para 1); and SDG 8 aspires to '[p]romote inclusive and sustainable economic growth, employment and decent work for all' (Global Goals, 2024b: para 1). Both goals have intertwined implications. As an example, the lack of higher education and vocational training opportunities, coupled with the absence of employment and entrepreneurial prospects, in Nepal have led to an unprecedented rate of outbound migration. A thematic analysis was carried out to classify major issues associated with the CSS (see Table 18.1).

Addressing CSS: Government and Industry Strategies and Policies

The preceding chapters indicate that there are both similarities and differences in the skill shortage priorities and associated industry sectors among the countries included in this volume. Similar identified shortages and/or skill mismatches exist in almost all countries, but their incidence and severity differ, as do the industry sectors in which they have been experienced. Accordingly, the strategic and policy responses to address them differ with respect to the involvement of multiple stakeholders (national and local governments, industry managers, vocational and higher education institutions)—holistic or fragmented approaches, industry structures and associated national priorities, demographic factors, and the urgency of skill development and redevelopment.

In general, larger developed and developing countries in the Asia-Pacific region report more integrated government-industry-educational institutional strategies, while developing and smaller countries tend to be engaged in partial or fragmented partnerships and selective industry and skill focuses. China, for example, has embarked on an ambitious nation-wide strategy to 'integrate skilled talents into its overall social development planning and government policies . . . in line with industry and local realities', focusing on such projects as a flexible (vocational and higher education) model, 'intelligent, high-end and green development', involving school-enterprise universities and a new skill evaluation system to support its dominant manufacturing sector (Yi et al. this volume). The strategy focuses primarily on building a resilient and sustainable industry and promoting inclusion and innovation. In contrast, India has focused on strengthening older workers' digital and technological skills within intergenerational workplaces to retain them for as long as possible and to address skill shortages caused by the declining birth rate. The Indian government's strategy emphasises the responsibilities of industry and individual businesses in concert with their communities to create 'inclusive and transparent cultures reflecting the different communication styles of different generations

Table 18.1 Comparative analysis of CSS in countries represented in this volume

Country	*Sector in Focus (SDGs)*	*SDGs Rank*	*Aggregate Labour Migration*	*CSS-related official recognition?*	*CSS-related issues*	*Key policy initiatives*
New Zealand	General (SDG1, 2, 3)	27	Inflow	Yes, for example, long-term skills shortage list (LTSSL) (New Zealand Government, 2023)	Skill shortages; labour shortages	Green list of highly skilled roles, spotlight skills recognition tool
South Korea	Education (SDG4)	31	Inflow	Yes, for example, OECD (2023) recognises chronic labour and skill shortages in various sectors, for example, manufacturing, logistics, social service, leisure, and hospitality sectors	'3D jobs' (difficult, dangerous, and dirty); younger South Koreans reluctant to take up blue-collar jobs	Skilled worker points ystem visa; employment permit system (EPS); incentives for STEM education
Australia	General (SDG4)	40	Inflow	Yes, for example, Priority Migration Skilled Occupation List (PMSOL) with 44 occupations with critical shortages (Australian Government, 2022)	Tight labour market; pandemic-related migration bottleneck	Australian jobs and skill framework; the skilled occupation list (SOL); jobs and skills Australia's survey of employers
Thailand	Manufacturing (SDG4)	43	Outflow	Not available, however, the 2020 OECD report recognises large skill shortages in the education, health, and social work sectors (Vandeweyer et al., 2020, p. 3)	An influx of migrant workers from neighbouring countries; ageing workforce	Graduate work readiness; emphasis on vocational education

(*Continued*)

Table 18.1 (Continued)

Country	*Sector in Focus (SDGs)*	*SDGs Rank*	*Aggregate Labour Migration*	*CSS-related official recognition?*	*CSS-related issues*	*Key policy initiatives*
Vietnam	General (SDG4, 8)	55	Outflow	No, and the World Bank (2014) report claimed technical skill shortages and gaps are not a matter of concern (p. 4)	Skill mismatch; TVET quality and relevance of education play; labour mobility	Emphasis on training and education systems that can meet the skill requirements of the industry
China	Manufacturing (SDG9)	63	Outflow	Not available, however, Premier Li Qiang has highlighted the need to develop skilled talent and accelerate the development of vocational education (Sun, 2023, para 1)	Ageing population; skill gap	Promote the employment of elderly talent; flexible educational and training model; certification systems
Singapore	General (SDG8)	64	Inflow	Yes, recognised in the Singapore Government's (2023) report on the skills demand for a future economy	Green skills; cutting-edge innovation to address the lack of natural resources	Reskilling and upskilling of the labour force in the context of climate change
Indonesia	Tourism and Hospitality (SDG8)	75	Outflow	Yes, for example, critical occupations list (COL) (CMEARI, 2020)	Digital divide; 4IR-related skills gap; capacity deficit in rural/regional areas	Super-priority tourist destinations initiative; making Indonesia 4.0 roadmap
Malaysia		78	Inflow	Yes, for example, Malaysian critical occupations list (MyCOL) (Malaysian Government, 2020)	Digital transformation; skills gap	National digital skills strategy, digital economy blueprint (MyDIGITAL); MADANI policy framework

(*Continued*)

Table 18.1 (Continued)

Country	*Sector in Focus (SDGs)*	*SDGs Rank*	*Aggregate Labour Migration*	*CSS-related official recognition?*	*CSS-related issues*	*Key policy initiatives*
Mauritius	Information & Communication Technologies (SDG9)	93	Inflow	No, however, the IOM (2016) report recognised labour shortages in the areas of manufacturing, agro-processing and construction, and skills shortages in the areas of tourism, ICT, and so on	Centralised wage-determination system	Strengthen policies targeted at developing skills that are in high demand; incentives for STEM education; reversing the brain drain
Philippines	Health/Nursing (SDG8)	98	Outflow	Yes, mission critical skills (MCS) (Government of Philippines, 2023)	Declining trade union density and collective bargaining coverage; economic push factors	Strengthen the protections for, and promote the welfare of, migrant workers and their families; stronger national coordination of efforts to fulfil the objectives of the global compact for safe, orderly, and regular migration (GCM)
Nepal	Tourism and Hospitality (SDG8)	99	Outflow	No, however, the Hoque (2017) report identified shortages in tourism, ICT, agro-processing, and manufacturing.	Outbound migration; limited employment opportunities; inadequate education and training	Tourism satellite account set up; employer-led labour market secretariat established; capacity development programmes aimed at returning migrants

(Continued)

Table 18.1 (Continued)

Country	*Sector in Focus (SDGs)*	*SDGs Rank*	*Aggregate Labour Migration*	*CSS-related official recognition?*	*CSS-related issues*	*Key policy initiatives*
Bangladesh	Construction (SDG9, 11)	101	Outflow	No	Poor working conditions; low proportion of female workers; outbound migration of skilled workers; equitable enforcement of labour laws	Accreditation schemes through universities to standardize higher-level workers and professional roles
India	Manufacturing (SDG4)	112	Outflow	Not available, however, recognition of a significant shortfall of workers across multiple sectors, for example, factories, engineering units, manufacturing and assembling plants, and infrastructure projects, have been widely reported in the media (Deshpande, 2024, para 6)	Multigenerational workforce; ageing workforce; greener pastures	Addressing wage inequality between skilled and unskilled labour; automation, AI and robotics
Tonga	General (SDG8)	n/a	Outflow	Yes, recognition to broaden the range of appropriate and aligned skills for both domestic and international markets (Kingdom of Tonga, 2023)	Labour mobility	Tonga labour mobility supply management strategy (TLMSMS); Pacific Agreement on Closer Economic Relations Plus (PACER Plus)

of workers, including establishing intergenerational dialogue forums, mentoring and team building programs at the workplace level to eliminate bias against older employees' (Dayaram et al. this volume).

Australia, on the other hand, under its new Labour Party-led federal government, has adopted a holistic approach by carefully identifying national skill shortages through its agency, Jobs & Skills Australia (JSA), and developing a national skills certification system in concert with key industry partners, aimed at meeting specific industry sectoral requirements, supported by both vocational and higher educational institutions. To bolster these goals, fee waivers for technical and further education (TAFE) and supporting apprenticeships and internships are key features. A number of the SDGs are addressed in this strategy, including SDGs 4, 5, 8, 10, and 17. Recognising the links between low workforce skills, low pay, skill shortages, and poor productivity, the New Zealand government has undertaken a major reform of the vocational education and training (VET) system and Fair Pay Agreements and established 'tripartite' Workforce Development Councils, Skills Leadership Groups, and Industry Transformation Plans to engage with industry in improving innovation, productivity, and quality of work in the eight key industry sectors. As in Australia, the NZ strategy has ambitious goals, incorporating SDGs 1, 2, 3, 4, 8, and 10.

On the one hand, the need for STEM education reform to ensure that its higher education system will focus on the cross-cultural competencies of schoolteachers in line with SDG 4 (quality education) has been identified as being significant in countries like South Korea. On the other hand, Singapore, a politically stable island state with impressive economic growth over many decades, seems to be focused on developing strategic solutions to the emerging skill problems associated with its ageing workforce and its over-use of migrant labour at both high- and low-skill levels. Using SDG 8 (decent work) and SDG 13 (climate action) as its primary goals, the Singaporean government, in concert with industry, is attempting, on the one hand, to provide safe and secure employment for foreign workers, especially those in potentially dangerous occupations, and on the other, training local workers with the skills required to develop and maintain a green economy but without over-dependence on expatriates. In contrast, neighbouring emerging economies such as Malaysia and Vietnam have adopted broader and multi-stakeholder strategies and policies to address their national skill shortage issues. For example, the Malaysian government has recognised the need to engage all stakeholders (government, industry, education providers, and employees) to 'collectively engender a framework to put Malaysia at the forefront of digital talent development', especially in the information technology sector, in order to develop practical and sustainable policies and programmes at the organisational level which can be implemented in consultation between managers and their employees (Turner et al. this volume). Vietnam has embarked upon significant educational reforms, including the accreditation of TVET providers, emphasising professional skill development, and attempts to reduce the number of jobs in the informal sectors. To do so, the government has, as in other regional countries, encouraged meaningful partnerships between the government, industry, and vocational and higher education systems.

Among the remaining developing and emerging economies, Indonesia, the Philippines, Thailand, Nepal, and Bangladesh have adopted more focused approaches to their skill shortages, reflecting their esoteric skill shortage problems. For example, Indonesia is concerned with promoting digital transition in the local tourism industry with a view to 'address the socio-economic inequalities associated with variabilities in the digital infrastructure in diverse regions largely through the Making Indonesia 4.0 government initiative'. In contrast, the emerging interest of the Philippines seems to be strengthening the health sector both locally and in relation to its significant government labour exporting policies. Another tourism-dependent economy, Nepal, has put policy emphasis on job creation and education and training in the tourism and hospitality sector, emphasising upskilling trekking guides better to fulfil their occupational health and safety responsibilities for tourists. Finally, facing a skilled labour shortage in the construction industry, Bangladesh's priority is to address CSS to overcome the growth aspirations bottleneck and increase female labour force participation in the construction sector.

CSS is also examined in small island economies: Mauritius in the Indian Ocean and Tonga in the Pacific. Both are small developing island states with very different social, economic, demographic and industry structural environments. For instance, the Mauritian government has focused on SDGs 4, 8, and 9 (quality education, economic growth, and innovation), with a special interest in its crucial ICT sector. In contrast, the Tongan government, rather like the Philippines, has focused on remedying challenges associated with labour export, including reducing gender, disability, and racial discrimination among its emigrant workers, and addressing exploitative labour practices and minimal employment rights, as well as incentivising local skills development and ensuring providing safe working environments in line with SDG 8 (decent work).

Concluding Remarks

Of necessity, each country's experience of labour, skills, or talent shortages differs according to the macroeconomic challenges, including but not limited to political, socio-economic, and demographic, and how the public, non-profit, and private sectors have strategically responded to CSS-related challenges. In this context, this chapter contends that the following four themes need policy and future research attention in the Asia-Pacific region and beyond.

- Upskilling and reskilling of the ageing workforce
- The 'brain drain' of the young workforce
- Socio-political dynamics of the inflow versus outflow migration
- Graduate work readiness

The book provides a snapshot of CSS challenges and policy responses. Since most countries are only beginning to recover from the COVID-19 crisis, the potential for primary data collection for research was limited in many cases. In addition, there are notable exceptions to the countries included, notably Japan and Taiwan, both of which are facing severe CSS. Covering CSS-related issues and strategies is not exhaustive across the countries covered. Future research could take these limitations into consideration.

Notes

* Corresponding author: a.nankervis@curtin.edu.au.

1 The SDG Index ranks countries based on their performance across 17 goals (UN, 2024: para 1).

References

Australian Government. (2022). *Priority migration skilled occupation list.* https://immi.homeaffairs.gov.au/visas/employing-and-sponsoring-someone/sponsoring-workers/pmsol

Coordinating Ministry for Economic Affairs of the Republic of Indonesia (CMEARI). (2020). *Indonesia's critical occupations list 2018.* Jakarta: Author.

Deshpande, P. P. (2024). *India's 'demographic advantage'—Benefits and concerns.* https://timesofindia.indiatimes.com/blogs/truth-lies-and-politics/indias-demographic-advantage-benefits-and-concerns

DFAT. (2017). *The 2017 foreign policy white paper.* Department of Foreign Affairs and Trade. https://www.dfat.gov.au/sites/default/files/minisite/static/4ca0813c-585e-4fe1-86eb-de665e65001a/fpwhitepaper/foreign-policy-white-paper/chapter-two-contested-world/indo-pacific-will-create-opportunity.html#:~:text=Some%20forecasts%20suggest%20that%20by,nickel%20and%20zinc%E2%80%94will%20continue

Dhakal, S. P., Nankervis, A., & Burgess, J. (2022). Comparative analysis of countries' ageing challenges and policies. In S. P. Dhakal, A. Nankervis, & J. Burgess (Eds.), *Ageing Asia and the Pacific in changing times: Implications for sustainable development* (Chapter 14). Springer Nature.

European Labour Authority. (2022). *Report on labour shortages and surpluses 2022.* www.ela.europa.eu/sites/default/files/2023-03/eures-labour-shortages-report-2022.pdf

Global Goals. (2024a). *The 17 goals.* SDG4. www.globalgoals.org/goals/4-quality-education/

Global Goals. (2024b). *The 17 goals.* SDG8. www.globalgoals.org/goals/8-decent-work-and-economic-growth/

Government of Philippines. (2023). *Philippine Overseas Employment Administration (POEA).* www.foi.gov.ph/requests/mission-critical-skills/

Hoque, S. (2017). Pathways to prosperity and inclusive job creation in Nepal background paper: Tourism sector. *ODI (SET), 14.* https://set.odi.org/wp-content/uploads/2017/10/6.-SET-Nepal-Tourism-for-ET_Oct-2017.pdf

IOM. (2014). *Regional guide to facilitate South-South labour mobility in Southern Africa.* www.iom.int/sites/g/files/tmzbdl486/files/documents/regional_guide_to_facilitate_south-south_southern_africa.pdf

Kingdom of Tonga. (2023). *Labour mobility supply management strategy 2023.* www.mted.gov.to/wp-content/uploads/2023/07/FINAL_Final-TLMSMS_23-March-20231.pdf

Malaysian Government. (2020). *Critical occupations list jobs.* www.ilmia.gov.my/bda-myjobprofile/col
OECD. (2023). *OECD Employment Outlook 2023.* Artificial Intelligence and the Labour Market. https://www.oecd-ilibrary.org/korea_262d4383-en.pdf?itemId=%2Fcontent%2Fcomponent%2F262d4383-en&mimeType=pdf
OECD. (2023). *OECD skills outlook 2023.* https://ageei.eu/wp-content/uploads/2023/11/OECD_Skills_Outlook_2023_EN.pdf
Singapore Government. (2023). *Skills demand for the future economy 2023/24.* www.skillsfuture.gov.sg/skillsreport
Sun, L. (2023). *Chinese premier Li Qiang urges better training for more blue-collar workers to plug skills shortage.* www.scmp.com/news/china/politics/article/3234864/china-needs-more-blue-collar-workers-says-premier-li-qiang
Suwannarat, S. (2022, 14 July). Labour shortages threaten economic recovery in Malaysia and Thailand. *PIME Asia News.* www.asianews.it/news-en/Labour-shortages-threaten-economic-recovery-in-Malaysia-and-Thailand--56263.html
United Nations Development Programme (UNDP). (2023a). *Human Development Index (HDI).* https://hdr.undp.org/data-center/human-development-index#/indicies/HDI
United Nations Development Programme (UNDP). (2023b). *Rankings. 2024.* https://dashboards.sdgindex.org/rankings
UNFPA. (2021). *Population trends.* United Nations Population Fund [UNFPA]. https://asiapacific.unfpa.org/en/node/15207
Vandeweyer, M., Espinoza, R., Reznikova, L., Lee, M., & Herabat, T. (2020). *Thailand's education system and skills imbalances: Assessment and policy recommendations.* https://one.oecd.org/document/ECO/WKP(2020)49/En/pdf
World Bank. (2014). *Preparing the workforce for a modern market economy. Vietnam Development Report 2014.* https://documents1.worldbank.org/curated/en/610301468176937722/pdf/829400AR0P13040Box0379879B00PUBLIC0.pdf

Index

Note: Page numbers in *italic* indicate a figure and page numbers in **boldface** indicate a table on the corresponding page.

For Product Safety Concerns and Information please contact our EU
representative GPSR@taylorandfrancis.com
Taylor & Francis Verlag GmbH, Kaufingerstraße 24, 80331 München, Germany

www.ingramcontent.com/pod-product-compliance
Ingram Content Group UK Ltd.
Pitfield, Milton Keynes, MK11 3LW, UK
UKHW020152200926
475702UK00016B/2675
* 9 7 8 1 0 3 2 4 5 8 7 1 7 *